Religious Beliefs and Knowledge Systems in Africa

Africa: Past, Present & Prospects

Series Editors: Toyin Falola (University of Texas at Austin) and Olajumoke Yacob-Haliso (Babcock University)

This series collates and curates studies of Africa in its multivalent local, regional, and global contexts. It aims fundamentally to capture in one series historical, contemporary and multidisciplinary studies which analyze the dynamics of the African predicament from deeply theoretical perspectives while marshalling empirical data to describe, explain, and predict trends in continuities and change in Africa and in African studies.

The books published in this series represent the multiplicity of voices, local and global in relation to African futures. It not only represents diversity, but also provides a platform for convergence of outstanding research that will enliven debates about the future of Africa, while also advancing theory and informing policy making. Preference is given to studies that deliberately link the past with the present and advances knowledge about various African nations by extending the range, breadth, depth, types and sources of data and information existing and emerging about these countries.

The platform created proceeds from the assumption that there is no singular "African experience", nor is it possible to, in any way, homogenize the identities, histories, spaces and lives of African people.

Titles in the Series

Ghanaian Politics and Political Communication
Edited by Samuel Gyasi Obeng and Emmanuel Debrah

Beyond History: African Agency in Development, Diplomacy and Conflict Resolution
Edited by Elijah Nyaga Munyi, David Mwambari and Aleksi Ylönen

Reflections on Leadership and Institutions in Africa
Edited by Kenneth Kalu and Toyin Falola

Imagining Vernacular Histories: Essays in Honour of Toyin Falola
Edited by Mobolanla Ebunoluwa Sotunsa and Abikal Borah

Insights into Policies and Practices on the Right to Development
Edited by Serges Djoyou Kamga and Carol C. Ngang

Guerrilla Radios in Southern Africa: Broadcasters, Technology, Propaganda Wars, and the Armed Struggle
Edited by Sekibakiba Peter Lekgoathi

Religious Beliefs and Knowledge Systems in Africa

Toyin Falola and Nicole Griffin

ROWMAN & LITTLEFIELD
Lanham • Boulder • New York • London

Published by Rowman & Littlefield
An imprint of The Rowman & Littlefield Publishing Group, Inc.
4501 Forbes Boulevard, Suite 200, Lanham, Maryland 20706
www.rowman.com

86-90 Paul Street, London EC2A 4NE

British Library Cataloguing in Publication Information Available

Library of Congress Cataloging-in-Publication Data

Names: Falola, Toyin, author. | Griffin, Nicole K., author.
Title: Religious beliefs and knowledge systems in Africa / Toyin Falola
    and Nicole Griffin.
Other titles: Africa: past, present & prospects.
Description: Lanham, Maryland : Rowman & Littlefield, 2021. | Series: Africa : past,
    present & prospects | Includes bibliographical references and index.
Identifiers: LCCN 2021019279 (print) | LCCN 2021019280 (ebook) | ISBN
    9781538150245 (cloth) | ISBN 9781538150269 (paperback) | ISBN
    9781538150252 (ebook)
Subjects: LCSH: Ethnoscience—Africa—Religious aspects. | Africa—Religion. |
    Africa—Religious life and customs.
Classification: LCC BL2400 .F58 2021 (print) | LCC BL2400 (ebook) |
    DDC 200.96—dc23

LC record available at https://lccn.loc.gov/2021019279
LC ebook record available at https://lccn.loc.gov/2021019280

Contents

Acknowledgments

TOYIN FALOLA

The drafts of the chapters in this book were read in multiple places—the University of Ibadan, Usmanu Danfodiyo University, University of South Africa, and various groups in Ghana, Mali, and the Republic of Benin. I am grateful to Professors Siyan Oyeweso and Adeshina, who invited me to give the Keynote Address at the Conference to mark the eightieth birthday of the Alaafin of Oyo where the series of essays on kingship in this book was presented. The entire drafts of this book, in manuscript form, were read by Drs. Bola Dauda and Michael Oladejo Afolayan. I owe them a debt of gratitude. Samson, Oko Yemi, left the village to Ibadan City to read some chapters as well. Samson, *mo dupe o*. The organizers of the annual Fela Kuti conference provided the space to speak to the cultural context of the Bible. I am grateful to Wole Ogundele for his kind invitation.

NICOLE GRIFFIN

I would like to thank Dr. Toyin Falola for his support of my interdisciplinary interest in African studies. He has been integral to my career, and I am deeply grateful. I'd also like to thank my mother, Michelle Griffin, for her support of my studies, as well as my grandparents.

Preface

In the past, I have written books that capture the essentialism of the African knowledge economy and the compelling importance it commands in information production, just like those coming from other continents of the world. Except those who are genuinely interested in scouting for knowledge regardless of the attendant challenges the process poses, only a few Eurocentric scholars have truly conducted emotionally disinterested intellectual adventures on African knowledge. In this category, we would find the efforts of scholars such as Uli Bier, Suzanne Wenger, and a host of others commendable for taking pioneering steps to shine light on the nature of knowledge and history of Africa and its people—both of whom have been the victims of mudslinging by those with limited understanding. On the opposite side, there are a plethora of books written by anthropologists of global fame—historians who were once considered as epitome of true scholarship, respected scientists, and vibrant literary scholars with celebratory ideas—all of whom have written about Africa and Africans. Their work rarely stems from an objective evaluation but from a Eurocentric positionality that reflects colonial and neocolonial interests at the expense of accuracy in African epistemology.

Woven through these scholarly materials filled with outsider interpretations of Africa are the political threads of orientalism underlying their assumptions. The colonization of Africa occurred under the myth of "terrium nullum," that the land was unclaimed or empty. This myth extends beyond disregarding not only African societies but also their knowledge systems. In other words, the promulgation of the African knowledge economy and history as nonexistent is an apparatus of colonial ideology. Upon discovery, African scholars who are aware of this epistemic violence and the corrugating consequences of allowing such narratives to thrive begin to undertake intellectual engagements of African values and ideas in an effort to kick-start the thorough process of decolonization. It is in this spirit that this book, in combination with the ones written by various Afrocentric scholars, seeks to extend the assignment of purging the academic space of the blatant misinformation, which it has been fed for centuries unchallenged. History can be a double-edged sword when not handled carefully. For one, it could be a potent instrument to conduct stealth wars on a people without appearing destructive on the surface. In this case, even those who are targeted may willfully join in the campaign to self-destruct, with the minutest of awareness about their destructive actions.

The African knowledge economy is the assortment of their religious inclinations, philosophical positions, epistemic realities, and intellectual insights. While foreign in contrast to the Western episteme, it makes sense to Africans who are the direct observers of these activities, how things work, and have a lived experience that attests to the claims that outsiders tag as bogus at some point. It is undeniable that people who remain distant, either physically or emotionally, to a particular lifestyle usually give biased projections to these things when making comments, even if unnecessary. This would, therefore, be escalated if they have the political wherewithal to air opinions about these things. Without doubt, this attitude was the norm a couple of centuries ago when Eurocentric scholars, including those who never visited Africa, gave excessive information about the continent and the people, and their material for a good part of the nineteenth and the twentieth centuries was used by the protruding audience of America and European countries to shape their ideas and understanding of Africans. This, therefore, necessitated that the first generation of African writers wrestled their names and identity from the mud that these uncanny universalists were dragging them in. Then, writings from the brilliant minds of Africa emerged.

This book, therefore, is an assemblage of African ideas and knowledge economies that have been used to shape the people and their perception of reality for millennia. Above all things, it has been able to establish basic knowledge-generation sources of the people and how they equally are fit to be recognized as such. Contrary to the orientalists' opinion, the African knowledge economy stands out with compelling characteristics and fledging attributes that would indisputably have foreboding impacts on the African people, and the world, when especially engaged. In spite of the continuous onslaught they have attracted from the world generally, these knowledge sources become more resilient and, therefore, have confounding contributions to make in advancing the course of the African people academically, scientifically, technologically, and also philosophically. Africans have come to an understanding that reviving their epistemological heritages promises to bring about the manifestation of change that they envision in their minds. Appropriating Eurocentric ideologies on the African realities is an additional challenge that inevitably proves unproductive regardless of how they are twisted and domesticated. Africans have not found their traction on development even though they have driven to accommodate other people's philosophies. The book is even projected to provoke an extraordinary amount of commentary that would tellingly reveal the existential epistemic crisis that has silently been going on in the global intellectual market. This is so because it makes bold claims, upon evaluation, about African knowledge-generation sources that have been denied adequate recognition for a very long time. It would generate some controversies in Euro-American intellectual communities over the contention that these claims are bogus, particularly when viewed from a distant position. Such categories of people are hugely miseducated on the African episteme; this is what this book has set out to do. People would be informed about African knowledge and how it is sourced from various angles in relation to how it has helped to shape the African space throughout time. On the other side, it would spark up an interest in genuinely curious ones who, like those in the past as cited above, are interested in learning about things they truly acknowledge their ignorance about.

For African scholars, the book will serve as a guiding light to open their eyes to possible and promising areas of scholarship that can be developed for adequate knowledge acquisition. The African people are mostly unaware that their histories and legacies are replete with sufficient items of events that would add substantial amounts of knowledge to the world when engaged properly. The book continues to debunk the failed analogy of the universalists, who use their Western and foreign standards to measure the extent and value of African knowledge and their perception of life. People differ in their experiences, and that could be a sufficient reason for people to understand the inviolability of different perceptions. This book widens the horizon of intellectual discourse that bothers on the celebration of African values; it unearths important topics and the underlying social values of the African world; it talks about how Africans see their reality in relation to how their day-to-day life is projected into the image already formed by the European imperialists. The publication of this book is hinged on an understanding that it provides an insider insight about these African knowledge-generation sources that have been subsumed into silence for so long.

BOOK OUTLINE

This book is divided into three different sections, each with captivating information covered about the African knowledge economy and production. The first segment, "African Worldview and Knowledge Systems," encapsulates three important items of discourse. It gives an insight into the concept of witchcraft and how it differs from the phenomenon in Western society of a similar persuasion. African witchcraft practices, it is discovered, are integral parts of the continent; however, their occupation of the African societies is not inspired by the intention to wreak havoc on the society, contrary to the stereotypes of the Western world. Their existence, rather, has been validated by the need for a balance of power since primitive and unadulterated primordial African societies. These groups, however, have been misconstrued by contemporary Africans whose understanding of them is basically shaped by Western education and Arabic teachings, leading them to launch against them virulent attacks that could eradicate their presence from African societies. African witches have, therefore, suffered unprecedented abuse by "postcolonial" Africans who mostly are unaware of their internalization of Western conceptions of witchcraft and subsequent self-epistemicide.

Also, it gives further information about Ifa and how it has been used to shape the worldviews of the Yoruba people, contributing profoundly to their knowledge production and social advancement. Ifa, being a compendium of the Yoruba people's history, epistemology, philosophy, and a host of others, has been in existence for thousands of years, far before the many civilizations and their claims to advancement. The segment affirms the concept of Ifa as intellectually and philosophically intelligible for providing unparalleled insight for the people even when there were, as we are now made to understand through the modernity of science, insufficient sophisticated materials to make such projections. The prescience of Ifa and the exactitude of its claims are incredibly insightful, making its authenticity undoubtful among the Yoruba people who are convinced of the reliability of the phenomenon. As such, the segment proposes Ifalogy, a field of study that will explore the inherent characteristics of Ifa and how it is used by the people to generate knowledge and information as regarding their world. Rather than being at variance with it because the Eurocentric interpretations of it connote some sense of degeneration, Africans, and the world, should find ways by which it can be learned.

In addition to this, the part talks about the valuation of age in the African worldviews. Africans who have spent considerable number of years on earth are repositories of knowledge and sources of reliable information. Unlike many other people of the world, Africans celebrate their elderly ones because of the understanding that this demographic has witnessed various issues, encountered multiple challenges, and lived a lifestyle mixed in turbulence and triumphs. This, therefore, gives them the opportunity to make projections about the future using their experiences as the data. While they do not always hold the right to be right at all times, they usually have sufficient experiences that can guide one from going wrong. This is the very reason African elders of the past did enjoy much social regard, because there was a mutual interest between them and other members of society. Even when Africans die, there is an understanding that their bond is not cut short because of their physical absence, as they make their way into the society of the ancestors, again making another round of contributions to the advancement of the lives of the living from the spiritual realm.

The second part comes with equally motivating packages that further stress the very importance of African knowledge essentialism. Tagged "Kingship Ideologies and Epistemologies," this section is an implosion of African political ideas that are entrenched in the monarchical arrangement used for centuries in developing the African societies. Kings are the political heads that symbolize authority, and they are the bodies through which the political policies are expressed. Representing power and authority, they are the ones through which the ideologies of a people are channeled and their communal progress is built around. Kingship, therefore, is a careful political concept in the African world because it involves systematic planning and democratic processes that invariably animate the importance of other members of the society, whose franchise is used to determine their choice of leadership. The economic and political advancement of the people is dependent largely on the soundness of the king's mind and the potency of his philosophy. Therefore, the choice is always hinged on the consideration of these things, in addition to some other factors put into place, such as the spiritual alignment of the chosen leader to the path of the people.

Therefore, the king's competence would be measured through his latent ability to show creativity in addressing political, diplomatic, economic, and social exigencies that have to do with the well-being of the people upon which he reigns supreme. The unfolding of emerging challenges becomes the grounds to test the leadership agility of the African kings because he is expected to develop an army of competent soldiers who would always defend their civilizations when challenged by external aggressors. This, therefore, becomes inquiry-worthy, as there are unending styles with techniques that can be learned from them to advance the contemporary world, contrary to popular belief that the African past is laced with deficiencies that cannot fit into the modern society. African kingships, just like their counterparts in the world around, created civilizing missions that helped in promulgating their ideas. Therefore, important things like their education, orature, arts, sports, and religion are the various ways through which their civilizations can be sustained. Africa has a body of civilizing ideologies that assisted them in spreading their influence over inferior areas and gave them prolonged relevance. When we see the artistic creations of African kingship surviving in an environment that is alien, that attests to the creative ingenuity built around their leadership style.

Against this backdrop, we are introduced to the epistemological valuation of the African kingship, and by this, we explain how African kingships can be studied in relation to how civilizations have been defended in the time past. What are the internal political permutations that go on in selecting the councils of elders who uphold the societal values and mores? What are those strategies, methods, and policies engaged to command such levels of respect among people, even to warrant building an empire? The Oyo Empire, for instance, lasted for centuries uninterrupted by foreign forces and internal disunity, affirming the strength of the philosophy used to uphold this status quo. Basing their government on the decentralization of power showed that past African political and ideological leaders are not devoid of ingenuity, as trumpeted by invaders who documented the African experiences by remaining deliberately blind to these angles of strength. Civilizations like the Benin Empire were strong in military and politics and very respected among different people at the time of their reign. All these are indicators of sturdy African ideologies.

The last part, titled "World Religions and Knowledge Systems," acknowledges the validity of these Abrahamic religions as other sources of generating knowledge because of their records in being the conscience of the people and deciders of their cultural direction. Quranic epistemology has been in serious critical onslaught by Western narratives in a competition to become the popular source of knowledge or truth generation. This epistemicide has contributed to the radicalization of Islam, including activities of conservative Muslims who have orchestrated violent crimes and attacks. The separation of science and religion in the Western episteme has been unable to process the Islamic culture as another knowledge-generation source, leading to the continuous desecration of Islamic knowledge. However, when closely considered, especially from the point of view of the very liberal Muslims who tenaciously hold the tenets of the religion with rapt interest, we would see the innumerable contributions of Islam and the unfurling Quranic epistemology. Generally, Islam is filled with an epistemic design that espouses a people's ideology.

This section also expressively talks about biblical sources of knowledge and how this has shaped the spiritual, physical, philosophical, and ideological perceptions of the Christian demographic in the world. Christian believers are convinced with such a knowledge economy that Christianity evinces. The religion is generally structured on the belief in an intersection between the physical and the spiritual world, where human's level of knowledge is directly proportional to the celestial inspiration they get. This is a creed maintained by a little less than two billion Christians across the world. Apart from making some claims to scientific knowledge in the Bible, the religion also is known for being a moral compass for the believers who have, upon their strong immersion in the teachings of the religion, built memorable relationships and interracial bonds all over the world. While the basis for Western scientific truth is empiricism, the background for religious truth is faith. This contradiction questions the deep-seated assumption that what we hold as truth is fixed and not rooted in personal and circumstantial convictions. There are various items of information that have been provided by some declarations made in the Bible and are today given contemporary interpretation when events prove them right.

The Pentecostal movement also is given a portion in this category because of the growing influence it is making in contemporary trends. Having the coloration of Christianity and indigenous philosophies, the group evolved from the emancipatory spirit of African Americans to nationalize it for common freedom. By relying on the information provided in the Bible that men are actually born equal, the enslaved Africans find solace and succor in marrying themselves to the word of God and project their collective agitations through the platform. The movement, with its transnational appeal, sources for patronage by individuals with Marxist values to engage the superstructure in a feast to ensure equity and tranquility. Pentecostalism challenges the masked imperialism of the missionaries who came with the insidious assignment to save the African people, laughably, from themselves. Such an attitude of hegemony is frowned at and called out at every opportunity. The pioneers of this movement recognized the irreconcilability of the treatment of Africans and Western claims to moral values. Immediately, the Pentecostal movement is laced with indigenous knowledge economy in order to excavate cultural relics that would help in reclaiming their lost identity.

Chapter 1

Belief and Knowledge Systems: Power, Eurocentricity, and Bias

Astronauts have photographed the Earth from space, showing it to be spherical. However, the shape of the planet has been the subject of debates throughout time and space. Pythagoras, from the sixth century BC, is remembered as the European philosopher who declared that the Earth was round. Similar concepts of a spherical Earth arose in the Middle East in the ninth century and in Ming Dynasty China during the fourteenth century. Despite these international sources calculating that the Earth was round, maps from nineteenth-century Europe continued to describe a flat planet. European geographers used passages from the Bible to shape their flat Earth maps, despite mathematical calculations proving the spherical shape of the Earth. Even today, in the presence of photographic imagery, Christian fundamentalists in the United States support the flat Earth model.[1]

It is easy to simplify the relationship between beliefs and knowledge as that of religion versus science, but this is inaccurate. The Quran asserted that the Earth was flat, but Islamic scholars interpreted it to mean "each little part . . . appears to be flat,"[2] allowing for the possibility of a spherical shape. There is no binary between religion and knowledge because all knowledge systems are based on validated beliefs. The reason why some Christians are more reluctant to accept the idea of a spherical Earth has to do with their philosophy of knowledge.

The good thing about science is that it's true whether or not you believe in it.[3]

I am the way and the truth and the light.[4]

And it is not for a soul to believe except by permission of Allah, and He will place defilement upon those who will not use reason.[5]

1

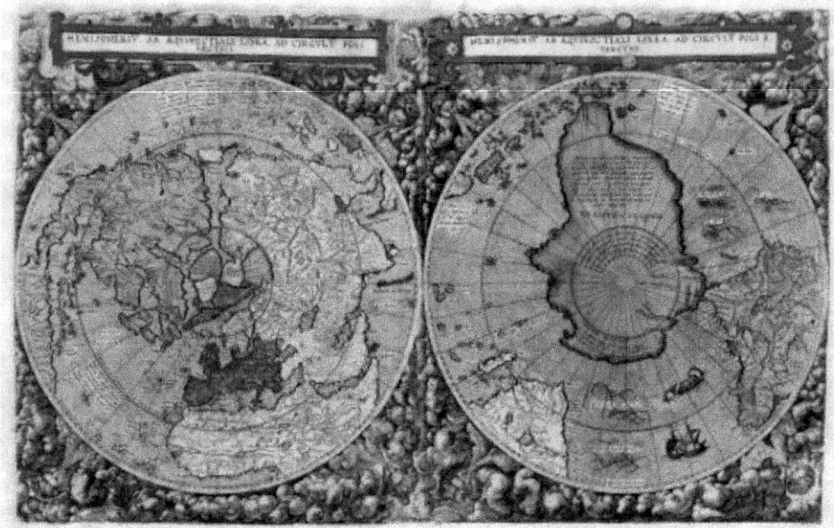

Figure 1.1.   Map of the globe. *Source*: "Antique map of World by de Jode." Archived from the original on May 9, 2008. Retrieved March 9, 2009, from https://www.sanderusmaps.com/antique-maps/world-and-polar-regions/world-_20635.cfm.

Consider these three quotes—each uses the term "truth" in a different discourse. Neil deGrasse Tyson views science as an indisputable truth that humans can discover. Through the word "science," he refers to empirical knowledge validated through the institutions and procedures of the scientific method. His assertion that science exists, "whether or not you believe in it," establishes a separation from any type of intangible dimension, whether spiritual, emotional, or moral.

In the second quote from the Bible, Jesus defines truth as that which is religious and knowable only through the divine. This definition of truth stresses a moral and spiritual dimension that is inaccessible in the absence of religion.

The third quote offers a definition of truth that strikes a compromise between the two extremes. Humans can gain knowledge, but that knowledge is not certain without the will of God. From this perspective, science has a clearly defined role while truth retains its empirical and abstract moral dimensions.

Neil deGrasse Tyson's assertion that science is indisputable can only be supported by valuing empirical evidence and disvaluing disembodied or intangible ways of knowing. However, these quotes about truth share the same implied values. Epistemology is a subsection of philosophy that seeks to understand the nature of knowledge—it is the philosophy of how we know what we know and an investigation of the underlying beliefs embedded in knowledge systems.[6] More directly, epistemology investigates whether institutions of truth are capable of delivering knowledge.[7] This field of study allows a deconstruction of the discourse of knowledge to uncover and ultimately question underlying assumptions. It challenges the relationship between knowledge in belief systems, breaking down the boundaries between science and religion.

This chapter will describe the history of epistemology and explore the concept of knowledge–power to conclude that knowledge is produced by powerful forces that validate beliefs. It will also apply knowledge–power to the current world system, applying theories of postcolonialism and the subaltern to knowledge. Finally, I will take a step back to explain the psychological relationships between beliefs and knowledge as well as how these tendencies also reinforce power.

PART I
KNOWLEDGE, BELIEF, AND POWER

Discourse on Western epistemology begins with a debate between Plato's rationalism and Aristotle's empiricism. Debates about the nature of knowledge took place throughout the world, but this specific debate's importance stems from its simplification of ideas that would become the basis of modern science. Plato argued that the limitations of human perception hid the true nature of reality. He articulated his value of rationalism in knowledge through a metaphor, asking his audience to imagine an individual living inside a cave. The individual is unable to see anything outside of the cave, only shadows cast by an outside light source. Someone who has only ever seen these shadows has a very limited understanding of the outside world. Their senses cannot lead them to understand the realities of the world outside, but reason may guide them to a deeper understanding. The allegory of Plato's cave represents his philosophy of rationalism: that there is knowledge beyond that which human senses can detect.[8]

Aristotle believed that knowledge could be gained through human senses. His philosophy of empiricism asserted that humans could only attain truth through sensory information—in this philosophy, anything that lies beyond the observable is beyond the realm of human knowledge.[9] Aristotle argued that anything can be justified through reason, but empirical evidence can validate a claim. Debates on rationalism and empiricism continued beyond ancient Greece to deeply influence Europe's scientific revolution.

Europe's Enlightenment period emerged from a history of war, religion, and nationalism. International trade opened up the world to exchange animals, plants, diseases, and ideas. The church's status as the sole source of

Figure 1.2.   Image of Shaka Zulu. *Source*: Sketch of King Shaka (1781–1828) from 1824. Attributed to James King, it appeared in Nathanial Isaacs' "Travels and Adventures in Eastern Africa," published in 1836.

knowledge, and the power that it held through that position, was challenged and religious systems fragmented.

In the early seventeenth century, Descartes revolutionized Western conceptions of knowledge through his philosophy of skepticism. Skepticism enabled a knowledge revolution because it insisted on considering the possibility of falsehood. Methodological skepticism saw truth as something that could be known by man but needed to be justified in the face of alternatives. Descartes practiced skepticism by rejecting his knowledge and then reconstructing it through justification.[10] Although Descartes was religious, his belief in God came from philosophical deduction instead of embodied thinking. Cartesian doubt, the process created by Descartes, developed new methods in mathematics, philosophy, and religion.

Various forms of scientific method existed throughout the enlightenment, but the version presented by Francis Bacon, in his 1620 book *Novum Organum*,[11] was the most influential. Bacon's method was the first "universal" approach to scientific information, and it was used by successors such as Isaac Newton. This method focused on either inductive or deductive reasoning, with a focus on empiricism and replicability.

Philosophers not only debated methodologies for finding truth, but they also debated the nature of truth, whether it existed, and whether it had limitations. In the 1920s, the Vienna circle developed the idea of logical positivism, that truth can be verified, but only that which can be physically observed can be known through science. This perspective leaves no room for religion or alternative ways of knowing outside of science. It sees truth as separate from humanity; it is that which does not have a function but just is.[12] Blanshard advanced the coherence theory of truth, arguing that truth is simply an agreement between judgments.[13] This is a superficial understanding in which truth plays no function and is not fixed. Bas van Fraassen's arguments from the 1980s to the early 2000s heightened the view of scientific realism, asserting that truth is black or white and awaiting discovery.[14] This view opened the doors of the scientific method, or similar principles, for other disciplines including the arts, humanities, and philosophy.

Although the nature of truth continues to be debated, I will conclude this history of epistemology with a definition of knowledge set out by Edmund Gettier in 1963. Previous to Gettier, the most widely accepted definition of knowledge was that of a justified true belief. It referred to the human dimension of truth—the extent to which truth is known by the human mind. Truth is seen as something that is fixed and knowable. Beliefs are what a human can claim to know, and justification is a series of logical steps proving a person's belief as truth. Gettier created the Gettier problem, which problematizes this definition of knowledge.

Gettier used a conversation between two American men, Smith and Jones, as a metaphor to explain the problem. Smith is told that "Jones owns a Ford." Jones does not own a Ford, but Smith believes so because he was told. Smith proclaims, "Jones owns a Ford, or Brown is in Barcelona." Serendipitously, Brown is actually located in Barcelona. Smith's statement, "Jones owns a Ford, or Brown is in Barcelona," is his belief, which is both justified and true. However, it is justified for the wrong reasons, based on misinformation. Gettier concludes that not only must knowledge be a justified, true belief, but there must also be causality between the justification and the truth.[15]

Consider a new example inside this framework: Western science might conclude that tea tree oil has antibiotic properties, and a group of indigenous people in Latin America may also believe in its healing properties. The groups have true beliefs that are justified differently. The scientist will have tested this hypothesis through empirical evidence, and the herbalist might have received the information from ancestors or religious ways of knowing. Because the indigenous group lacks a scientific justification for knowing about the healing properties, their justified true belief is "accidental" and not validated by modern science. This example represents the limitations of the modern philosophy of knowledge—it presents a single, narrow pathway to truth.

The modern academic system is built on a distinct set of historical philosophies. This Eurocentric approach to knowledge not only developed from European philosophies but also based on Western values, including individualism, disembodied thinking, Cartesian thinking, secularity, and empiricism. There are some minor deviations, but all studies within the modern university cling to these values as tightly as possible. Putting aside the modern historical context of epistemology, it is possible to connect the relationship between knowledge and power.

Beliefs and knowledge do not exist in an ahistorical relationship; they are functions of power in society. "Ideology," a normative and nonepistemic set of beliefs among a group,[16] is the term I will use to examine power's role in the relationship between knowledge and beliefs. Although ideology is typically used in political terms, in this context it describes any sort of power held within or between societies along with the beliefs that maintain that power balance.

Two theorists are well known for identifying connections between power and knowledge: Karl Marx and Michel Foucault. Marx asserted that history functions in a cyclical pattern due to capital accumulation. The bourgeoisie class accumulates capital exponentially, increasing inequality. The proletariat class, which has little capital, must constantly sell its labor to survive. The bourgeoisie's accumulation of capital and political power lowers the wages of the proletariat class, and more labor must be sold merely to earn a "starving wage." According to Marx, these inequalities grow more extreme until the proletariat organizes a revolution to overthrow the ruling class. This event can be postponed through ideology.

Marx viewed religion as an ideology, claiming that it was "the opium of the people." This referenced the common political ideology claiming that the ruling class held its place because its members were favored by God.[17] Such ideologies encouraged people to sustain their own suffering through passivity, believing that the current world order is the will of God. From a Marxist perspective, the ideologies held by large groups work to oppress the proletariat class. The scientific method stems from a history of politically influenced beliefs that created the secular democratic state and the unique character of scientific knowledge; the Marxist perspective identifies the foundations of modern knowledge as a creation of the ruling parties used to sustain their power.

Michel Foucault was the other theorist who wrote about ideology as a function of power. Foucault explained the idea of the power-knowledge nexus, describing it not in terms of a historical struggle but as two interrelated concepts. In the power-knowledge nexus, power is that which creates and validates knowledge. Knowledge, in turn, is able to reinforce and validate power. In Foucault's analysis, the institutions of power, which are changing and complex, reinforce their power through their disciplinary policies.[18]

Although the history of epistemology is diverse, Western philosophers have largely held the view that the nature of truth is stable. They viewed history in terms of Weber's modernity as rationality.[19] Viewed through the Enlightenment, history begins with the arguments of Aristotle and Plato, progressing to the advent of modern science. However, the arguments of Marx and Foucault dispel the notion that truth can exist without the influence of power. This link between truth and the shifting forces of power requires truth to have an aspect of relativity. It is impossible to perform a neutral identification of an ideology because the researcher is positioned either within or against it. The theories of Marx and Foucault allow us to deconstruct Western epistemology as an ultimate truth, and the idea of knowledge as justified true belief is heavy with historical context, unwritten values, and power dynamics.

The modern world order's philosophy of knowledge was developed primarily by white men in Europe and America. The narrative's beginning in ancient Greece implies democratic values, and its progression through the Enlightenment invokes an age of reason and secularity. It continues through societies that practiced capitalism and exploited other countries through systems of colonialism. These Eurocentric philosophies were born from systems of racism and patriarchy, in which the elite had few limitations. Although nationalistic movements weakened the power of these empires, the ideology of Western science remained. This is evident through the Western academy's dominance throughout different cultures and the hegemonic forces of Western epistemology.

PART II
APPLICATIONS OF BELIEFS, KNOWLEDGE, AND POWER

Evolutionary political theory explains that political bodies developed from kinship groups. As these groups became larger, their size forced them to decentralize and a central government was necessary to maintain order. This is the origin of the leader or king.[20] Historically, this leader was not democratically chosen. A leadership position creates order, but it also creates power dynamics. From a Foucauldian analysis, power dynamics ultimately lead to control of knowledge. The interplay between power and knowledge will lead to a widespread ideology that is often, but not always, religious in nature. Historical examples link power, knowledge, and beliefs in ways that are related to modern times, the epistemology of the subaltern, and the idea of epistemic violence.

Figure 1.3. Bust of Plato. *Source:* The Wellcome Collection. Accessed July 29, 2020, from https://wellcomecollection.org/works/v9mqh7zb.

Shaka Zulu was a great leader of Southern Africa who expanded the Zulu Empire to include 250,000 subjects occupying more than 11,500 square miles by 1828. He expanded this empire through relentless violence, but he maintained it through power-knowledge and beliefs. Shaka Zulu reintegrated his conquests into a cosmopolitan Zulu identity. He exercised control over the breeding of women and cows along with the consumption of milk—the practice of drinking milk from the cow established a hierarchy in which the king gathered milk first, then the military, and then the rest. The flow of milk in the kingdom symbolized the flow of power.

In a study on perceptions of Shaka Zulu, interviews found that people who knew him loathed him for his ruthless conquests, while the people who knew of him both feared and admired his genius and violence.[21] His spirit is honored today in Southern Africa, showing the relationship between religion and power over time. Shaka's rule represented a power-knowledge nexus with violent and religious foundations. The values of violence, kingdom, and hierarchy sustained his rule over a large territory. These values were beliefs, but through power, they were validated as knowledge.

Christianity is another example of a modern-day kingdom maintained by beliefs and power-knowledge. Over one-third of the world identifies with some part of the Christian church.[22] The church asserts its authority by defining the Bible as an epistemic text or an all-encompassing truth.[23] The Christian church asserts that the Bible is truth, and it uses biblical verses to reinforce its power. This power is not the physical disciplinary power identified by Foucault and applied by governments to shape society's behavior. Instead, it is a spiritual disciplinary power, demanding that adherents obey spiritual rules to be rewarded in the afterlife.

It may seem difficult to identify today's ideologies due to superficial secularity, but the absence of religion *is* a religious perspective.[24] A modern institution can be stripped to reveal its own power-knowledge nexus similar to that of the historical Zulu kingdom or Christian church. Academia validates knowledge through the institutions and processes of modern science and the university, and the underlying values of this system are Eurocentric, with individualistic, capitalistic, and democratic undertones. Money gives universities the power to validate knowledge, and this money comes either from the state or from prestige and individual donors and students. The neutrality of knowledge is impossible in both cases; universities must serve the customers that fund them. In the modern world, this means that the colonial powers have the most influence over academia and that which is regarded as "world knowledge."

Power can validate beliefs as knowledge. Power is also a factor of historical circumstance, changing over time. I have deconstructed the philosophy of knowledge through the history of epistemology validated through Western philosophy, referring to epistemology in its singular form. The term "epistemologies" can be used to discuss the variety of epistemic norms that exist throughout the world.

Western dominance in global knowledge and the singular use of the term "epistemology" represents a hegemony. This widespread cultural dominance—which has its roots in colonialism—is so entrenched in the current world order that it often goes unnoticed. Postcolonial theorists such as Walter Mignolo have noted the inseparable relationship between knowledge production and the political power of colonizing nations. Mignolo is a postcolonial writer who views the world in terms of knowledge, beliefs, and power within a historical context. Mignolo's work developed from previous postcolonial work on the colonial matrix of power, especially that of Anibal Quijano. Mignolo uses the historical context of colonization, where the Western world systematically took over countries in Europe, Asia, and Latin America. Colonization was a political process that weakened the structural institutions of nations and their people. This global exercise of power came with a "West knows best" ideology. Knowledge of other countries was acknowledged, but those countries were mostly commodified and exotified, conceptually devalued as inferior alternatives to the gold standard of Western science.

Although nations have gone through decolonization, Mignolo has noted that the structural and ideological remnants of colonialism remain.[25] Previously colonized nations are now nation-states possessing structures that had been designed to serve the empire, not the local citizens. The most harmful of colonialism's remnants is the idea that Western concepts are superior to those of other cultures. Extensive educational and missionary efforts etched this idea into the minds and infrastructure of other nations, leaving the ideology difficult to deconstruct. Mignolo asserts that the production of knowledge, with its Western epistemological and scientific foundations, maintains neo-colonial relationships in which Western countries continue to exploit former colonies politically and economically.

The physical institutions of modern science are those of academia, and their structure evolved from historical ideas about epistemology, including a history of colonialism and a distinct separation from the church. Western universities, which are the dominant institutions for producing knowledge, are continually validated through rankings, income, and publication. Modern academia emphasizes the peer-reviewed journal, which depends on the written word and institutions of approval along with skepticism through relevant scholars. Journals have the power to publish what they please and the authority to validate knowledge, while books and nonreviewed sources are dismissed as less credible. Modern academia has no disciplinary limits to its knowledge; peer-reviewed journals cover subjects that range from psychology to religion.

Postcolonial researchers seek not only to deconstruct the colonial matrix of power but also to create new epistemic foundations and institutions.[26] Postcolonialism tends to reject meta-narratives and generalizations that homogenize individual cultures. It also rejects the "othering" frequently done by Western anthropologists in the absence of context to understand societies that are different from their own. A postcolonial epistemic perspective would question the scientific method's Eurocentric foundations and allow new methodologies to flourish. These might include autoethnographies, storytelling, religious ways of knowing, oral traditions, and the more contextualized practice of social sciences.

Spivak's article "Can the Subaltern Speak?" takes postcolonial epistemology a step further.[27] Spivak does not define herself as a postcolonial theorist; she advocates for the subaltern. In contrast to Western hegemonic knowledge, the subaltern includes ways of knowing that are marginalized. These knowledge systems are plural, diverse, and ever-changing. They are also complex, and Spivak heavily emphasizes the compacted marginalization of women's perspectives in discourse. Subaltern ways of knowing include herbalists, religion, spirituality, emotionality, and experimental methods that transcend the limits of science, but they are often viewed as beliefs, rather than knowledge, because they lack the power to validate their perspectives.

Hegemonic Western knowledge conducts epistemic violence against subaltern ways of knowing—widespread cultural trauma is caused when an indigenous knowledge system is lost, and communities lose their identity, becoming vulnerable and disempowered. Epistemic violence occurs when communities have their stories told for them. The effects of this violence frequently include actual violence; such processes can amplify inequalities of power.[28]

Now that the lines between belief and knowledge have been blurred, and now that I have defined what they are in the West and problematized the Western definition, I will present two alternative models to knowledge. The first is De Santos' model of a constellation of knowledge,[29] where knowledge does not exist in a singular form as expressed by the West. Instead, knowledge exists in a plural, coexisting way that is dependent on cultural values; different people may choose to use different systems of knowledge that are all of equal value. The second is Walter Mignolo's border thinking, where knowledge exists together but each knowledge system has its limits. Individuals are encouraged to wisely decide which system of knowledge is most relevant for the situation.[30] For example, the same individual who uses traditional prayers to treat mild fevers may use a doctor's expertise to treat cancer. Border thinking allows coexisting knowledge to have pragmatic applications.

PART III
BIAS: PSYCHOLOGY'S THEORIES OF KNOWLEDGE AND BELIEFS

Psychology is infused with the Eurocentric value of individualism, but the field should not be disregarded. Instead, it should be questioned each time it is applied. This section relates the themes of knowledge and belief to individual and collectivist psychological theories. I previously discussed knowledge and beliefs in relation to larger political and historical processes, but this section isolates the processes in which beliefs influence knowledge.

In psychology, a cognitive bias describes an individual's psychological reasons for believing in something that is untrue. The most famous is confirmation bias, the tendency for individuals to overvalue information that supports their previously held opinions.[31] The idea of these biases assumes that truth has degrees of certainty. However, biases also refer to relative truth, such as opinion or perception—they can show us the metaphorical pathway taken by the brain as beliefs influence "knowledge."

Another cognitive bias is the availability heuristic, where an individual's thought processes are biased by their personal experiences.[32] For example, the word "cat" represents a small house cat for most people, not a lion or cheetah. People who do not have personal experience with large cats think of the most relevant "cat" in their lives. The availability heuristic interferes with the way an individual justifies their beliefs through their underlying assumptions. Media reports might lead a person to think that they are more likely to die from a shark attack than from a tornado, even when the opposite is true, because information about shark attacks is easier to recall.

Emotional thinking can also be a cognitive bias. In *Thinking Fast and Slow*, psychologist Daniel Kahneman describes the brain's two systems of thinking—slow reason and fast emotion.[33] The "fast" response is often emotional, reactive, and separate from reason. The "slow" system can conduct a thorough analysis and arrive at a different conclusion. Such thinking is inherently separatist and reductionist, but these systems reveal how beliefs influence knowledge. For example, a statement challenging the existence of God might provoke a reaction of fear and disgust from a highly religious individual because emotional responses interfere with the ability to evaluate conflicting arguments.

One type of "fast" thinking is in-group bias, or identity protection. Studies have found that individuals think in ways that protect their own identity. They identify with different in-groups, seeking information that holds their own group above others. They are also attracted to information that blames or devalues out-groups. This constant filtering process collects information that not only validates the individual's current position but also that of their group.[34] At the same time, their emotional responses repel offensive information that devalues their group in society. For example, Americans who identify as Republicans are not likely to read material that casts Democrats in a favorable light, and vice versa.

We have already discussed Gettier's problem: knowledge had been defined as a justified, true belief until Gettier showed that there must also be causation between the justification and the truth. Cognitive bias accounts for false justifications between belief and truth. An individual's opinions, identity, emotions, or experiences can alter their perceptions of reality. Although the scientific method has removed some of these biases to reveal pure knowledge, the historical context of epistemology and the existence of power-knowledge structures question the very existence of a singular knowledge. The systems that seek knowledge as truth may be ignoring their own underlying beliefs as they use them to validate that truth.

One psychological theory transcends the realm of cognitive biases to understand the relation between power and knowledge. It is an extension of the identity protection theory called the White Male Effect,[35] which holds that individuals believe information when it validates their group's place in society. The theory also explains how power combines with identity protection. Current society operates under hierarchies of racism and sexism, and identity protection systematically works in favor of those with power to make the perspective of white males more validated in society. This is problematic because white males are less likely to experience systemic problems with poverty, discrimination, climate change, or violence. The privileged roles of white males—who hold the majority of leadership positions in Western nations, transnational corporations, and intergovernmental organizations—make them less likely to feel threatened by these risks, and they avoid taking action to change a system that continues to disadvantage the underprivileged.

The concept of cognitive biases reflects the Western epistemic value of disembodied thinking. The idea that thought and reason can be separated from personal, emotional, or even spiritual experiences is based on a false pretense. Using Mignolo's border thinking, knowledge does not have to separate itself from that which extends beyond reason. Instead, it can be explored as it reveals itself. Reflexivity in research, along with new epistemic traditions, may be able to strengthen the relationships between beliefs and knowledge instead of ignoring them.

CONCLUSION

This work has established beliefs' deep entrenchment within knowledge systems, it has highlighted power's role in validating beliefs as knowledge through the power-knowledge nexus, and it has deconstructed Western epistemology and that of Western science to reveal distinct historical values. I have presented subaltern epistemology as a field that defies Western hegemonic knowledge and nurtures alternatives. And psychological analysis shows that ways of knowing are not only historically dependent and heavy with values but also that these values affect our interpretations of knowledge. Cognitive bias reveals that not only should diversity in knowledge be embraced but also diversity in researchers. The strong connections between knowledge and belief systems mean that different sides of truth can only be revealed by viewing knowledge through a variety of lenses.

Part I

AFRICAN WORLDVIEW AND KNOWLEDGE SYSTEMS

Chapter 2

Witchcraft as Ideology and Knowledge

From the Salem Witch Trials or the Eastern European myth of Baba Yaga to the Kalku in Chile, almost every culture has an interpretation of witchcraft. Western representations of witchcraft typically center around women conspiring with the supernatural through despicable means. Given the incredible diversity of Africa, with an estimated between 1,500 and 2,000 independent languages spoken, it is only intuitive that Africa is also home to the most culturally diverse and unique witchcraft beliefs.[1] Witchcraft beliefs challenge the division between knowledge and belief in a way much similar to world religions; however, it fails to fall exclusively within the categories of either religion, ideology, or knowledge. In this chapter, the function of witchcraft as ideology and knowledge will be explored within the modern postcolonial context. This will include understanding the epistemology of witchcraft, how witchcraft has been portrayed in the colonial ideology and the ideological function of witchcraft itself.

A 2010 LiveScience article entitled "Belief in Witchcraft Widespread in Africa" claims that the majority of Africans believe in witchcraft. The article highlights some of the consequences of witchcraft belief that have been in the news, including a disengagement with public health across the continent, horrific murders of people accused of witchcraft in Kenya, and hunts for albinos in Tanzania.[2] Similar stories of violence related to witchcraft include "Tanzania 'witchcraft' murders," "our son was robbed of his future,"[3] and "witchcraft belief is a curse on Africa."[4] A stroll around Nairobi will reveal several ordinary signs for "waganga" to practice "juju" to help with lost love, politics, or career goals.[5] Not only is witchcraft widely experienced as a reality in Africa but also in African communities abroad, such as the Nigerian elite in New York City.[6] Online discussions expound the consequences of witchcraft to political corruption, war, and violence motivated by romance or greed.[7] Witchcraft beliefs in Africa today are both highly prevalent and relevant in world news.

Critical to any international discussion is the discrete enunciation of the assumptions. On a subject such as witchcraft, which has vastly different connotations based off of culture, this is of special importance. Perpetuating binaries is inherently deceitful given the falsehood of localism and the growing globalization of the modern world. However, simplification of the Western and the African perspectives of witchcraft will prove essential to understanding relevant literature. Since the majority of literature about witchcraft in Africa is written from the Eurocentric academic perspective, it is best to first describe the assumptions of those writings. European literature on witchcraft in Africa typically begins with the assumption that witchcraft is a "primitive" belief, not comparable to world religions (see, e.g., the works of Foucault or Evans-Prichard). Anthropologists have spent much time trying to understand why Africans *still* believe in witchcraft. They note the negative effects of such belief as perpetuating underdevelopment and poverty. The European perspective also typically emphasizes accused witches as a human rights issue.[8] These writings all work through the underlying assumption that witchcraft is a *false belief*.

In light of the literature of postcolonialism and the ongoing Africanization of knowledge in academia, literature on Africa must always use the African ideology.[9] Given that most Africans view witchcraft as a reality, the entire workings of European literature on African witchcraft prove irrelevant. Whether witchcraft exists or not, it does not change the lived reality of witchcraft experienced by many Africans and abroad.[10]

While I will define key terms associated with witchcraft, it is essential to point out that witchcraft itself is an English and, therefore, Eurocentric term. The idea of witchcraft in Africa is a socially constructed idea shaped by historical and cultural interactions in the context of colonialism.[11] That being said, witchcraft is irrational in the same sense that any religion can be irrational; they are based on faith and spirituality, not the secular. Given its spiritual nature, witchcraft has behavioral effects on African people on a multilateral basis. This includes changing how they interact with each other on a personal and community level to a societal and national level.

Not all Africans attest to the realities of witchcraft, as some also attest to its contributions to the cycle of poverty.[12] For the sake of this analysis, I will approach the topic of witchcraft from the perspective of its lived reality. This perspective emphasizes phenomenology and epistemology, including works from the West only with critical analysis. This is a postcolonial perspective that does not assume the existence or nonexistence of witchcraft but instead analyzes the current debates on the topic and the consequences that witchcraft has. I acknowledge the inherent generalizations that will take place in such a broad topic as "witchcraft in Africa" and will attempt to cite culturally specific beliefs whenever possible.

PART I
THE EPISTEMOLOGY OF WITCHCRAFT

But the layman's ground for accepting the models propounded by the scientist is often no different from the young African villager's ground for accepting the models propounded by one of his elders.[13]

Due to the history of colonialism in Africa, African religions have been both overgeneralized and demonized. A trademark methodology of European missionary work was the demonization of traditional African religions as "worshipping the devil." Since witchcraft in the Christian, biblical perspective is associated with pacts with the devil, witchcraft in Africa was given the same reputation. Witchcraft became a term synonymous with African religions, divination, traditions, ancestry, and traditional healers. Since these terms each have significant and distinct meanings, it is essential to redefine these terms before exploring literature on witchcraft in Africa. The use of English to explain an African concept inherently has a limiting effect. For anyone trying to understand witchcraft in Africa, Western associations with the term must be deconstructed.

African Religions

In 2010, a report on the religions of sub-Saharan Africa reported that the population is about 62 percent Christian and 30 percent Muslim. The "other religions" category makes up less than 1 percent of the population.[14] Yet, these numbers are extremely misleading, as even the most orthodox of Christian or Muslim Africans practice hybridity in their religion. They may use the Bible or the Quran but in relation to their African spirituality. African spirituality differs depending on the country, region, and tribe. Yet there are a few traits that can be generalized about African spirituality.

The first is the inseparability of African spirituality from other aspects of life in Africa. Whether it is politics, romance, family relationships, or business, spiritual sayings and traditions play an integral role in every part of Africa. Spirituality is integral to the Africanization of knowledge, as it is a validated way of knowing for most Africans. Asante makes the distinction between the natural, supernatural, and the paranormal in African spirituality.[15] The natural includes relationships that people have with each other and the environment and the moral standards that uphold those. Supernatural includes

Figure 2.1.   A Niam-Niam witch doctor. *Source:* The Wellcome Collection. Accessed July 29, 2020, from https://wellcomecollection.org/works/jrtdnvfb/items?canvas=1&langCode=eng.

relationships with ancestors of one's family or tribe, the people of the past. It also includes relationships to any gods or spirits of the natural. Finally, the paranormal includes African mythology. This ranges from animals that have abilities beyond the natural to people with the ability to channel the spiritual world for good or evil. In particular, African spirituality puts emphasis on ancestors and validates spiritual experiences as a way of knowing. Many African religions attribute spiritual causation to events that natural observation cannot easily explain, such as luck or death.[16]

Magical Thinking

The word "magic" comes from the Greek word "magike," an etymology that underlines the Eurocentric tones of the category. Magic is a social construct, as it explains what often is unexplainable. It is worth noting that there is typically no direct translation of "magic" into many African languages; instead, it is built into the language itself as an underlying assumption. While many European religions such as Christianity also use faith to explain the unexplainable, such as Jesus' healing powers or turning water into wine, this is seen as religious and not magical. The idea that magic is somehow something separate from religion can be traced to the Torah, in which "pagan" religions were deemed as using magic.[17]

Many anthropologists have described magical thinking as "false science,"[18] the "science of the concrete,"[19] or "African science." It has also been called the "natural attitude" or a cultural interpretation of science.[20] With technology, magic is often dubbed African's interpretation of modernity.[21] A worldview that includes magic in Africa often does not see magic as the replacement for the observable but an explanation for the unobservable.[22] Consider Evans-Prichard's example of a Zande house collapsing. The Azande clearly understood that termites were the cause of a house collapse and that this was preventable. They used witchcraft, a magical belief, to explain *why* they thought the termites had chosen this house in particular.[23] Magical thinking often does not replace the observable *why* but offers insight into the unobservable *how*.

Some magic has a dark connotation, such as "juju." This might involve using body parts in dark rituals to increase the powers of individuals for war or political campaigns, such as "muti." Magic, in general, describes cultural knowledge about spirituality and healing and is given to every member of a community.[24] An example of specialized magical knowledge is the Zulu "Izangoma," who are called to the role by the ancestors trained to mediate human concerns with the spirit realm.[25] Magic describes the phantasmagoric, that which is virtual and beyond the realms of physical space. It includes healing, interaction with the spiritual world, sorcery, and witchcraft. Yet, despite the religious nature of magical beliefs, they are still often seen by outsiders as below the status of both science and religion.[26]

Witchcraft, Healing, and Sorcery

So far, I have described magical thinking as characteristic of African religions. I've also described the hybridity of African religions and the hypocritical bias in which Eurocentric religions use the term "magical thinking." Stories of witchcraft, healing, and sorcery are prevalent in every world religion, in particular all mentioned individually within the Bible. Whereas biblical references to witchcraft, healing, and sorcery are seen as manifestations of the cosmic struggle between God and the Devil, such discussion in Africa religions are ridiculed from the outside as folklore. Concepts of witchcraft, healing, and sorcery in Africa must come from a place of religious respect and understanding—a perspective that does not assume their inherent falsehood. Instead, they must be looked at as characteristics of every religion that take on a particular form in many African religions.

As an anthropological perspective—which is the only useful perspective given that magic and associated terms are Eurocentric labels for the "other"—witchcraft, healing, and sorcery have in common that they are ways that humans can manipulate or channel the spiritual. Witchcraft differs from sorcery in that witchcraft is inherent to the person. Therefore, in witchcraft beliefs, witches have the ability to perform witchcraft, which the layman cannot perform. Sorcery, on the other hand, can be used by anyone.[27] Healing, in the sense when it is miraculous, is often an example of sorcery beliefs or religious from channeling ancestors or gods. It is important to note that, despite these anthropological definitions, witchcraft is a constantly constructed and culturally relevant term.

The term "witchcraft" has an inherently Eurocentric origin. Its use in the modern-day sense emerged from the fusion of Wicca and old Victorian ideas.[28] The phenomenon of witch hunts in the Western world accompanied Christianity in that it characterized witches as women who had made a pact with the devil to perform sinister tasks. The translation of this term to Africa occurred during colonialism in which missionaries performed the "white man's burden" of "civilizing" African nations. In the process, missionaries sought to convert people to Christianity, demonizing their indigenous religions as satanic and, therefore, witchcraft. Christianity and colonialism applied the English term "witchcraft" to Africa; however, concepts of African "juju" or dark magic existed far before this encounter.

For the purposes of this analysis, I define witchcraft as the intentional use of magic toward sinister acts by an individual. This definition differs from the anthropological definition in that it includes both cultures that believe that people are "born witches" and those who believe people "become witches." It includes African indigenous religions and their witchcraft perceptions as well as African Christian or Islamic witchcraft perceptions. I've included sorcery within the category of witchcraft for the purpose of this analysis. I am excluding nonsinister magical acts from witchcraft. This includes divinations, prophets, healers, and spiritual leaders. Their categorization within witchcraft is a misunderstanding that comes only from the Eurocentric view that non-European religions are associated with the devil.

Epistemology of Witchcraft

From an outside perspective, as has been stated by many Eurocentric researchers, witchcraft seems an irrational belief. Evans-Pritchard's analysis of the Zande's beliefs of witchcraft admitted the logical nature of witchcraft. Although Evans-Pritchard's study showed progress in European understanding of African beliefs, the fundamental issue of epistemology was not addressed. Witchcraft in Africa must be analyzed and discussed through an African epistemology.

Eurocentricity in the use of the word "witchcraft" has been discussed, as the application of this word to Africa has heavy implications that come from the use of the English word in the Christian religion and history of missionary work and colonialism. This is not unique to the term "witchcraft" but reflects the larger colonial matrix of power in which secular academic epistemology exists. The colonial matrix of power is the physical and ideological systems that European domination in economics and politics created to maintain their power.[29] Key to this is the secular and modern epistemology of academia, which defines knowledge only as that which fits into the framework of the Enlightenment.

This European epistemology that dominates modern academia has several key features. First, it is a Cartesian philosophy, separating the emotional from the cognitive as a way of knowing. Following is the aspect of secularity, which denies the religious or magical any space in the theory of knowledge beyond the humanities. Next is objectivity, or the personal detachment of the individual from the object of study. In particular, standard modern epis- temological practice is to follow the scientific method and to use academic journals to critique current findings. Among the problematic aspects of this epistemology are illusion of secularity, as nonreligious knowledge is religious in that it does not include religion.[30] Also, the entrapment of this system of criticism within the European academic system disallows the subaltern to publish itself.[31] Finally, European epistemology is limited to singular truth and way of knowing. The pluralist idea of multiple ways of knowing does not connect to current scientific idea of knowledge taught in universities. This limits the amount of knowledge and the timbre of that knowledge available in global academia and on the university level.

Given the superficial summary of European epistemology that I've pro- vided, my analysis of an African epistemology will be similar. My focus here is on witchcraft and its role within a larger system: thus, I utilize a false binary and generalizations of macrosystems of knowledge to analyze witchcraft only. Given the diversity of Africa, a singular African epistemology is not possible: thus, I will describe what I will call themes in African epistemolo- gies. It is important to note that epistemic reasoning is not indicative of cog- nitive performance. A person who holds witchcraft beliefs is part of a system of historical and cultural justification of that system of knowledge just as a scientist in America has been taught to praise the scientific method.[32] What is immediately obvious to the reader of Afrocentric knowledge is its insepa- rability from knowledge, the innate rejection of the secular. African ways of knowing especially validate that which is subjective or personal experience, including the emotional and intuition. Often misunderstood about African epistemologies is their emphasis on testimony, validating that which has been passed down from ancestors as the most sacred.[33]

Understanding themes in African epistemologies explain the epistemol- ogy of witchcraft. Ideas about witchcraft are passed down in community and social contexts. They are perpetuated by emphasis on testimony and ancestral knowledge as truth and validating intuitive, spiritual, and emotional knowledge as truth.

Case Studies in Witchcraft

The best way to understand the sheer diversity and complexity of witchcraft beliefs in Africa is to highlight some specific cultural beliefs. These examples can serve as anchors in which witchcraft beliefs can be understood and analyzed, as well as examples of variance across cultural groups.

"Mangu" and the Azande

Any analysis of witchcraft in Africa would be incomplete without mentioning Evan-Prichard's anthropological analysis of Zande witchcraft beliefs. The Zande people live in southern Sudan and are a melding of various ethnic groups that previously lived in the region. The region and the Azande fell under Belgian and French rule and the British until the independence of Sudan in 1956. "Mangu" is the Zande word that roughly translates into "witchcraft" in English. The Azande believe that witchcraft is genetic; for an individual to utilize witchcraft, a child must be born from a same-sex 'witch' parent as well as make the choice to be a witch. Witchcraft is thought to be utilized through sheer will, and thus the intent to hurt someone else itself can cause harm even if the witch does not perform a charm or spell. The Azande believe that witchcraft is a physical substance that clings to the intestines and is discoverable upon the death of a witch. Like in many places in Africa, Zande people believe that witchcraft is an everyday part of life and a major cause of misfortune and death. For the Zande, witchcraft can often be a slow process and families often consult a healer or an oracle to seek help to combat the dark magic if witchcraft is suspected.[34]

Of special note is the Azande use of the "poison oracle." This practice is of special note because it is a practice across many cultures in Africa that has to do with witchcraft. In this practice, a decision is made by poisoning a fowl and observing to see if the fowl lives. The decision typically surrounds the guilt of a person, especially one who practices witchcraft. Therefore, it serves as a truth-finding system of justice.[35]

"Thakathi" in the Zulu

Another anthropological study on witchcraft in Africa is Ashforth analysis of "muthi" and "thakathi" in South Africa with the Zulu. The Zulu people believe in witchcraft in everyday life and as a cause of death, but they do not believe that it is genetic. Appearing closer to sinister sorcery, the Zulu believe that witchcraft is when a person uses supernatural herbs and traditional medicine to harm others. According to Ashforth, the only difference between witchcraft and healing is the moral intention of the "spell." The harmful substances that are used for witchcraft as called "muthi" or "muti," translated as "medicine" or "poison." The "thakathi" is distinct in Zulu culture from the "sangoma," translated as "diviner," "shaman," or "healer." The "sangoma" serves to heal people from any disease or acts of witchcraft using "muthi" for morally sound intentions.[36]

The Banyang Were-Animals

The Banyang live in the southwest region of Cameroon. They have several beliefs related to witchcraft including belief in supernatural agencies and an ultimate deity and a cult of the dead. In one tradition, they believe in witchcraft in the dimension of possession of animal counterparts, "were-animals." Every person has a were-animal, but the were-animal they possess and how they instruct it to act is the window of opportunity for witchcraft. Not all were-animals do harm or are associated with witchcraft, but some are more susceptible to witchcraft than others. This act of using one's spiritual were-animal to cause harm to others is called "debu."[37]

Counterexamples of Witchcraft

Along with examples of witchcraft, I'd like to include two examples that are distinctly not witchcraft. The first is the example of basket divination in Northwest Zambia. This practice is not limited to the region but is practiced in various dimensions throughout the continent. In basket divination, diviners pass spiritual knowledge and skills through generations. In particular, these skills involve mixing a basket of magical items. The diviner is taught how to read the meaning in regard to the spirit world of the objects based off of how they land in the basket. Sometimes, diviners use this tool to identify witchcraft. Still, divination is not an act of witchcraft itself because it lacks malice.[38]

A similar example of a diviner using their connections to the spiritual world to seek out witches is the people of Kongo using the "nkisi" to detect witchcraft. The object, the nkisi, is not purely of this realm but channels a spirit who inhabits the object.[39] Special about the nkisi is that the tradition of using them also migrated with Africans during the slave trade to influence African American Christianity. The nkisi is also a symbol of African art, often labeled with terms such as "primitive" or "fetish" art. It has been the object of Western interest in Africa and European imitation. Like the divination baskets, the nkisi does serve to connect humanity with the spirit world but not

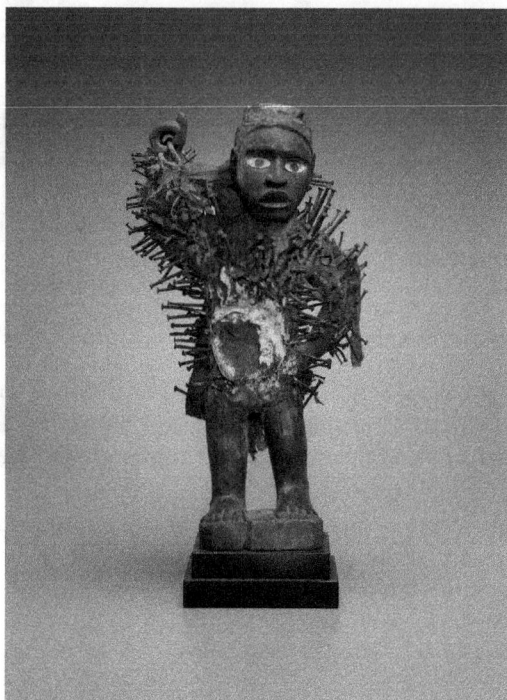

Figure 2.2. Nkisi, believed to inhabit spirits in some tribes in the Congo. *Source*: Yale University Art Gallery. Accessed July 29, 2020, from https://artgallery.yale.edu/collections/objects/84739.

for means of malice. Therefore, the nkisi can be used to detect witchcraft but is not an act of witchcraft itself.

Cultural Collectivism and Witchcraft

It is worth noting that the bulk of literature on witchcraft in Africa is anthropological work done by Western scholars. As I explain some of these theories of witchcraft, keep in mind the epistemic context of these researchers and the biased perspective they have as European people studying the "other."

Evans-Prichard's study in 1937 with the Azande is the foundation to most works in the anthropology of witchcraft. It is evident from his writings that previous to his writing, witchcraft beliefs were viewed as simply "irrational." Earlier, I described the belief of the Zande people with the termite example. To reiterate the famous example, a person's house had collapsed due to termite infestation. The Azande attributed this misfortune to witchcraft. To the outsider, the answer is obviously termites and in that time the Azande were viewed as unable to understand the science of that. Despite this assumption of the irrationality of the Azande, they did have extensive knowledge about the relationship between termites and the collapse of the house. Witchcraft did not function as a replacement for lack of science, but rather witchcraft explained the causality of this misfortune. Evans-Prichard used his analysis to describe the rationality of the Azande and the idea of cultural relativity. He stated that it wasn't that the Azande were illogical but that their logic existed within the confines of their culture.[40]

An interesting introduction to Evans-Prichard's landmark paper provides justification for why an outsider must study the Azande. He asserts that the Zande people are unable to explain their own beliefs about witchcraft because they are so ubiquitous within their lives.[41] This perspective outlines the assumptions of anthropology and its relation to the "other." This traditional perspective denies that the "other" is able to speak for themselves because they are unaware of their own beliefs, uneducated, and unable to analyze their own culture. In the later discourse of postcolonialism, the idea of autoethnography as a tool of epistemic disobedience will challenge this idea.

Cultural relativism implies neutrality as a term, yet in practice, anthropological interpretations of the cultural relativity of witchcraft continued their assumption of primitivism. Schutz defined witchcraft as a "natural attitude." This is, simply speaking, the most straightforward conclusion for people to make about mysteries of their world based on their religious, cultural, and educational environment.[42] Levi-Strauss, a bit more radical, denoted witchcraft the "science of the concrete." He attempted to strip the hierarchy from beliefs systems and analyze them for what they were. He saw magic and science as essentially the same, with not one inferior to the other.[43] Yet, the placement of his chapter "the science of the concrete" within the larger text of his book *The Savage Mind* retains the inherent racism of the day. Furthermore, his inability to give a voice to the people whom he studied earned his work a space within the colonial matrix of power.

A fairly recent perspective on witchcraft beliefs is that they are formed or reinforced by economic factors. This theory comes from the idea that most African cultures are more collectivist than the West. The result is that the globalization of capitalism causes ideological conflicts on the community level. This doesn't mean that African countries do not have markets where goods and supplies are exchanged. Most villages have a village market where goods can be purchased and exchanged. But, usually, this happens within the community context where friendship, familiarity, community, and kinship ties are an essential part of the economic interaction. Growing large corporations and access to the global economy disrupt the regular economic patterns of the community, causing one person or family to gather extreme wealth. The norm in these collectivists communities is that families help each other in times of poverty and the community gains wealth as a whole. The idea of an individual gaining wealth while the community stays at the same level leaves no explanation except for witchcraft.[44]

The economic causal theory of witchcraft beliefs reflects the larger idea of normative ambiguity. The idea of normative ambiguity causing witchcraft beliefs is that "witches" are targeted when their action doesn't fit the societal framework of how they "should" behave. When something happens out of the ordinary that cannot be immediately decided as proper or improper behavior, witchcraft is suspected. This includes when one person in the community suddenly has more power or wealth.[45]

A 2014 analysis in South Africa found significant xenophobia toward non-South African blacks fueled by witchcraft beliefs.[46] Foreigners in South Africa were seen as taking the wealth of South Africans, setting up tourist shops or restaurants that became successful quickly in a way that could only be explained by witchcraft. This is an example of the economy creating social tension that results in witchcraft accusations. But also, the influx of foreigners disrupts the dynamics of South African society, which creates normative ambiguity. The foreigners aren't necessarily doing something morally wrong, but they are coming from outside the community context, which results in distrust.

Witchcraft as Knowledge in Modernity

Throughout literature about witchcraft in Africa the question permeates, "How is witchcraft still practiced in Africa?" The inquisition is problematic because the assumption is that witchcraft is not modern. This has shown up throughout my analysis as witchcraft beliefs have been described as "pre-religion" or "beneath religion" as well as "primitive" or associated with Social Darwinism. As I stated at the beginning of the discussion, witchcraft is a lived reality—and, therefore, a knowledge system—for many people around the world. The tangible physical, economic, and behavioral effects of witchcraft beliefs make it a modern reality.[47]

Modernity as a concept has historically been associated with current Eurocentric values. Among these today are secularity, democracy, capitalism, technology, and individualism. The concept developed from Western Enlightenment ideals that, while developing in a specific culture and historical framework, are often used as a sort of measuring stick for the rest of the world. Postcolonial scholars reject this concept of modernity and the ensuing definition of development. In Africa, scholars search for Afrocentric development and define modernity by Africa's current lived realities.

Evidence for the modernity of witchcraft comes from two factors. First, that witchcraft is currently believed in by a wide variety of Africans and around the world. Second, that the epistemic justifications of witchcraft have not remained stagnant, thus making the question 'why people still believe in witchcraft' irrelevant. It is not a question of *still*, but *now*. Analysis of witchcraft beliefs shows that they are adapting and strengthening in response to pressing modern factors of growing global inequalities and rapidly developing technology.[48] For example, the anonymity of cell phones has sparked witchcraft beliefs specifically related to cell phones. Namely, that witches can cast a spell on someone through a phone call.[49] Through a normative ambiguity analysis, this belief may come from the cultural clash of the ability to remain anonymous in collectivists and community-based societies. Another example is the modern academic environment. This Eurocentric system rewards successful academics who play by the rules through promotions, money, and titles. This individualistic practice also prompts heightened witchcraft accusations.[50]

It is a limited point of view to ask how witchcraft beliefs can exist within modernity. This is because modernity is not singular but plural; multiple modernities exist as lived experiences of people around the world. And thus, witchcraft exists as modernity in Africa.[51] A further topic of discussion is the implications of the modernity of witchcraft for the development of Africa. Many scholars have argued that witchcraft is an impediment to the development of Africa.[52] This is part of a much larger discussion about the Eurocentric and singular pathway to development that is touted by the West. The possibility for multiple pathways to development requires Afrocentric thought and a humanistic assessment of the practicality and tangible needs of Africa. Frankly, witchcraft beliefs impede with the development of Africa in the context that development is defined as likeness to Europe.

PART II
WITCHCRAFT AND THE COLONIAL IDEOLOGY

Until the lions have their own historians, the history of the hunt will always glorify the hunter.[53]

It is widely accepted that motivations to spread Christianity and the "civilizing mission" were at the root of colonialism. In many ways, this is a humanitarian effort—at least at the surface. The ideological justification for colonialism was the helping of poor, uneducated, and demonic "children of God" to be civilized Christians. Africa was seen as the "dark continent," despite the complications of preexisting Christianity in the North. Africa was not absent of religion but teeming with indigenous religious beliefs that Christian outsiders equated with demonology. The process of Christianizing Africa required coordinated church efforts, resources, and time. This gap between indigenous beliefs and Christianity is where colonialism interacted with witchcraft beliefs.

To help Africans to adopt Christianity, a common tactic was for missionaries to learn the local religious beliefs and, in a sense, meet people where they were. The window of opportunity that missionaries saw for saviorism was witchcraft beliefs. Systematically, missionaries used the fear of witchcraft beliefs as evidence of the devil. From that binary, they were able to customize local beliefs into Christian doctrine.[54] Even today, missionaries in Africa note that fear of witchcraft is key to spreading Christianity, as this fear has heightened due to threatening forces of the HIV epidemic and globalization.[55]

In practice, historical colonial missionaries validated witchcraft as the work of the devil, whereas colonial law undermined magical thinking as irrational. A 2003 study on women inflicted with madness in South Africa up until 1914 found an underlying conflict between the nature of madness in local and colonial dominant contexts. The South African indigenous groups were likely to attribute madness to witchcraft, whereas colonial law deemed it a mental health issue. This dissonance in epistemic foundations, different systems of knowledge, would have practical implications in regard to medical treatment and the law.[56] The result was epistemic violence.

Although causality is difficult to prove in retrospect, it is highly likely that the trauma of colonialism heightened witchcraft beliefs. Colonizers brought along oppression, diseases, and ideas that caused normative ambiguity and economic chaos—along with physical and epistemic violence. Christian missionaries took advantage of indigenous witchcraft beliefs, melding them with ideas of demonology to their own benefit. The result was the even further heightening of fear and dark magic within communities. Modern Christianity in Africa carries on this legacy as it often reinforces modern witchcraft beliefs.

Academia also works within the colonial matrix of power. In this system, outside scholars write *about* Africa. Although anthropology has validated witchcraft as logical through the guide of cultural relativity, the primary issue is that writing on Africa is still not coming from an Afrocentric perspective. Institutions that talk about Africa, from academia to NGOs to government agencies lack recognition of witchcraft beliefs for the reality that they are in Africa.[57] The title of the journal article "World View: Writing about Africa without Mentioning the Role of Tribalism and Witchcraft Is Like Writing about British Fox-Hunting without Mentioning Class" says it all.[58]

As an example, consider the United Nations Development Program's (UNDP) rhetoric on human security. This conversation took place in 1994 and focused on global politics that were humanistic and closer to the reality of individuals. UNDP defined human security as the "legitimate concerns of people who sought security in their daily lives." Yet, their extensive descriptions of concerns to the security of Africans did not include the spiritual issue of witchcraft. As stated earlier, whether the UNDP officially recognizes witchcraft as a reality does not matter—because witchcraft inarguably is a lived reality for most Africans. This is what Ashforth described as "spiritual insecurity," a divide between how the UNDP enunciated the concern of people of the Global South versus their actual felt insecurities.[59]

African studies is a field that developed within Western thought. Historical circumstances create gaps in understanding, which limit the ability for Western research about Africa to be accurate. This literature tends to describe the Global South based on what they "lack" in comparison to the West. Accurate literature on the continent requires an understanding of the life realities of individuals within their own cultural context. The solution is a new wave of literature that takes the local social and political contexts seriously while at the same time being globally reputable.[60]

PART III
THE IDEOLOGY OF WITCHCRAFT

Understanding the Ideology of Witchcraft

In the light of postcolonialism, magic and witchcraft are socially constructed categories. Their status as somehow less than religion, instead of taking the form of "superstition" or the "other," comes from the development of comparative religions and anthropological foundations such as Social Darwinism.[61] Social Darwinism, in particular, labeled witchcraft beliefs as pre-religion, as if humanity develops on a scale that Africans had not yet progressed. Postcolonialism deconstructs, as I have attempted to do throughout this essay, the historical and cultural factors that shaped current realities and perceptions of witchcraft.

Moving forward, African educational systems continue to model the European value of secularity, pushing away ideas about witchcraft from the conversation. This process perpetuates epistemic violence, which does not allow African students to reach their full potential. It, instead, teaches children separatism in their identity and the foreignness of academia.

A global example of normative ambiguity, as I earlier described, as an anthropological theory is that of African perceptions of European witchcraft. Through surveys and interviews, scholars have found over and over again mentions from Africans about Europe's relationship to witchcraft. The common response is either "Europe has relinquished witchcraft"[62] or that "Europe's wealth come from witchcraft."[63] The former is more modern while the latter is the traditional response that models my earlier hypothesis that witchcraft beliefs are associated with capitalism being practiced in collectivist societies.

Despite assertions such as in Social Darwinism that witchcraft beliefs are "pre-religious" and that Africa will develop out of them, witchcraft beliefs seem to be steady or heightening in Africa. The increase of globalization and ongoing crises threatening African countries only heighten these beliefs, as I will discuss later in witchcraft as modernity. The economic causation theory of witchcraft was created to explain interactions on community levels, yet it can be seen even in international interactions. For example, the sex tourism industry in Kenya leads hopeful Kenyan women to witches in the south and in Tanzania and Zanzibar. Access to a "mzungu" can change your life, provide for your family, and maybe even your village if they start a business or NGO. Therefore, women work hard to purchase expensive spells that might increase their attractiveness to foreign men.[64] NGOs have also been historically accused of heightening witchcraft beliefs, as local conflict comes from competition to reach the limited resources of the organization.[65] International witchcraft beliefs are more recently tied to the increase of HIV lab testing, especially in South Africa. Rumors circulate that Western doctors sell South African blood off or even are poisoning those being treated.[66] Continued misunderstanding between Western actions in African nations and wealth and education inequalities have historically heightened witchcraft beliefs and will continue to do so.

Historical Analysis of Witchcraft Ideologies

I have distinctly stated the difference between witchcraft ideas of the West and Africa, including how heterogeneous witchcraft beliefs in Africa are today. Many scholars see human culture through anthropology as a continuum of development. This scale puts witchcraft beliefs before formalized religion. This is ahistorical because witchcraft beliefs heightened in Europe in tangent with religion; thus, it is more accurate to say that witchcraft is a symptom of religion than a precursor to it. However different the historical and cultural circumstances are, theories about witchcraft beliefs in Africa exist in a globalized definition of witchcraft. The literature exists in the same sphere as literature on sociological and anthropological justifications of the witch trials of Europe and colonial America. Thus, I will cite some of the theories of witchcraft in Europe, as to why it functions in society, only to provide it as context to the debate in and on African witchcraft.

First, there are those who speak of the criminology of witchcraft. As witchcraft in Europe is famous for discrete accusations of individuals for their crimes, the question goes—how did these witches suddenly become criminals? The answer to this is often cited as 1484, when Pope Innocent IV wrote that witchcraft was a real and serious crime facing the Christian world.

Thus, in most Christian European countries, witchcraft became illegal on the national level. In England, witch hunts took on a more local-entrepreneurial level. Thus, the justice system had the objective to incriminate witches through a repressive justice system that targeted church dissenters and accused witches.[67] In a sense, the rise of witchcraft on a micro-community level came from the global and national laws.

The congruence between this theory and witchcraft in Africa is that many African nations have outlawed witchcraft. In South Africa, the Witchcraft Suppression Act of 1957 outlaws any activity related to witchcraft—based on the 1735 witchcraft act of England. So, although ideas about witchcraft in Africa developed independently and with different motives than those in Europe, they are related. First, because colonialism merged witchcraft ideas with Christianity for many people. Second, because colonial laws of Europe about witchcraft translated to their understanding of African witchcraft. This bill has influenced South Africa through outlawing "claiming supernatural powers" and thus repressing indigenous African religions and traditional healers while also making the lived reality of witchcraft a taboo. Since the law defines deviance, it also validates witchcraft as evil and perpetuates the urge to seek witches within the country. Similar laws exist in most other African nations, also with colonial influence.

Earlier, I mentioned the economic causality theory of witchcraft. For Europe, unique economic conditions that affected society coincided with the rise of witchcraft. Consider the European tale, "Rumpelstiltskin." In this story, a poor cloth weaver is desperate for a way out of poverty. She trades her firstborn child to a mythical creature in exchange for riches. This tale reflects several social conditions that relate to witchcraft: the women being a cloth weaver, the cloth weaver being poor and rejected from society, and then the female cloth weaver being seen as desperate enough to use despicable means to achieve economic justice. The tale reflects the reality of rural female cloth weavers gaining "riches" as demand for cloth increased with the transatlantic trade. The result was suspicion, jealousy, and accusations of witchcraft. These accusations come both from patriarchal forces attempting to reinforce gender norms and economic jealousy.[68]

Other theories of witchcraft's rise in Europe similarly focus on dissent on social pressure to take down those who do not belong. This includes homosexuals,[69] women who expressed their sexuality,[70] or rebels.[71] It also includes people who were mentally ill or hysterical for medical, emotional, or spiritual reasons.[72] Interestingly, it also includes those healers who were misunderstood as practicing witchcraft, when in fact using traditional healing methods.[73]

Many of these themes seem familiar in discussion of witchcraft in Africa, especially the themes of feminism, disease, misunderstanding, and economic or social inequality. There are many limitations as witchcraft in Africa has long stood the test of time in contrast to Africa. Furthermore, African witch-craft beliefs take a wide diversity, whereas Europe had relatively homogenous perceptions of witchcraft within the church. The European scare of witchcraft might have begun, or been snowballed, by the proclamation of a singular pope—whereas African witchcraft has been validated by individual religious leaders, politicians, and colonial regimes throughout history. Furthermore, whereas witchcraft in Europe seemed to die down in a few hundred years, African witchcraft has not declined, and if anything, intensified.

A Feminist Perspective on Witchcraft Ideology

The gendered dimension to witchcraft is core to its function in society. His-torically, most witchcraft accusations as well as violent persecutions have been against females rather than males.[74] A 2012 survey of perception of witchcraft in Ghana found that 82 percent of descriptions of witchcraft used feminine pronouns or associations. In function, women are seen as more likely to employ witchcraft due to jealousy in love, even in the case of polygamy.[75] According to UN Women, women in sub-Saharan African represent less than 15 percent of landowners.[76] Sub-Saharan Africa's gender parity index (GPI) of gendered literacy was .75—only second to the lowest in the world of .70 in Southern Asia.[77] In West and Cen-tral Africa, about four out of every ten girls are married before their eighteenth birthday.[78] In feminist theory, witchcraft in Africa can be analyzed as a piece of the larger patriarchy. On the other hand, it is possible that witchcraft beliefs natu-rally target the weakest in society as scapegoats, this being women and children. Either way, the gendered dimension to witchcraft cannot be ignored.

A Dangerous Ideology?

The primary reason that scholars argue that witchcraft is detrimental to Africa's development is that it is a hindrance to scientific thinking. Much emphasis in development discourse has been put on the capacity for STEM education to bring technological development. It is perceived that witchcraft beliefs are incoherent with modern science and thus harmful to this effort. Counterevidence suggests that the poor science performance that does exist for African students comes from lack of jobs to make those skills applicable.[79] Another argument for witchcraft's harm to development is that of social capital. The idea is that witchcraft beliefs erode social trust, which decreases the ability for people to start businesses and maintain relationships.[80] This may be true, given the relationship between individualism and capitalism to witchcraft accusations.

The Western model of development is critiqued for many downfalls, an urgent one of those being poor environmental management. Although witch-craft beliefs have been accused of being counter-development, they may be one of the reasons that Africans practice better environmental management. Ideas that relate witchcraft to nature including natural gods and cursed forests may be key to environmental protection.[81] In terms of pedagogy and curriculum concerning witchcraft, it is most practical to teach witchcraft and all other indigenous knowledge systems, as they apply to the people studying, along with critical thinking skills. Promotion of critical thinking skills maximizes the strengths of these beliefs.

One of the most tangible ways that witchcraft beliefs are seen in Africa is through their effects on health-related behaviors. A 2012 analysis on South Africa found that around 8 percent of premature deaths were seen as attributed to witchcraft.[82] The mythology of witchcraft often includes symptoms similar to diseases such as slow death, premature death, and death of several relatives. Symptoms of malaria such as hallucinations or yellowed eyes may be interpreted as related to witchcraft.[83] On one hand, diseases may go untreated as a result of attribution to witchcraft whereas science may be able to easily provide a cure.

On the other hand, strict rules about local healers not able to practice because of overgeneralized witchcraft laws may hinder the healthcare options for many Africans. With extremely limited access to money, qualified physicians, and acceptable facilities, many Africans receive local healer care as their primary health care. Restricting access to this care is not only an act of epistemic violence but it also physically limits individuals living in poverty to health care.[84]

The relationship between witchcraft and rising HIV rates is particularly interesting. Deaths from to HIV due to their apparent lack of causation are often interpreted as caused by witchcraft.[85] Traditional healers are highly likely to identify HIV as a form of witchcraft.[86] In fact, the rising rates of HIV have coincided with heightened witchcraft beliefs.[87] A study in South Africa found that people who had misconceptions about HIV were more likely to believe in witchcraft.[88] The epistemic of HIV in Africa is the sight of tragedy and shock. The nature of the disease and the rising prevalence may have heightened witchcraft beliefs. Leftover colonial distrust matched with Western humanitarianism, clinical trials, and experimental medicine heighten the mystery of the disease. Whether this indicates causation or coincidence, witchcraft beliefs are much overlooked in most of the literature concerning HIV rates in Africa.

CONCLUSIONS

To start a conversation with "witchcraft is a problem in Africa," two people from different cultural backgrounds might both agree—for different reasons. The Western humanitarian might see witchcraft as a problem of women and child rights, patriarchy, and missed health care. From the African perspective, witchcraft as a problem might involve the heightened activity of witchcraft in the modern world. This may even connect to HIV as an agent of witchcraft, Western or government conspirators, and oppression of local cultures.

Witchcraft is a lived reality for most Africans and many of African descent. While most literatures on witchcraft focus on disproving its existence or condemning witchcraft accusations, it is disconnected from this reality. A close understanding of witchcraft, as well as associated concepts such as African religions and healers, in a local context is the only starting point for conversation on witchcraft. The validation of witchcraft as an epistemology, therefore, has much to contribute to postcolonial discourse and understanding of Afrocentric knowledge. The result would have much to contribute to global discussions on topics ranging from politics, health, human rights, and education.

Chapter 3

Elderhood and Ancestorhood as Ideas and Beliefs

Aging, or old age, is a universal phenomenon, an irreversible biological process that is integral to understanding societal and human development. Sagner and Kowal argue that aging is socially constructed; in other words, they recognize old age as inevitable but attribute the definition and meaning to societal opinions and conceptions.[1] Aging is sometimes associated with wisdom and infallacy, while youth is seen as a time of naivety and recklessness. This is especially true in African cultures, where elderhood is a strong organizing force of society. In recent times, age is measured and described using a chronological counting system. Prior to this Western hegemonic adoption, Sangree denotes that Africans described old age through a hierarchal placement of persons based on generations. These placements are often known as age groups, where the top hierarchies and their members are often considered older generations.[2] Other times, naming patterns reflect the sociocultural and historical events of a particular era and give away a person's elderliness or youth, therefore attracting due treatment.

Oftentimes, the notion of age tends to be conflated with seniority; as noted by Baker and Eaton, the view of chronological age as an avenue for certain privileges is clearly meaningless without an understanding of seniority.[3] They also denote that age is only a meaningful and important concept in organizations or institutions where the conventions of calendars and clocks determine an understanding of time, which is ultimately any formal institution in the present society. In other words, age without seniority will be relatively inconsequential in formal institutions in the society, although age is often considered a near-accurate index of seniority. An understanding of the concept of seniority is necessary to make meaning of the previous sentence; therefore, seniority, as examined by Baker and Eaton, is viewed as "the duration of membership within a local social system."[4] Although age is often a marker

37

of seniority, with the definition previously presented, this is, however, not always the case.

Spending more time or number of years at a place of work often places an individual at a place of authority and seniority irrespective of their age. In some occupations like sports, where experience measured as opposed to age, the ideology of age as an indication of seniority does not apply. In other words, any newcomer to the sport is considered inexperienced and young in the field irrespective of their chronological age. However, since time offers advantage to older people, that is, since older people tend to get into various systems earlier than younger people, it complicates and conflates the perception of age and seniority in formal institutions. It is often a tricky business to distinguish both concepts, which, therefore, provides credence to Baker and Eaton's claims that most scholars will consider the quest to provide conceptual distinctions as pointless.[5]

In contemporary times the most obvious definition for old age in Africa emanates from a chronometric description of human progress—that is, the reflection of age in numbers. This, therefore, gives credence to Sagner and Kowal's description of old age as a product of the passage of time, which is measured using days, months, and years. Following a number of researchers, they note that in Africa, the ages fifty, sixty, and sixty-five mark the commencement of elderliness or the twilight years of a person's existence. This is culturally represented in Adeboye's description of old age as "ojọ alẹ"—the metaphorical representation of old age as the twilight of a person's life among the Yoruba people of Western Nigeria.[6] Old age as the passage of time also plays out in the retirement of people in Africa; in other words, toward the aforementioned ages, most African workers get closer to their eligibility for retirement and pensions. Age, as observed by Baker and Eaton, is the most pervasive basis for social organization.[7] It is often part of the requirement for employment and retirement.

Considering that old age is an inevitable and important social organizer, conceptions of old age have an impact on several spheres of society across cultures. In Africa, cultural conceptions of elderhood find expression in areas of society such as household politics, societal politics, judicial matters, religious affairs, education/academy, and in the workforce. Having understood the parameters for the definition of old age in Africa, it is necessary to understand the various conceptions and opinions attached to old age in Africa so as to examine their interactions with, and the effects on, the society.

The following chapter will serve to explore the impacts of elderhood on the production of knowledge in Africa. The first part explores the cultural meaning of elderhood in Africa and its impacts on knowledge in the contexts of everyday life and academia. The second part will engage in a comparative study of African, Eastern, and Western conceptions of old age to reimagine the role of elderhood in Africa. The words "old age," "elderhood," and "ancestorhood" will be used interchangeably in this work; although old age can be understood in light of the various parameters for definition provided so far, they tend to connote similar meanings even though elderhood and ancestorhood refer more to the cultural significance of the former in the African society.

PART I
UNDERSTANDING THE EPISTEMOLOGY
OF ELDERHOOD

Cultural Significance of Elderhood and Ancestorhood in Africa

Culture refers to the people's way of life; it reflects the people's values and norms and how these factors help in structuring human interaction in the said society.[8] Wisdom, reverence, honor, and spirituality usually come to mind in discourses of elderhood and ancestorhood in Africa. They constitute ideologies, philosophies, and values associated with old age in Africa. Old age has a huge cultural significance in Africa, which impacts intergenerational and social interactions in the continent. Traditionally for the African, age is a marker for seniority and seniority in turn equals power and privilege and constitutes a huge aspect of social relations within the continent.[9] Given the social ordering of Africa by seniority, the question and expression of seniority in understanding the cultural conceptions of elderhood cannot be overemphasized.[10] Seniority is also coterminous to privilege in Africa; it begets the conferment of certain statuses and privileges in African culture. Authority, respect, and reverence constitute one of the major privileges of the state of elderhood in Africa. Kenyatta puts it succinctly in the following statement:

> As a man grows old, his prestige increases according to the number of age grade he has passed. It is the seniority that makes an elder an almost indispensable in the general life of the community. His presence or advice is sought in all functions. In religious ceremonies, the elder holds supreme authorities. The custom of the people demands that the elder should be given his due respect and honour.[11]

The passage of time is believed to afford the elderly a wealth of wisdom, knowledge, and experiences; they are equally believed to enjoy proximity to the ancestral world and are, therefore, viewed as living representatives of gods and ancestors.[12] Adeboye, in his description of the Yoruba cultural inclination to ancestorhood, does not classify the elderly as ancestors but rather links and mediums through which the living can have a relationship with the ancestors.[13] Among the Igbo people of Eastern Nigeria, Okoye also notes that the people perceive their elders as links to ancestral spirits and are therefore assumed to receive firsthand the instructions from the ancestors.[14] However, according to Apt, the Shona people of Zimbabwe do not view the elderly as mediums but rather as ancestral spirits among the living.[15] Following these opinions, Kopytoff, in his examination of ancestor human relationship in Africa, reemphasizes the ancestral proximity of African elders; in his opinion, he states:

> Ancestors are intimately involved with the welfare of their kin-group but they are not linked in the same way to every member of that group. The linkage is structured through the elders of the kin-group, and the elders' authority is related to their close link to the ancestors. In some sense the elders are the representatives of the ancestors and the mediators between them and the kin-group.[16]

Following Kopytoff's line of thought, it is easy to identify the functionality associated with the state of elderhood in Africa. Although elderhood might be viewed as a state of being, it is also accompanied by an array of functional roles that define its very essence and emphasize its significance in the society.

From the excerpt, a clear deduction can be made of the need for mediation between the ancestors and the living; this is meaningful given the pervasive religiosity and supernatural belief of people in sub-Saharan Africa. Ancestral worship is an integral part of traditional religion in Africa; therefore, ancestors are believed to play tangible roles in the affairs of the living. With that in mind, Kopytoff observes that the conception of ancestor and the living relationship is dependent on several factors; in more specific terms, he describes it as "ambivalent, as both punitive and benevolent and sometimes even as capricious."[17] Given that the ancestors are believed to possess supernatural powers and authority, there are certain actions and behaviors expected of members of a particular kin or family to attract the benevolence of the ancestors and other actions that are bound to set off the ancestors and attract their punitive response. These dos and don'ts are believed to be understood by the elders, which, therefore, emphasize their functionality in issues of divinity. Elderhood is also associated with divinity in most African cultures, especially since the diviners, herbalists, and healers usually emerge from the pool of the elderly.[18]

Also, stressing this concept of functionality and social responsibility in relation to old age, the impartation of the supposed accumulated wisdom in conflict resolution, life decisions of younger people, and other sociological issues emphasize the functional role and authority of the elderly in African societies. Although this notion of accumulated wisdom is an age-long opinion

Figure 3.1. Wooden ancestral effigy. *Source:* The Wellcome Collection. Accessed July 29, 2020, from https://wellcomecollection.org/works/hnuzmejk.

that expresses the cultural values and regard for the elderly, the question is, is there a chance that these ideologies are misrepresentations of old age? Old age also tends to usher in varied medical conditions, some of which include cognitive decline, thus eliminating the ability for coherent thought processes.[19] Mbele also seems to express these doubts in the following thoughts:

It is common, however, to romanticize the image of the African elder, imagining the elder as the repository of a society's values and wisdom, which apparently have remained unchanged over the ages.

We associate the notion of the elder with respect, wisdom, power, and authority. How truthful is this perception of the image and role of the elder in Africa? It appears to me that this view of the elder both reveals and conceals the truth about the elder in African society.[20]

Irrespective of this skepticism, the cultural notions of old age have continued to thrive. In Africa, there is only one opinion to it, and that is that the elderly is filled with wisdom and maturity and is almost infallible.[21] Therefore, the elderly are often known to preside over important matters in the society; their authority in the society is akin to that of a parent or king while the younger ones assume the roles of children or subjects who have no traditional right to question the authority of an elder. Okoye goes ahead to lend credence to this notion in her submission of the Igbo cultural appellation for elderly people in the society. The honorific use of Nna anyi and Nne anyi, which is simply translated to mean our father and our mother, emphasizes this parental regard and respect for the elderhood in the African society.[22] Noting this status conferred on the elderly in Africa, Eboyehi attributes this to the influence of the sentiment or value of parental respect and reverence ingrained in the African worldview as well as the existence of the practice of ancestor worship in sub-Saharan African communities. More specifically he notes:

> Among the Esan, the aged occupied a special place in the heart of Esan families and communities. Like every other African society, old age in Esan had a sacred status. An older person was seen as drawing closer to the spiritual dimension, and therefore more in touch with the source of knowledge, greatness and discernment. He was seen as a representative of the ancestors who holds the "okpor" (family staff). He communed with the ancestors and informed members of his family who was to be blessed or warn them against any danger. His decision in the family is final and no other member of the family has any right to question his decision or authority. He commanded a lot of respect. He is addressed as the "owanlen" (the wise one). Under this situation, everybody aspire to grow old.[23]

Also, the aged or elderly in Africa play the role of oral historians for the society; in other words, since literacy in Africa is rather a modern invention, the elderly engaged in recounting the history of the people, most of which they witnessed or some which were told to them by their foreparents. They also occupy the position of storytellers, especially folktales for the entertainment of the listeners who are usually younger people or children. Owing to Okoye's affirmation of their responsibility in educating and inculcating morals and cultural values, one can easily understand their adoption of the folktale, which is inherently an aspect of folklore designed for moral education and entertainment.[24] Therefore, very much like the primeval African griot, African elders are held in high regards due to their roles as historians and storytellers.

Furthermore, old age in Africa is often perceived to be a privilege and blessing; therefore, it is a state of being that is often desired and appreciated.[25] Also, Apt observes that the reflection of old age in many African languages is often in reference to its importance and high esteem. Adeboye notes the reference to the elderly as *agba* among the Yoruba tribe of Western Nigeria, which ultimately connotes a list of supernatural forces, some positive others negative, the major reference being toward a supernatural ability that superseded that of the mere mortal. Although she states that the interpretation does not fully apply as a lot of negativity is subsumed within that single conception, she does not negate its significance to the perceived relationship and proximity of the ancestors to the elders. Among the Igbo people of Eastern Nigeria, the filial reference to the elderly like the use of Nna anyi for the male and Nne anyi for the female speaks of the regard and honor ascribed to the elderly in the culture and how these factors order social relationships within the continent.

Also, in reference to female subjugation in Africa, the aging of women in several cultures within the continent tends to eliminate their alienation from various societal issues such as politics, judicial processes, economics, education, religion, and so on. As noted by Brown, the attainment of the state of elderhood elevates a woman's status in relation to her male counterparts.[26] Udvardy and Cattell are of the opinion that by the time most women in Africa reach middle age, the cultural regard for old age affords them greater authority and special statuses.[27] In some cultures, with the attainment of elderhood comes high-ranking positions in several sociopolitical offices; they also preside over family functions while, in other instances, certain activities will not even take place in their absence. Using the illustration of several Samia women, Udvardy and Cattell explore the expression of the aforementioned opinion in the women's growing control of their very own affairs by rejecting certain demeaning gendered practices such as wife inheritance. They examine how the contemporary African woman in Southern Africa at the attainment of elderhood has the liberty to go about engaging in social activities; they are able to engage in taboo activities for women without the regular gendered cultural restrictions.

There is almost a defined attitude toward the elderly in Africa as explored and presented by the examined scholars. These attitudes are integrated value systems that guide social relationships and actions in the African society. It is, therefore, unsurprising that these values tend to reflect in the various areas of the society. They color the lens from which the society in Africa is viewed; they provide justifications for different actions and responses to diverse issues concerning elderhood in contemporary society.

Also, as noted and explored by Eboiyehi, chronological age is not the only marker for elderhood, seniority, and respect.[28] In an extensive examination of the Esan people of South-Southern Nigeria, seniority is attained in reference to a person's achievements. As much as the Esan people value and respect age, they also recognize the place of achievement, activities, and exceptional abilities. The more responsibilities a person takes on successfully, the more respect and honor such a person accrues to himself. This method of allocating honor is, however, more operative in the contemporary dispensation where Western parameters for defining honor are redefining Africa's conception of seniority and elderhood. Also, with the growing globalization and modernization of African societies some of these values associated with chronological age and elderhood seem to be constituting problems of interaction between the elders and youths, especially given the gradual erosion of youthful affinity to African cultural practices. It is, therefore, necessary to explore the reflections of these attitudes and value systems in modern institutions and other areas of the society.

Cultural Reflections of Elderhood in African Politics

Politics has the do with the act or methodology of governance and leadership of a state.[29] Governance, on the other hand, is viewed as the process of controlling or managing a society. It is characterized by the exercise of authority by select individuals for social control and development.[30] Political institutions that exercise governance have long existed in precolonial Africa, and with its implication of authority, elderhood and age hierarchy have played a huge role in its activities. In fact, as noted by Ogo, the concept of elderhood in Africa often translates to leadership.[31] Berton and Panel opine that the selection of traditional rulers or chiefs was usually from the pool of the most elderly of the people particularly the men.[32] However, in monarchical systems where inheritance and royalty were the major determinants of leaders, Mbele denotes the following:

> Even where monarchs ruled; they were assisted by and responsive to a councils of elders. The elders played central roles in rituals as well; for example, they controlled the "Poro" secret society of the Mende of Sierra Leone.[33]

While examining the political system among the Igbo people of southeastern Nigeria, Mbele opines that the elders were the custodians of power and authority and constitute a majority of the decision-making body of the government.[34] This claim goes ahead to validate conceptions of value and honor attached to old age and elderhood in Africa. Following the history of Africa's democracy, Adebayo examines harmful reflections of the performance of elderhood in the continent's politics.[35] For one, the unwavering grip of the older populace on the continent's politics since authority is viewed as their birthright continues to alienate the youth from government and eliminating youthful ideologies and opinion in societal development. He also goes ahead to state that there are multifaceted reasons for the alienation of the youth from government affairs in the continent. Asides the opinion of elders as the residuals of knowledge and wisdom and therefore naturally fit to lead, Adebayo observes the notion of the infallibility of elders in the continent. This notion is even supported by indigenous African proverbs. Among the Gikuyu people of central region of Kenya, the following saying exists in reference to elderly superiority and advantage: "what an elder sees sitting down, a young man cannot see even if he stands."[36] This saying corroborates the perceived advantage of old age in terms of knowledge and wisdom.

This conception creates an inability to question elders especially by younger people. Younger people are unable to demand leadership in the presence of the perceived wise and knowledgeable superiors. Although it is clear that old age does not necessarily translate to uncanny wisdom and knowledge and that it is quite possible for younger people to be wiser and more knowledgeable, age and elderhood have continued to influence leadership positions in the society. While examining the said situation, Adeleke cited in Adebayo puts it succinctly in the following statement:

> The elder can say whatever he wants to the youth, he can be rude to the youth, he can disrespect him and talk down on him, even when he (the elder) is at fault, and the youth must take it because he is the youth. This is often reflected at grassroots levels where, in villages and wards, elders hold all the key positions. There is even a saying in a Nigerian tribe that "when elders are talking, the youth must be quiet." When you take this idea and magnify it, you start to see how the culture is already rigged to make elders think that youth have nothing beyond physical strength and youthful exuberance to offer when they (the elders) are around. The few times young people are allowed to lead are times when they are leading their peers, as seen in student unions and community age groups.[37]

Adeleke's perception, which is a proven reality, is not without its consequences on the developing nations of Africa. The alienation of a nation's youth from political affairs on the basis of their perceived and culturally sanctioned subordination denies the nation the possibility of fresh and effective perspectives to socioeconomic and political affairs of the nation. In the first place, the cultural factor serves as an obstacle for youths to obtain the necessary political experience necessary to address complex sociopolitical issues in the continent. This is because their interaction with political offices are monitored by cultural values and expectations of respect and deference to the elders, therefore naturally they are exempted or given a back seat in the affairs of society; besides, when elders are speaking the youth is expected to keep shut and observe. Following a research conducted by Ogo who describes youths as persons within the age ranges of fifteen to thirty-five, out of eleven countries in Africa, namely Burkina Faso, Cameroon, Democratic Republic of Congo, Egypt, Ghana, Nigeria, Senegal, Sudan, Tanzania, Uganda, and Zimbabwe, only one country presents the age of thirty as the minimum age for contest of the office of the president while about four present age thirty-five and rest forty.[38]

However, this is an unfortunate situation given that a fraction of the population who in this case are the elderly—people within the ages of sixty and above have monopolized the government alienating the youth who constitute 35 percent of Africa's population and still counting.[39] Adebayo denotes that Africa's politics and governance have refused to make a generational change from the leadership of the old to the young. The political system and its policies of election and office have been designed to prevent the entrants of the youth. He also carefully examines the trend of leadership in Africa and using the following recent statistics, he concretizes his claim that Africa has refused to include the youth in its political offices, particularly the office of the president:

> Recent elections on the continent do not offer much hope of a generational shift. President Muhammadu Buhari was elected as Nigeria's president in 2015 at the age of 73; Ghana's president Nana Akufo-Addo was also 73 years old at the time of his election in 2017; Malawi's president, Peter Mutharika was elected in 2014 aged 74; South Africa's president, Jacob Zuma was re-elected for a second term in 2014 aged 70. Suffice to add that there have been attempts by younger men to vie for political office across the continent but with little or no success.[40]

In fact, as observed by Ogo in her 2015 publication, by the year 2020, "3 out of 4 people in Africa will be on average 20 years old."[41] Unfortunately, the continent continues to recycle thought processes emanating from the same geriatric fountain, some of which are not applicable or tenable to the changing and evolving society. This therefore justifies the consistency of Africa's challenges. Experientially, addressing challenges with the same ideologies and approach over and over again is bound to continually provide the same results.

Some of these said challenges include the unstable economy and the prevalent poverty in Africa. These are some of the major issues the continent continues to experience without remedy, which is in itself proof that a consistent approach has failed to tackle the problems of the continent. Also, as noted by Olaiya, the economic condition of the continent implies that the larger population of the continent who are generally the youth are adversely affected and cannot be able to meet the social demands and responsibilities expected of them, which leaves them disempowered and unable to interfere and intervene in the sociopolitical affairs of their various nations.[42] Their inability to break into the political scene early enough means that they are unable to create the necessary political network and experience to cater for the political needs of the continent. Reiterating this opinion, Ogo goes ahead to state that

> the notion of elders as leaders perpetuates a vicious cycle in which young people in Africa are unprepared for the challenges of leadership, development and nation-building. Thus, leaders, although "mature" and "elders" are ill-equipped to effectively tackle developmental problems.[43]

Also, given the magnitude of the monetary implications of elections and campaigns in the continent, the youth is naturally sidelined, economically and culturally, which further complicates and undermines their chances of participating and interfering in political matters.

The subject of economic challenges as a barrier against youth elections in the continent cannot be overemphasized. With the attainment of political independence by most African countries, a privileged few members of society got political control, which translates to economic empowerment one that has so far remained in the hands of the privileged few most of whom constitute the current elderly leaders of the various nations of the continent. The absence of the necessary head start on the political front for the African youths coupled with the underlying economic challenges of the continent places them at a disadvantaged point. The problem of unemployment means that a good portion of African youths lack the necessary economic stability to live their personal lives let alone embark on political ambitions. Therefore, aside from the subordination of youths using the cultural perception of elderhood as tantamount to wisdom, economic stability or material wealth is indeed another factor preventing youth leadership and retaining elderly governance in the continent. To express the true depth and implication of money and leadership in the continent, Adebayo states the following:

> Electoral outcomes, especially in the context of African democracies, have frequently been influenced by the wealth of the candidate(s) or their parties. This is not a new phenomenon, given that rulers and contenders for public office have throughout history leveraged power through the wealth they own or control. Equally, the economic strength of their political base gives them an edge over rivals, competitors, and detractors. The modern political landscape is replete with political systems in which rulers and governing bodies across continents— monarchs, military dictators, elected heads of state, and legislatures—rely on their economic and financial influence, whether ill-gotten or legitimately accumulated, to gain access to and/or maintain political power.[44]

Furthermore, as much as it is a herculean task for youths to participate or control political affairs in the continent, it is not unheard of. In fact, in a study conducted by Ogo, 56 percent of African youths show a lot of interest in the political affairs of their various nations even though a fraction of this percentage only get to contest political offices and an even lesser number get to be voted in.[45] However, so many questions usually come to mind in discourses of young people in politics in Africa. For instance, does the conception of youth subordination affect their optimal performance in their political offices? Can they truly hold their older colleagues accountable? Are they truly opportune to express their views on critical societal issues or are they silenced as is expected culturally? Also, is there a meaningful collaboration between the youth and the elders in politics and governance in Africa?

The cultural expectation to keep silent in the presence of elders as noted by Hamzat cited in Ogo continues to play out in governance of various African societies. She notes that the elders among politicians tend to rely on the expectations of deference to escape accountability and scrutiny from their younger colleagues. Hamzat even goes ahead to explain the long-term effect of the cultural expectations of silence and deference from the young political leaders in their relationship with their older colleagues:

> When the elderly person is doing things wrongly, things that are destroying or capable of destroying both the old and the young, both the present and future generations, the young is expected not to question that action even though he or she would be affected in the consequences of the wrong actions of the elder/leaders.[46]

The obvious frustration of the youth in these situations answers the question of their optimal performance in governance. To be perceived as subordinate and given little or no regard as a result of one's youth is arguably very frustrating and could lead to the natural death of one's ability to question the world around them or demand that things be done in the right manner. Often times when the youth break cultural protocols and question elderly actions, they are often shunned and cast in a negative light as cultural offenders. However, given their inability to disregard these cultural expectations, many tend to exhibit and adopt the bandwagon syndrome; in other words, since they can't question or reprimand the actions of the elders, they join them. This falls in line with Sung's description of the acquiescent respect as a form of elderly respect peddled by African and Asian cultures across the globe.[47] This scenario might therefore be able to account for the growing corruption and uniform approach to issues in different institutions around the continent. It further implies that there is very minimal meaningful or gainful collaboration between the elders and young people in Africa's political scene.

Performance of Elderhood in Academia

Age deference remains an integral part of African life and culture even in this era of modernity and globalization. This factor continues to reflect in the interaction between society, its institutions, and its elders. The attenuation of the cultural expectations of deference to an elder as a result of the ongoing Westernization of the African society has created an awkward atmosphere for social relationships in formal institutions. In fact, one might dare say that age in contemporary Africa has become a principle of social inequality. The concept of ageism is often used to explain a discrimination or negative behavior expressed toward an individual on the basis of the person's age.[48] It is a term often used to examine discrimination against the elderly; however, in this context, it will be adopted to examine the privileges of elderhood at the expense of youth in African academia.

With the growing Westernization of African societies and universities in contemporary times, the practical traditional age etiquette that includes a full prostration of men and the overt kneeling of women among the Yoruba people of southwestern Nigeria barely plays out in university contexts. However, this does not mean that expectations of age deference are absent. In fact, in the absence of overt displays of deference in the academia, the formal environment has created alternate expressions of deference and performance of elderhood.[49] In the absence of kneeling and prostrating, there are tentative approaches to an elder and the overt hierarchies between students and

Figure 3.2.   Hemba male ancestral figure. *Source:* Yale University Art Gallery. Accessed July 29, 2020, from https://artgallery.yale.edu/collections/objects/134639.

teachers can be seen and felt. This is usually externalized in the use of lin-guistic honorifics and other actions like picking up a teacher's bag or reliev-ing him/her of any other luggage as a sign of respect; there is also the slight bowing of head for the men and the cautious attempt to kneel by the women in the presence of perceived elders.

Following Van Den Berghe's line of thought, he reiterates that the struc-tures of seniority based on age are still persistent, hence the consistent expectations of deference from younger people in daily interactions. He also notes that to surmount the growing challenge of navigating the culturally sanctioned deference on the basis of age and the egalitarianism encouraged in formal institutions like the academia, these persons especially in Anglophone African nations adopt the use of formal languages like the English language that has a neutral linguistic approach and make no demarcation for familial and neutral expressions. However, this approach does not always apply in conversations between persons of same ethnic groups. In other words, the continued use of their local language retains the hierarchy of seniority and invokes its accompanying etiquette.[50]

With the staff, the performance of elderhood and the deferential response of the younger/subordinate is quite obvious. The younger staff is often sad-dled with the responsibilities of attending to various errands and activities, often attending to rambunctious first years or moving files from one depart-ment to the other. The older staff members are often alienated from these responsibilities by virtue of their age and maturity. The responsibilities often seem cumbersome and overwhelming for these young staff members and are considered a rite of passage in these institutions. Also, the young staff is not at liberty to report or express any form of distress but is rather expected to take on these duties without complaints because after all if he/she doesn't, who will? As observed by Van Den Berghe, the age hierarchy is often in cor-respondence with the status of seniority in the occupation, that is, the older staff member could be a senior lecturer or a doctorate degree holder while the younger staff might just have master's and enrolled for a PhD.[51] In this case, the performance of elderhood on the basis of experiential seniority is almost justified; however, this is not always the case.

In reverse cases where the younger faculty or staff is in a position of author-ity, this usually constitutes ethical and interpersonal constraints; the younger staff often feels inadequate or in no position to question or reprimand the activities of the older staff. In relation to the traditional etiquettes of senior-ity, Eboiyehi opines that younger persons are often in no position to sanction elders; they are not permitted to be rude or even chatty in the presence of elders.[52] This provides credence to Van Den Berghe's opinion that "aggres-sive behavior and over-talkativeness are resented from a person who is too junior, and sometimes academics in their fifties will contemptuously refer to rival colleagues in the forties as 'small boys.'"[53] This factor also affects the recruitment of staff as potential older staff members are often avoided for fear of being unable to sanction or reprimand them when needed. Therefore, the academia loses out on the value such older applicants might provide as a result of the culturally instituted power distance.

In the absence of nonteaching or junior staff members, the younger academic staff members naturally fill in these spaces. They are often found at the beck and call of the older staff members. It is almost a common sight to see them following the elderly staff members from one place to another. Van Den Berghe denotes that it is not strange for them to be referred to as "small boys" by their older contemporaries or superiors.[54] The filial sentiment toward the elderly in Africa always supersedes any occupational hierarchy. This might therefore account for the parental references (mama, baba, mummy, or daddy) often employed when addressing the elderly members of staff. It also gives credence to the following statement that examines and emphasizes the sentiment and value of parenthood and by extension elderhood in African societies:

> There were strong relationships between the aged and the young adults. These relationships do not necessarily have to be familial as they cut across families and communities. In these societies, children provide care and support for their aged parents "as a means of repaying the tremendous debts . . . owed their parents for producing and caring for them in infancy and childhood.[55]

Oftentimes, as noted by Van Den Berghe, the traditional notion of elders as storehouses of knowledge and wisdom and, therefore, deserving of authority and power interferes with judgment and decisions in the academia.[56] Naturally, in university settings, leadership usually goes to the eldest person in a group, especially among the junior staff in the various organizations who still adhere strictly to the etiquettes of seniority and age deference.[57] Therefore, among the staff, particularly the junior staff, age is a crucial determinant of a person's status and authority in the academic work space. Using the Nigerian example, Van Den Berghe notes that oftentimes claims to university chancellorship are based on age and seniority.[58] Although this might be justified by Lienard's opinion of age in the following statement and therefore eliminates the notions of partiality in the choosing of persons for such a weighty position:

> Age might constitute an adequate proxy for authority, as an older individual is likely to have more experience, greater knowledge and social skills, larger social networks, and more group affiliations than younger individuals.[59]

This ideology, although not explored in clear terms, is usually the reason for the attributions of wisdom and knowledge to the elderly and therefore often stands to justify situations that might not reflect these claims; in other words, not all elderly/older persons possess more wisdom, skills, and even networks than younger people. However, in most cases the elderly continue to sail on these preconceived notions sometimes cheating deserving younger colleagues out of these positions. It doesn't help that these notions are further reinforced by the traditional principles of honor toward constituted authority, hence the inability to question these leadership arrangements. In fact, indigenous saying and proverbs consolidate these notions and are often called upon for the defense of the elderly. According to Ogo, the following Sierra Leonean proverb is generally a reflection of the people's opinion toward elderhood and youth:

> "An Okro plant cannot grow taller than its farmer." (Creole, Sierra Leone) Meaning: The youth (Okro plant) is planted by the farmer (elder) to whom it owes its existence and sustenance. Thus, the youth cannot be greater than the elder.[60]

In Swahili, she identifies another proverb that conveys the same thought pattern providing proof that the myriad cultures within the African continent share the same value in reference to age and seniority, which accounts for the uniform alienation of youth from leadership positions, in general politics and academics.

> "When a kid goat bends down, it sucks from its mother's breast." (Swahili) Meaning: Youth are admonished to defer to elders, and reap the reward of nurturing.[61]

These sayings reveal the depth of these opinions and account for how this factor of age and deference tends to affect the quality of leaders and people's approach toward societal and academic politics.

The same factors apply also in student and staff relationship, their interactions usually reveal an obvious gap sometimes as a result of the privileges bestowed on them by chronological age and seniority.[62] On the part of the staff, there is a performance of elderhood that encourages that gap. Students are often unable to question their lecturers in cases where they have opposing or conflicting opinions. This situation obviously stifles student's curiosity and creativity equally eliminating any traces of critical thinking or the ability to question the world around them. There is an absence of a necessary mentorship and camaraderie between students and their teachers creating an atmosphere of subservience, ingratiation, and sycophancy, an express route toward eliminating productivity and innovativeness in the academia.

To further expand the practice of ingratiation brought on by the performance of elderhood and the resultant subservience, Shankar et al. opine that ingratiation is generally enabled or discouraged by the atmosphere of organizations or academic environments.[63] While examining the distribution of power in various organizations, they examine the social conditionings of various institutions and very adequately classify them as participatory and authoritarian climates. For the former, they identify features such as "team spirit, group decision making, high goals and supportive relationships," which are clearly inhibitory factors for the thrive of ingratiation, sycophancy, and subservience.[64] The aforementioned features are clearly features that ensure the conduciveness of the academia as a place of learning and innovation. However, in the examination of authoritarian climates, they identify features like the overindulgence on status and power or in the case of the academia, the privileges of seniority.

There is also the demand for blind obedience or, if not in spoken words, the nonverbal expectations of deference and blind honor as well as personal loyalty. These factors comparatively explored by Shankar et al. proffer a clear picture of the implications of the overreaching performance of elderhood and deference in the academia. Although Africa continues to be an age-valuing society, in the recent times, the rapidly Westernizing continent is beginning to adopt a new approach and orientation toward the value of age. This accounts for the ongoing redefinition of elderhood in formal institutions; in other words, age is no longer the only marker for seniority and seniority continues to play an important role in formal and informal institutions in the continent.

As a result of several factors such as education, economic status, and military rank in the larger society substituting age as metaphors for seniority, the academia is also experiencing a redefinition of the concept of seniority. Since military rank applies only in military institutions, economic status and level of education seem to be the most common factors at play in the substitution of age as a symbol of seniority and authority in the academia. Adeboye notes that the distribution of power in African societies is often dependent on seniority; with that in mind, it is necessary to note that the same pattern is bound to play out in the academia.[65] Therefore, power lies within the corridors of seniority, which asides from age is determined by economic status; in other words, the richer a member of staff is, the more he or she is respected and valued for the mere idea of being rich and also there is more likelihood for such a person to be given leadership positions. In fact, given the economic emphasis of modern Africa, social status is almost completely dependent on wealth and economic achievement.[66] The fact that wealth connotes power around the world influences the understanding of seniority, which also plays out in the academia.

Given the formal atmosphere of the academia, it is, however, unsurprising that educational attainment is a basis for status attainment. In the academia, the higher a person's educational achievement the more a status of seniority is conferred on him/her against the lesser achieved contemporaries. This form of seniority is primarily based on the conception that experience begets wisdom and knowledge. It is further consolidated by the acquisition of Western skills and opinions that tend to be "relevant" in the modern African society. It also stems from the notion of Western knowledge as ultimately superior to the African knowledge system, therefore having acquired as many of it as possible, the person in question is treated with a new defined deference made for persons who had acquired superior knowledge and experience. Therefore, certain positions are acquired by persons who have attained a certain level in education irrespective of age.

PART II
REIMAGINING ELDERHOOD AND KNOWLEDGE

African Notions of Elderhood versus Western and Eastern Notions of Elderhood

Age as the chronological marking of the passage of time is indeed a universal concept, although the notions of age tend to differ from society to society. The ongoing globalization and the disintegration of geographical barriers with the advent of technology are gradually neutralizing the cultural ideologies and values of age and elderhood in Africa. Some scholars like Nwachukwu-Agbada consider this neutralization to be harmful to the African cultural heritage and value system.[67] However, having established that Africa as continent values and reveres the elderly considering them as the locus of wisdom, knowledge, and authority, it is therefore necessary to comparatively examine the notions of elderhood and age in Western and Eastern cultures across the globe. Given the negative effects of Africa's excessive elderly reverence, the comparative study is primarily to identify possible meeting points for the aforementioned cultural ideologies so as to mitigate the negative implications of these excesses on Africa's sociopolitical, economic, and educational development.

The African concept of respect in reference to age and elderhood is founded on an existing filial piety. The respect and reverence for the elderly in the continent tend to affect the social and political interactions of youths and elders in the contemporary society. Some of these interactions have been identified to be leading causes of the alienation of the African youth from leadership positions in various formal and informal institutions in the continent. This notion of elderhood and reaction to elders by Africans is very similar to the conception of elderhood in Eastern or Asian cultures. In more specific terms, Chen and Chung state the following in reference to Asian cultural values for elderhood:

> Most Asian nations, especially those influenced by Confucianism in East Asia such as China, Japan, and Korea, also highly value seniority, which refers to both age and length of service in an organization. . . . in Japan the aged enjoy a high status not only in the family, but also in the work force and community. The practice can be demonstrated by the honorific linguistic codes used to show respect to the elderly, by the special treatment of the elderly in the household, and by the national policy that is designed to protect the elders' welfare.[68]

Also, just like the African values toward the elderly, Asian elder–youth relationship is equally based on filial piety. This, however, makes sense given the internalized familial and communal orientation of these cultures. The communal orientation implies a respect and regard for one's parents and extended older relatives, one that colors their perception of other elderly people, relatives, and non-relatives. However, Western cultures sport a bright contrast to the explored notions and values of old age in Africa. As examined by Chen and Chung unlike the aforementioned cultures, Western cultures encourage individualism as opposed to the communality that emanates from filial piety and other family values.[69] The United States as a representation of the Global North is considered by Chen and Chung as a youth-valuing society; in other words, physical strength or vigor is emphasized, aging is associated with decline and disease, therefore productive aging is encouraged while the welfare of the aged in that culture is primarily left in the hands of the government.[70] The philosophy of individualism influences people's attitude toward their families and consequently their elders. The looseness of family ties in these cultures eliminates the strong family bond and dependence that is existent in Asian and African family, therefore the attendant independence and culturally instituted individuality equals minimal regard and respect for the immediate and extended families, which finds its way to the general relationship of the youth and the elderly in these cultures.

   Also, the earlier established African/Asian regard and respect for elderhood is externalized in various categorizations examined by Sung, which include care respect, acquiescent respect, linguistic respect, consultative respect, salutary respect, and precedential respect, among others.[71] The care respect has to do with showing concern to elders, helping them out with household chores, and being there for them in health-challenging situations as well as showing all other interpretations of care. To express the depth of this regard for the elderly, recent laws in China are against the neglect of the elderly. As noted by Martinez Carter, children who fail to cater for their parents or make constant trips to see them face the risk of being jailed or fined.[72] Although there are no known legitimate laws enforcing caring for the elderly in Africa, there are unspoken cultural expectations to care for the elderly; children are taught value and care for their aged parents. In fact, among the many reasons for child birth in the continent, the notion of having a person who is culturally obligated to cater for one at old age tops the list. To strengthen this belief system, spiritual myths are often employed as in the case of the Esan society in South-South Nigeria, where a blessing is attached to catering for one's aged parents. Eboiyehi notes that the abandonment of the elderly often attracts the wrath of the ancestors and tends to rob the perpetrator of certain blessings. In his very words, he states the following:

> Among the Esan of south-south Nigeria, it was believed that the spirits of their ancestors were always around them to bless and favour those who take care of their aged parents and punish those who abandon their elderly parents. Thus, in traditional Esan society, old age was perceived as a blessing and those who cater for their aged parents will partake from the blessing.[73]

Therefore, the care-respect just as in Asian cultures is an integral aspect of the concept of African elder respect. The second form that is the acquiescent respect equally plays out in the African cultural scene. Acquiescent in this context has to do with showing deference and submission to one's elders. Apparently, this cultural expectation plays out in Asian families and is not restricted to them. In the African family context, it refers to agreeing with parent's decision without question, especially in reference to life decisions such as choice of schools, marriage, career, lifestyle, religion, and so on. Generally, an African child is expected to comply with his/her parents' lifestyle and value system without complaints. To do otherwise is to be disrespectful and desecrate the sanctity of eldership as well as attract ancestral wrath. Also, the concept of linguistic respect is well represented in African languages; the use of honorifics while addressing the elderly in various cultures across the continent is a clear indication of linguistic elder respect. The cultural-induced inability to refer to an elder by their first names exemplifies the cultural use of honorifics and special pronouns in addressing the elderly in Africa.

    In recent times, this hyper-respect culture and the use of honorifics is represented in the attachment of sir/ma while conversing with the elderly; age hierarchies for the African person are revealed in the compulsive use of honorifics in elder–youth conversations and relationships in Africa, such as sir, ma, chief, Prof., Dr., daddy, or mummy (for nonrelated elders). The latter is often employed to express the depth of one's regard for an elder. This reference comes with its own specific performance of deference. To view and refer to such a person as family is indeed the height of social and personal regard. Also, Sung identifies another form of elder respect known as the consultative respect. This form of respect is expressed by reaching out to elders especially family members for conflict resolution or other issues. Here the conception of elderly wisdom comes to play as they are expected to provide practical and functional advice in dire situations. Salutatory respect as stated by Sung is rather a visual expression of respect; in other words, it is a way of showing respect to elders by bowing, kneeling, hugging, shaking hands, or kissing.

Although the later hardly plays out in traditional African settings, bowing and kneeling is rather common in many African societies. Among the Yoruba people as earlier established, the men are customarily expected to bow or prostrate in deference to elders, while the women are expected to kneel. Asian and Western cultures, however, permit kissing and hugging as forms of elderly recognition and respect. Precedential respect also constitutes a form of elder respect identified by Sung; it is a form of respect where elders are given certain privileges like opening doors for them in public places or giving up your seats for them or serving them first before others. The list of the various forms of respect goes on and on. The expectations of respect in both African and Asian cultures are integrated in the people's lifestyle.

So far, this chapter has explored the cultural conceptions of aging in Africa while extracting similarities from Asian cultures; it has equally dwelled on the negative effects this excessive indulgence on age, seniority, and the attendant respect has on the growth and development of the sociopolitical and academic spheres of the African society. Although the Western situation appears cringeworthy, it is not without its merits. This does not imply that Western cultures are completely and utterly oblivious of the concept of seniority and respect. It is rather an examination of the difference or depth of the meaning and expression of seniority, elderhood, and respect in these aforementioned cultures. In fact, in a cross-cultural study conducted by Sung in reference to the expressions of respect among Americans and Koreans, he notes that respect for the elderly among the Americans just like as earlier examined for Africans and Asians is expressed in several ways some of which are included in the following analysis:

Acquiescent respect was the most frequently cited form among the Americans (50% of all the participants). Care respect was the second most frequently cited, and was followed by linguistic respect, salutatory respect, consulting respect, and precedential respect. The rest of the forms were cited by 5% or less. In terms of importance, care respect was the highest rated form (3.67, in the four-point scale), followed by consulting, acquiescent, salutatory, linguistic, and precedential. Care, acquiescent, and consulting were roughly extraordinarily important, and salutatory, linguistic, and precedential were extraordinarily to highly important. Although rated as important, six other forms—presentational, public, celebrative, gift, spatial, and victual—were rarely or minimally practiced by the young Americans (These forms were excluded from the subsequent analyses.)

Combining the results of the analyses of frequency and importance, six forms—care, consulting, acquiescent, salutatory, linguistic, and precedential—are found outstanding; these forms were practiced more often and are rated more important than others.[74]

In another study conducted by Kusserow, he examines the early inculcation of individualism in American children. Using the Parkside Pre-School in Manhattan, New York, he explores how teachers are obligated to help students build a sense of self while encouraging an egalitarian atmosphere that is primarily found in public institutions across the country.[75] Using several methodologies like letting children color and draw without the restrictions of specificity, and avoiding imposing restrictions on children's writings and paintings, they help the children understand the importance of personal creativity and imagination.[76] This in turn becomes the bedrock of innovation and ingenuity that spills into to the wider society catalyzing inventions and technological and social growth. The teacher without fear of challenge often tries to eliminate the difference of hierarchy between them and a student by often squatting to meet the student's level or engaging in conversations with the students as they will an equal.[77]

Western cultures as the case may be equally encourage respect for parents and elders; however, their culture of individuality continues to find expression in their intergenerational relationships. Individuality in this context has to do with an emphasis on personal freedom. That is, these cultures recognize the place of independent thinking and free will, and the concept of seniority and social status is awarded on the basis of personal achievement, innovations, and discoveries, not on the basis of one's chronological duration on earth.[78] Therefore, since there is no unreasonable demand for deference from the elderly among them, there continues to be an egalitarian atmosphere in their various institutions and organizations while the interpersonal relationship of the young and old is primarily nonhierarchical. The absence of an expectation of deference implies that people are accountable to each other; the concept of elderhood ceases to be a tool for the elimination of accountability on the part of older colleagues in public institutions. Persons within these cultural spaces make personal choices and chase personal interests without fear of a culturally expected deference or submission to elderly consent or fear of being shamed by culture and society.

This situation as observed by Gorodnichenko and Roland creates an environment for culturally motivated innovations, critical analysis of situations, and invariably growth and development in the society.[79] From this perspective, among other things, one can attribute Africa's persistent underdevelopment to the culture of deference and submission with its attendant sycophancy, ingratiation, and the absence of independent thinking and personal creativity.

The compulsive sense of duty that African youths have for their elders eliminates their ability to think independently and even pursue personal ambitions.
Choices and actions are made based on the consent of elderly authority while
the likelihood for elders to capitalize on this compulsive piety to be authorita-
tive and irrational is very high.

Collaboration of Cultures for Africa's Development

The presence of filial piety as earlier established often translates to a life
dictated by elderly doggedness and a perpetual submission to the will and
dictates of elderly family members. It is very well captured in the term "filial
stupidity" as coined by the psychologist Edward Shen.[80] The concept of independent thinking is clearly eliminated from this equation. Therefore, there is
or there will be an inevitable lack of innovation as the latter concept emanates
from critical and independent thinking. This situation equally breeds unaccountability as the younger generation is too "respectful" to hold the older
public officeholders accountable—hence the continued rot of the very foundations of the different spheres of the society.

Individualism has been proven to decrease the frequency and quality
of interpersonal relationships. In this context, it decreases the relationship
between parents and their children. The child–parent synergy is lost, which
consequently trickles down to the rest of the elderly population, which often
times affects the general well-being of the society. This generates a vicious
cycle as the current youth cohort would not occupy that position permanently.
The youth-valuing society of the West is setting its seniors up for abandonment and psychological imbalance and as aptly noted by Sung, respect and
regard for elderhood is necessary for the general well-being of the young and
the old; it is in fact a huge factor in determining a society's quality of life.[81]
Encouraging positive attitudes toward old age and the position of elderhood
is indirectly a personal investment for one's old age as well as this could
enlighten the society on the inevitability of psychological and physical degeneration as well as ensure the collaboration of the young and old to promote a
healthy and functioning environment.

Juxtaposing both cultures exposes an existing imbalance; a level of balance is necessary for the growth and development of society. A de-emphasis
in the expressions of Africa's notion of elderhood is necessary, so is that of
the West as both values will be undoubtedly useful in contemporary society.
Africa's value system toward the elderhood fosters respect for seniority and
age, which in turn institutes a social order where the concept of time and
experience is valued by those who will most likely benefit from it. Although
this social regard is often misused by the favored party, this is not always the
case, when such authority is properly handled; it begets a mutually benefiting

relationship between both generations. Adeboye's examination of some Yoruba proverbs in reference to elderhood in the culture reveals the ideal intentions of these said values attached to elderhood. Some of those proverbs and their translation and significance are as follows:

Proverb: *Owo omode ko to pepe, ti agbalagba ko wo keregbe Ise ti ewe ba be agba, ki o ma se ko o Gbogbo wa ni a ni'se a jo nbe ara wa*
Translation: The hand of the young does not reach the high shelf; that of the elder does not go into the gourd. The work that a child begs an elder to do let him not refuse to do it, we all stand to benefit from mutual cooperation.

Proverb: *Omode gbon, agba gbon, la fi da ile Ife.*
Translation: The wisdom of the youth was as important as that of elders in the establishment of Ile-Ife.[82]

The philosophy of valuing elderhood emanates from the understanding of the obvious need for complementarity, collaboration, and mutual respect between diverse generations, as it is rather clear that no one person has the monopoly of knowledge or wisdom. It stresses the relevance of youth and old age for a functional and effective society.

These African values with all their shortcomings cannot be totally dis-carded for the much-needed development to occur. In fact, an understanding of the very reasons behind these values will set the society on the right path in its intergenerational relationship. Elderly deference is no doubt a way of ordering the interaction of the old and young. It is a way of humbling the impatient youth so as to benefit from the wisdom and knowledge of the elder. This, however, does not imply that the elders have monopoly of wisdom but rather an acknowledgment that the older person with more years and experi-ence on earth is more likely to understand the ways of the world better than the younger person. However, with the technologization of society in contem-porary times to address contemporary issues in more sophisticated and novel ways contrary to what the elder is used to, the proverb stating the elder's inability to put his hand into a childish gourd as in the proverb previously mentioned suddenly makes sense.

The concept of deference should not translate to fear or authoritarianism; young people should be perceived as wise in their own might and in tune with the ways of their generation and therefore capable of making decisions beneficial to them. An understanding of this will most likely eliminate the reckless abuse of the regard for elderhood in African communities. Elderhood will no longer be an avenue for reckless unaccountability. In public offices, young people should try to uphold these cultural values by maintaining and expressing a meaningful amount of regard and respect for their elderly colleagues and bosses, while at the same time being bold enough to question or hold accountable the elderly when necessary. Respect is indeed reciprocal; therefore, if both parties respect and regard one another with proper understanding of their weakness in regard to their age and experience public, offices will undoubtedly function at optimum level. With these in mind, the concept of deference can now be viewed in a different light; if respect and deference is properly handled by the elders, the society stands to gain from elderly experience and wisdom while the elderhood will continually retain its relevance to society.

Generally, it is not unnecessary to seek elderly advice and guidance when faced in difficult times. Seeking elderly support is first an understanding of one's weakness and need for social and familial support, which constitutes the bedrock of sane and psychologically balanced individuals. Maintaining a strong filial bond continues to apply in African societies; the culture of community has been noted by Fenton and Draper to aid the ageing process of elderly people and also helps the younger society understand and appreciate the cycle of human existence.[83] Although the society continues to change, certain life principles remain constant; some of these life principles have been lived, understood, and mastered by the elderly generation, hence the need for society to protect and preserve intergenerational relationships. The concept of elderly respect expands the general principle of respect; if one is able to show respect to the elderly, then the person can express respect to other individuals irrespective of age.

However, the adoption of individualism though in small doses is equally relevant to Africa, that is, the ability to think independently and critically cannot be overemphasized. Therefore, as much as elderly respect is encouraged, the ability to express oneself freely albeit respectfully regardless of one's age is equally necessary for the progress of society. Dictatorship as a result of the position of elderhood should be greatly discouraged while the elderly members of society should not act like they have monopoly of wisdom and knowledge. They should often times pay keen attention to the younger generation, show interest in their perspective of life as this will promote mutual respect, and encourage societal development and a conducive atmosphere for human productivity.

CONCLUSION

So far, this chapter has been able to examine the general conceptions and definitions of old age and elderhood in the society. More specifically, it explored the African notion of elderhood and ancestorhood while analyzing the performance of elderhood in the society. It evaluated the impact of this performance and conception in the sociopolitical and educational institutions in the African society. It identified the African conceptions of the elderly as links to ancestors and storehouses of wisdom and knowledge. This in turn justifies the subordinate position of the youth in the society and provides reasons for the alienation of the youth in sociopolitical issues. In contrast to Africa, this chapter further revealed that the Western notions of elderhood tend to exercise a form of filial piety, which influences their relationship with the elderly; the West, on the other hand, is rather youth-oriented and more individualistic. In a juxtaposition of both cultures, the study advocates a blend of both cultural orientations of elderhood so as to achieve the much-needed development in Africa. Elderhood is a valid qualification to the creation of knowledge, but knowledge cannot be dependent on this characteristic alone.

Chapter 4

Ifa Divination and Society

The inquisitive attitude to know and understand the world is a trait found in human beings; the inclination to gather information through experience and interaction with the social institutions in the community is regarded as knowledge. Knowledge cannot be separated from human activities as it balances the human inquisitive nature to understand the shape and organization of the world one inhabits. The process and act of seeking for knowledge predates the modernity of science; it has been the subject of human fixation from the preliterate era. To define knowledge may be a herculean task as the depth of the concept evades a monolithic definition. Modern Eurocentric theories on the subject of knowledge can be categorized into two angles, those of empiricism and rationalism. These two perspectives on the theorization of knowledge have this basic assumption "that knowledge is a justified true belief."[1] In the introduction to this book, knowledge was stripped of this certainty and the role of values and beliefs in knowledge was revealed. Olusegun observes that indigenous system of knowledge has its foundation in interaction with the immediate community.[2] Thus, the aim of this chapter is to establish the Ifa system of knowledge and its inherent values and beliefs.

Indigenous knowledge is home-grown knowledge that enables communities to make sense of who they are and to interact with their environment in ways that sustain life. It is knowledge that arises from life experience and which is passed down from generation to generation through words of mouth in the form of folklore, idioms, proverbs, songs, rite of passage and rituals. It equally covers the broad spectrum of life and therefore there are different types of indigenous knowledge ranging from people's beliefs, medicine, arts and crafts etc.[3]

The need for human beings to search for answers to unravel complex situations is not the occupation of science and technology alone; it has always been the preoccupation of the preliterate African communities to understand and preserve their culture, values, philosophies, and traditional systems of worship. Knowledge is an extract from varied experiences, customs, philosophies, folklore, proverbs, language, and realities found in a specific community but may possess similar characteristics in other communities. The social institutions in the society strengthen and expand the agency of indigenous knowledge system. And so, knowledge is spread through the process of socialization in that particular society. This system of knowledge is usually based on a broad structure of values, beliefs, religion language, rituals, and culture of that particular society or group of people who possess a common ancestry and origin. Knowledge system is a product of a society's culture, religion, value system, and literature. Olusegun observes that indigenous knowledge systems have certain special features that distinguish them as a field of study.[4] One of the unique features of indigenous knowledge systems is that no one can claim ownership of them; they are the collective result of the culture, values, arts and crafts, and mores of a society. These systems of knowledge have been in existence for more than thousands of years and are owned by the community. This collective knowledge is mostly transferred orally from one generation to the other in the preliterate society. This kind of knowledge is not written down but engraved in the minds of the community's wise men and women who may be bards or historians, physicians, and traditional rulers. Olusegun states that

> Ifa as an indigenous knowledge refers to the system of divination and the verses of the literary corpus. Yoruba religion identifies Orunmila as the grand Priest; as that which revealed oracle divinity to the world. Such is his association with the oracle divinity: in some instances, the term "Orunmila" is used interchangeably with Ifa.[5]

Ifa is a system of knowledge that reflects the culture, tradition, values, traditional religion, language, and history of the Yoruba people. This system of knowledge is a structured method of guidance that is connected to the physical and psychological state of the Yoruba people, supplying answers to events, issues, and problems in an explicit way that explains the outcome, shape, and result of the issue as it is in the present time. The Ifa literary corpus is passed orally from many generations of the Ifa initiates to the other successive generations. Ifa as a system of knowledge encompasses traditional medicine, arts and crafts, innovations, religious practices, values, and thoughts of the Yoruba people.

Karenga notes that Orunmila discussed that the attainment of good life is the acquisition of knowledge.[6] That knowledge aids the achievement of a good life is hinged on its multifarious importance to human existence.

Through Ifa, the wisdom and intelligence to lead a meaningful life and make smart choices and decisions cannot be underestimated as humans seek fulfillment of their destiny.

PART I
YORUBA CULTURE AND PHILOSOPHY

The Yoruba are a group of people from the southwestern part of Nigeria spread across Oyo, Lagos, Ekiti, Ondo, Osun Kwara, and some parts of Kogi state. According to Olu–Osayomi, the number of the Yoruba people in Nigeria is about 20 million.[7] The sacredness of Ifa corpus is hugely known in the Yoruba epistemology and traditional religion. The deity, Orunmila, is the originator of Ifa and is known as the deity of wisdom. In the Yoruba traditional religion, Orunmila is believed to be the wisest of all the deities and ancestors that the Yoruba Supreme Being, Olodumare, trust enough to allow to witness the creation of the world. In the Yoruba belief system, the earth and the whole activities of human beings are controlled by the legion of divinities, deities, ancestors, and spiritual beings because they have been imbued with special powers from Olodumare to attend to human beings. These divine beings are representative of the Yoruba Supreme Being and are capable of manipulating and interfering in the activities of human beings.

In the Yoruba worldview, the world is structured into two divisible but inseparable parts: the physical world (aye) and the spiritual world (orun). These two domains are structured in a way that is interconnected to each other. The physical world is inhabited by humans while the spiritual or celestial world is dominated by gods, goddesses, and the spiritual bodies. The past is never gone as it is retrievable and accessible to the Yoruba people.[8] The two worlds operate in a coordinated flow of interactions and this belief is strongly held in the Yoruba tradition and culture. There is also a fluid communication channel between these domains, which is coordinated by one who can traverse both worlds. There are so many philosophical beliefs among the Yoruba people; the system of knowledge is grounded in the ancient religion and Ifa tradition. The Yoruba believe that the dead can communicate with the living and human beings can also speak with their dead ancestors. The reincarnation of the dead and the world of the Abiku is a system of thought and philosophy of the Yoruba people, which is also shared among some other African communities and tribes. To begin the exploration into Ifa and how it is a system of knowledge, it is important to first of all establish the origin and significance of Ifa in the Yoruba traditional religion and culture.

Orun is inhabited by Eledumare and several divinities such as the deified ancestors, Orisha. Drewal categorized these gods and spiritual beings into two broad groups: the temperate gods and the temperamental gods.[9] Among the calm and mild gods was Orunmila who possessed wisdom through his existence during the creation of the world; he was charged with the responsibility of divination and guidance. All the secrets, mysteries, and knowledge of the world is bared to Orunmila.

> The Yoruba believe that the four-hundred and one divinities mentioned above descended from the skies into the city of Ife. At that time there were no creatures of any kind on the earth. The divinities were the first inhabitants of the earth, and Ife was the first place on earth inhabited by human species.[10]

Ife was the birthplace of the Yoruba people according to the myth of creation, which narrated how the earth was filled with water and was made solid by the dispersal of dirt by a hen. The first settlement for the divinities when they descended from heaven was known as Ile Ife, and Orunmila secured his roots in Oke Igeti. The history of Orunmila the god of wisdom is narrated and codified in the Ifa literary corpus.

Orunmila: The Voice and Wisdom of the Divinities

Orunmila was sometimes interchangeably substituted for Ifa, the deity who is acclaimed to be the one with wisdom and intelligence to guide humans and act as an intermediary between Olodumare, the Supreme Being, and his subjects. Orunmila was purportedly the deity of knowledge and intelligence in the Yoruba folklore about the deified ancestors and gods. Orunmila was not a god but a human who was venerated into an Orisha; scholars like Abimbola talked about Orunmila as one of the "four hundred" and sometimes "four hundred and one" Orisha sent down to Aye, the world by Olodumare (the god-head).[11] Orunmila was synonymous with wisdom as his popular praise name was (Akerefinusogbon) the Little One with the belly of wisdom. Abimbola posited that Ifa, not only was he a major divinity he also regulates every aspect of the Yoruba people, as they depend on it for direction in all of their ceremonies, rites, and moral principles.[12]

> Orunmila stands in a unique position to advise all of the other deities, as well as human beings. The myths of Ifa recount that he was the first creation of Olodumare, and as such, has eternal knowledge of all that was and is and is to come. He declares the will of Olodumare to man and god alike, and serves as the mouthpiece of the other Orisa. Since leaving the world, Orunmila speaks through Ifa divination, one of, if not the, main mode of communication between mankind, the Orisa, and Olodumare, and between Heaven and Earth.[13]

In the preliterate Yoruba society Ifa is perceived as the speaker or representative of the spiritual beings, deities, ancestors, and so on, and the path to ancestral intelligence. From the mythological narratives, history, spirituality, and herbal medicine of the Yoruba people, Ifa remains a central philosophical and epistemological figure. The word that proceeds from Orunmila, the divinity of traditional intelligence, is known as Ifa. Like the other divinities are given roles and functions to perform, Orunmila is charged with the act of divination to be performed for human beings when they need to seek knowledge. When he descended into earth, he employs his wisdom in creating order. Orunmila had to return to heaven but revealed the sixteen sacred palm nuts as a divination tool that will assist human beings during difficult times.

The Origin of Ifa

Olodumare the Supreme Being in Yoruba cosmology is perceived as the creator of all beings, who is the origin of all intelligence, knowledge, and power (ase). Ifa is both the name and religion of Orunmila, who is the progenitor of the system of divination. Ifa is based on the mores, social and communal relations, the human and supernatural relations, and the Yoruba philosophy of the world. The revelation of the sixteen scared nuts for divination was a landmark in the organization and traditional religion known as Ifa. After the

Figure 4.1. Ifa ritual bowl known as "Adjella-ifa." *Source*: The Wellcome Collection. Accessed July 29, 2020, from https://wellcomecollection.org/works/d33m5m5y.

departure of Orunmila to Orun (heaven), one of the myths narrated how he revealed the secret of knowledge to his children after their plea for him to return to earth failed. He instructed his children to pick the sixteen palm nuts as the divination tool whenever they seek knowledge.

> Ifa is a system of geomancy, one of the divinatory techniques used by the Yoruba to gain knowledge of their complex cosmos and understand the intellectual configurations of our human universe. It is generally regarded as a process of the pursuit of knowledge about the course of life, and it is consulted at successive stages in people's lives.[14]

Ogunnaike observes that Ifa has multiple meanings and definitions with epistemological, philosophical, and metaphysical value; the foremost meaning recognized is connected with divination as a system of knowledge associated with Orunmila, while the second meaning is the deity himself, and last, the religion as a system of worship.[15] Ifa as a branch of Yoruba religion occupies a unique position in the traditional religion as a result of his intermediary activities between the divinities, ancestors, and humans. The divination system is the bridge between humans and their deities, because without the system communication with these divinities will be impossible, which will hinder access to celestial and divine resources.

> Ifa represents a special branch of Yoruba religion because of its intellectual outlook and its stock of traditional academic men. In this sense, Ifa is more than a branch of Yoruba religion. Ifa is a means through which Yoruba culture informs and regenerates itself and preserve all that is considered good and memorable in that society. Ifa is Yoruba culture in its true dynamic and traditional sense. Ifa is a means whereby a non-literate society attempts to keep and disseminate its own philosophy and values despite the lapses and imperfections of human memory on which the system is based.[16]

The Ifa religion is arguably the most influential in the traditional Yoruba religion because it is a religion with an academic foundation and collection of literature. Ifa with its tripartite metaphysical meanings and values holds a regal position among the plethora of Yoruba deities, which has a system of regenerating the customs and rites in the Yoruba cosmology. The dimension of this religion is broad with aspects such as spirituality, morality, sustenance, provenance, wisdom, and philosophy. The philosophies of the Yoruba are codified and regulated in the Ifa religion, and ideas about almost every human activities and life can be found in the literary corpus of Ifa. Ifa is consulted before a child is conceived and still remains relevant throughout the birth and lifetime of the child. At every stage of the child's life from infancy to adulthood, Ifa remains a constant figure and keeps the order of life proceedings.

The importance of Ifa cannot be overemphasized in the preliterate Yoruba society as all the ritual and rites of passage are endorsed and certified by Ifa.

> Ifa L'o ni Oni
> Ifa l'o ni Ọla
> Ifa l'o ni Ọtunla
> Ifa l'o ni Ireni
> Ọrunmila l'o ní ọjọ mẹrin
> Orişa da si ayé. (Abimbola 1977, 170)

Ifa is the omnipresent and omniscient divinity—having control of the past, present, and future. In the Ifa literary corpus, the Yoruba myths, thoughts, and philosophies are established and illustrated with stories that are poetic.

PART II
IFA IN YORUBA RELIGION AND SOCIETY

In Yoruba traditional religion Orunmila is notably one of the oldest deities in the primordial Yoruba society as observed by Olu-Osayomi. In Yoruba folklore, Orunmila is believed to oversee the affairs of both divinities and man. However, there exists a higher being, Olodumare, the Almighty Being, that controls the affairs of the divinities by putting them in charge of different power to perform some specific roles. To understand the Yoruba people, history, myths, and culture is to understand the knowledge that Ifa possesses. It is not an overstatement to say that the foundation of the Yoruba people and cosmology is found on its many gods and goddesses who are the progenitors of this tribe of people.

> Ifa represents a special branch of Yoruba religion because of its intellectual outlook and its stock of traditional academic men. In this sense, Ifa is more than a branch of Yoruba religion. Ifa is the means through which Yoruba culture informs and regenerates itself and preserves all that is considered good and memorable in that society.[17]

In traditional Yoruba religion, Ifa is revered among the many divinities and deities because it is the most intellectual religion of all. It is a religion that keeps the life cycle regulated right from the time of birth and the regeneration of the Yoruba belief and value system. Ifa is a link that other divinities speak through and keep getting their dues in form of sacrifices. Ifa is indispensable in the traditional Yoruba religion because of its powerful agency and role in traditional medicine, divinities, and ancestral worship. Ifa is consulted during coronation ceremonies as well as during funeral to seek the goodwill of the divinities.

Dramaturgy of Ese Ifa

The Ese Ifa is a body of subtexts or poems that contain prerecorded events, myths, stories, history, and narratives to unravel a mystery. The Ese Ifa is rendered in a kind of dramatic performance that is preceded by the idafa (divination). The divination that is acted out in a script-like form starts with the diviner, babalawo, casting the opele (divination string), or Ikin (sixteen palm nuts) to read the Odu that is formed on the divination powder. The odu, which are sixteen figures, lead to the subtext or verse to be chanted. The Ese Ifa is the poetic narrative tied to the Odu that has been revealed by the casting of the opele or ikin as the case may be. It is in the rendition of the Ese Ifa that the answers to the client's enquiry or questions are being revealed and solved. There is no fixed number for these Ese Ifa for the Odu, which means the diviner can have at least four or more Ese Ifa verses to elucidate the Odu.

> Once the diviner has thrown his figure, the divination proper can begin. Each figure has several pieces of literature (ese) specifically connected with it, and it is in the words associated with the figure thrown that the answer to the client's query must be found. There is no definite number of pieces for each odu, but a diviner would not normally begin to practice unless he knew at least four for each (thus involving mastery of at least one thousand in all); good diviners are said to know about eight of the pieces for each of the 256 figures and many more for the important figures.[18]

The primary function of the Ese Ifa is to direct the client who has consulted the babalawo for divination and seeks knowledge to the appropriate action or decision to take. The Ese Ifa almost always suggests the required

Figure 4.2.   Palm nuts. *Source:* The Wellcome Collection. Accessed July 29, 2020, from https://wellcomecollection.org/works/tene7e2c.

or appropriate sacrifice to make or offer through a precedent action narrated in the verse. The Ese Ifa sets a prototype of a similar incident, the injunction, decision, and outcome and systemically guides the inquirer to make a comparison between his issue and the one narrated. The Ese Ifa may expressly or implicitly state the advantage of heeding the advice or solution provided in the prosaic verse.

In any Odu the Ese Ifa attached to it is not usually in the singular form but often in the pluralistic mode, which attests to the existence of preliterate wisdom. The Ese Ifa attached to the Odu may be chanted randomly (not in a fixed structure), with different narratives but with the same message and code, and it is the duty of the seeker of wisdom to unlock the code and message in the verse. The diviner may assist the client in decoding the message; it is, however, the client's prerogative to choose the Ese Ifa that is applicable to his problem.

There are many historical allusions in the process of consultation and chanting of the verse and it is dramatic in its presentation. The language of the Ese Ifa is mystical and esoteric that commands attention and diligence in order to extract the meaning embedded in the verse. Usually there is a recognized pattern for the verse, which is noted to include the propitiation action, the diviner's name, the client, and the outcome of the divination.

> The practical point of these pieces is to guide the inquirer by suggesting a sacrifice or type of worship, by indicating his likely fortune, and by referring to a precedent from which he can judge his own case. Since more than one piece can be quoted for whatever figure is thrown, these are recited at random one after the other, and it is for the client, not the diviner, to select which applies to his particular case.[19]

There are many allusions in the verse chanted, which is a creative way to give answers rather than bluntly give it away. These allusions build up the narrative in the verse and set the mind of the client on the course of answers. These poems of Ifa may also be proverbial in the sense that it takes a scenario and philosophizes about the merits of imbibing a particular positive attitude. The disadvantages of embarking on the wrong course of action or character may be dire and are emphatically enunciated in these poems. These Ese Ifa are deep but may sometimes have short, witty, and simple stories attached to them.

The structure of the Ese Ifa couched in the lyrical narrative states the Ifa diviner's name, followed by the inquirer's name, on whose request the divination process is initiated. According to Finnegan, the characters in the Ese Ifa may include humans, animals, objects, and nocturnal beings and deities.[20] The characters or actors in the Ese Ifa are often imbued with intricate and poetic nomenclature, which may have significance on the narrative. The Ifa poems can have characters such as trees, fruits, animals, rivers, stones, and so on, as the mythological figure who has asked the divination be performed on his behalf. The Ifa poems contain numerous characters and characterization whose names may sometimes be short, as in one word, or long like a couple of words or a phrase.

> Expressed in poetic language and sometimes chanted all through. This part is concerned with setting out a precedent in terms of a previous divination. First often comes the name of the priest of Ifa who is said to have made the prophecy in the precedent cited, and the name of the client(s) for whom he was divining— these may be people, deities, animals, plants, inanimate objects. Thus the client may be told that on the previous occasion.[21]

The length of the Ese Ifa varies from one to the other; a verse may be cryptic and short as having few lines and as lengthy as several lines and stanzas containing a dramatic narrative. The concluding part may be closed with a song-like epilogue by the diviner. The narrative plot of the Ese Ifa usually has a chronological arrangement that is usually the prologue, the plot, and finally the epilogue or conclusion. The conclusion is direct and signifies the end of the divination or consultation process.

> They can be about animals, gods, legendary humans, natural phenomena like rivers or hills, plants, and even inanimate things like metals or shells, and they may take the form of a simple story about a man going on a journey, an account of the founding of a town, a philosophical discussion of the merits and demerits of monogamy—"there is . . . no limit to the subject-matter which Ese Ifa may deal with." The outcome often takes an aetiological form with the present nature of some plant or animal traced to its imaginary actions in the story—in particular its obedience or disobedience to the injunctions laid on it by the oracle; its characteristics in the world today thus provide a kind of imaginative validation of the truth of the story.[22]

The subject matter and characters in the Ese Ifa are diverse and filled with various characters who bring the poetic narrative to life in a quasi-magical recitation or the semi-spiritual interpretation. The diviner does not sway from the verse text; however, his professionalism comes into the performance by using many mnemonic devices and stopgaps to change the tune or the ambience of the verse to suit the situation of the divination. Finnegan considers the Ese Ifa as a religious poetry of the Yoruba people, making comparison between the Christian hymn and Islamic poetic scripture.[23] The Ese Ifa can last for about few minutes or extend up to an hour depending on the selected poem chanted by the Ifa priest.

The topics and subject matter in the Ese Ifa are numerous in such a way that every human situation and issues are captured and dealt with, with possible solutions to them. The scope of the topics may range from communal living, the importance of honesty and hard work, and the philosophical debate on the acquisition of wealth to simple issues of life as friendship, betrayal, and revenge. The plot of each Ese Ifa is carefully laid out with precision to highlight the upside and downside of complicated issues. The Ese Ifa will be examined later in this chapter to demonstrate that Ifa is a well-constructed knowledge system of the Yoruba people, which is also relevant in this modern era.

Babalawo: The Custodian of Ifa and Knowledge

The custodian of the Ifa corpus is the qualified babalawo who is immersed in the lore, religion, and verses of the Ifa corpus. He goes through series of trainings from his formative years to his adult age till he is tested and certified by the teacher and trainer who is a professional of the occupation. The babalawo who has been charged with the art, verse, and religion venerates the sacred art of Ifa and the secrets of the religion.

> The qualified priest is a totally divine person versed in the taboos, rites, recitals, and ceremonies of the cult. He guards jealously the paraphernalia of his profession, venerates his own mission and entirely respects the secrets of his client. He is usually full of assurance, of a settled disposition and dispassionate in his approach to men and matters.[24]

The priest of Ifa is an instrument of knowledge and usually leads a procession of the worship. In the primordial Yoruba society, the babalawo is respected for his intuition, wisdom, and dexterity in handling difficult and confounding issues. The babalawo is reputed to know mysteries that are naturally obscure to human beings, through several tutelage and teachings they have undergone. The Odu or Ese Ifa is orally recited, learnt, and chanted, which requires a lot of attention and a retentive memory. The training of the Ifa priest requires learning the Odu—the structure, verses, the divining procedure, and rituals. The years for the training are usually not fixed but Finnegan notes that it could be up to seven or ten years and even so the learning does not end then; it takes a lifetime to attain the mastery of the Ifa system of knowledge.[25] There may be a leader of a group of diviners known as Olori Awo in a community depending on the structure of the profession in the place.

The training of the apprentice deals with a lot of memorization of Ifa poems, sacrifices, materials, language, and craft. The years dedicated to the memorization of the literature of Ifa are usually long but may differ from one trainee to the other depending on his ability to memorize and chant appropriately. Each of these Ifa poems and Odu is connected to the Yoruba divinities that have some special powers to act on the activities of humans. Learning and knowledge are continuous exercises and are especially so in this kind of traditional knowledge system of the Yoruba. The intense training of the Ifa priest is highly metaphysical and philosophical, combining several aspects such as healing through herbs and plants, guiding rulers and monarchs, and prescribing and interpreting spiritual codes.

Ifa priests are not only reputable diviners; they are also trained and professional physicians who have knowledge of many herbs and plants, treatment, and application of this knowledge to heal, mend, and cure people from diverse ailments even before the advent of Western medicine. These ailments vary from the mild ones like cough, rash, and diarrhea to complex and highly sensitive ones like infertility, psychological disturbances, sterility, and so on. The list of ailments and diseases that can be treated and cured by these Ifa diviners is also based on Ifa's knowledge about life, healing, and herbs. Ifa priests are also trained bards, chroniclers, and historians, who have been trained to not only memorize, recite, and chant but also on the act of delivery, theatrics, and performance. These Ifa priests can tell and narrate the history of the Yoruba people and how each of their ancestors and deities became who they were. This trait is not too far-fetched as Ifa; the deity of wisdom is known as a grand historian. In the Ifa literary corpus, the etiological stories of the Yoruba people are narrated and it is not too ambitious to say that if one seeks to study to know about the Yoruba people, the best place to start from is to read the Ifa literary text. Ifa divination can be studied as a site of performance with the different paraphernalia and audience, which highlights the indispensability of this system of knowledge. There are many Ifa poems from the literature that have myths and stories about the different herbs and their functions in traditional medical practices. These Ese Ifa document the Yoruba system of healing using the indigenous methods and herbs to cure and bring relief.

> In the traditional Yoruba society, Ifa priests were the physicians, psychiatrists, historians, and philosophers of the communities to which they belong. It is therefore not surprising that an elaborate system of training involving so much time and patience is marked out for all who aspire to become Ifa priests.[26]

Ifa priests are also reputable philosophers who through Ifa have been able to acquire knowledge of the world and its application to extant situations. Ifa literary corpus is a repository of philosophies about life, knowledge acquisition, morality and religion, healing, and wealth acquisition. The vast themes and subjects in the Ifa literary corpus are inexhaustible—as each verse takes an aspect of human activity and problem and explicates the nuances of life and how complex situations could be maneuvered, to achieve either a good result or cope with such issues that one must encounter. These priests themselves learn from the great philosopher, Orunmila, and many of his philosophies are codified in the Ifa verses. The years of training that are estimated to be about ten to fifteen prepare them for the tenacity and ability to philosophize. The training sharpens their intellect and broadens their horizon to the mysteries in the world.

The training of an Ifa apprentice is systematic and well structured with each stage designed to stimulate the trainee to yield to the ultimate goal of becoming a renowned Ifa priest. Abimbola recognizes about five levels of training for the apprentice which includes:

> First, the handling of both the divination string and the sixteen palm-nuts, which is important as the proper operation of these instruments of knowledge, is essential to the whole training process. This stage also involves the learning of the sign, symbols and names of the 256 Odu verse-texts. The learning of these verses requires dedication, intelligence and a good memory, and so this initial stage of training may be referred to as the learning of the Ifa literature.

The second level of instruction includes the learning of the poems (ese Ifa), the subverses attached to each of the Ifa figure (Odu). It is important to note that the method of training and dissemination of the poems by the master who is also the priest is oral. The priest chants a verse and the apprentice repeats after him, and so this is done continuously till the trainee gets a grasp of the verse.

The third stage involves the trainee watching the priest divining for a client and how he applies the different ingrained knowledge of the verses to the divination. This part of the trainee's education requires him to make mental note as he watches his master gathering material and performing sacrifices on behalf of his clients. The apprentice may also participate in getting the required materials and in the process learns from participating in the performance of the propitiatory sacrifices.

In the fourth level of training is the acquisition of knowledge of different types of sacrifices and the appropriate materials. In each poem attached to the Odu is a specified sacrifice to be carried out and the significance of that sacrifice lies in its appropriateness to the poem. The method of carrying out the sacrifice is learnt and also the places where the materials can be purchased are also learnt in this stage. The deity who should be offered the sacrifice is also important in this part of the training. There are different kinds of sacrifices offered to each divinity connected to the Odu, because each of the Odu is also regarded as a spiritual entity.[27]

> The Odu themselves are not regarded as mere chapters of text or collections of words, but are understood as spiritual entities with distinct "personalities" and characteristics in their own right.[28]

And last, the learning of traditional medicine, which is an important aspect of this Ifa training. The sufficient understanding of herbs in the treatment of various ailments is essential to the craft. The herbs and plant could be prescribed for an ailing client, which are codified in the numerous Ifa poems.

Initiation into the Ifa cult is the final rung of the traditional system of graduation from the school of Ifa training. The initiation process involves seasoned senior Ifa priests who will test the trainee and conduct the ceremony in the forest; the senior priests test the trainee on different aspects of his education to ascertain his intelligence and completion of the training. The trainee is advised to stick to the ethic of his profession with all honesty and also abide by the codes and secrets of the cult when he starts practicing. However, the initiation does not mean the end of the learning process for the new priest but the beginning of a lifelong education and practice of Ifa divination. He may consult other revered senior priests when he needs help on difficult issues when divining for clients.

The education of the Ifa trainees signifies that before Western education, African societies like the preliterate Yoruba society have systems of academic education though informal but effective in organizing, preserving, and conveying knowledge to generations of their descendants. The inscription of Ifa figures on the divination system is also an organized system of writing with its deep semiotic interpretation. Writing as a system of knowledge preservation and dissemination was not alien to the African preliterate society; these societies possess their own systems of education, codification, signs, and symbols and most importantly knowledge, which are passed on orally.

PART III
IDAFA AND THE WEB OF INTERDISCIPLINARY DISCOURSES

> The Ifa divination system is a highly elaborate one. It rests on a series of mathematical permutations, the principle of which must be grasped in order to understand the way in which certain pieces of literature are associated with each of these. The permutations of figures (odu) are based

on two columns of four units each, and the different combinations which these eight units may form between them. The total number of figures is 256, each with its own name and associated literature. It is only after obtaining one of the figures to form the basis of his utterance that the diviner can proceed to the divination itself.[29]

In the primordial era in Yoruba communities whenever people need advice on several issues ranging from mundane issues like a change of occupation to more serious ones on life and death, they visit the babalawo to perform Ifa divination for them. There are several kinds of divination system in the Yoruba culture and traditional religion. The didafa also known as idafa is the most revered and respected one because of its intellectual position. This system of divination has been studied as a mathematical permutation that involves the binary multiplication of the Ifa figures to produce the 256 Odu. The generation of the Odu, which is based on this complex system of multiplication, connects it to the field of mathematics. The divination system has also been compared to the system of coding and programming in computer science. The Ifa divination system has been proven to have some similarities with coding system of computer science.

> The Ifa divination codes have symbolic characters in the Yoruba language. The characters thus have no numeric and no alphabetic. These codes refer to the 8-bit code of order 16 formed by the signature such that each word of the code is a juxtaposition of two elements of the Ifa hex code.[30]

Ifa is a system of knowledge of the Yoruba people, which is found on ancient philosophy, myth, folklore, belief system, and culture of these people. Scholars in cultural studies have connected this system of ancient Yoruba knowledge to a mathematical combination. The combination works with the juggling of the ikin (beads or nuts) to achieve a binary composition, which connotes the specific Odu for the divination system. The divination itself is an art that has connection with several other disciplines like computer science, mathematics, mobile engineering, and so on. The divination works with several other props and devices to kick-start the mathematical calculation.

Idafa is the process of divination using the string of beads and palm nuts. Idafa is a communication link between the babalawo and the extraterrestrial world of knowledge, which transcends the human world but has a link in it. The divination process begins with the communication of the seeker of wisdom or knowledge (client) with the ikin Ifa (the totemic beads).[31] This process of conversing with the palm nuts is initiating the knowledge acquisition and it is usually done with the intent of knowing that which is obscure to the human physical eyes (oju ita). The babalawo (father of secrets) is the diviner and interpreter of the knowledge revealed. The babalawo begins the process of knowledge finding with the Opele, the strings of knowledge, which offers a systemic code of knowledge preexisting before time immemorial. The idafa is the whole process of search, which the client or seeker of knowledge has initiated with the quest for wisdom into the unknown.

> There are two main ways of obtaining the figures. The first, less elaborate mechanism consists of a chain or cord of eight half-seeds (often split mango stones), divided into two portions of four half-seeds each. When this is thrown down by the diviner, the resultant figure makes two columns of four units each, the exact combination depending on whether the seeds have fallen convex- or concave-side-up. The other way of obtaining a figure, a longer method used in important consultations, is with a set of sixteen palm-nuts and a small board.[32]

The divining system can be categorized into two different ways based on Finnegan's observation of how the Odu can be obtained. The first system is conducted with an opele (string), which when cast on a round- or square-shaped board shows either a binary combination of beads having pros or cons, and the second system is considered more elaborate and usually conducted during an important situation with ikin Ifa (nuts) that are sixteen in number on the opon Ifa (tablet). These two systems are very important and in no way less significant to the dispensing of wisdom. Although the second system involves a lot of juggling and indentation on the opon Ifa to mark the figure, the two systems will provide the same Odu. Finnegan states:

> The diviner throws or passes the nuts rapidly from one hand to the other. If either one or two nuts are left in the right hand, the throw is valid and he makes a corresponding mark on his board: a double mark for one nut, a single for two. The process is repeated eight times and eight marks are thus made in the dust on the tray; these start from the bottom right-hand side and are laid out in the form of two parallel columns of four sets of marks each. This gives the same result as the eight-seed chain, the double mark corresponding to a seed convex-side-up, a single mark to the concave.[33]

The babalawo rapidly transfers the nuts from one palm to the other and makes a vertical stroke on the divination powder based on the number of nuts left when transferring these nuts from the right or left palm. This is done rapidly for about eight times to complete the indentation of four lines each on either side of the divination board. When the two columns have been successfully marked on the tray, the Ifa figure is pronounced, which leads to the recitation of the Ifa poems. Sometimes, the knowledge is embedded in a cipher the babalawo has to decipher; the code may be layered in several poetic or prosaic texts. The idafa continues till the full meaning or code is cracked to reveal the kernel of the matter. The system is so elaborate that it involves series of theatrics—the rhythmic tap of the iroke and cultic chants of the Ifa texts, bodily movements of head and hands.

> If the picture is not clear enough the priest may seek further aid in the effica-
> cious sacred cowries and the sacred piece of bone. These are used in the manner
> of a touchstone mainly for casting lots. The priest is not limited to a single throw
> of the chain. In practice, he casts his chain several times recording the forma-
> tion of the nuts in the yellowish powder, iyerosun, contained in the ornamented
> divining tray. To stimulate his memory and create a conductive environment, the
> priest uses a short ivory staff, iroke, to tap the tray rhythmically while he chants
> the relevant Odu from the almost endless and untiring corpus of Ifa poems.[34]

The idafa is not a mindless throwing of the ikin or opele but a systemic arrangement of possibilities that any human situation can be placed on. These possibilities that are represented by the Odu are on the sixteen figures that are broadly in total of 256 possible outcome or potential models. The 256 possi-ble figures are more of a guide that is deeply reflective of human experiences and situations and ways of understanding, responding, and interpreting them.

Ifa is a system of knowledge of the Yoruba people that is considered as a science of knowing the past, present, and future. It is a system grounded on unraveling mysteries and hidden knowledge. Through Ifa the cistern of knowledge is made accessible to humans, such as pieces of advice on mar-riage, work, friendship, trust, obedience, and on many other areas of life.

> Ifa has a special position among the gods. He is both the deity who acts as the
> intermediary between men and gods, and also in a sense is the impersonal prin-
> ciple of divination by which mankind has access to what is otherwise hidden
> from them. Ifa thus, as god and as oracle, plays a central part in Yoruba religious
> and everyday life.[35]

From the 256 Odu at least one of the possible scenarios or outcomes will be relevant to the problem of the client. The client will recognize similari-ties between his or her issues with the poetically illustrated event in the Ese Ifa. When the client's issue has been referenced to the precedent event in the poem, the Ifa priest will proceed to explain the story and give the interpreta-tion relevant to the present situation. The Ifa poem may carry a condensed message or code that may prove too complex for the supplicant's understand-ing but the diviner is always capable of detangling the veiled message of Ifa.

Odu Ifa

The Odu Ifa are figures or symbols of knowledge etched as vertical lines or marks made on the powder of the Ifa tablet that contains Ifa knowledge figures and signs. The Odu are principally sixteen in number and replicated on the binary permutation. Abimbola stated that the 256 characters in the Ifa literary corpus are individually known as Odu with a distinct sign and symbol.[36] Attached to the Odu are poems known as Ese that supply it with depth and mythic-religious symbolism.

> The Yoruba believe that the Odu are diviners in their own right and they, like the other divinities, descended from orun into the city of Ife. It is also believed that the Odu were sent by Olodumare (the Yoruba High God) to replace Orunmila on earth after the return of the latter to orun.[37]

The Odu Ifa is an enormous body of literary narratives that evokes the knowledge and experiences of the Yoruba people.[38] The Odu is a sixteen by sixteen divination system with significant symbols, nomenclature, and signs. Abimbola stated the number of Ese attached to each Odu is about 600; these body poems consist of different verses with allusions and poetic properties.[39] The thorough education of the Ifa priest and apprentice helps him to distinguish one poem specific to a particular Odu from the other without committing errors of substituting a poem for Odu Eji Ogbe for Otua Meji. The Yoruba mythological stories stated that the Odu are also believed to possess special powers of divining for humans as Orunmila was taken away from them. The Odu are representatives of the power of divination that Olodumare has given Orunmila, the wisest divinity. The Odu is filled with myths, spiritual codes, and mores to guide human beings to lead a good life when they have applied the knowledge Ifa has revealed in the Odu.

> Nowhere is the profundity and beauty of African spirituality more apparent than in the Odu Ifa, the sacred text of the spiritual and ethical tradition of Ifa, which is one of the greatest sacred texts of the world and a classic of African and world literature.[40]

Karenga speaks of the beauty of the Odu Ifa, the sacred text of the Yoruba people that existed even before the introduction of writing. The Odu is a large body of oral literature filled with history, folklore, proverbs, myths, songs, and spiritual instructions on diverse issues. He noted that in Africa, Ifa literature had existed for generations through the medium of the fathers of mysteries who were initiated into the profession of old. The Odu Ifa proves that the possession of a body of literature is not alien to the African people, which many Eurocentric scholars have claimed not to exist because it does not conform to the Eurocentric definition of literature.

The Odu that are about 256 volumes of independent texts are derived from sixteen basic names; each of these names is a derivative of the sixteen probable models of divination symbols marked on one side of the vertical lines etched on the divination powder. However, Ilori also acknowledged the existence of about 249 shorter poetic texts that are chanted as prefaces to the main texts. She also notes that the Odu is accompanied by significant tune and strokes during the divination process. Odu Ifa is known for its expansive subjects and possibilities that are achieved through the binary multiplication and interpretation of the divination beads. The sixteen models of the figures are arranged sequentially based on the order of superiority and are listed here:[41]

I	II	II	I	I	II	I	II
I	II	I	II	I	II	I	II
I	II	I	II	II	I	II	II
I	II	II	I	II	I	II	I
(1) Ogbe	(2) Oyeku	(3) Iwori	(4) Odi	(5) Irosun	(6) Oworin	(7) Obara	(8) Okanran
I	II	II	II	I	I	I	II
I	I	I	II	II	I	II	I
I	I	II	I	I	II	I	II
II	I	II	II	I	I	II	I
(9) Ogunda	(10) Osa	(11) Ika	(12) Otuurupon	(13) Otua	(14) Irete	(15) Ose	(16) Ofun

The Odu 256 in number are then cast in two sets, making the foremost set Oju Odu the major text. The sixteen principal figures are reduplicated on the basic sixteen aforementioned models. The divination string and sixteen palm nuts are read from the right side to the left with the strokes on the right considered the principal figures whereby the sixteen basic names are derived from. Every Odu has a connection with a divinity, and so the Odu contains myths and stories about that particular divinity. The connection with the divinity will also stipulate what sacrifices should be offered to that deity who will assist the client in solving his issue. The Odu Ifa gives direction and elucidation to the mystery that has been brought to the Ifa's priest. The plethora of spiritual, ethical, and moral subjects in these poems are easily known and categorized through the Odu Ifa.

> The Odu, however, in spite of its variety, its often expansive and almost limitless details, is not something structurally indeterminable. In fact, it has now become clear that the priest when chanting the Odu is not engaged in some unconscious process but in a highly controlled and artistically structured activity.[42]

Abimbola, an Ifa scholar, notes that the Odu Ifa has about eight significant features in the recitation of the verses.[43] The Ifa signature (Odu) carries a prefix or suffix denoting the binary duplication of the sixteen principal Odu. Thus, the manipulation of the divination chain and sixteen palm nuts will provide vertical strokes on both the left- and right-hand side of the divination powder. When this binary duplication is achieved on either side the sign is accompanied by the prefix "Eji" or suffix "Meji," that is, having Ogbe strokes on both the right and left side will interpret to having Eji Ogbe.

> Wande Abimbola, a noted Ifa lorist and researcher, has identified eight typical features of the basic Ifa poem. Though he does not discuss their role, these features are not more functional than stop-gaps or stanza margins intended to give the priest a moment to catch his breath or more, shuffle the details of his chosen poem—especially when he has to recite, sing an declaim, in turns, parts of these details. The competence of the priest is, among other ways, reflected in how carefully and correctly he can pick his way through the meaning, message and rites structurally integrated into each Odu.[44]

The Odu is acclaimed to be the largest Yoruba literature of the myths of creation, etiology, ethics, and morality. The linkage of each Odu to a divinity opens a medium between these spiritual beings, ancestors, and human beings to communicate and seek for assistance for whatever issue that may be bothering them. The Odu Ifa brings the divinities and their human worshippers closer to each other in a way that both entities benefit from this intermediary activity, making Ifa the true representative of these deities and ancestors.

The arrangement of the poems is divided into eight maximum and a minimum of four formats; the poems with the eight organizational patterns are known as Ifa Nla, lengthy verses of Ifa, and the Ifa poems with the four structure are called Ifa kekeke, short verses of Ifa. The arrangement of the Ese Ifa follows the pattern recognized by Finnegan.

> The corpus of Ifa divination verses was the largest archive of myth and cosmology available to the Yoruba, and (since most people consulted babalawo occasionally and heard some of these verses) was probably the most widely available source of general religious knowledge of Ifa itself, more shortly.[45]

In the verses of texts (ese Ifa) selected the narration of the precedent event is cited, which involves the diviner, his client, and the reason for the divination. The purpose of the divination, the procedure to be carried out, compliance/noncompliance of the client to the injunction, the outcome of the clients action, the reward of the action taken, and finally the lessons drawn from the prosaic text are the eight-structure division of the verse texts the babalawo follows to deliver the outcome of the divination, which Ilori has delineated in her article. The Odu is lyrically chanted, which emphasizes its literary adornments and musical qualities.

Ifa Divination System

> Divination is a practice, usually involving the use of supernatural means,
> that seeks to reveal or discover hidden knowledge or occult realities.[46]

Divination is more than a practice of jostling of Ifa divination tools; it is an organized system of thought of the Yoruba to gain knowledge, advice, and opinion of the deities about the affairs of humans and the effect of their action. Adegbindin discusses the different types of divinatory systems in the Yoruba society, which are ways of getting instructions on how to lead a good and successful life on earth.[47] The divinatory systems are about five in number in the Yoruba traditional religion and culture. The Yoruba thus employ such divinatory methods like Olokun-awo, Agbigba, Obi Dida, Eerindinlogun, and Ifa divination. Divination enhances the Yoruba people's action on political, marital, social, and religious matters wisdom and direction. Thus steering them to the right path and making good decisions on any issue through the consultation with Ifa.

The system of "knowing" involves a series of knowledge band—knowing the unknown, knowing the past, knowing the present, and knowing the future. The knowledge is achieved by the priest through the series of rigorous training and mental exercises. It is not a system based on spiritual possession or trance-like performance. These Ifa priests "know" because they have been schooled on the system of memorizing the Ifa literary corpus and manipulation of the divination equipment.

> Ifa, however, relied not on its babalawos being possessed by their orisha but
> on their mastery of a technique that entailed the capacity to remember a vast
> corpus of verses. The babalawo began by manipulating a handful of palm
> nuts to produce one of 256 (16 × 16) configurations (odu), to each of which
> corresponded a sequence of verses that described mythical precedents; these
> were then recited by the babalawo, and the client selected one that spoke to
> his situation. The source of the problem and the steps to be taken to resolve
> it, by a specified sacrifice to a particular orisha, would then be clarified by
> casting lots in response to the client's questions. Though Orunmila thus sus-
> tained the system of orisha cults as a whole (which indeed he belonged to),
> he also represented himself as somewhat above and outside it, as the sole
> channel of wisdom from the supreme being, Olodumare, who was the source
> of the Ifa verses.[48]

Before the commencement of the divination, the client must first pay homage to the Ifa priest before making his intention of communing with the divinity known. The priest then begins the divination process by laying the divination string before the client, who converses quietly with a token or an equivalent of this. The client expresses the reason for the consultation to the token and drops it on the divination tool. The client's act of whispering his issues or problems to the token before the commencement of the divination is symbolic; communication and gift are mediums for opening the portal for knowledge. Abimbola notes that the client could also decide to commune with the string of divination in some cases.[49] The significance of communing with the divination instrument or token is the connection of the client's ori, which gives direction to a man's destiny in life, to the divinity, Ifa, who gives direction in the world.

The diviner starts divining by picking the divination bead and singing the praises of Ifa, saluting his prowess in giving wisdom, direction, and guidance to humans. In his salutation, the Ifa priest often entreats the divinity of knowledge to provide the right answers to the client's mystery or problem. The Ifa priest throws the chain, reads the code, and declares the Odu, which appears on the string. The Odu is the key to the client's dilemma, which shows that every problem has a precedent action and Ifa divination is an established system of knowledge into hidden mysteries of the world.

The next point of action after discovering the Odu is to chant the poem (ese Ifa) attached to the Odu. The expertise of the Ifa priest to recite as many verses as he can recall from that particular Odu testifies to the mental process involved in this system of knowledge. When chanting these Ifa poems the client listens and watches the priest's voice, tone, body movement, and pitch, which show the seasoned process of training the diviner has undergone. It is in the recitation of these verses that the client will choose the verse appropriate to his situation. These verses, though poetic, are stories related to the subject of consultation. When the client has successfully recognized and selected the appropriate verse, the diviner will proceed to interpret the verse and state the sacrifice that needs to be done.

> Sometimes during the process of divination, the client will recognize certain poems the content of which contain problems similar to the problems of certain members of his family. He may also recognize a poem which relates to other personal problems of his own different from the original one on account of which he has consulted Ifa. It may also happen that the client does not know which poem to choose out of the poems chanted by the Ifa priest. In all these cases, the ibo will be used to clarify and elucidate the actual message of Ifa.[50]

The rendition of the verses might continue for a while if the appropriate one has not been recognized by the client. The appropriateness of the verse is very important as it will also lead to the successful completion of the knowledge and sacrifice. The sacrifice is an important part of the divination process as it binds the client, Ifa priest, and divinity together. The client may either choose to pay the diviner in the absence of getting the propitiation materials required of him or he may decide to carry out the sacrifice himself.

Sacrifice is therefore central to Ifa divination and to Yoruba traditional religion as a whole. Sacrifice keeps the belief system going and links the client, the diviner, the divinities, and the ancestors together through a system of service and reward. When the supplicant refuses to perform the sacrifice, he makes it impossible for this system of service and payment to be completed. Such a client therefore commits a taboo, which might be punishable by the divinities or the spiritual beings in charge of such disciplinary actions because of his fraudulent action of cheating the divinities out of their dues. The Ifa priest too is cheated from receiving the payment for services rendered, because some of the items of the sacrifices serve as part of his reward. The performance of sacrifice marks the completion of the divination process for all the parties involved.

Instruments of Ifa Divination

Iroke Ifa

This is a short metal or wooden figurine that the babalawo uses to tap the divination tray while consultation is in progress. This is noted to also invoke the deity of knowledge to make the divination a success. Abimbola notes that this carved wooden figure is representative of the supremacy and authority of the diviner. The sizes of this figure may be in smaller pieces or large ones, which are carried by the priest's apprentice or assistant before him during an important outing.

> The iroke is carved with ivory or wood in small and large sizes. On some iroke, a human figure or the head of a human being is carved. The upper part of the iroke is carved in a long, sharp and conical shape. The bottom part is thick so that it can support the upper part when the instrument is made to stand erect.[51]

The bottom of the small iroke is held by the priest when divining, while the head of the piece is used in tapping the tray. This instrument serves as an aesthetic component of the traditional system of knowledge, which also beautifies the Ifa priest's house or temple.

Ikin Ifa

The ikin Ifa that are sixteen palm nuts are reputably the ancient and most crucial tool of Ifa divination. The origin of the ikin Ifa is traced back to the myth of Orunmila's angry departure from aye (earth) to Orun (heaven). Abimbola noted that the ikin is extracted from a specific palm tree (ope Ifa).[52] The significance of the ikin rests on its usage on important occasions or divination ceremony such as the installation of a new king or monarch, initiation of

Ifa apprentice, and during the priest's personal divination. These palm nuts are secured in a lidded bowl at a specific corner of the room or shrine with limited movement or transfer from this spot. The removal of the nuts from this location is usually based on the purification purpose to invoke its power and effectiveness. The ikin is used alongside the sacred powdery substance, iyereosun, which could be yellow, white, or creamy in color.

Abimbola notes that the sixteen palm nuts are transferred from one hand to the other in a swift deft motion, and the number of nuts left on the previous palm determines the mark that will be made on the Ifa divination tray.[53] The nut(s) that is left on the previous palm is usually between one and two. To arrive at the figure of knowledge, Odu, the number of marks on the divination tray must be four on both the right and left sides.

> If two palm-nuts remain in his palm, he makes one vertical mark on the powder of divination. If one palm-nut remains, he makes two marks below the first mark. But if he succeeds in taking all the palm-nuts at once so that none remain in his palm, he will make no marks at all. In the same way, if more than two palm-nuts remain inside his palm, he will not make any marks on the powder of divination.[54]

These marks are interpreted as divination signage; when a singular stroke is made on the tray on both the left and right sides four times, the name of the figure is called Eji Ogbe. And when double marks or two vertical strokes are etched on the tray on both sides four times, the divination figure is called Oyeku Meji. These patterns are in the total number of 256 in the Yoruba ancient knowledge system of Ifa divination.

Opele

The Opele is an open-ended string of attached nut used also for divination, which may be made of a soft cotton rope or metal. There are about four open nuts attached to both sides of the string or chain. The string is held in the middle at the top end by the diviner who throws it on the ground or whatever platform created for the divination process. When the divination string is thrown, the nuts attached to the string are either inside and outside upward or downward. Abimbola opines:

> There are 2 possibilities of this form of presentation each time he Ifa priest throws his chain. Each of these possibilities of possibilities of presentation is known as an Odu or chapter in the Ifa divination corpus.[55]

The divination bead and sixteen palm nuts may not follow the same process but essentially determine the same figure of odu. For instance, when the eight nuts-string is thrown and are all inside up or face up, the figure is also called Eji Ogbe, and when the nuts are all outside up or backside up, the figure is Oyeku Meji. Abimbola notes that the divination bead is often used in the search of knowledge than the sixteen palm nuts.[56] The string is more of an everyday consultation instrument than the sixteen palm nuts. These instruments are important in the divination system as they help elucidate and achieve the deposition of knowledge.

Apo Ifa

The chain and other materials for divination are stored in the priest's bag known as apo Ifa. The bag may be cotton or made of animal skin and slung around the diviner's shoulder when he has an engagement outside his house. The Apo Ifa also serves as part of his costume when the Ifa priest goes for functions, ceremonies, and festivals requiring his presence and attendance.

Iyerosun

This is the powdery substance that is used during the sixteen palm nuts divination system where imprints are made to reveal the cipher. The color of this substance varies from white, cream, to yellow. The significance of the powder is powerful beyond its use as inscription material on the tray. Abimbola states that the powder is extracted from the Irosun tree or extracted dust from dry bamboo, which is spread on the surface of the divination tray as a medium between the sacred palm nuts and the code of message.

> The powder of divination is highly regarded by Ifa priests as a sacred symbol of Ifa. Particles of this powder are sprinkled on sacrifices to insure acceptance by the divinities. The client is sometimes asked to swallow some of the powder and rub it on his head to forge a bond of unity between him and the divinities so that he may get the satisfaction that the divinities are in support of his cause and have approved of his action.[57]

The significance of the divination dust lies in the binding of the client, divination, message, and sacrifice to the ancient Yoruba system of knowledge. The ingestion of the iyerosun foregrounds the acceptance of the knowledge revealed; eating the powder is synonymous with taking in knowledge and safeguarding it in one's belly. When it is also smeared on the head, it binds the knowledge to the symbol of one's destiny (ori). Rubbing the powder on the head signifies that the head and the mind is where knowledge is embedded; the head is the seat of wisdom and the stomach is where knowledge is processed and churned out.

Ibo

In the process of divination, the ibo is used by the priest to get more information as regard the interpretation and appropriateness of the Ese Ifa. The ibo is cast to further locate the target of the message, the method of propitiation or sacrifice, and which divinity will be offered the sacrifice. The ibo is an assurance medium to which the client will be guided toward the knowledge of the present consultation's outcome, whether the divinities give their blessings or not to the knowledge revealed.

> The basic instrument in the ibo are a pair of cowry shells tied together and a piece of bone. The cowry shells stand for an affirmative reply while the bone stands for a negative reply from the divinity in respect of every question posed. But several other instruments are also used as part of the ibo to symbolize different things. For example, a piece of rock stands for good health while the black ake-apple nut represents Orunmila himself.[58]

Abimbola notes that the client and Ifa priest believe in the efficiency of the Ifa tool to reveal the mind of Ifa to them and also to determine the exact person the message in the verse is directed to.[59] This ibo has a way of determining and unraveling difficult questions during the divination process; it is a communication system between the divinity of knowledge and the Ifa priest. The ibo is placed in the client's palms while the Ifa priest continues to seek for clear direction; the cowry and bone are separated into different palms, each of the item may be on the right or left palm. When the priest asks a question through the handling of the divination chain, the Odu that comes after the first one will determine which of the palm to be selected. The palm that contains the bone signifies that the answer is negative and before this is concluded the Ifa priest must have done it twice.

Opon Ifa

This is the divining tray, plate, or board, Opon Ifa, which is a wooden flat surface where the Ifa priest makes imprints during the divination process. This tray is usually used when the sixteen palm nuts are employed for divination. It is on this tray that the divination powder is spread and the strokes are being etched to reveal the Odu that Ifa has orchestrated.

PART IV
THE LITERATURE OF IFA APPLIED

The Ifa literary corpus is an oral documentation of the Yoruba thoughts, beliefs, customs, rites, philosophies, and epistemological innovations. Ifa

codifies how the Yoruba people think, eat, and relate with divinities and fel-
low human beings. The Ifa literary corpus explores their beliefs on the myth
of reincarnation, predestination, etiology of the Yoruba people, language, arts,
and craft. Few of the Ifa Odu and Ese Ifa will be stated here and the connection to the knowledge system of the Yoruba will be established through its
interpretation and analysis.

> *Oyeku Meji, Ese Ekini*
> Oyeku, mo ba o mule
> Mo mo se da mi.
> Inu bibi eru ni i peru;
> Edo fufu iwofa ni i pa Iwofa;
> A dia fun Oofua.
> Nigba ti n be laarin ota aye.
> Bi iku ba n sa egbee mi pa,
> Oto ni Oyeku o maa sa mi si.
> Bi arun ba n ss egbee mii se,
> Oto ni Oyeku o maa sa mi si.
> Gbogbo alawe obi ni ikuu pa,
> Oto ni a a yo oofua obi si.
> Iku ma pawo mo o,
> Iku ye lori awo.
> Oto ni a a yo oofua obi si.
> Iku ma pawo mo o,
> Iku ye lori awo.[60]

In this poem Ifa discloses that when a covenant is struck between Oyeku
Meji and any human, death cannot overcome such a person, and he
becomes invisible to death. He has cheated death because of the agreement with Oyeku Meji. Whoever consults Ifa and the Odu that appears
on the divination tray is Oyeku Meji, and proceeds to offer the sacrifice
attached to the Odu has succeeded in averting an imminent death or
threat to his life. He may be among many who have been earmarked for
death but will be saved from this disastrous end because Ifa has revealed
that an agreement with Oyeku Meji will save and shield him or her from
this evil.

The poem could also be interpreted based on agreement or covenant making and betrayal; this may be between friends or a group of people. This
particular covenant is between the client and his ancestors or deity attached
to his lineage. When the person has been faithful in his ritualistic worship and
service to his deity, the divinity should never betray his follower whenever
he is in need.

Another part of the poem also talks about anger and a hot temperament—
the inclination of being aggressive and displaying excessive anger, which the

Yoruba mythological story philosophizes about. Ifa discouraged the display of anger and hot temperedness, which is narrated in this Ifa poem. The display of anger to one who is superior is highly discouraged and frowned upon; after all, what will the angry slave do to his master but to be seriously punished for deigning to display unbridled anger toward his boss? This part of the poem is illustrated in lines 3–4:

> Inu bibi eru ni i peru;
> Edo fufu iwofa ni i pa Iwofa;

In the concluding part of the Ifa poem, there is a play on a particular word from the name of the Ifa signature, Oyeku Meji. The word is extracted from the Odu to emphasize the main subject of the poem that whosoever has reached an agreement with the divinity and an ardent worshipper of Ifa will be protected from untimely death or disaster. The word, "ye," a syllable from the figure "Oyeku," is symbolically used at the end of the verse to yoke the deliverance from death to the name of the Odu. This verse narrates the moral instruction that is passed to the client who may choose from any of the part of the poem that deals with his problem. This Ese Ifa philosophize about issues of agreement and the consequences of breeching this agreement between human beings and divinities and among themselves. There are about three layers of knowledge embedded in this Ifa poem:

> The first wisdom that has been provided is the restraints from breaking covenant and agreement between humans and the spiritual beings and also amongst humans themselves. At the level of human relationship, Ifa knows that a breach of agreement destroys one's integrity and invites consequences that may be very dire. The second layer talks about temperance and civility even when one is confronted with aggravating issues. There is wisdom in refraining from excessive display of rage as when one is consumed by that emotion it may lead to series of actions that one may later regret. Rage should never cloud one's reasoning to make an individual overlook the place of superiority. The final strand of wisdom which is hidden in the poem is the connection to Ifa and the worship of this divinity. The relationship with this divinity opens one's external and spiritual eyes to be sensitive to oracular instructions.

> *Owonrin Meji, Ese Ekinni*
> Owon omi, owon omi
> Owon loruko ti a a pe Owonrin.
> Owon ojo ni a a pe leerun.
> Akitipa, akitipa, akitipa;
> Owo sisi, owo sisi.   5
> Awooda okuuru, awooda okuuru, awooda okuuru,

Owaara, owo sisiisi.
Owaara, owo sisiisi.
Bi won ba n ro,
Won ki I da mo.
Eji a ya sile; eji a ya soko;   10
Abata regede a si dodo.
A dia fun Owo-winiwini,
Ti i somo Olokun, seni ade.
Omo a woo mi kuuru gba jo;
Owo sisi, owo sisi.[61]   15

    This Ifa poem is discussing rain as part of the weather and the description of how a torrential rain can be. This interpretation is the surface interpretation as there are two levels of interpretation that can be detangled from these Ifa poems. The first line of the poem describes how the rain pellets hit the ground and the kind of sound it makes. During a torrential downpour there is a particular sound that emerges from the contact with the roof of a house or on plants and this sound is described by the repetition of the word "akitipa." When the shower begins fully it is usually forceful packing a lot of power in its wake, and at every stage of the torrent it gives a particular sound. However, after some time the rain will begin to subside to a trickle that it started with in the beginning till it finally stops. The high-low rhythm of the rain is significant to the deeper level of the Ifa poem. When this poem is chanted to a client it could mean one or two things to the client.

    First, there is an abundance of blessing or good things coming to the client, which the Yoruba believe that rain brings blessing, bountiful harvest, prosperity, and generally peace. The regulated rhythm of the rain that intensifies after some time is symbolic to the plentiful goodness that should be expected. The second interpretation could be literal in that it is significantly about rain for farmers and everyone. Rain is significant for growth, expansion, goodness, and calmness, which human beings need to lead a good life. Rain has so many proverbs in Yoruba depicting its effects and importance for the continuance and sustenance of life. Rain brings longevity to humans, plants, and animals. Therefore, when chanted by those who consult Ifa, this poem brings positivity to those it is chanted for.

    In the Ifa poem, the downpour flows and becomes a river or stream that is tied to a divinity called Olokun. The Yoruba believe that for each body of water there is a specific divinity connected to it. At the end of the Ifa poem, the connection is made to Olokun the divinity of the ocean, who is the overseer of this body of water. When a person is asked to make a sacrifice after the divination, he makes the offering to this divinity or any of the water divinities. This poem of Ifa is also calling drawing our attention to how torrential rain floods and becomes a large body of water. This is why scholars of Ifa have made a connection of Ifa to science, which before the advent of modern science and technology can describe the weather and accurately make predictions about the weather, to warn people of an impending shower or draught.

Ifa divination is a system of knowledge of the preliterate Yoruba society, which works on a series of precedent stories and myths narrated in the Ese Ifa to give knowledge about certain issues because there is absolutely no new situation or problem that does not have a precedent, which has occurred before. Ifa is an organized system of preexisting knowledge that sets a base for the interpretation of complicated issues. In the Ese Ifa narrated previously, Ifa has revealed a knowledge of how rain works and its relationship to the sustenance of life.

Owonrin Meji, Ese Eketa
Atelewo o lee hunrun ihere ihere;
Ko se ferefere,
K'ori ferefere bi ala
A dia fun Mofeeni,
Ti n lo ree kowo lodoo Kiifeani.   5
Oju ni n pon Mofeeni,
Lo ba lo kowo lodoo Kiifeani.
Won waa n wa oku adie
Ti oba o fi se oogun
Ki omoo re kan soso o le ye.   10
Won wa okudie naa titi, won o ri
Ti won fi wa a de okoo Gbamiorami,
Nibi ti Mofeeni ti n singba l'odoo Kiifeani.
Mofeeni si ni akuko adie kan,
Akuko adie naaa si ku sinu ago.   15
Nigba ti awon onise-oba de,
Won bi Kiifeani pe ta l'o ni in.
Kiifeani ni oun ko o.
O ni olorun mo jee ki oun o de
Akuko adie t'o ti ku mo'nu ago ni toun.   20
O se bi oba fee mu eni ti o ni akuko naa ni.
O ni iwofa oun, oloriburuku kan bayii,
Lo ni akuko adie naa.
Were, o ti rannse si Mofeeni
Ni okoo Gbamiorami nibi t'o gbe n sise asedoru,   25
Nibi t'o gbe n singba, ti n sesin.
Ti n sisee boo-ji-ojimi,
Ti Mofeeni gbe n sise asedaajin.
Nigba ti Mofeeni de,
Won bi i pe se oun l'o ni un pe oun ni.   30
Akuko adie t'o ku s'inu ago naa.

O si dahun pe oun ni.
Won ni awon fee ra a ni.
Ki Mofeeni o too yanu fohun,
Won ti fun un ni opolopo owo,
Won ni owo akuko adie re nu-un,   35
Ni Mofeeni ba di oloro, o dalaje.
O ya enu koto,
Orin awo ni n ko.
O ni, "Mo fe,
N o loowo o,   40
Iyere.
Mo mo mo fe,
N o biimo.
Iyere.
Iyere titi l'a o fi oni sun,   45
Iyere."[62]

This Ifa poem narrates the story of a slave who became wealthy through the sale of his dead cock that was needed for the resuscitation of the king's son. The slave, Mofeeni, is serving his master, Kiifeani, who was too quick to blame his servant for the death of that animal. The king sent his messengers to search for anyone who owns a dead cock so as to prevent the death of his only child. When these messengers approached Kiifeani and was asked if he was the owner of the dead animal, he quickly denied the possession of the dead cock, thinking whoever owns the cock will be arrested. He quickly summoned his servant, Mofeeni, to bear the brunt of the allegation, but fortunately for the slave, he became wealthy as the purpose for the dead bird was revealed. He was given a lot of money for the purchase of the bird.

The moral lesson or knowledge that Ifa is trying to impact in this poem is to desist from underestimating and downgrading people because of their present predicament or situation. And servants and slaves should be treated with respect and compassion. When people are in the position of authority, power, and wealth, it is important that they imbibe the spirit of compassion and humility because whoever is at the bottom of the rung today may have his luck changed to replace whoever is at the top tomorrow. The future is unpredictable and dealing with people in a humane way is always the best thing to do. This is an admonition to the rich, wealthy, and people in the place of power to not take advantage of the poor and wretched by abusing and mal-treating them. These people might turn out to be more than they used to be.

The poem also comforts those who have been treated badly to be cheerful because there is always light at the end of the tunnel. People who are passing through difficult and hard times should persevere because at the end he will reward them with good fortune. Ifa reveals that whoever consulted Ifa and the Odu cast was Owonrin Meji has been going through difficult times, but should not be weary because he will receive good fortune at the end of the trial. This is a knowledge system that the Yoruba believe to reveal their fortune for them when they are passing through hard times. The significance of the poem as a system of knowledge of the Yoruba people assures them that tough times do not last forever, and perseverance is necessary in life because hard times are inevitable and are meant to strengthen human's resilience to succumb to these periods of trial. Ifa is knowledgeable on all issues and his assurance and wisdom on matters that are beyond human control. The Ifa poems are filled with many subjects, themes, and philosophies about many aspects of life that are hidden to mortals. Through Ifa divination, the knowledge and experience of those characters such as deities, ancestors, and inanimate objects are made plain to human beings to give them direction on how to go about their lives and tackle complex situations.

> *Otuurupon Meji*
> Ologbon kan o ta koko omi seti aso,
> Omoran kan o moye eepee 'le;
> A dia fori,
> A bu funwa.
> Ori ni ire gbogbo le to oun lowo bayii?   5
> Won ni o rubo
> O sir u u.
> Igba ti o rubo tan,
> O si ni gbogbo ire ti o nfe.
> O ni bee gege ni awon awo oun   10
> Nsenu reree pefa,
> Ologbon kan o ta koko omi seti aso,
> Omoran kan o moye epee 'le;
> A dia fori,
> A bu funwa.   15
> Ori pele o,
> Ori abiye.
> Eni ori ba gbeboo re,
> Ko yo.[63]

This Ifa poem talks about wisdom and predestination that is controlled by the divinity, Ori, which has control over the acquisition of wisdom and every other thing. The poem talks about the impossibility of a wise person scooping water and knotting it on the edge of his cloth, and counting the dust on the face of the earth. This divination was performed for Ori and Iwa (personality) who sought Ifa for answers on goodness. Ifa prescribed a particular sacrifice for Ori to offer and he hearkened to Ifa's instruction by performing

the sacrifice, which ushered in immense goodness that Ori wanted. He testi-
fied that Ifa delivered exactly as the diviner promised the result will be. The
poem started by declaiming that the wisest of all human beings will still not
be able to figure out spiritual things without the help of his Ori and Ifa. It is
important that one's Ori be connected to the right source as it will bring in
goodness. The Yoruba believe in predestination and the input of one's divinity
represented by Ori. However, there is also the believe in Yoruba cosmology
that this divinity can be bewitched and manipulated by forces greater than it,
which renders it impotent in defending and attracting good things to such a
person.

The Yoruba people believe so much in the power of this divinity that sacrifices and prayers are offered to it to secure its effectiveness. Ifa codifies the
myths and belief system of the Yoruba people, which also serves as a compass
for navigating discourses of folk medicine, philosophy, religion, and spiritual
practices. Ifa is a system of knowledge of the preliterate Yoruba society that
gives an in-depth analysis and explanation of the origin, organization, culture,
and religion of this group of people. Ifa tells the history of the Yoruba people
starting from the creation of the earth and the subsequent spread of the different deities and divinities on earth. This Ifa poem reveals how the divinity, Ori,
is connected to the failure or success of a person in the Yoruba thought system. Ifa philosophizes about knowledge, which no man can solely lay claim
to and the emptiness of human knowledge without the input of divinities.

> *Otua Meji*
> Ayooro enu,
> Ayooro enu,
> Ebiti enu o tase;
> Eno oforo nii poforo,
> Enu oforo nii poforo,   5
> Enu foroforo nii poforo.
> A dia fun okere
> Ti yoo mule lebaa ona,
> Won ni ki okere o sora
> Nitori pe enuu re ko bo.   10
> Won ni ko mo moo fi gbogbo ohun ti o ba ri
> So fun eeyan mo.
> Okere o gbo.
> Igba ti o ya,
> Iyawo okere bimo meji leekanaa,   15
> Igba ti inu okere dun tan,
> To di ojo kan,
> O ni okere bimo meji,
> Ile kun teteete,

Gbogbo ero ona,   20
E ya waa wo o.
Igba ti awon aye gbo,
Won ya bo sinu igbe,
Won nawo gan ile okere,
Won si tu u wo.   25
Igba ti won o dee inu ile okere,
Won ba omo meji ti o ni naa.
Ni won ba mu won lo sile.
Igba ti awon omo aye dele,
Won fi awon omo okere leri iyan,   30
Won si ba obe lo.[64]

This Ifa poem narrates the story of squirrel that is talkative and could not keep secrets to himself but goes on to babble to everyone on the street. A divination was performed for Squirrel the protagonist of the narrative, who was counseled to refrain from talking too much because of his inability to keep issues to himself. He was cautioned against revealing everything he knows to people around him but refuse to listen to this advice. The Squirrel's wife gave birth to two children, and the Squirrel became very happy that he could not curtail his joy and keep the good news to himself. On a fateful day, the Squirrel decided to share the news with everyone, stating that he has two children and his home is filled up with children. Unfortunately for Squirrel while he was out spreading the news, human beings heard the news and decided to see for themselves if what the Squirrel was saying was true. When human beings got to the Squirrel's house and confirmed that truly he had two children, they decided to take the young ones home to make a good meal of pounded yam and soup of them. This is the literal interpretation of the Ifa poem on the talkative that is a snare unto itself.

From the Ifa poem the moral or lesson Ifa is impacting is the prudence of keeping one's mouth shut at the appropriate time. An individual who talks too much cannot keep a secret to himself and opens himself to danger. Ifa warns against divulging one's secret to many people as it opens a door for the enemy to attack once the secret to a person's power is laid bare for everybody. A person who talks too much is vulnerable to attack and snare that one may unintentionally lay for one's self. This Ifa poem calls for caution to the person Ifa divination is performed for; the advice is to be tactful and refrain from unnecessary loquacious personality. This poem expands on the knowledge of Ifa the divinity of wisdom to guide the Yoruba people in the preliterate society on the imprudence of being too wordy. Ifa is a system that teaches and philosophizes on issues that are very important in life. Lessons are learnt from the precedent stories narrated in the Ese Ifa; these lessons have been culled from series of experiences and intelligence of the ancestors.

From the recitation of the Ese Ifa attached to the Odu, the series of possible scenarios and narratives provided will lead the client(s) to the appropriate poem connected to his problem. When he has identified the Ifa poem connected to his issue, the knowledge embedded in the poem is then expatiated and interpreted by the Ifa priest to reveal the kernel of the advice or solution Ifa is providing. The Odu and Ese Ifa are by themselves pieces of knowledge embedded in these narrative poems, and thus when the client consults the diviner for divination, it is because the client believes that Ifa will provide the right answer to his problem. The 256 Ifa poems are possible templates that address many issues, subjects, and philosophy about the world.

Ogunda Meji
Gbongbo se woroko fi woroko jana;
A dia fun fekun
Nijo ti i lo oko ode.
Oko ode ti oun nlo yii,
Oun le rise bo mbe?   5
Ni ekun dafa si.
Won ni ki o rubo elenini.
Ekun nit a ni o selenini oun ekun?
O ni oun o nii ru,
Laipe, ekun kori soko ode.   10
Esu di ategun,
O tele e.
Igba ti ekuun doko ode.
Lo ba ri ira,
O si pa a.
Nje ki ekun o maa da ira ni inu lu,   15
Ni Esu ba ja eso igi afon kan,
O so o mo ekun ni bara idi.
Bi o ti ba ekun ni bara idi tan,   20
Esekese ni ekun sa lo.
Ki o to pada de,
Esu ti gbe eran lo.
Igba ti ekun pada de,
Ti o wa ira titi, ti ko ri i,
Lo bat un wa eran mii lo,   25
Sugbon bakanaa lo ja si.
Igba ti ebi waa bere sii pa ekun,
Ere lo sa rubo.
Igba ti o rubo tan,
O tun pada lo si oko ode,   30
Esu ko si deru ba a mo.
Ijo ni njo,

Ayo ni nyo.
O ni gbongbo se woroko fi woroko jana.   35
A dia fun fekun
Nijo tin lo oko ode.
Won ni o kaaki Mole,
O jare,
Ebo ni o se,
Kee pe o,   40
Kee jina,
E waa ba ni ni tisegun.[65]

This Ifa poem is about a divination performed for Lion when he was about to go hunting in the forest. Lion consulted Ifa to know if he will be successful in hunting game and the instruction given to him was to offer sacrifice in order to overcome his adversaries. However, Lion refused to offer the sacrifice before embarking on the hunting outing, claiming that he is beyond any adversary's machination against him. He set out into the forest to hunt and Esu, the mischievous divinity, decided to teach the lion a lesson after he had transformed himself into wind. Lion caught an animal, ira, but could not succeed in dissecting it because Esu had hit Lion's buttocks with the afon tree fruit he threw at him. Lion was afraid and took to his heels and Esu went away with the game of the hunt. After some time, Lion returned to pick up the animal but discovered that it has been taken. Lion decided to hunt for another animal and had a similar experience of what had happened earlier and then remembered he was asked to offer a sacrifice, which he ignored.

Lion decided to heed the instruction to offer sacrifice to overcome his adversaries after the failure to capture animals. After he had offered the sacrifice, he went back to hunt and was able to overcome Esu's plot to scare him away from his prize. Lion became joyful and sang the praises of Ifa, noting that he was warned and instructed to appease the divinities before setting out to hunt. This poem of Ifa reveals the Yoruba thought system that is codified in the Odu and Ese Ifa about the importance of heeding advice of the divinities. The Ifa poem discouraged the reliance on one's ability in flagrant disobedience to the instruction of the wise men and deities. The Ifa poem symbolizes the thought system, culture, religion, philosophy, and attitude of the Yoruba about life. When a client consults an Ifa priest and this poem is chanted, the client's problem is modeled on the story narrated in the poem. The Odu and Ese Ifa deal with several subjects like marriage, divorce, disobedience, justice, temperance, and so on.

These Ifa poems are important aspects of the Yoruba people in terms of traditional medicine and healing. Ifa has also been closely linked to the field of modern medicine in the way the divination is performed for an ailing client.

When the divination string is cast and the figure appears on the divination powder, the Ifa priests interprets the Odu and recommends herbs, medicines, and sacrifice for that particular ailment to restore the ailing client and keep evil forces away. In some cases, the client may not even be aware of an affliction or even have physical exhibition of the disease or ailment but when Ifa is consulted and divination is carried out these diseases and sicknesses are revealed and the appropriate cause of action is stated. The curative method for the client may be prescribed herbs that will be eaten or swallowed, used on the body as either lotion to smear on the skin, used for bathing, and most often the offering of sacrifices to the gods and goddesses. The exact kind of sacrifice and method of disposal is prescribed so as to offer the right sacrifice to the right divinity. Ifa may also instruct the client to avoid certain things or situations that may act as triggers to such disease or ailment.

Ifa is a system of knowledge like psychology, which reads psychological and psychical energies of an individual who has come for the performance of Ifa divination. Through Ifa divination, the client's Ori (psychic divinity) is connected to his destiny, and his purpose on earth is revealed. Ifa system of knowledge is psychotherapeutic in nature as it dislodges mental strains and energies in the client, whose Ori has been connected to the divination and appeased for good fortune. When the divination process has been completed there is always the purgation of dark emotions and energies the client is carrying. The evil emotions trapped in the body and head are drawn through the offering of sacrifice to the divinities. The Yoruba belief in predestination and the power of spiritual forces in determining how a person turns out in life and so, Ifa divination is usually performed to get this knowledge. Many of the Ifa poems are codification of this Yoruba belief in fate, death, and reincarnation.

CONCLUSION

This chapter has traced Ifa as a knowledge system in the preliterate and modern era, which is passed down orally from generations of babalawo, who are generally regarded as fathers of mysteries. The chapter began with the meaning and type of knowledge, which makes Ifa a type of indigenous knowledge because of its unique characteristics that have been in existence over thousands of years before the advent of modern system of documentation. This system of knowledge is a product of a community's culture, values, customs, religions, and history. The knowledge system is communally owned and reflects the myths, innovation, and practices of that community or group of people. This chapter proceeds to state how the Ifa literary corpus is a knowledge system of the Yoruba people and its spread in many other communities.

The chapter also explored the place of Ifa in the traditional Yoruba religion stating the important position it occupies. Orunmila is interchangeably used for Ifa, as the divinity who was present during the creation of the universe. The praises of Ifa reflect his important role as the mouthpiece of the other many Yoruba divinities and spiritual beings. Ifa is the link between human beings and these ancestral beings; the intermediary role of Ifa makes it a divinity that is omnipotent and omniscient as he sees the past and beyond the present to the future. The study also discusses the Odu Ifa as a body of knowledge that is generated through the operation of the sixteen sacred palm nuts (ikin Ifa) and divination bead (opele). The Odu Ifa is about 256 with numerous subtexts known as Ese Ifa, and it is impossible to state the exact numbers of poems in the Ese Ifa.

The study also examined the training of the Ifa priest otherwise known as babalawo. The training usually takes about five to ten years depending on the trainee's decision to take it as a full-time profession or not. However, Ifa scholars note that the training does not end at the initiation of the trainee in the forest but continues to the demise of the priests. The Ifa education is a lifelong process that an Ifa priest goes through due to the expanse of the literary corpus. Some of the Ifa tools are stated and explained in the course of the study. The Ifa equipment are important to the craft as some are symbolic to the divinity of wisdom, while others are part of the diviner's costume.

Finally, the study explored how the Odu and Ese Ifa reveal that Ifa is indeed a system of knowledge of the Yoruba people. This part of the study takes on the analysis of some selected Ifa poems and explicated how these poems are oral documentations of the Yoruba folklore, myths, legend, culture, religion, mores, and spiritual practices. The Ifa poems reveal innovative aspects like folk medicine, agricultural practices, time management, and weather forecast of the Yoruba communities. The thoughts, beliefs, values, language, arts, and crafts of the people are codified in Ifa literary corpus. These poems narrate indigenous knowledge, morals, lessons, and philosophies of the Yoruba people. Ifa tells the history of the Yoruba gods, goddesses, and traces the origin of the people to their ancestral home, Ile-Ife. Ifa is known as the grand historian who is knowledgeable on all things because of his relationship with the Yoruba High god—Olodumare.

In conclusion, Ifa is not only a branch of the traditional Yoruba religion; it is a system of knowledge that is present at the beginning of life and explicates the mysteries that are hidden to mortals. Ifa is a system of knowledge that regenerates Yoruba cultural materials, language, values, folklore, and spiritual practices. It enhances the continuity of intelligent ritual materials, festivals, and sources of oral literature of the Yoruba people. Ifa as a system of knowledge is found and studied in the diaspora as an important field of interdisciplinary discourses. The system of knowledge is relevant both in the preliterate society and the modern era. Ifa will continue to remain relevant in the field of science and technology, agriculture, computer science, mathematics, psychology, anthropology, and so on, because of the structure of knowledge embedded in it. This study and many other extant works on Ifa cannot exhaust the dimension of the Ifa system of knowledge. This study, however, reiterates that knowledge is a product of a people's custom, tradition, rites, philosophies, and metaphysical beliefs and materials in a given society. Therefore, Ifa is a broad system of knowledge of the Yoruba but has transcended its etiological mold to infuse different aspects of modern epistemology in different parts of the universe.

Part II

WORLD RELIGIONS AND KNOWLEDGE SYSTEMS

Chapter 5

Quranic Epistemology

Alif, Lam, Meem, Ra. These are the verses of the Book; and what has been revealed to you from your Lord is the truth, but most of the people do not believe.[1]

Islam is the world's fastest-growing religion. There were about 1.8 billion Muslims in the world in 2015, with an expected increase to 3 billion in 2060.[2] By this estimate, Islam will soon replace Christianity as the largest world religion by population. There are about fifty nations globally that have an Islamic majority. The influence of Islam is not limited to the Middle East, as more than two-third of the world's Muslims live in the Asia-Pacific region. In regions such as Europe and the Americas, Muslim populations often fall at about 5 percent or less of the population.[3] Still, Muslims represent a significant minority with an estimated over 25 million Muslims in Europe in 2016.[4]

The growing global dependence on oil has brought much attention to the politics of the Middle East. The influx of oil money has increased political tensions and created humanitarian crises. Additionally, attention is brought to Muslim minority populations globally due to the large percentage of Muslim immigrants and the threat of terrorism from extremist groups.[5] The inseparability of Islam and politics has given Islam its influential power in contemporary political issues that deal with Muslim countries and peoples. Global collaboration and understanding of these problems require basic comprehension of Islam. The problem with the increasing relevance of Islam to global politics and economics is the simultaneously occurring misrepresentation.[6]

The misrepresentation of Islam stems from the clashing of cultures between the Western and Islamic world. This clash originates from Western

Figure 5.1.   Mosque. *Source:* **Toyin Falola.**

colonization and Eurocentric domination of world culture, politics, and economics. This domination combined with the inherent incompatibility of Western culture to traditional Islamic values causes Islamic demonization of Western culture. Extremist Muslims, through their association with terrorists such as the events of 9/11, prompted Western demonization of Islam. Additional topics of global importance such as oil exportation, immigration, terrorism, and Western military involvement in Islamic nations have heightened these tensions. The rhetoric of some Western leaders, such as Donald Trump, on topics such as politics in the Middle East and issues of immigration tends to distort the nature of Islam, at times promoting Islamophobia.[7]

Understanding Islam is vital to the successful resolution of global political, economic, and humanitarian problems. A simple summary of the beliefs of Islam is not enough to bridge this intellectual gap. Islamic and Western scholars have different standards of knowledge, different epistemologies. Epistemology is interrelated to ideology, ontology, and values. This includes the idea of truth, whether it exists and whether humans are capable of finding it. The ideology of a people determines what they define as truth and their ontology determines how truth relates to their lives and beliefs. For example, Islamic scholars believe that the Quran is truth. They believe this because they value religion and believe Allah is the center of being. This cornerstone belief makes the standards of truth in Islam fall under the framework of Quranic epistemology. In order for non-Islamic peoples to successfully communicate and problem solve with Islamic scholars, they must understand the rhetoric of Quranic epistemology.

The problem with the term "Quranic epistemology" is it puts a non-Western concept in a Western framework. The concept of epistemology developed from discussion in ancient Greece between Socrates and his students, Plato and Aristotle. This foundational argument debated the importance between a rationalist or empiricist approach. Plato argued that reality can be deceiving and that only reason could look past this false veil.[8] Aristotle countered that reality can be deceiving, but reason alone has no relevance to reality.[9] The Western conception of epistemology in philosophy begins with this argument in ancient Greece and was revived during the Enlightenment, as outlined in the introductory chapter. Scholars such as Descartes revisited the nature of knowledge and introduced skepticism.[10] The revival of these ancient discussions and creation of the field of epistemology were undoubtedly tied to religious skepticism in the West. Biblical scholars such as Thomas Aquinas used epistemological arguments in order to defend their religion beliefs. Other scholars such as Voltaire and Hobbes used epistemology to argue against religion.

From the epistemological discussion of the enlightenment grew the philosophy of Western science. Gettier solidified the definition of truth in the Western perspective as justified true belief.[11] Other scholars such as Bacon published the scientific method, a methodological approach to obtain a justified true belief.[12] Karl Popper continued to critic what could be identified as "true" science and reinforced the role of criticism and empiricism in science.[13] There are two outcomes of the Western etymology of epistemology, which make it problematic to compare cross-culturally. First, that epistemology is associated with modern science. This science takes a particular form of empirical, peer review through Western-validated institutions. The second outcome is the idea of the secular as the only pathway to knowledge. Mainstream academia, in its Eurocentric nature, values first knowledge, which is secular. It is not that this literature denies religion outright, but it is able to exist separate from it, without discussing implications for religion.[14]

Islamic scholars base their knowledge off of Quranic epistemology. Quranic epistemology by no means exists in a vacuum from Western epistemology; Islamic scholars both influence and were influenced by the ancient

Greeks. And the globalization of knowledge and interconnectedness of phi-losophy in the world cannot be denied. I do not claim that all Muslim scholars follow a particular set of ideas about the nature or conditions of truth. Instead, I seek to generalize some of the patterns in Quranic epistemology to give an introduction to the topic. I do this through explaining foundational concept of Islam and the Quran. Then I explain the history of Islamic philosophy before outlining the basic arguments of Quranic criticism. Finally, I analyze the diversity and applications of Quranic epistemology.

PART I
FOUNDATION OF ISLAM

Muslims understand their world through the framework of Allah's final word to man, the Quran. Quranic epistemology is the foundation of Islam. But to understand the Quran and its approach to knowledge, I will first explain themes in the Quran. The Quran is the most important book in Islamic litera-ture. The ability for the Quran to be intellectually relevant as well as sacred exemplifies the center point of Quranic epistemology, the togetherness of spirituality and intellect. The Quran is a spiritual foundation of Islam but also a logical system with great complexity.[15]

Islam is a reformative religion that branched off of Christianity in the sixth century. Discussions of the Quran are inseparable from discussions of Muhammad. Muhammad was the founder of Islam and author of the Quran. Muslims believe that Allah had sent many prophets before Muhammad to humanity such as Jesus Christ. They believe that Christians make the mistake of equating the prophet with Allah. Muslims do not worship Muhammad as Allah; rather, they venerate him as an agent of Allah who was able to deliver his final message to humanity. Muhammad received this message through revelation throughout his life and spread the message through speech. These speeches were written down by the followers of Muhammad who were able to compile them into the Quran after his death so that his message would live on. The word "Quran" means "he read" in Arabic. Thus, the Quran is the message that Muhammad read as written by Allah.

> And it is not for any human being that Allah should speak to him except by revelation or from behind a partition or that He sends a messenger to reveal, by His permission, what He wills. Indeed, He is Most High and Wise.[16]

Since Muhammad is central to Islam, it is important to understand who he was. Muhammad was born in about 570 CE, an orphan who grew up poor and illiterate. He was a devout religious man who often secluded himself to pray. Muhammad began to announce his religious revelations when he was about forty years old. In his early religious movement, he had few followers and heavy opposition from Meccan polytheists. He migrated from Mecca to Medina in 622; this event became known as the Hijra and became the beginning of the Muslim calendar. Muhammad took on a strong political role in Medina and united forces against the Meccan. His religious role always had political implications. His lack of education is part of his identification as the "illiterate scholar." The word for this in Arabic is Ummi. Ummi is the argument that Muhammad's lack of education makes his revelations more authentic, as they are not inspired by any previous religious works.[17]

Unlike the Bible, which was edited and compiled over hundreds of years, the Quran was compiled within about twenty years of Muhammad's passing away. Each revelation, or ayah, that Muhammad had was written down word for word by his followers, as they believed it was the direct word of Allah. The Quran is organized into chapters called surahs. Each surah has several ayat. The Quran can also be grouped in other ways such as in ruku, which have ten ayat each to facilitate reading. The Quran is also not the only text important in Islam, as the Hadith is a separate text that also is meant to detail the life and teachings of Muhammad. While the Quran is the direct word of Muhammad coming from his revelations, the Hadith is collection of the words, silent approvals, and actions of Muhammad. The relevance of the Hadith to Muslims varies within the religion, but the Hadith does form important foundations to the Sharia, Islamic religious law. Verses in the Quran support that Muslims should strive to act like Muhammad but give them few practical avenues for this. The Hadith provides more practical guidance on how a Muslim should live their life. Some Muslims, called the Quranists, reject the Hadith altogether as relevant to Islam.

The Quran's role in Islam is to be an inspiration to beauty and morality as well as a tool for understanding Allah's intentions. The practice of Qira'at is a ritual and art in which the Quran is read artistically to reveal the beauty in the verses. This recitation is song-like and is often used for public performance with highly trained professionals rather than for everyday interpretation. The interpretation of the Quran is called the tafsir, analysis that varies based off of the Islamic perspective of the interpreter. The Quran can be analyzed in various ways, primarily either thematic or verse by verse.[18]

"Islam" means submission in Arabic. Beliefs in Islam focus on submission of the self through the will of Allah. This cannot be forced or from fear but must come from genuine love. There are five pillars and six articles to the Islam faith. The first pillar is shahada, profession of faith and submission to Allah. Second is salat, prayer that happens five times a day, typically in the direction of the city of Mecca. The third pillar is sawm, which includes Ramadan and fasting in appropriate time periods. This fasting is able to purify followers, making them more devoted to Allah. Zakat is the value of charity, giving the poor, which is also thought to purify followers from sin and is expected to increase during holy periods such as Ramadan. Finally, the Hajj or the pilgrimage to Mecca at some time during their lifetime is expected to reaffirm the faith of followers.[19]

There are six articles of belief that the Muslims must acknowledge to be a follower under Allah. These include belief in Allah, angels, revelations, prophets, judgment, and predestination. About one-third of the Quran is about eschatology, the afterlife. Muslims do not necessarily believe in the existence of a soul but believe that the Allah that gives them life now will also give them life in the afterlife. The prevalence of eschatology in the Quran is indicative of the religions focus on judgment and law, which translates to political matters.

A particular sin that influences the judgment is shahada. Shahada is the idea that watching sin happen and not intervening makes the follower a sinner as well. This idea encourages conversion efforts by Muslims including their colonial and missionary efforts to spread the religion.[20] Shahada explains why globalization is incompatible with Islam. Islam cannot embrace the secular because it is a sin to not try to convert non-Muslims.

Islam is inevitably tied to politics. When Muhammad traveled to Medina he became the ruler of the city because of his role as the prophet. This was also when he gained the most followers. His role as prophet and his political leadership became intertwined, inseparable. His political leadership supplemented his role as the prophet to create religious law, which became known as the sharia. His effective military leadership allowed for expansion that lasted for centuries to build the Ottoman Empire. The successors of Muhammad who ruled this empire were called the four rightly guided caliphs. Even the division of Islam into the Sunnah and the Shia was based off who the political successor of Muhammad would be. The idea of separation of church and state is unique to Western worlds and does not exist in Islamic epistemology.[21]

One implication of the lack of separation between politics and religion is that the collective memory of Islam is relevant to international politics in the region. This collective memory of Islam is influenced by disagreements in the nature of Islam, theological disagreements, as well as in who should be leading the Islamic state and how and political disagreements. The collective memory is threatened by globalization and Western influences that threaten the morality and integrity of Islam. From this threat to the collective identity of Islam came political discourse and extremist groups such as that of Wahhabism.[22] To understand and improve these global tensions, there must be a global collective effort to understand Quranic epistemology.

PART II
PHILOSOPHY OF TRUTH IN ISLAM

Quranic epistemology describes two different philosophical discourses. The first of those is the Quran as an epistemological text and the second is the epistemological justification of the Quran as truth. The Quran can be read as an epistemological text by Muslims in order to understand the nature of truth. It reinforces itself as a bearer of truth by stating that only through Allah is anyone able to find truth. Then, it states that Allah was able to deliver his message only through prophets, which he did to Muhammad. The Quran describes itself as the sacred word of Allah as spoken through Muhammad. Through its ayat, the Quran presents three primary tenets of truth. First, that there is a singular truth that is found in the Quran through Allah. Second, that this truth is only possible because it is created by Allah; he is the cause of all that is true. Third, that anything that contradicts the idea of Allah being the bearer of truth and solidifying his word through Muhammad is false.[23] It also reveals that the methodology in which truth can be obtained is only through religious technologies including study of the Quran, prayer, revelation, and reason through Allah.[24]

The second dimension to Quranic epistemology is defense of the Quran as truth. The Quran can be read as an epistemological text, which reinforces beliefs of itself, prayer, and revelation as truth. Yet, an additional dimension of epistemological justification is necessary for modern populations to read and apply this ancient text to their lives. The Islam religion, through religious leaders and philosophers, has been able to provide a variety of justification as to why and how the Quran should be read as an epistemological text.

A foundational argument of the Quranic epistemology is the idea of the Quran as existing outside of time and therefore applicable to any historical context. The eternality of the Quran relates to three interconnected ideas in Islam, the Haqq, Hikma, and the Ma'arifa. The Haqq is the idea of truth in Islam, which is something constant and unchanging. This is the epistemological assumption that there is a constant truth. The Hikma says that because truth is constant, there is a balance of truth in every historical moment. The Ma'arifa is the Islamic methodological approach to search for the objective and constant truth. This includes through using the technologies of prayer, revelation, and the Quran to understand the nature of reality.[25] A way to understand the eternality of the Quran is to view it as a phenomenon rather than an event. If the Quran was an event, it describes only the historical context and situation of the time that it was created. This would mean that it would not be generalizable to present-day circumstances. Instead, Muslims view the Quran as a phenonium, something that was an event part of the larger pattern of reality. In this view, the events of the Quran are as old as time and applicable to the future.[26]

Along with the eternality of the Quran, Muslims claim that it is inimitable. No text could replace it in the future, nor could any of it be changed to better fit Allah's intentions. The idea of imitability is that the Quran was Allah's final message to his creation. It was delivered through Muhammad but was not created by him, as he was the messenger of Allah only. Through imitability, the Quran was not created, but a truth that has always existed.[27] A problem with the concept of the inimitability of the Quran is it was only indirectly written by the prophet Muhammad. It was written from accounts of his speeches by his followers. The topic of whether or not the Quran was created is a topic of division among Muslims. Some see the Quran as something such as Allah that always was and always will be. And others see the Quran as something that was created through an enlightened follower of Allah but still a product of historical situations.[28]

A similarity between Quranic and biblical epistemology is sacred protection from corruption. This is the argument that the religious text is the work of Allah and cannot be altered.[29] This argument is vital to biblical epistemology because the Bible has been altered and compiled by so many different religious institutions. The Quran has undergone far less editing since the bulk of the text was written and compiled within twenty years of Muhammad's death. Still, different translations and versions of the Quran exist. Their existence depends on the idea that the Quran has sacred protection and thus individual ayat cannot ever be discounted for poor editing or translation.

A problem with a complex logical system such as the Quran is that it is long and covers many of the same topics. Inevitably, the Quran contradicts itself at some points. This is a similar situation to the Bible in Christianity. Observe the following two verses.

> Indeed, Allah does not forgive association with Him, but He forgives what is less than that for whom He wills. And he who associates others with Allah has certainly fabricated a tremendous sin.[30]
>   The People of the Scripture ask you to bring down to them a book from the heaven. But they had asked of Moses [even] greater than that and said, "Show us Allah outright," so the thunderbolt struck them for their wrongdoing. Then they took the calf [for worship] after clear evidences had come to them, and We pardoned that. And We gave Moses a clear authority.[31]

The first verse asserts that Allah does not forgive those who worship false gods, yet the second verse clearly states that He does. Unlike other religious texts, the Quran has a system for reconciling these contradictions. While religious texts such as the Bible are compilations of many different sources, the Quran is primarily a chronological account of Muhammad's teachings. When there are teachings that contradict each other, it is assumed that more was revealed to Muhammad and the later verse is the one that is more enlightened.

Figure 5.2.   Hands and Quran. *Source:* Toyin Falola.

This concept is called Naskh. In this example, the second verse is regarded as more truth to Allah's intentions. While idolatry is a huge sin, it can be forgiven according to the Quran using Naskh.

There are two primary ways in which the Quran can be interpreted. The first is through tafsir tartibi, sequential interpretation. In this ayah by ayah reading of the Quran, individuals follow the exact wording of the ayah as the word of Allah. According to Naskh, in issues in which the Quran contradicts itself, interpreters use the later version as truth. This is because of the assumption that Allah had revealed more to Muhammad as time went on.[32] The other way to interpret the Quran is through tafsir maudu'i, thematic interpretation. In this technique, the individual is either dealing with a religious question not answered in the Quran or an issue that has contradictory ayat in the Quran. The follower resolves the question by abstracting themes from the Quran and applying them to various issues.[33]

History of Islamic Philosophy

> And do not pursue that of which you have no knowledge. Indeed, the hearing, the sight and the heart—about all those [one] will be questioned.[34]

Key to Quranic epistemology is the relationship between religion and reason. While Western sources see these two as separate, through Cartesian thinking, Islamic scholars see Allah and reason as the same. The question of whether the Quran is a text of reason has evolved of the centuries and remains the key discussion for Islamic scholars. The idea is that Allah has "freedom limited to reason," therefore he is not separate from reason.[35] Because of the direct relationship between Allah and reason, many Islamic scholars pursue science and empiricism, believing that the Quran is an empirical text.

> It is He who created for you all of that which is on the earth. Then He directed Himself to the heaven, [His being above all creation], and made them seven heavens, and He is Knowing of all things.[36]

The tradition of philosophy connecting the pursuit of knowledge and Allah traces back to Al-Kindi, an Islamic philosopher in the ninth century. Al-Kindi was greatly inspired by the musings of Greek philosophers as well as the work of the Islamic philosophers before him. In particular, Al-Kindi was inspired by Platonic realism. This worldview asserts that the material world corresponds to universal forms in the supernatural realm. Platonic realism is an epistemological perspective that diverges from empiricism by asserting that there are things that exist in which we cannot see. It assumes that we can access these things through thought. By the logic of Platonic realism, every-thing comes from something else. Thus, everything must have come from a starting point. Platonic realism calls this starting point "the one." Al-Kindi interpreted the one as Allah, the makers of all things. Through this ontologi-cal perspective, everything that exists, all materials and consciousness, comes from Allah.[37] This is one of the first examples of Islamic philosophy using rationalism to defend the existence of Allah.

Al-Kindi defended the idea of revelation as thoughts coming directly from "the one," Allah. Rather than discounting philosophy and seeing prophecy as the key to enlightenment, Al-Kindi saw them as two different paths to the same answer. Prophecy was knowledge directly obtained through Allah, while philosophy was knowledge obtained through the reason that Allah gave humanity. He argued that while philosophy is able to reach the same answers that are given through prophecy, prophesy is the direct word of Allah and, therefore, more accurate. Ultimately he saw philosophy and prophecy as equally capable of truth, with prophecy being the more straightforward way to discover it.[38]

Ibn al-Haytham, a tenth-century philosopher and father of modern optics, also saw scientific research as a religious act. Unlike scientists such as Coper-nicus who had to fight against the church in order to pursue their research in the Christian world, Ibn al-Haytham had the support of the Muslim com-munity. Together Islamic philosophers such as Ibn al-Haytham and Al-Biruni built the idea of empirical science in the Muslim world.[39] They were inspired by the theories of Aristotle but framed everything within the larger picture of science as Allah's creation.

Al-Farabi was also a tenth-century Islamic philosopher who took inspiration from Al-Kindi. He was often known in the Islamic world as the "second teacher," with Aristotle being the first. Al-Farabi took great inspiration from the ancient Greeks and went to great lengths to preserve their writings. Al-Farabi expanded on Al-Kindi's platonic worldview by saying that everything comes from something, "the one." Yet he took it further to say that Allah didn't create the world, but rather that his existence caused the universe to be. He developed the idea that philosophy is a religious act by describing our universe into three layers. He said that humans only exist between the upper and lower world; they can only reach happiness through connection to Allah through constant intellection. He spent much time thinking about the nature of intellect and described potential, actual and acquired intellect in which the agent, the knowledge of Allah, is the light that allows us to see the truth. He found the value in reason to include both the happiness generated from it and the capacity for voluntarism that comes from knowledge.[40]

Suhrawardi was an Islamic philosopher in the twelfth century who designed the school of Illuminationism. Illuminationism developed from the layered philosophies of previous Islamic scholars who combined Quranic readings with the platonic worldview of "the one." Illuminationism argues that all light is an extension of the original light. The original light is Allah and all of the light that comes from him is the good in the world. Illuminationism heavily relies on the binary of light and dark. The light is everything that is good, moral, and true. Everything that is not touched by the light is in darkness, which is evil. Thus, everything that is not touched by the influence of Allah is in the dark.[41]

Later in the twelfth century emerged the philosophy of Averroes. Averroes revived Aristotle's work for the Islamic world in the twelfth century, reviving discussions about the nature of knowledge in Islamic epistemology. He believed in the view of Platonism, that there are things beyond which we can see but can access through reason. He found this reason through the words in the Quran and philosophy. Averroes believed that because of Platonism, everything emerging from "the one," humans are united as extensions of the same being. This is the being that gives everyone consciousness and the ability to reason. Thus, he concluded that all humans shared a part in the same intellect.[42]

Modern Islamic philosophers such as twentieth-century Muhammad Iqbal and twenty-first-century Nidhal Guessoum build their understanding of the Quran based off of these traditional theorists. Muhammad Iqbal argued for the empirical nature of the Quran in a world with a growing binary between religion and science.[43] Nidhal Guessoum reaffirmed this through a thematic analysis of the Quran in which it encourages the pursuit of truth and knowledge with a special emphasis on truth.[44] Islamic epistemology focuses on understanding the nature of truth in relation to Allah and validating the perusal of truth with the religious act of becoming closer to Allah. It sees truth and Allah as one in the same, and thus the pursuit of one is the pursuit of the other. Modern Islamic epistemology focuses on the tawhid, the oneness of Allah and the Divine Law in which everything is either seen as truth, Haqq, or falsehood, Batil. This is inspired from the contrast of light and dark in the perspective of illuminationism. Haqq can be founded from reasoning or prophecy, which is understood through the ayat of the Quran.[45]

So far, I have explained what the Quran says about truth and how this idea has developed through the history of Islamic philosophy. Now I will explain key aspects of Quranic epistemology so that the Islamic perspective can be understood from an outsider's point of view. Key to the Quranic epistemology is the immanence of Allah. This idea is best understood through comparative religions. Religions in general have the perspective of either an immanent or a transient Allah. An immanent Allah is fully accessible to the physical world. They are not only able to influence but are inherently inseparable from day-to-day life. Through this perspective, empiricism that focuses on that which can be seen is religion because it is studying the work and nature of Allah. A transitive perspective sees that the nature of Allah is beyond the physical world and accessible only through human thought. This perspective of Allah is rejected by Islam by most Muslims.[46]

Key to Quranic epistemology is the idea of knowledge by presence. Knowledge through presence is able to explain how Muslims know what they know about Allah. Critics often say that there is not enough empirical evidence to support the existence of Allah. They cite that the existence of Allah cannot be tested in a scientific way and is thus not provable. Islamic scholars argue that they know of the existence of Allah because they exist. The argument goes: because I have consciousness I exist. Because I exist, I must have come from somewhere. Because I came from somewhere there is a god.[47] This is similar to Descartes argument: "I think, therefore I am." Yet it translates more to "I think, therefore Allah is." A common metaphor for understanding knowledge through presence is the suspended man. Imagine a man who is suspended in the air, not able to perceive anything through his physical senses. Unable to see, hear, touch, or speak, he is still able to think. This proves the existence of something that is beyond the body, an existence of a light inside which comes from the power of Allah.[48]

Quranic Criticism

One way to understand Quranic epistemology is to hold it up to Quranic criticism. The catalyst for discussions of Quranic epistemology is skepticism and doubt. From this criticism, Islamic scholars are able to explain their thought processes on the nature and methodology of finding truth. The largest criticism of Quranic epistemology analyzes the Quran as a text. It juxtaposes the Quran to other religious Meccan and otherwise texts of the time and sees the continuities that make the content of the Quran not unique. Quranic epistemology relies on Muhammad being an illiterate scholar who knew little of other religions or philosophical texts. Thus, the Quran is unique and the authentic word from Allah. Continuities between the Quran and other religious and philosophical texts of the time are evidence of the Quran as a cultural product.[49] The similarities between the Quran and other texts imply that it has a human origin and thus cannot be the work of Allah alone. The Quran is a development from the historical situations of the time that it was created and not the singular generalizable truth.[50] Defendants of Quranic epistemology would argue for the view of the Quran as phenomena, taking place in a historical situation but generalizable. They would argue that Allah has revealed truth through other prophets and Muhammad's consistency with past prophets supports its authenticity as the word of Allah. The idea of a prophet through Quranic epistemology is not one who is the literal relative of Allah but instead one who is more able to access the logic of Allah.[51] This is that all thought and all creation comes from the first light, that of Allah's intellect. Allah is able to send specific messages to people known as prophets to make his word heard. This is not the work of a philosopher who has discovered Allah's work but that of someone who received the message completely.

Another critique of the Quran is its vulnerability to editing and translation. After the death of Muhammad, the Islamic community remade the Bible to match the new religion. The construction of the Quran included Iran Islamic poetry and Bedouin speech together. There were originally seven versions of the text eventually turning into fourteen. All of these versions also had various translations. Even the first few lines of the Quran can be translated in various ways, leaving the text vulnerable to manipulation.[52] Quranic epistemology defends the Quran as having sacred protection from manipulation. However, how could this be truth when so many contradictory versions and translations exist? This brings into question which version of the Quran is closer to the intentions of Allah. Finally, it questions why Allah would send Muhammad into the world as a prophet with his message if it was so unambiguously documented.

Next are the technical contradictions of logic in the Quran. For example, how could the speaker of the Quran be Allah when Allah is addressed many times in the text. This would mean that Allah was addressing himself. A counterargument would be that it was angels speaking.[53] Also, there are many miracles in the Quran that are impossible. These are present in the context of Quran but not seen in modern day. It is possible that the miracles are metaphors.[54] Another evidence against the divine nature of the Quran is the mentioning it has of the Meccan gods. In doing so it is contradicting itself by containing these "satanic verses." These are either signs of evil within the Quran or discredit it altogether. Furthermore, new scientific discoveries can discredit the Quran. The best known of these is that of evolution. Evolution is not mentioned in the Quran and it is said that Allah created the world. This means that either the ayah requires interpretations to become the truth or is inaccurate. Defenders of Quranic epistemology chose to either defend the creation of the world or embrace a thematic interpretation of the Quran consistent with modern science.

One of the most compelling Quranic critiques is that it is interpreted in various ways. People tend to pick and choose what they want the Quran to say, especially in the face of highly controversial issues. The most famous example is that of veiling. The Quran supports veiling, yet many Muslims believe this was a decree for the Medinan community and is a historical circumstance. This is a radical view as most modern Muslims believe the entire Quran is divine and none of it created from political necessity. The idea that some part of the Quran could be from political necessity puts the entirety of the Quran into question. If some things were added for nonreligious reasons, the Quran is no longer the word of Allah.[55] The interpretive nature of text means that there will never be a perfect interpretation of the Quran. Phenomenology says that every interpretation is infected with individual perception. People will undoubtedly pick different interpretations of the Quran and apply them differently in various situations.[56]

PART III
THE QURAN APPLIED

The Quran and Science

A key piece of Quranic epistemology compared to other religious epistemological perspectives is the way that it encourages scientific exploration. Consider the Christian foundational religious tale of Adam and Eve. In this story, Eve ate an apple from the tree of knowledge, which was the original sin. Knowledge is explicitly equated with sin and evil. Instead of negating science as evil or misleading such as Christianity, the Quran embraces science as a form of worship, a way of getting to know Allah. This is connected to the way that the Quran defines Allah with nature. The Quran even asks in several ayat for proof of knowledge before accepting it.[57] The Quran does not discourage scientific methodology but categorizes it as a form of religious way of knowing, in which there are many others. Physicists and devout Muslim, Abdus Salam said, "This in effect is the faith of all physicists: the deeper we seek, the more is our wonder excited, the more is the dazzlement of our gaze."

Despite this underlying encouragement of science, the tensions between the dichotomy still exist in subjects such as the existence of Allah or creationism. These can be categorized into the secular, synthesis, and apologetic solutions (Hedin).[58] The secular solution to Quranic criticism is saying that religion is a personal choice. This involves separating Islam from political and social matters. This is very difficult to do since Islam has always had a political side to it.

> Say, "Indeed, I am on clear evidence from my Lord, and you have denied it. I do not have that for which you are impatient. The decision is only for Allah. He relates the truth, and He is the best of deciders."[59]

The secular solution is largely Western and incompatible with the religion. The apologetic solution to this dichotomy is that human knowledge and values change over time while the Quran is constant. From this point of view, scientific knowledge can be incorrect. The apologetic solution also argues that the Quran has few statements that can be scientifically proven wrong or not interpreted as metaphors. The synthesis solution incorporates science and Quranic epistemology. For example, a religious scientist might say that evolution is the physical manifestation of how Allah was able to create humanity.

Diversity in Quranic Epistemology

There are several different interpretations of the Quran; there is not a singular Quranic epistemology. The major split in Quranic interpretation is that between the Sunni and the Shia. This divide happened early after the death of Muhammad. The divide was over whether the successor to the Muhammad's state should be his close aid or his closest family member Ali. The Shia support the caliphate going through Muhammad's bloodline only. This political division lead to religious schism.[60] The political division lead to different religious beliefs as Sunni Muslims take a more individualistic approach to religion while Shia Muslims rely on orthodox interpretation of ayat.

Another major variation is that of Sufism. Sufism was a seventh-century reform of Islam that took an approach of mysticism. Sufis were named after the wool garment that they so often wore. These mystics thought their religion had become too material, with focus on technical social and legal codes. They wanted to return the religion to the internal emotional struggle with Allah. There are many different sects of Sufism with different Quranic interpretations.[61]

Another variation of Islam is Wahhabism. This was an extreme reform movement that occurred in the eighteenth century and focused on returning to fundamentalist Islamic values. For example, Wahhabists focused on destroying idols in the church such as saints. The religious movement was intertwined with a political alliance in central Saudi Arabia. This ultraconservative group has been historically associated with terrorism and destruction of religious buildings. Their extremism is due to a different epistemological perspective and different analysis of the Quran.[62]

Along with various divisions within Islam are the regional differences. African interpretations of Islam take place in different cultural and historical contexts, often leading to different interpretations. There are global and intellectual biases against Islamic philosophy that originates in Africa. Often this Islamic perspective is denounced as "too African" to represent Islam. African Islamic philosophy proved effective and well thought out during slave trade. West Africans were able to use rhetoric from the Quran in order to protect their rights. Thus, the African Islamic philosophies flourished, including epistemological perspectives. These differ from traditional epistemological perspectives because they are shaped by the traumatic effects of slavery and influence of traditional African religions. African Islamic perspectives are often ignored because they are too African for Islamic scholars and too Islamic for African scholars.[63]

The different interpretations of the Quran lead to several different implications of the Quranic message. As mentioned previously in this paper, a controversial issue in Islam is the way in which it treats women. The oppression of women in Islam includes veiling, having multiple wives, and the sanctioning of punishing one's wife. Some feminist perspectives that argue against these practices in Islam argue that the Quran's oppression of women was a sacrifice Muhammad had to make in order to get the message of Allah heard.[64] Others believe that the Quran is the exact word of Allah and women are only respected and valued if they are veiled and obey their husbands. These different interpretations of the Quran show how there are different epistemological perspectives about the Quran, whether it is truly the word for word Allah's intentions or influence by historical circumstances.

Another controversial topic in the Quran is its teaching on war and peace. The Quran has an association in the Western world with terrorism. Terrorists groups only represent a small percentage of all Muslims. Many of these extremist groups believe the Quran clearly says that violence to protect Islam must occur at all costs.[65] They believe that death in war is one of the few ways in which they can be guaranteed paradise in the afterlife.[66] Other interpretation of the Quran is that its call to violence should only be used in the face of defense and not against nonbelievers.[67] Despite the violent interpretations of the Quran the Quran can also be interpreted with peace.

Fight in the way of Allah those who fight you but do not transgress. Indeed. Allah does not like transgressors.[68]

For example, Gandhi believed that the Quran was a strong supporter of the nonviolence movement despite the fact that it is so often interpreted with violence. He was able to gather support from Muslims for his non-violence movement for Indian independence. He was aided by the paci-fism advocacy of Khan Abdul Ghaffar Khan. Ghaffar Khan interpreted the Quran to support nonviolent protest against British rule of India. He was a close friend of Gandhi and influenced Muslim support in Gandhi's efforts.[69]

I've made arguments about the controversial issues of the oppression of women and use of violence in the Quran for a purpose. This is that both key issues have heavy consequences for their practical application, yet the Quran's message is so unclear that it can be interpreted toward various extremes. This again is one of the primary issues with Quranic epistemology, that it can be interpreted in many different ways. The ayat within the book are not clear going either way. Therefore, although the Quran praises the word of Allah through the prophet as the highest form of knowledge, this knowledge is too ambiguous to achieve practical implications.

CONCLUSIONS

Quranic epistemology is shaped by religious, political, historical, and philo-sophical forces. It has many faces and is able to change over time. What has stayed constant is its dependence on platonic realism, the symbolic nature of the world, and the ability for reason to access truth. Muslims see the world through a perspective of illuminationism, that everything touched by the Islam religion is truth and morality and everything untouched by it is false and corrupt. They believe in knowledge by presence, that their very consciousness is the only evidence of Allah that they need. Quranic epistemology believes in a singular truth that is consistent with the will of Allah. It touts that the way to find truth is only through prayer, prophecy, or religious philosophy, with prophesy holding the highest privilege. Quranic epistemology supports the practice of scientific empiricism, although it interprets empirical evidence as Allah's will. Therefore, the synergy between Islam and science has a limit.

The variations on Quranic epistemology such as Sufism and Wahhabism represent different interpretations of the Quran. Quranic epistemology is highly variable based off of the way the reader interprets the message of the Holy Book. This leads to political and religious fissions within the Islamic world that can escalate into political or violent struggles. Through under-standing Quranic epistemology, world leaders can use the tenets of Islam to bring the light of Allah to complex matters. In this way, they can use the Quran to advocate for peace and humanitarianism. Understanding the mechanisms of the religion will reduce the dehumanization of Islam, as it has much in common with other world religions such as Christianity. Most importantly, validating and acknowledging Quranic epistemologies will allow for understanding and constructive collaboration between Islamic and secular scholars.

Chapter 6

Biblical Epistemology

Jesus answered, "I am the way and the truth and the life.
No one comes to the Father except through me."[1]

The Bible cannot be ignored in understanding Africa and a vast array of knowledge generated about the continent. The Bible's impact is everywhere, expressed as ideas and ideologies, as representations of Christianity, as a source of conflicts in plural societies, as a way of living, as values that shape people's behavior, as a tool and resources to build communities—moral, economic, educational, social, and political—and as a political text that allows people to tap into stories, statements, insights, wisdom, and knowledge. Africa can no longer apologize for being part of a Christian world, and the Bible has become one of the most preeminent books that millions of Africans read on a daily basis. A short, two-time survey of what people read during a flight between Lagos and Atlanta consistently reveals that the most popular is the Bible.[2]

The Bible is revered as the word of God in Christianity, the most influential religion in the world. Christianity is practiced by over one-third of the world's population.[3] The distribution of Christianity has spread significantly over the last century to the Americas, Africa, and Asia.[4] Translated into over 2,400 languages, the Bible is perhaps, if not, the most read book ever published.[5] With billions of individuals proclaiming their faith in scripture as the word of God, the Bible is ubiquitous. Scripture is inscribed in ancient tombs, university halls, and public domains. Concepts from the Bible are referenced in the constitutions of several nations, notably in the United Kingdom, the United States, and Italy. Missionaries, spreading the word of God through Jesus Christ, have shaped the course of history. The Bible is often a moral foundation to the philosophy of law. It lays at the center of global cultures, social norms, and moral standards. The same Bible was used to ignite the crusades and justify the Holocaust. It has also been the center of hate crimes against nonconformists.

At the same time, scripture inspired the charitable efforts of organizations such as the Red Cross. It is used in human rights rhetoric such as in apartheid South Africa. Scripture has saved the lives of individuals on the brink of death by providing them hope of redemption. Like a double-edged sword,[6] the Bible is a powerful tool capable of both violence and liberation.

The Bible is a self-proclaimed truth. Yet, the value of this truth has come into question. Other religions, such as Islam, are soon to surpass Christianity in global populations.[7] The prevalence of other world religions, for many, questions the status of the Bible as the sole source of truth. Historical and scientific evidence also undermine many biblical claims. One example is the debate between evolution and creationism, as well as the debate within creationism itself.

Christianity and the Bible, which is derived from the religion, have undeniable powers.[8] Yet, what is the relationship between that power and its truth value? Epistemology is a field of philosophy that analyzes human knowledge. Different epistemological approaches represent different standards of knowledge. For Christians around the world, the Bible serves as a theological, spiritual, and an epistemological text. It does not describe in a philosophical language what it means to know something. It is a functional foundation for creating and evaluating knowledge. Through the Bible, Christians seek truth. The use of biblical epistemology defines scripture through faith as truth. As a consequence, biblical epistemology, some have argued, discounts reason and science.[9] This chapter will be divided into two sections. First, the philosophy of knowledge presented by the Bible is examined in detail. Then, applications of the Bible as a system of knowledge in Africa is examined in a grounded narrative.

PART I
THE BIBLE AS AN EPISTEMIC TEXT

Epistemology utilizes topics in metaphysics such as the nature of reality, perception, and existence. It applies metaphysical concepts to their implications for human knowledge. It can be used to evaluate whether institutions of truth are capable of delivering. Evaluating these institutions requires analyzing the underlying assumptions and values involved in the production of knowledge.[10] Epistemology seeks perspective. It strives to distance philosophers from their individual experiences to better understand truth. Epistemology deconstructs the factors and sources of knowledge production. It analyzes the environmental, metaphysical, cultural, and historical circumstances of ideas.[11] It discusses human limitations of knowledge, questioning whether knowledge is attainable. Epistemology notices that multiple, well-reasoned answers to the same questions exist simultaneously. It seeks to bring collective knowledge closer to universal truths.

An Epistemic Dichotomy

As epistemology examines different standards to truth, the epistemological dichotomy I seek to explore is that between the logical philosophical and biblical standards of knowledge. These different standards of knowledge lead scholars to drastically different conclusions, based off of the same evidence. Tina Beattie defended biblical epistemology in her 2007 book, *The New Atheists: The Twilight of Reason and the War on Religion*, by stating, "Western science is just one way of interpreting the world."[12]

This quote is not her own but repurposed from Richard Dawkins' book. Dawkins is a renowned scientist and outspoken atheist. Beattie is a faithful professor of Catholic studies at the University of Roehampton Western. Both agree that science has its epistemological foundation in empirical evidence through the scientific method. Each confirms this as one of many possible ways to interpret the world. Yet, these scholars differ in how they apply these ideas to epistemology. To Beattie, this idea discredits traditional epistemology and justifies biblical epistemology. In contrast, on biblical epistemological arguments, Dawkins states,

> Faith is the great cop-out, the great excuse to evade the need to think and evaluate evidence. Faith is belief in spite of, even perhaps because of, the lack of evidence.[13]

Dawkins acknowledges that science has limitations. Yet, he sees it as a stronger epistemological foundation than faith. He does not discredit modern science but puts it into perspective, acknowledging its limitations. Beattie and Dawkins are examples of two scholars with different standards of evidence worthy of knowledge. Understanding the foundations of scientific and biblical epistemologies showcases the underlying incongruencies. These differences explain how two acclaimed scholars have such contrasting claims to knowledge. Both biblical and scientific epistemologies have extensive histories and layering philosophical foundations.

Defining Biblical Epistemology

While traditional epistemology has various perspectives on knowledge, biblical epistemology provides a different standard for knowledge. Biblical epistemology does not use the foundation of empirical evidence and reason that Plato and Aristotle debated. The Bible states that only faith can lead to the acquisition of knowledge.

> Trust in the Lord with all your heart,
> and do not lean on your own understanding.
> In all your ways acknowledge him,
> and he will make straight your paths.[14]

> Heaven and earth will pass away,
> but my word will not pass away.[15]

This first quote discounts the role of rationalism. It states that humans are not capable of understanding truth but only receiving it from the Bible. The second quote discounts the role of empiricism. It states that physical evidence of this world is temporary, while the word of God is eternal. These two arguments represent a form of skepticism to traditional standards of knowledge. This skepticism allows individuals to build their knowledge on the basis of the scriptures. It is similar to Descartes' skepticism because it requires a central point to build all other ideas on. Biblical epistemology uses the Bible as this central point. Instead of skeptical reasoning, it encourages skeptical faith.

The Bible claims that it is the word of God and the only avenue to truth. Consider:

> All Scripture is breathed out by God
> and profitable for teaching, for reproof, for
> correction, and for training in righteousness.[16]

This scripture defines knowledge. Instead of knowledge based in the pursuit of evidence, it encourages knowledge through faith in the word of God. Through this perspective, the Bible is God's word to each human being, the only way to salvation.[17]

The Bible serves as the foundation of knowledge for many Christians around the world.[18] The Bible has authority; it defines knowledge as found through faith in scripture. Consider:

> Every word of God proves true;
> he is a shield to those who take refuge in him.[19]

Through this scripture, the Bible validates its own contents by proclaiming itself as the only source of knowledge. This verse reinforces the idea of "biblical inerrancy." Biblical inerrancy is the concept that the Bible is accurate in all aspects, because it is the word of God. It is primarily embraced by fundamentalist Christian groups.[20] It explains how ideas such as creationism can persist past scientific counterevidence. Biblical inerrancy is one concept that separates biblical and Christian epistemology. Christian epistemology relies on two primary sources of information, the Bible and testimony. Not all Christians believe the Bible is inerrant; many believe that chapters in it are allegorical. Individual testimony is an important source of knowledge for the Christian religion because it provides individual accounts on how the Bible can change lives.[21] Biblical epistemology is limited to the reading and study of scripture.

There is also a distinction between religious philosophy and biblical epistemology. Philosophy of religion debates the theoretical conceptions of religion. This may include the role of the Bible or more broad questions about the existence of God. Philosophy of religion is not limited to one religion but explores many religious beliefs. It may use biblical epistemology to prove the existence of God. It may also use the justification of natural religion through reason and science to justify the presence of a God. For example, natural religion might cite the complexity of human DNA as evidence of a God. While biblical epistemology uses scripture to support its arguments, philosophy of religion primarily uses traditional conceptions of knowledge to support its arguments.[22] An example of a religious philosophical debate is that of Kant, advocating for a natural religion. This religion would not be based off of the Bible but used as evidence from science and philosophy to prove the existence of God.[23] Biblical epistemology is related to yet separate from Christian and religious epistemologies. It describes the presence of God and Christianity only through the literature of the Bible. Biblical epistemology is a pattern of rhetoric used by Christians around the world to justify their beliefs but is not equivalent to religion or Christianity.

The Bible is a distinct epistemological text because of its incompatibility with philosophy or science. Philosophy champions reason, science champions evidence, and the Bible champions faith. These differences represent inconsistent ideas about what constitutes legitimate knowledge. Because of these epistemological differences, philosophers and theologians are unable to have coherent discussions about the same topics.[24] Some scholars suggest that biblical discourse is not a separate epistemology from science or philosophy. Instead, it is a different ethical standard. In this view, biblical epistemology does not have a different standard of knowledge but is not receptive to alternative perspectives.[25] This argument has merit. Yet, championing the revision of theories over the static doctrine of the Bible implies a scientific epistemological approach. The definition of knowledge presented in the Bible is the word of God, which is infallible and present in every sentence of scripture.

The History of Biblical Criticism

Biblical and traditional epistemology are not mutually exclusive. Western philosophy flourished in the Enlightenment, in the context of a powerful church. Enlightenment philosophers were trained in the rhetoric of the Bible and heavily influenced by the institution of the church. It put pressure on philosophers to either support or avoid writing about biblical issues. Still, many philosophers did indirectly relate their philosophies to the Bible. Biblical criticism examines the problematic nature of a biblical standard of knowledge. Biblical criticism evaluates the Bible based off of reason, including the historical accuracy and the logical consistency of the Bible. Through these reason-based and empirical arguments, biblical criticism seeks to disprove biblical inerrancy.

Biblical criticism is often sparked by controversial biblical verses. Although many verses preach love, the Bible is also saturated with violence and oppression. Consider the following verses:

> Slaves, submit yourselves to your masters with all respect,
> not only to the good and gentle but also to the cruel.[26]

> "I do not permit a woman to teach or to
> have authority over a man, she must be silent."[27]

> This is what the Lord Almighty says. . .
> "Now go and strike Amalek and devote to destruction all that they have.
> Do not spare them, but kill both man and woman,
> child and infant, ox and sheep, camel and donkey."[28]

> Then the Lord spoke to Moses, saying,
> "Bring the one who has cursed outside the camp,
> and let all who heard him lay their hands on his head;
> then let all the congregation stone him."[29]

These are just a few of the many biblical verses that can be used to support violence. The first has historically been used to support the idea of slavery. The next supports the oppression of women through silence. The next is an example of genocide, as God supports the murder of an entire race for the victory of another. The last supports the practice of stoning as punishment.

Contrast these biblical quotes from another:

> God is love.[30]

These verses seem to contradict each other. The same God that supports violence is also equated with love. Under biblical inerrancy, these quotations create a truly fearful Christian. In application, these verses can be used to support horrendous acts. Skeptical thought questions how a good-willed God could speak such violent words about His children. Such biblical verses sparked biblical critics to evaluate their significance.

One of the first biblical critics in the enlightenment was Voltaire. Voltaire took a historical approach to the Bible. He compared historical text in the Bible with other documents for consistency. He sought to verify that the Bible was mostly consistent with other historical documents. Voltaire's findings were limited by the archaeological and linguistic discoveries of his time. Yet, he had enough information to conclude that the Bible is historically inconsistent within itself and with the historical record. This assertion challenged the idea of biblical inerrancy and undermined the biblical authority of the church. As a reaction to Voltaire's findings, church leaders attempted to amend or omit passages from the Bible to fit the historical record.[31]

While Voltaire focused on the historical consistency of the Bible, Richard Simon focused on its translational consistency. He found several passages that were missing in Greek or Latin verses. One of those additions was the verse that supported the Holy Trinity, one of the foundations of the Catholic church. Translational inconsistency added to doubt of biblical inerrancy. Jean Meslier combined historical and translational analysis through the mythology in old pagan texts. He found many passages of the Bible similar to pagan texts. These myths were both venerated as scripture and condemned as paganism. He came to two possible conclusions about the use of pagan writings in the Bible. Through the logic of the church, pagan texts are wicked, thus the Bible must be corrupted by wicked texts. Alternatively, the passages were insignificant and did not hold holy or wicked meaning. Either way, the discovery undermined the status of the Bible as God's word.[32]

Other philosophers were less direct in biblical criticism. They expressed concerns about the influence of the Bible and its inconsistency with philosophy. Diderot's philosophy focused on only believing that which can be directly observed. He made vague comments about Christ; he had never seen a resurrection and thus did not believe in them. Thomas Hobbes was concerned with the historical inaccuracy of the Bible because of its use in public education. He argued that the more rational parts of the Bible should lay unamended, while irrational parts should be discarded. John Locke made a similar argument, arguing that reason should override faith when possible. Both of these philosophers' indirect views on biblical matters reflect the application of epistemology through reason and skepticism.[33]

Indirect biblical criticism through notable philosophers was later applied to support more blatant biblical criticism. For example, Locke's philosophy was so often applied to biblical criticism that his writings were banned by the church for heresy. It wasn't Locke who challenged the church but Ayers who used his philosophy to argue against religion. His arguments sparked religious backlash. Bishop George Berkeley was a philosopher who responded by defending the church. He argued against the application of philosophy to religion. He equated the abstract and eclectic rhetoric of philosophy to foundational atheism. Locke tried to destroy preconceived notions by stating that every individual sees situations through different eyes. Berkeley countered that religion was the common candle that brought truth to light, despite individual perspectives. He criticized science as atheistic in nature. Newton's science claimed matter could not be created or destroyed. If matter could not be made or destroyed, then God could not have made the world from nothing. Berkeley further divided the fields of philosophy and religion by advocating for the legitimacy of biblical epistemology.[34]

Traditional epistemology did not develop independently of religion but in tangent with the rhetoric of the Bible. The Enlightenment did not completely overcome the influence of the church present in the Dark Ages. It simply allowed reason to supplement that religion. The power of the church did not allow for outright biblical criticism. Modern scientific discoveries such as archaeological and geological evidence that contradict the Bible did not exist at the time early biblical criticism emerged. Because of their historical circumstances, Enlightenment philosophers typically endorsed the Bible or did not discredit it outright. Many were content with separating their philosophical and religious views. They articulated the historical and conceptual inconsistencies in the text, starting the conversation on biblical criticism.

Contemporary Arguments in Biblical Criticism

Traditional epistemology supports the use of reason and empirical evidence to evaluate knowledge. Contemporary knowledge from this school of thought refutes the legitimacy of the Bible. Modern biblical criticism refutes the truth value of the Bible based off of historical, scientific, and philosophical arguments.

Voltaire's analysis inspired later scholars to question the historical context of the Bible. The Bible is a collection of different genres. It includes texts classified as history, poetry, epistle, and literature. Many of these passages began as oralities, passed down through words of mouth to support Christianity and Jesus Christ. These oralities were eventually written down in Hebrew, Arabic, and Greek and were translated to hundreds of languages over time.[35] Understanding the processes that shaped its writing, translation, and editing naturalizes the Bible.[36] It demystifies the Bible as the word of God. Biblical history underscores the amount of human alteration that has gone into the Bible over time. This view undermines the idea that the Bible is the unadulterated word of God.

It is impossible for a text to remain the same word for word, across translation and editing. Many scholars claim to have evidence for half of the New Testament being forged in the name of the supposed authors.[37] The possibility of forgery is supported by the contradictory verses in the Bible. Several translational analyses done in the tradition of Simon's work have found several other later insertions to scripture.[38] Many advocates for biblical epistemology acknowledge that literary criticism is a necessary part of interpreting the "true meaning" of scripture.[39] In the next section, I will explain the allegorical interpretations of biblical epistemology, which stands in contrast to biblical inerrancy. The idea of literary critique being necessary brings up the problem of biblical selectionism. Modern historical analysis has repeatedly found that many biblical texts are distortions of earlier versions through editing or translational errors.

Scientific evidence against the knowledge presented in the Bible is extensive. Stories such as creationism, the garden of Eden, and Noah's Ark are scientifically unsubstantiated. Geology, archaeology, and biology all provide evidence that the earth is much older than stated in the Bible. No scientific evidence has been found to support most of the events explained in the Bible.[40] Biblical epistemology can produce skepticism about abstract scientific concepts such as evolution. The Bible is also inconsistent with many simpler scientific concepts. For example, the Bible provides inaccurate descriptions of basic human anatomy.[41] This misinformation implies that the Bible either can error or has been translated or edited incorrectly. Either way, the description of human anatomy presented in the Bible is counterevidence to biblical inerrancy. Refer back to John Locke's suggestion that what reason cannot explain can be left back to faith. For much of the time that the Bible has existed, scientific and historical evidence against it did not exist. Now that that information is available, it is nonsensical to ignore it.

There are several modern philosophical arguments against the God portrayed in the Bible. These arguments are useful in evaluating the legitimacy of the Bible. One argument that pokes holes in biblical epistemology involves the silence of God. The Bible portrays God as all-loving and all-capable. God has a purpose for humanity and intends for us to fulfill it. Yet, the previously stated concerns about the Bible, its ambiguity and historical and scientific inaccuracy, provide controversial evidence to His existence. If God is loving, powerful, and wants us to fulfill a purpose, why does He have such an unconvincing evidence of His existence? This argument juxtaposes His silence with His proposed nature in the Bible, stating that the two cannot exist simultaneously.[42]

One philosophical commentary on God's silence by Antony Flew is the gardener parable. In this parable, you enter a garden that is perfectly maintained. You look for the gardener and are told that he is invisible. You try to set a trap, to catch the gardener. Yet, you do not catch him. You are told he is also intangible. The contradiction is this: if a gardener is invisible and intangible, what is the difference between that and no gardener at all?[43] This parable supports the contradictory nature of God's silence and His nature as presented by the Bible. It also serves as a thought experiment that undermines one of the basic weaknesses of biblical epistemology. The Bible is a self-endorsed text. It gains legitimacy only through its own scripture and the legacies of that scripture in church and testimony. It is impossible to disprove biblical epistemology because there is no evidence to support belief. Biblical epistemology is based on legitimizing the unfalsifiable knowledge of the Bible through faith.

A philosophical argument that makes this point is the Five-Minute Hypothesis. The Five-Minute Hypothesis argues that the Earth was created five minutes ago. Five minutes ago, every fossil was created exactly how it is now. Our brains were implanted with memories of our lives. History books were written with histories that did not happen. The Earth was created with coffee shops, the Eiffel Tower, and the Pyramids already in existence.[44] This argument is not a religious philosophy followed by individuals or churches but a thought experiment. It makes the epistemological argument that just because something can't be proved wrong doesn't mean it is true. Any physical evidence against the Five-Minute Hypothesis can be justified as created five minutes ago. The hypothesis is unfalsifiable, just as the Bible is in Biblical epistemology.

Consider Descartes' radical skepticism. He rejected all his beliefs and found central concepts to rebuild them. He rebuilt all of these ideals on two

Figure 6.1.   Hands praising Christ. *Source:* Toyin Falola.

concepts. First, that he knew that he was a thinking, individual mind. Second, that he believed in the existence of God. He built off of this second idea to state that an all-loving God would not allow him to be deceived and eventually built up his previous religious beliefs based off of this argument.[45] This is how biblical epistemology is justified. Biblical epistemology is only justified through its own text, on the basis of faith. This can be applied to any knowledge presented in the Bible. Any argument against biblical concepts can be argued as how God created the Earth. Physical evidence such as fossils that predated the biblical age of the earth can be justified as the work of the devil. Such an argument is unfalsifiable. Biblical epistemology would fit Karl Popper's idea of pseudoscience. It presents itself as legitimate knowledge yet is unable to predict the future or develop beyond inherent preconceived notions.

Interpretive Biblical Epistemology

Most of my arguments against biblical epistemology have been based off of the problematic nature of biblical inerrancy. Through the assumption of biblical inerrancy, it is simple to discount the Bible based on my previous historical, scientific, and philosophical arguments. This is only a simplified version of how modern mainstream (nonfundamentalist) biblical epistemology operates. Interpretive biblical epistemology argues that the Bible is not perfect. Some of the ideas from this school of thought are that the Bible is limited to the scientific thoughts of the time it was written, and it works under the assumptions that many passages are allegorical. It also takes into account historical context to discount ideas such as the oppression of women. Interpretive biblical epistemology allows for the Bible to be a more flexible source of knowledge, compatible with other disciplines and religions.

Thomas Aquinas is often cited as the father of allegorical biblical interpretations. He founded the idea of Thomism, that reason was found through God. He did not argue that the Bible overrides scientific and historical findings. Instead, he argued that many stories in the Bible were allegories for how Christians should live their lives or maintain their relationship with God. In this perspective, editing and translation did not have the power to override the messages symbolized by biblical stories. The Bible was always accurate, provided that an educated biblical scholar analyzed the meaning of the text.[46] The arguments presented by Aquinas were initially rejected by the church but are now widely practiced. Many modern biblical schools advocate for symbolic interpretations of the Bible based on its historical context.[47]

A 2014 TED talk by Amir Aczel, a physicist and preacher, explained the synchrony between biblical teachings and modern science. Aczel connects abstract concepts in physics such as the theory of relativity to the idea of God's omniscience.[48] His ideas do not fall under biblical or traditional epistemological backgrounds. They represent a hybrid manifestation of both. He does not champion the ideas of modern science or the Bible over one another. Instead, he hybridizes the ideas of the Bible through scientific concepts. In doing so, he is following in the evolved philosophical tradition of Thomas Aquinas. The idea that science relates and supports the ideas in the Bible is a common Christian belief that has gained traction in recent years.[49] This interpretive biblical epistemology does not emphasize the physical events of the Bible for literal interpretations. Instead, it focuses on their symbolic meaning about the nature of God and our relationship to Him.

Interpretive biblical epistemology uses the Bible and science both as legitimate sources of knowledge. It takes many different forms. Yet, often it uses modern science as a guide to interpret the symbolic nature of the Bible. Christians following this epistemology do not support biblical inerrancy but a modern form of Thomism. They understand the scripture as something that is flexible, meanings that are uncovered over time. For example, someone may believe that God guided the process of evolution. They might also support that in the Bible's description of the Earth's seven-day creation with each day representing millions or billions of years. Interpretive biblical epistemology is ambiguous. Scripture can be interpreted through several symbolic avenues.

A problematic aspect of interpretive biblical epistemology is that it uses symbolic interpretation for the entire Bible. Symbolic interpretation is a tool of literary analysis. Literary analysis is used for works of literature that were written with artistic intentions. The Bible does include passages written as literature, poetry, and prose. Yet, much of the Bible is not literature but a series of historical and epistle accounts.[50] To analyze the whole Bible in a symbolic nature is to inappropriately apply literary critic to different genres.

Another issue with biblical epistemology is selectivism in which passages of the Bible are symbolically or literally interpreted. Followers may choose to disregard certain passages altogether, taking others at face value. The problematic nature of biblical selectivism is exemplified in how the Bible can support several different religions. Take, for example, the split of Mormonism from Christianity. In the 1820s, Joseph Smith claimed that he had directly received word from God that the church had strayed from His intentions. He created a supplemental doctrine to the Bible, the Book of Mormon. The Church of Jesus Christ of Latter-day Saints, Mormonism, was built off of this doctrine as well as the Bible. Mormons interpret passages of the Bible in such a different way than other Christians that their churches are incompatible.[51]

Traditional biblical epistemology works under the pretext that the Bible is clear and literal in meaning. This is disproven by the contradictions in the Bible and its incompatibility to modern science and history. Interpretive biblical epistemology operates under the pretext that the Bible is plain in symbolic interpretation. The interpretations of the Bible such as that of Joseph Smith show how ambiguous scripture is. Their biblical interpretations show the nature of the Bible as able to support many diverse religious philosophies.[52] Each of these individuals used the Bible through their own personal experience, relating it to the problems and concerns of their generation to gain religious traction.

I presented two versions of biblical epistemology. The first is literal biblical epistemology, using biblical inerrancy to establish the Bible as the source of knowledge. The problematic nature of this perspective lays in its contradictions within itself and between history and science. The second is interpretive biblical epistemology that allows the Bible to act as a flexible source of knowledge. The ambiguous and contradictory nature of scripture makes it unable to exist without interpretation. Therefore, biblical epistemology is always interpretive. The problem with the interpretive nature of biblical epistemology is that it defines knowledge as something symbolically interpreted through scripture. Knowledge that is presented symbolically is ambiguous in language. Consider Wittgenstein's concept that knowledge must be clear in language in order to have a singular meaning and truth value. The interpretive nature of scripture does not hold up to this standard. This knowledge can be used to support a wide variety of concepts. It does not have a direct truth value and cannot be knowledge.

Interpretive biblical epistemology uses faith to evaluate the truth of scripture. It is flexible to science, culture, and time. The ambiguous nature of the Bible is both its fault and merit. It can be used by various groups, to justify different knowledge about God. Yet this quality is what makes the Bible so popular with changing values over time and across cultures. I've made the point that biblical epistemology is always interpretive because of the ambiguous nature of scripture. Therefore, I will for now on refer to interpretive and literal biblical epistemology as biblical epistemologies. I've presented various reasons that biblical epistemologies are problematic. Yet, these standards of knowledge continue to hold great global influence.

Biblical Epistemologies in Context

Psychology investigates the cognitive processes behind biblical epistemology. It studies individuals with fundamentalist religious views to understand the underlying motivations for their ideological tenacity. Experiments in cognitive psychology show that individuals with strongly held religious views do not consider information contradictory to their beliefs. Their adherence to biblical epistemology makes them unable to hear any other argument as inherently false.[53] This is not unique to religion but a common cognitive bias in which all people tend to see themselves as correct. This phenomenon is amplified in the context of religion. Part of the reasons for this cognitive bias

Figure 6.2.   Christian symbols. *Source:* Toyin Falola.

is identity protection. The Bible is a deeply personal text that integrates itself into people's self-identity as Christians. Psychology shows that individuals have especially strong cognitive biases to ignore evidence that threatens their personal or community identities.[54] Some Christians have flexible religious views that consider different perspectives. Still, very intelligent people adhere to fundamentalist biblical views due to psychological and social reasons.[55]

There are various societal consequences for acceptance of biblical epistemologies: they affect the cultural norms, education systems, and social structure of communities. One documented effect of the acceptance of biblical epistemologies is on scientific literacy in America. Scientific literacy is important in America for voters to understand contemporary issues such as the significance of climate change. A statistical analysis done in 2011 found religion to be more predictive of scientific literacy than either race, gender, or income.[56] Acceptance of biblical epistemologies creates voters who are less likely to consider factors such as climate change in elections. The inability for scientific literature to fit the standard of biblical epistemologies has tangible effects for society.

Given the large Christian population and strong influence of biblical epistemology, it is vital for researchers and policy makers to understand it. Biblical epistemology has a distinct rhetoric, including a pattern of selectivism and allegorical interpretation of scripture. In nations with large populations of Christians, the influence of the Bible can be ubiquitous. Many institutions, including the school system, are based off of the Christian calendar, symbolism, and methodology.[57] The rhetoric of politics often includes moral and logical references from the Bible.[58] It is important for individuals within and outside of the Christian religion to evaluate biblical epistemology. Through this, they can untangle biblical references from other societal influences to work toward critical evaluations of truth.

Summing Up

Traditional epistemology developed through Western philosophy to support modern scientific discoveries. Biblical epistemology responded by becoming more interpretive. I've divided biblical and traditional epistemologies into binary categories in order to differentiate them. I simplified this difference as the justification of knowledge lying in either faith or reason. Yet, these two epistemologies are intertwined in application. Through isolating biblical epistemology, it is possible to analyze how individuals use the Bible as a basis of knowledge that guides them through their everyday lives. It lets us understand how the Bible can serve as a foundation for knowledge in community and international discourse.

The effect of the Bible as a guide to knowledge in any capacity is that it can be interpreted to support contradicting ideas and religions. It often does not consider arguments different than its own. Its interpretation may change but scripture is meant to remain stagnant. That scripture contains verses capable of supporting genocide, torture, misogyny, and slavery. The knowledge presented in the Bible continues to contradict current historical, philosophical, and scientific ideas. When the scripture is spread, it takes on different interpretations. These interpretations can be used to take advantage of populations, psychologically forcing them into submission.

A problematic feature of the Bible is its advocacy for spreading international Christianity. Attempts to spread Western religion have been successful but at a great cost. Colonialism was founded on the spread of the Bible, disrupting the order of colonial nations, enslaving large populations, and causing continuous suffering. The Bible is also based in Western concepts and biblical epistemology is culturally inappropriate to many non-Western nations. It is the ambiguous nature of scripture, culture of closed-mindedness, and faith-based epistemology, which allow these atrocities to happen. It places the only foundation of knowledge in the Bible, which has historically led to the destruction of cultures through acts such as book burnings. Nations that have new populations of Christianity may not be aware of the historical context and usage of the Bible in order to interpret it loosely. These populations are vulnerable to extremism and biblical fundamentalism. Modern missionaries seeking to spread scripture must critically evaluate the benefits and methodology of spreading biblical epistemology cross-culturally.

The largest difference between biblical and traditional epistemology is that the Bible is unfalsifiable. Although significant evidence discounts the legitimacy and pristine nature of the Bible, Christianity continues to thrive off it. The idea that the Bible is God's word is like Descartes' evil genius or the Five-Minute Hypothesis. These ideas all create skepticism in traditional knowledge and place belief in unlikely and unsubstantiated ideas. Biblical knowledge has the unique support of the institution of the church, in its various forms, which is embedded into the culture, infrastructure, and institutions of modern societies.

Biblical epistemology is an influential, yet problematic field. The teachings of scripture influence individuals, societies, and institutions at every level. Scripture is a versatile tool able to legitimize wars or liberate nations. The Bible has provided a basis for charity as well as violence. Yet, biblical criticism has established these scriptures are interpretive, contradictory, and self-legitimizing. If the unfalsifiable knowledge of scripture is accepted as an epistemological text, it can be used in unlimited contexts. Biblical scholars seek an unknowable truth, but their evidence is unconvincing leaving their biblical "knowledge" unjustified. Only through faith, and not reason alone, is the Bible a convincing perspective in epistemology. Through cross-epistemological conversations, traditional and biblical scholars can each improve their understanding of the nature of knowledge.

PART II
THE BIBLE AND AFRICA

Assuming you are not a trained philosopher, by now you would be seeing messiness in my preceding presentation. Epistemologies may lose touch with reality if they are left untranslated into narratives. Narratives are grounded in different ways of thinking, which, in turn, lead to several debates. Narratology itself has the capacity to alter the way we see events and construct causations, thus creating additional complications. If you are committed to an epistemology grounded in faith, it shapes the way you construct narratives.

The Bible, in the various manifestations of its epistemologies, even in their messiness, has become an integral part of the narratives on Africa; this includes how Africans construct narratives and how various ontologies have emerged as products of specific narratology. The application of the Bible to the understanding of Africa—the emergence of various narratives and ontologies—requires not just an essay but many books. Here, I can only provide a few aspects of the integration of the Bible to African knowledge as well as the intersectionalities the Bible has created with a myriad of themes and topics. I will focus on three broader themes of interest: politics, nationalism, and the Bible as a "literary" text.

The Bible, Politics, and Power

The connection between the Bible and politics operates as ideas, theories, and practical realities. Africa has been part of this triple connection. The origins of modern Africa, in its colonial foundation, cannot be divorced from some of the ideas in the Bible, the role of missionary agents, and the concept of "civilization" promoted by the colonizers as a tool of conquest, control, and exploitation. Modern politics are also very much connected with the Bible in terms of the continuity of politics in postcolonial Africa, the connections of leadership with the church, and the political role of preachers and pastors. Variants of Christian expressions are also connected with the economy and politics of the state. The commercialization of the church profits enormously from how modern economies are also organized by the state. To develop many of these ideas fully, there is the need to provide a larger context on the Bible and its theory of power.

Ideas and Theories of Power

Throughout history, Christianity, and more specifically the Bible, has shaped just about every facet of modern civilization. In the public sphere, many laws and societal norms find their origins from the Bible itself. In this section, I hope to explore the complex relationship between the Bible, power, and politics and how the religious doctrine has been used to both legitimize and challenge authority and hegemony in both the biblical and historical context. It is vital to understand how the Bible has been modified and utilized over time to achieve agendas throughout history. By analyzing these complicated relationships, I hope to understand not only what the Bible says about power and politics but how power and politics, and more importantly who holds power, have influenced the interpretations and use of the Bible for endeavors that are outside the realm of religion. Furthermore, the Bible and various biblical figures are inherently political because they challenged empires, rulers, and ideologies. Anything that causes mass mobilization of people can be considered revolutionary and political, even when they are presented as theological.

A number of African Christians have divorced politics from the activities of biblical figures, presenting them strictly in theological terms. Many biblical characters, including Jesus Christ himself, actually speaks directly to politics and political engagements. The most cited characters, when it comes to the merger of theology and politics, are David, Moses, and Jesus.

The Bible gives distinct examples of what power and politics, in a religious context, should look like. It deals with many instances of politics, power, and more importantly what it takes to be a fair or just ruler in the eyes of God. In the New Testament, King David was revered as a significant figure in the Bible, called "the man after God's own heart." When the Bible discusses fair rulers and kings, some of the characteristics mentioned are just rule, trust, and belief in God, humility, and mercy. After David rose to power after Saul, he treated the Saul's grandson, Mephibosheth, with a great deal of respect and mercy. Perhaps more famously known for his battle with the giant, Goliath, David had an outstanding amount of trust and faith in God. When people doubted David's ability to beat Goliath, he famously stated, "The Lord who rescued me from the paw of the lion and the paw of the bear will rescue me from the hand of his Philistine [Goliath]."[59] This belief in God against such great odds is a characteristic that is heavily revered in the Bible as a characteristic all believing Christians should try to emulate. David's story is not one solely of righteousness and good deeds, he made mistakes as well. Another story of David is that he slept with Bathsheba and had her husband strategically killed afterward. This was one of David's most well-known sins but after a conversation with Nathan, a biblical figure, he admitted his wrongdoing and began asking forgiveness from God.[60]

In the Old Testament, the oppression and enslavement of Hebrews under the Pharaoh, Ramses, is constantly used as an example of how not to rule. African Christians have used this example in a countless number of ways, using it as their experience under colonial rule, military dictatorship, and oppressive regimes. The rule and role of the Pharaoh in Egyptian society is imperative to understanding why Moses' character played such a significant part. The Pharaoh ruled ancient Egypt with a force unmatched. As a ruler, the Pharaoh was arrogant, stubborn, and cruel. As the Bible tells it, when Moses and Aaron came forth to ask Pharaoh to free the Hebrews, he refused. Ultimately, after the plagues hit Egypt the Pharaoh allowed Moses to lead in the Exodus. Ancient Egypt, while not monotheistic in practice, was heavily spiritual. Society as a whole and the Pharaoh himself believed that he acted as a divinely appointed viceroy on earth, a mediator between celestial beings and the masses. Though he was not the first or last person to defy an authority figure, the immense regard for the Pharaoh is what made Moses such a prominent model. Moses disrupted the social and political hierarchy and fabric in ancient Egypt in startling ways. Africans, both seeking power and those oppressed by power, have turned to the story of Moses to explain their situations.

The most prominent figure in Christianity, Jesus himself, can be seen as a rebellious, nonconformist, paradigm-shifting political figure given the context in which he was born. Jesus was a political icon. At the time of Jesus' birth, there was a rigid caste system; Jesus occupied one of the lowest classes, just above the beggar and slave.[61] Although the relationship between Jews and Romans during the Roman rule of Judea was primarily harmonious, Jews were the religious and ethnic minorities and thus were deemed outcasts.[62] Romans and Jews lived in harmony for a time until tensions between the two reached a breaking point; this was the point in time which Jesus was born into. This was a perfect concoction of conditions and circumstances to create a jarring political figure. The political and social fabric of the Roman Empire at this time was one of hierarchy and exclusion; only the most prominent and privileged classes were afforded certain rights, such as practicing commerce, voting, and holding office.[63] In turn, these practices excluded the lower-caste peoples. As such, people of differing religious ideologies, specifically the Jews, bore the brunt of these sociopolitical systems. For this reason, Jesus' teachings of equality among all men became popular with the most marginalized groups in society: the poor, the sick, the sinners, and the outcasts.

In Reza Aslan's book, *Zealot: The Life and Times of Jesus of Nazareth*, we see Jesus depicted as this revolutionary character that defied the most powerful empire the world had ever seen. Moreover, he defied the Romans on behalf of the outcasts, people the elites did not even recognize. The ideology that Jesus ushered in was one that roused and uplifted the marginalized and dispossessed and caused massive social and political upheaval tremendous enough to threaten Roman rule. Jesus uttering the words "I am the Messiah" was treason against the state and ultimately against the Roman emperor, rather than a simple religious proclamation.[64] The mainstream view of Jesus as a detached, divine entity only concerned with the afterlife is not consistent with the way officials treated him—as an individual with the potential to undermine the stability of the state.[65] Jesus was a political figure as much as he was a religious one and this is an idea that has been brushed over countless times by historians and theologians alike.

The charges Jesus was tried and convicted of had little to do with theology as much as it did with political motivations. In his trial, Jesus was convicted of sedition, a crime against the state punishable by crucifixion. Whether by claiming to be the King of Jews, an act undermining the rule of Roman authorities, or the cleansing of the Temple in which Jesus and his disciples threw out all money changers (modern-day bankers) and vendors from the establishment even though there was no law against conducting business there. The intricate relationship between vendors, priests, and Roman nobility made it that Jesus' attack on business in the Temple is as good as an attack on the state itself.[66] Finally, the method in which Jesus was killed was highly political. Under Roman rule, crucifixion was reserved for enemies of the state or slaves. Most were familiar with crucifixion as a torturous punishment, but not many were knowledgeable of its background as a political tool used with the intention to terrorize subjects into submission to the Roman hegemony.[67]

While the role of politics in the Bible is often disputed, it is clear that politics, authority, and power are overarching and very apparent themes within it. The Bible provides guidelines about how a ruler should or should not behave in order to be just and fair to his constituents. With Jesus' own example, we found a man set on being the gatekeeper of a massive paradigm shift that goes on to shape and reshape much of the world and history as we know it. The message of Jesus, at the time of the Roman Empire, was one of undermining the status quo and the state; if that is not intrinsically political, I do not know what is. While the Bible may not refer to politics outright, the text has been used countless times to legitimize and delegitimize rulers and empires and for this reason the Bible has a very close, almost indistinguishable ties to power and politics.

Biblical Evidence of "Church and State"

The role of the church and government, that is, politics, in the lives of Christians began to morph after Martin Luther's proclamation of the "95 Theses." Luther's ideology was staked on the idea that humans attain God's salvation through God's mercy and faith alone, not good deeds or works the way the Catholic Church taught.[68] Luther believed the church's practice of selling indulgences to be corrupt and blasphemous. Luther's significance to Christian philosophy and theology does not end here, however. Luther also put forth an idea known as "the two kingdoms doctrine," which states that God rules all institutions and beings, but that there was a separation between the spiritual kingdom, that is, church, and the secular kingdom, that is, government.[69] This was one of the first prominent pushes for something resembling the separation of church and state.

The two kingdoms doctrine was birthed from a biblical precedence. Romans 8 distinguishes between the physical body and the Spirit,[70] and in Matthew 22:21, Jesus is recorded as saying, "Render unto Caesar what is Caesar's and to God that which is God's."[71] These are believed to be instances within the Bible itself that call for a separation of church, the spiritual self, and state, the physical state or at least a slight disconnection of the two.

The Church, Bible, and African Colonization

But as history has shown, the separation of church and state is not something that is easily accomplished. While the Bible has been used to legitimize rulers, empires, and conquests, it has also been used as a tool of mass oppression and subjugation. This relationship between the British monarchy and Christian missionaries illustrated that. These actors worked in tandem to infiltrate Africa, specifically Central and West Africa.

The Bible has been utilized throughout history for the purposes of politics, power, and authority; from this we learn how power, or lack thereof, has shaped the course of modern history. The fact that Christianity and the Bible have been used as tools of oppression and conquest is not surprising; the church's role in upholding the institutions of colonization and slavery is well documented. The introduction of Christianity in Africa was, in many ways, the precursor to colonization. Albeit the missionaries' main goal was to promote Christianity, they acted as agents of the state and were used to gain the trust of Africans, scope out the area for potential natural resources, and played a vital role in the slave trade.[72] In the view of the state and church, being European and Christian was the pinnacle of civilization and these missionaries believed they were bringing civility and modernity to the "natives" through their work and gospel. This view was held most notably by David Livingstone, a missionary turned explorer and the first European who arrogantly claimed to have been the first to discover and name Victoria Falls in southern Africa.

The relationship between these two institutions, the state and the church, worked in an interesting way. The state provided protection and the necessary resources for missionaries to sustain their work in Africa and in turn the missionaries helped to establish commerce and a new market for British enterprises.[73] Emmanuel Ayandele, the prominent Nigerian historian, treated Christian missionaries as no more than the "spiritual wing" of colonial power and imperialism.[74] Celebrated Guyanese historian and activist, Walter Rodney, explains that missionaries were indeed agents of imperialism because of their extensive role in providing a colonial education to many of the African communities they inhabited. Missionaries, he says, were vital to determining values and attitudes during colonial rule and thus missionaries preached about humility, docility, and complacency in the face of oppression and subjugation.[75] Almost everywhere, the missionaries, interpreting the Bible in various ways, had a definitive impact on African culture and society.[76]

The intricate and often times unclear link between the Bible, power, and politics allows the biblical text and the precedent within it to be utilized in a plethora of ways. In it we find illustrations of good and unjust rulers, revolutionaries shaking the foundations of entire empires, and even justification of acts and institutions deemed corrupt and destructive. The Bible has been modified and interpreted in many different ways to justify and uphold differing political, social, and economic agendas. In relation to power and politics, we find the Bible providing models of fair and unjust rulers and how they should behave toward their subjects. In relation to power and politics, we find the Bible being used to legitimize power in the hands of those who use it as a tool for such. What I have found is that there are many different ways in which the Bible discusses power and an equal number of ways in which those in power influence what is interpreted from the Book.

The Bible and Nationalist Insurgency

African nationalism was not just a political movement; it was also a religious movement. When Christianity was brought to the continent—even if it was initially brought by colonialist force—the Christian teachings instilled a sense of zeal in the African converts. This zeal was based upon Christian teachings of inner dignity and uniqueness, as well as God's calling for all to love one another as equals. For the African people, these teachings were inherently anti-colonial in nature; thus, they had justification from the Word of God to take back the land that was rightfully their own and to reclaim their own individual pride as human beings and children of God. With this zeal, the African people established Africanized churches and created prophets among themselves that led the continent on a sort of exodus from Western domination. Eventually, this exodus became political; however, without Christianity and African interpretations of the Bible, the political exodus would have taken a different trajectory.

Since the mid-twentieth century, there has been a general agreement among scholars from the West and the African continent that Christianity, and particularly biblical passages, helped incentivize African nationalism. Throughout much of the continent, due to colonialism, Christianity is prominent. In many countries outside of North Africa, at least one-fourth of the people are Christians, divided evenly between Protestants and Catholics.[77] It is in these areas where Christianity is the most prevalent across the continent, and consequently, it is in these areas where higher rates of African nationalism exists. In fact, it has been shown that areas colonized by missionaries who established greater emphasis on Christian education later had higher rates of African nationalism. This means that, paradoxically, while Europeans attempted to suppress the African people, they also unwittingly gave the African people the chance to overcome the European influence.[78]

Missionaries established Christian schools across the continent with a strong focus on biblical text. However, interestingly, the Bible was not necessarily taught in English or another European language. In many places, missionaries translated the Bible into around 500 languages or dialects that were common to the African people. The missionaries did this for practical reasons: they wanted to use the Bible as a means of very basic educational instruction. The missionaries also figured, logically, that the Holy Word would be better grasped if the people heard it in their own languages. Indeed, because the Bible was translated into African languages, Christianity resonated with the African people, so much so that its teachings gave birth to an African nationalism that grew at the same pace as European nationalism.[79] According to René Lemarchand, translating the Bible in the Belgian Congo allowed the people to gain insight into their own ethnicity: they were able to use both the secular and religious literature to retain "recaptured the cultural identity" of their nations and groups.[80]

Biblical translation also caused newspapers to be written in African languages. The Mau Mau movement, with its highly nationalistic nature, was brought about by the nationalistic language in the press created by the Kikuyu of Kenya. In Uganda, similar patterns occurred. Newspapers were written in the Luganda language and served as inspiration for anti-European rhetoric among the people.[81]

But what exactly about the Bible allowed this surge of nationalism? Scholars note that the basic tenets of Christianity stirred the Africans' desire for freedom and equality as, the Africans argued, Jesus would have desired. In the New Testament, a common theme is to "love thy neighbor"—and by "neighbor," this means anyone who is similar to oneself and anyone who is different from oneself. In other words, according to the New Law of Jesus, it is important to love all people, for all people are neighbors. As it is written in John 13:34: "I give you a new commandment: love one another. As I have loved you, so you also should love one another."[82] This was a revolutionary concept, as it changed part of the premise of power to love and duties. To Africans who organized themselves into different kinship and identity clusters, it was also a transformational concept. Now, with the universalist attitude of love, bonds extended past one's own group. In a sense, then, Christianity allowed all Africans to come together and find how they related to each other, particularly with two things: nationalistic pride and faith.[83] In the Belgian Congo since 1934, for example, Protestant missionaries have encouraged the people to think of themselves all as members of the same Church of Christ in the Congo, not as individual entities.[84]

Christianity expands on this teaching by saying that all should love their neighbors, irrespective of their background and, by implication, the color of their skin. In John 7:24, Jesus said: "Stop judging by appearance, but judge justly."[85] In Galatians 3:28, Paul said: "There is neither Jew, nor Greek, there is neither slave nor free person, there is not male and female; for you are all one in Christ Jesus."[86] Consequently, the African people saw a striking contradiction: while the Europeans taught not to discriminate, they themselves were discriminating. Yet the teaching of loving one another, regardless of skin color, allowed the African people to long for freedom all the more.[87] While Christianity in the Bible also teaches the importance of loving all people, it also teaches the importance of the inherent value that every individual possesses at birth. Every person was made by God and created in His image, according to Genesis 1:27;[88] therefore, every person has dignity and worth, as is shown, for example in Jeremiah 1:5: "Before I formed you in the womb I knew you, before you were born I dedicated you, a prophet to the nations I appointed you."[89] This central teaching of Christianity helped bring life to the African nationalism movement because it allowed the African people to see the great injustice of Europeans preaching Jesus' teaching of the value of every human being while also oppressing the African people and treating them as subhuman. This meant that, for the African people, they needed to reassert themselves in the name of Jesus' Law of Love because they deserved to be treated with respect as God intended. With these Christian teachings, African people gained a sense of unification and self-love that made the entire nationalism movement possible.[90]

Lessons taught in the Bible helped incentivize the African people to seek independence. However, it was also the European missionaries' decision to "Africanize" the clergy that made independence come to pass at all.[91] In tropical Africa in particular, the Europeans first granted Africans the power to lead in church rather than in the government. Therefore, when the Europeans allowed African people to lead their own churches, they ultimately introduced them to their first sort of "governing" experiences that gave them the skills and the faith to be effective leaders in political movements. In fact, during the time when Africans first entered into the clergy, it was they who asserted that they were just as intelligent and capable as their white authorities. It was also these same Africans who used their newly found self-confidence to demand that other Africans be placed into government positions.[92]

Being leaders of the church not only taught Africans the self-confidence skills useful in asserting themselves but also the practical skills necessary to properly run a political campaign or administer a political service. In the church, Africans learned how to manage property and accounts, raise funds, organize committees, publicly speak, and arrange an orderly democracy.[93] Thomas Masaji Okuma said that the parallels between successful churches and political campaigns are undeniable. The skills that church leaders learned, with some adjustments, served as the foundation for a nationalistic campaigns and governments.[94] It is also worth noting that a major incentive that ties all of these factors together is Christianity's lesson of always remaining hopeful in times of distress. In the Bible, it is written that those who are inspired by God will be the proper reformers of society. Similarly, those who are the dejected will see a better future with God's help.[95] Thomas Lionel Hodgkin stated that by the mid-twentieth century, Africans were fully aware of the oppressions of colonial war and found solace in the Christian idea of the broken people being God's chosen people. They saw stories in the Bible as being allegories for their current circumstances. The Belgians, British, and French were associated with the biblical Romans, Philistines, or Egyptians. The African people were associated with the biblical Israelites. The African people saw that, as the new Israelites, they would receive divine help that would send them on a sort of new exodus. This exodus would in turn deliver them from their suffering and into a new, brighter future.[96]

These biblical teachings inspired certain Africans to spark nationalism by making themselves into prophets of sorts before they considered any form of political office. For example, in 1950, a mission school graduate, Azikiwe, said that he would not go so far as to say that he is the "New Messiah" but that he is "one of the apostles of the new Africa."[97] Another example, quite infamously, is "Osagyefo" Nkrumah who deliberately baptized himself as a prophet when he inscribed on his own statue in Accra, Ghana: "Seek ye first the political kingdom."[98] This, of course, is a satire of sorts of Jesus' Sermon on the Mount in Matthew 6:33: "But seek ye first the kingdom [of God], and his righteousness; and all these things will be given you besides."[99] According to Herbert Spiro, this particular action from Nkrumah is especially significant because it shows how African politicians often transformed relevant biblical passages to suit their own purposes. These politicians knew that by using words so deeply personal to the African people, they could convince the African people to follow them.[100]

So far, this section of the essay has concentrated on twentieth-century political movements that were sparked by Christianity. However, it is also important to discuss how African's early encounters with Christian teachings in the Bible gave rise to early forms of anti-colonialism. Let us consider the Kongo kingdom. In 1491, the king, Nzinga, converted to Christianity. The kingdom then remained somewhat Christian for the next two centuries, likely either for economic or political motivations. Scholars dispute the extent to which the kingdom remained Christian and for what reasons conversion took place, but there is definitely a scholarly consensus that leaders of the kingdom did communicate with European religious and political leaders like the Pope. Furthermore, between the late fifteenth and late sixteenth centuries, the Kongo kingdom spanned more than 115,000 square miles and was thus one of the largest sub-Saharan African kingdoms, as well as one of the wealthiest. The kingdom traded extensively with the Christian Portuguese, so by converting to Christians themselves, the Kongolese could maintain prominent trading patterns and the region's general prosperity. This means, then, that while politics were an important reason for conversion, economics were probably the most important reason.[101]

However, the Portuguese did not remain friendly to the Kongolese. By the seventeenth century, the Portuguese attacked the Kongo kingdom, especially at the Battle of Mbwila in 1665, when the Kongo king Antonio I was killed. This started the general deterioration of the kingdom. By the beginnings of the eighteenth century, the capital of Kongo, Mbanza Kongo (otherwise known as São Salvador), was deserted. The kingdom then broke into small territories that were dominated by Kongo's nobility and warlords. However, it was Catholicism that had existed in Kongo since the fifteenth century that people used as an impetus for returning to the "glory days" of the kingdom. An upper-class Kongolese woman, Dona Beatriz Kimpa Vita, founded Antonianism, which was the most prominent movement using Christianity in an attempt to restore the kingdom to its previous state. In 1704, Dona Beatriz became sick and claimed that the reason for her sickness was the possession of Saint Anthony. She also claimed that it was Saint Anthony who spoke through her to the people. The reason she could do this, she said, was because she was a *nganga marinda*, someone trained to communicate with the supernatural world.[102]

Dona Beatriz said that the Kongolese people must resist Portuguese oppression by relying on their Catholic roots. After all, she said, the kingdom prospered the most right after conversion, so she felt that revitalization of the faith was necessary and essential. According to her, there was an "Africanized" version of Christianity that might help people believe. If one believes in Christ, she said, one shall be part of the African Holy Family. Through the vision of the African Holy Family, Jesus was not born in Bethlehem but in Mbanza Kongo. Jesus was also not baptized in Nazareth but in Nsundi while his mother, the Virgin Mary, was a slave to a Kongolese nobleman. Overall, the entire understanding of Christianity was rewritten, with a few exceptions. Dona Beatriz respected the Pope and the Vatican, but she also resented European Catholics who she considered to be unempathetic to the needs of the Kongolese Catholics. She felt she did not need European influence to make an impact; and indeed, she made an impressive impact. She and her followers lived in Mbanza Kongo for some time. There, she sent messengers to spread the Antonianism teachings. There, she also encouraged the rulers of the divided Kongolese regions to reunite under one leader. Sadly, however, Dona Beatriz' ending was a sad one. In 1706, King Pedro II captured her and burned her at the stake under the accusation of heresy. Even though Dona Beatriz's movement was brief, its impact was felt even after her death. Because of Dona Beatriz, sculptures in brass, wood, and ivory were erected of Saint Anthony. His image was also placed on pendants, for he was considered to be a protector of mothers and their children.[103] Most importantly, Dona

Beatriz was one of the earliest examples of an impassioned person using the Bible as a tool of progress, according to an African vision. She is significant for twentieth-century African Christian leaders who led the Africans to independence, making her horrific death not be in vain.

Whether one considers leaders from hundreds of years ago or leaders from the past century, it is clear that the Bible had tremendous influence on African leaders—so much so that their churches with nationalist agendas still exist to this day in the form of African Independent Churches (AICs). They also are identified as other names such as African Instituted Churches and African Initiated Churches. The first AIC as founded in 1870, but AICs currently represent over 10,000 independent African Christian denominations. They are all over the continent, but they are mostly concentrated in southern and western Africa. There are of course some differences between these churches, but they all share one important commonality: they were founded by Africans and not by foreigners. This means that these churches also have a specific African agenda and not a foreign agenda. All of these churches also use the Bible as a way to justify African culture into the practice of worship. Some scholars even say that these churches are in some ways syncretic or acculturating in their practices because they seem to meld African religious beliefs with traditional Christian beliefs. Indeed, some of these churches have denominational names like Pentecostal, Anglican, or Roman Catholic. Even with these names, however, these churches do not identify with European Christian traditions wholeheartedly. These churches are also strongly missionary; almost all of the Christian conversion throughout the continent in the twentieth century was brought about because of these churches.[104] The first AIC leaders knew that their mission was to provide what they knew the African people needed, not what Europeans thought the African people needed. Happily, the AICs continue this mission to this day, spreading their teachings to a total of 110,000,000 estimated adherents.[105]

Africans were not intellectually incapable of reclaiming their own land and identity prior to Christian biblical influence. To say this would be to imply that Africans are somehow lesser than Europeans, which would contradict everything that African nationalism and scholarship stand for. However, it is a beautiful irony that it was the Europeans, the oppressors, who gave the Africans the very tool needed to form a powerful rhetoric and skill set that could institutionally overthrow them. Christianity offered Africans lessons on self-love, inherent dignity, and unity. These lessons incentivized the nationalist movement and the process of casting out the physical presence of the Europeans, even if ultimately a metaphorical presence still remains. With Christian institutions, Africans gained a sense of purpose and acquired the skills necessary to lead millions of followers.

Christian messages of hope galvanized the common people and inspired future leaders to serve as messengers of God, as well as deliverers. While Africa of course had a beautiful cultural history before European contact, it was European-given Christianity that offered the cultural change necessary to progress through physical and spiritual independence. Perhaps, then, E. Bolaji Idowu did not exaggerate when he said that the church was the pioneer, or the author, of African nationalism.[106] Without the Bible Church, Africans could not have used European's own power against them and indeed replicated a modern, poetic retelling of the Israelites resisting their enemies to fight their own cause.

The Bible as a Secular Text

Like the use of African proverbs, parables, idioms, tortoise stories, and all other forms of orality, many Africans invoke passages in the Bible to serve the same purposes. They even seek equivalences between those African proverbs and statements in the Bible. It is also not unusual to combine elements of African orality with lines in the Bible. In so doing, the Bible is not being referenced as scripture but as a text containing relevant ideas. Nollywood, the large-scale Nigerian film industry, thrives as a combination of African worldview and those of the biblical and the Qur'anic. Eclectic words are drawn from so many sources: the Sufi-oriented Imam in Lagos can draw words from the Bible as he presents the leather-bound charm to his clients. The Babalawo (diviner) can start with Ifa lines and take one or two lines from the book of Psalms. Politicians invoke words from the Bible. The oral space is suffocated with words and lines from the Bible. In treating these words, we cannot just locate them in the religious and spiritual realm, but we should also see them as the conversion of the Bible to a secular text, that is, a work of literature that produces significant outcomes.

It must also be noted that the Bible shares certain things in common with African orality and religious texts like Ifa: the journey of the Bible started as oral texts, like the Odu Ifa, and then converted into a written text. The Bible, as a written text, contains the key elements of orality. This orality approximates, in many ways, the expressive forms of many African cultures, that is, those who are grounded in the use of proverbs, idioms, and didactic stories have little or no difficulty in processing, understanding, and using the Bible. Instead of using a Yoruba proverb, they can find an equivalent in the Bible. Instead of telling a didactic tortoise story, they can find something similar in the Bible. The same is true of drama: the early works by Hubert Ogunde and Adebayo Faleti drew extensively from the Bible, as they related them to Yoruba ideas and story lines or as they related them to the politics of the time. The David-Goliath story draws strong parallels between the struggle of

Nigerian nationalists and the British colonizers. Rather than an ethnographic compilation of words and statements that have regarded the Bible as a political text, I want to provide a larger reading on this aspect.

The Phenomenology of a Secular Text: Conversational Tropes

How do Africans read the Bible through a secular lens? It is, by all means, an ancient collection of religious documents written from particular theological viewpoints. These different viewpoints all have distinct biases and can be interpreted in a variety of ways, depending on the reader. Every biblical contributor had a particular framework, an objective to teach truth about God and God's relationship with humanity.[107] They wrote from a position of faith and assumption, rather than neutrality, based on what they had been taught and how they viewed the world.

From Nollywood, analysis of newspaper writings, and scores of interviews in different African countries, I attempt here what Africans take away from the Bible. This is a phenomenological approach that presents how people present their own experiences and consciousness without the scholar attempting to doubt the data or questioning the validity of the data itself. Instead of interpreting biblical stories as absolute truth, I focus on how individuals project their values and life lessons as connected to several biblical passages. By focusing less on what could be considered myth and more on moral truth, people may present their reality as finding inspirations and guidance for their everyday lives. When they draw lessons of individual concerns in relation to personal lives, the Bible plays a critical role in instructing a good and moral lifestyle as each person defines it. Whether or not we believe in a deity and/ or an afterlife, there are certain principles present throughout the Old and New Testament that many Africans seem to adopt into their lives or claim to subscribe to.

A caveat is necessary here. A phenomenological approach carries a great intellectual risk: When you describe a Yoruba god or goddess among the Yoruba, you may be misinterpreted as if you are an advocate when you may be an Anglican reverend making a living by teaching African Traditional Religion at the University of Ibadan. My analysis of the tropes may sound like "preaching" but it is a summation of individual experiences, as I have collected and understood them, and not the expression of my own religious beliefs.

I will point to the most recurrent values that are presented in my data as most essential to living a life dedicated to serving others, seeking joy and respect, and making the most of each and every day. I am not questioning the values and tropes as they are presented in my data but identifying them in relation to biblical statements.

Grace

One of the most radical principles of life discussed throughout the Old and New Testament is the concept of grace. Grace is essentially "giving people more that they deserve irrespective of the cause of their need and without regard to national, cultural or religious boundaries."[108] Africans mention the word "grace" in routine conversations, whenever they refer to survival, endurance, attainment of old age, overcoming a serious illness, escaping death from a serious car accident, and many other calamities. While the concept of grace is essential to the Christian faith, it seems, from the evidence, that it may not be limited to those who believe in a higher power. The task of treating others with absolute respect, kindness, and understanding, whether or not they deserve it, is a challenge for anyone. We all come from different backgrounds, have different interests and experiences, and we all make countless mistakes. If a person, religious or not, understands that humanity is both flawed and capable of positive change, then they communicate to others that they not only strive to live by grace but they believe in the capacity of grace to protect them.

At its heart, grace is about people caring for other people. While the Bible teaches us that grace is a gift from God, the important thing to take away from the African conversational trope is that grace can save people and it can be conferred without asking for it. While nonreligious people might disagree about the idea of sinfulness, most would agree that as humans they strive for connection, acceptance, and love for one another,[109] or, at least for the people they know. They might not believe in God or the theological implications of grace, but they present the evidence that they find meaning and acceptance by understanding and caring for someone—children, family members, friends, and colleagues at work. When a colleague dies, they contribute money for the burial ceremony.

Luke 6:31 reads: "Do to others as you would have them do to you." This verse is essentially the famous "golden rule," which is present throughout the Bible and a vital part to understanding the meaning of grace as Africans tie this to notion of Ubuntu and *Omoluwabi* (among the Yoruba). The Bible explains that, as we are all flawed, we deserve forgiveness, love, and respect as much as anyone else and therefore should give everyone else that which we think we deserve. This connects to the Yoruba concept of *idariji* (forgiveness). Unsurprisingly, the concept of treating others the way you want to be treated is included in many different religious texts, including Buddhism, Islam, Hinduism, and a number of African faith systems.

Hope

Hope is not a guarantee that bad things will not happen in the future nor is it simply looking on the bright side but in fact an encouragement to cherish the good aspects of life and to take leaps of faith to overcome challenges.[110]

Hope translates to notions of *ireti* (expectations) and *itelorun* (contentment). The Bible never says that we won't have problems but instead tells us to take courage in the hopes of overcoming the world. The biblical definition of hope is like that of faith, meaning that although we cannot see what the future holds, it is important to not give in to doubts and fears but remain hopeful for positive change.[111] The Yoruba, in their concept of *ayanmo* (destiny), anticipates elements of hope—as long as you remain alive, you cannot tell what you will become, from a poor man on Monday to the most wealthy on Wednesday.

To those who don't believe in God or life after death, they still communicate the impression, in interviews, that they strive to put this attitude toward hope in humanity here on Earth. They say that there is no reason to not have hope for a better future, especially as having hope does not concern itself with evidence or proof. For nonreligious people, "hope can be a way to have the benefits of faith without necessarily believing in God."[112] Whether Africans put their trust in God or in each other, they appear to be encouraged to look beyond threatening situations and immediate problems and believe that they have the power and capability to live better lives.

Love

The third most common trope is that of love. The true meaning of life, according to the Bible, is without a doubt unconditional love. The Word teaches us that love is patient and kind and says that there is no greater commandment than to love our enemies as we do ourselves, indicating that self-love and respect is just as important as loving others. Love is named as "the fulfillment of the law" and has the power to "cover over a multitude of sins." In other words, love is everything.

The Bible talks about love more than anything else and speaks on love for and from God, friendship, family, romantic love, self-love, and even love for our enemies. It teaches us that love is powerful, especially when it is offered to those who feel neglected, cast down, or do not love in return. Regardless of whether or not someone believes in God, they tend to revel in the knowledge that there is no shortage of love in the universe and it endures all things. As humans, many Africans are portrayed in many films as if it is their purpose to love and to give. To live a purposeful life, Imams, Babalawo, and Pastors tell their clients to be caring, patient, and truthful in love and stay away from arrogance, jealousy, and selfishness.[113]

Justice

Biblical justice differs from the typical definition of "equality" (where every person is treated the same no matter the circumstance) and refers more to restoration and liberation of those who face injustices such as abuse, poverty, and discrimination. The justice of the Bible stems from grace and righteousness, as those capable of action are called upon to live selflessly and overturn injustices to help out those in need.[114] It emphasizes in the Bible to focus on doing good and serving others, rather than seeking revenge or trying to get even with oppressors and wrongdoers. As mentioned before, the Bible teaches us to love our neighbors, including those who seek to harm us or cause us injustice. True justice is that of compassion and mercy. Africans invoke this a lot, and the intense criticisms of politicians and the rich focus on their lack of compassion, injustice, and corruption.

Religious or not, we can learn from the concept of biblical justice to focus our attention on providing for the needy, protecting those who face abuse, caring for the disadvantaged, and showing hospitality to everyone. The Bible teaches us not to get caught up in trying to blame or punish people for the unfairness and corruption in the world but dedicate ourselves to liberating the victims of injustice. By working as doers of justice, we can hope that our actions are recognized and replicated by others. This value may have driven anti-apartheid resistance in South Africa.

Joy

Joy, as discussed in the Bible, is recognized as an essential part of life, but as a social value it is often neglected in pursuit of other things. Joy in the Bible is understood as fundamental and sustainable happiness and comes from transforming people's lives in a positive way and building relationships with people. 2 Corinthians 6:10 reads: "We have access to subterranean joy that is simultaneous with, and deeper than, our sorrows." The Bible encourages us to find comfort in what we have achieved and what we are blessed with, even when times are hard, and to celebrate the happy moments in our lives.[115] Oral data coming from postwar Liberia and Sierra Leone tend to reinforce this notion of joy.

The lines on joy in oral data are repetitively predictable: all people should adopt the idea that joy is not optional but should be considered an essential part of life. Even when we face suffering, stress, misfortune, and so on, we should take comfort in knowing that joy is possible. Whether people believe in a deity or not, a life dedicated to changing other's lives for the better is never a life wasted. The common belief is that by loving people as well as us, and celebrating with people in their accomplishments, we can find our own sense of lifelong happiness.

Peace

In the Bible, the concept of peace refers to a number of different things, including the absence of war or violence, peace with people and God, positive harmony, health, and spiritual well-being.[116] Just as the case with joy, peace is described as an important aspect in people's lives and should be sought out both personally in private and on a worldly scale. The Bible encourages us to find peace within ourselves and among other people to find harmony and understanding. Peace can be found through working for justice and following the example of Jesus Christ, who is often named the "Prince of Peace."

Many Africans do not fully understand peace as a positive concept and only see it as the *absence* of trouble. Biblical peace can be described as the "quiet goodness of life," unaffected by the problems and sorrows of the world.[117] An example of this comes from Jesus the night before his torturous death, who knew his fate but still spoke with a message of peace—"Peace I leave with you; My peace I give to you; not as the world do I give to you. Let not your heart be troubled, nor let it be fearful" (John 14:27). All people, including those who do not believe in God, still strive toward living a life grounded in peace and justice. Like joy, true peace comes from giving and serving others, which despite the incredibly hard work, can give lasting rewards. In countries like Nigeria and South Sudan where conflicts and violence are endemic, conversation on peace and security has become the routine of living.

CONCEPTUAL ANALYSIS

In this closing section, I want to put the aforementioned text—literary, political, and secular—in a larger context of the overall relevance of the Bible. Why does the Bible work as a text? Multiple Western and Western-imposed ideologies stem from the text, stories, and morals presented in the Bible due to its centrality in the Christian religion that has dominated the world for numerous centuries. While Christianity contains varying beliefs about the relationship between God, humans, and Jesus, the Bible behaves as a source of guidance and unification of these sects. However, the Bible, in its use for religious practices and education as well as its proliferation among individuals with various motivations (unification of people, conversions, etc.), may also be approached using historical and literary ideas through its story-based explanations and alternating narrative approaches.

The historical influences of Christianity continually emerge within the timeline of many societies, from the establishment to common societal morals, roles, and attitudes to the defending of the religion through wars, treaties, and the building of empires. Along with the patrons and core edifices of the religion, the Bible has continued to be translated, preached, and uplifted in societies.

The visualization of the Bible as a book with typed and printed font is a commonplace practice in the current society, though this image of the Bible as a compiled work that is used to spread the ideals of Christianity as well as serve as basis of literacy supports the idea of the Bible as a secular text. A text, defined as the "abstraction of verbal content from its origins . . . copresent with the reader . . . and given a material embodiment in the process of publication."[118] This context examines the textualization of the Bible in history from its revelation to its compilation and mass publication. The messages of the Bible, the preaching of Jesus Christ, and the stories of the Prophets and other narratives found in the text of the Bible were oral traditions passed through the tradition of storytelling as found in the Israeli culture of the period. Therefore, the compilation of the contents of the Bible does not conform to the Western style of literature with single authors and one perspective of writing. In this manner, the Bible seeks to reflect more heavily on its readers than its writers than claiming a single authorship.[119] Analyzing the Bible in its structural form creates multiple questions regarding its compilation into a single book, its timeline of revelation from the Old Testament to the New Testament.

While the New Testament of the Bible is comprised of definitive Christian beliefs, the existence of biblical texts originates from the Hebrew tradition as upheld by both Christian and Jewish individuals. Many historians debate the initiation of written sources of biblical text, with ideas of scrolls going back as far at the sixth century BCE.[120] Nevertheless, the initial script of the Bible is seen as rivaling the oral traditions popular to the common classes of the people in the Middle East, during the time.[121] As oral histories were more prominent to lower classes, written traditions were reserved for those of a higher status. These conditions not only limited literacy but also created a symbolic status of written works as a form of higher communication with ideals of divine intervention.[122] Access and promotion of the written editions of the religion were not complete rivals to the oral tradition but these works were often restricted to temples and priests,[123] thus allowing the Bible in its textual sense to behave as a symbol of both literacy and social stratification. In efforts to maintain the prevalence of Christianity among the community and encourage communication, increased literacy was a definite condition that citizens had to meet to benefit from a written script. Formation of educational structures and role acquisition of priests as teachers became a practice to allow individuals to understand and learn of the message preached by Jesus as well as compile the oral histories maintained by the people. Christianity took hold of the codex quickly[124] wherein the Bible became a source of learning as a secular text for individuals of the community.

The adaptation of the written source of the Bible created parallel practices within communities, one that maintained traditional structures of oral messages to maintain beliefs and ideas and another that altered the access of education to individuals while also changing the capacity of influence of those in charge of maintaining religious practices and education. In addition to challenging oral traditions, the Bible as a text demonstrated an authority of writing by which social understandings, attitudes, and practices could be changed by the publication of literature. In addition to the centralization of education within the societies of the period, the documentation of the Bible also challenged traditional ideals of individual and communal infrastructures. The interjection of a single author of the Bible centered on a predominant philosophy regarding the prioritization of the individual; however, the maintenance of a collective effort in the recording and compiling of the word afforded both its readers and writers a unique complexity in the manifestation of a compiled text.

The structural compilation and formatting of the Bible assisted in maintaining this capacity of change and perspective. Due to the unique structure of the text with its multiple sections and combinations of narrative stories with moral messages, the Bible allows for its readers to form their own interpretations of passages and ideas. By extending literacy to multiple classes and the uses of religious texts as basis for understanding, individuals were able to challenge the practices observed by the faith and refer to the Bible as a textual guide to develop new practices and interpret passage in alternate capacities. For example, Martin Luther's[125] interpretation of the text presented in the Bible most famously provided a basis for the theological revolutionary to adopt a differing method of not only practicing Christianity but also perceiving the structures of the church and their role in the lives of the individual and the collective community. The use of the Bible in these historical contexts demonstrates the influence of the Bible within the realm of the secular environment in previous as well as more recent communities.

Within its historic impacts and significance, the Bible presents varying texts and scripts from which many possess literary tools. Both the Old Testament and New Testament books within the Bible address many narratives of individuals and prophets. These narratives tell stories with levels of imagery[126] and fascination with the human aspect of the characters.[127] The narratives of the Bible also distinguish themselves through their alternating of voice. Narratives simultaneously contain dialogues of characters as they contain a narration of action[128] as well as the perspective or voice of God.[129] These narratives, while seeing to provide moral guidance, also appeal to the humanity of individuals and create a concrete depiction of issues relevant to the readers. Along with narratives, the Bible is known to contain elements of poetry[130] within its text. Similar to the narrative, the poetry found in the Bible in both sections focuses on experiences held by characters of specific motivation and purposes.[131] The poetry, like the narratives, inclines the characters and the readers to seek the truth and the divine presence; however, the poetry of the Bible further inclines individuals to the power of God and evokes a sense of passion and devotion through its use of melody. Biblical poetry further encourages the use of vast imagery to appeal to the sense and intellect of the reader.[132] The multidimensional writing of the Bible allows the reader to comprehend literary devices and figurative language to examine perspectives, morals, and the devotion to the God.

The Bible, as understood through multiple lenses of history, sociology, and literature, functions as an introspective work from which many fundamental ideologies and concepts stem. The Bible as a secular text displays many literary achievements while also creating a foundation for the separation between the knowledge and belief systems of the individual.

It is precisely the relevance of the literary achievements of the Bible that allows Muslims to invoke it; that provides resources for Nollywood to deploy it; and that supplies limitless words, concepts, and ideas for millions of people to invoke it, whether they are religious or not. As a political and literary text, the Bible remains arguably the best-cited literature, far more than the combined works of William Shakespeare or the entire literary output of all African creative writers.

Chapter 7

Pentecostalism and Its Knowledge System

In postcolonial studies, there is an ongoing depiction of Christianity as a missionary project of the West. The phenomena of Pentecostal mega-churches both conform to and challenge this narrative. The Pentecostal religious movement has defied the expectations of scholars through a demographic shift into Africa and Latin America. While the estimated world population of Pentecostals is about half a billion, Pew Research Center estimates that 43.7 percent of these followers are located in sub-Saharan Africa.[1] This indicates a heavy concentration of the Pentecostal movement, not only within the "developing" world but also within sub-Saharan Africa. According to an online database on African churches, seven out of the ten largest churches in sub-Saharan Africa are in Nigeria. The largest of these is Deeper Christian Life Ministry in Lagos, which has a reported weekly attendance of over 65,000.[2] For this reason, this study will heavily draw upon Pentecostal movements in West Africa, particularly Nigeria, to understand African Pentecostalism. An analysis of the Pentecostal movement in this geographical context shows extreme divergence from other Christian missionary waves in so as African Pentecostalism functions both as an import and innovation of Africa. This chapter will serve to understand Pentecostalism as a knowledge system within its historical context. Due to the embodied nature of knowledge in Pentecostalism, this will be followed by a discussion on godmentality and how Pentecostalism is internalized and performed. The resulting grounded narrative will provide insight into understanding the Pentecostal knowledge system within Africa.

PART I
UNDERSTANDING PENTECOSTALISM

Defining Pentecostalism

It is important to clarify the heterogeneity of Pentecostalism. Its transnational application to Europe, the Americas, Asia, and Africa manifests in very different forms. Better understood as Pentecostalism, the phenomena represent a paradox of both difference and uniformity as cultures tend to perform Pentecostalism differently but share a transnational identity.[3] They join together only in a Manichean "war against Satan," the vagueness of which can be used by different cultural and political groups to achieve various agendas.[4]

The perceived beginning to contemporary Pentecostalism is the Azusa Street revival. This unorthodox Christian meeting to place on April 9, 1906, in Los Angeles, California. The leading preacher, William Seymour, was an African American man who was born to emancipated slaves in Louisiana. The revival stood out from orthodox Protestant practices through exaggerated demonstrations of faith and worship including speaking in tongues, testimonies of miracles, highly emotional worship, and divine gifts. A frequent report of attendees of services on Azusa Street was that they saw God's divine fire on top of the church. This report was so frequent that the fire department was called to put out the fire. Many leaders from the Azusa Street revival spread the religious movement to other areas of America and abroad. Azusa Street today is pinpointed as the starting point of the Pentecostal and Charismatic Christian religious movements.[5]

Growth of the Pentecostal movement in Africa happened almost simultaneously with the pan-African movement. Seymour's *Apostolic Faith* newspaper spread throughout the continent along with the tenets of Pentecostalism. In as early as 1906, Lucy Farrow, niece of Fredrick Douglass, was preaching Pentecostalism through Liberia and in 1914 William Wade Harris, a Liberian-born theologian, through the Ivory Coast and Ghana.[6] The prominence of powerful black men and women in the Pentecostal movement challenges the traditional narrative of the colonial missionary. African nations were still political colonies in the early twentieth century, and a prominent narrative for this colonization was the perceived need for white missionaries to save "the dark continent." The Pentecostal movement broke this narrative because it was led primarily by the African diaspora. African Americans used Pentecostalism to connect to their African roots and people living on the African continent. In many ways, the movement created a foundation for early pan-African movements and postcolonial nationalism.[7]

The Azusa Street revival represented a discontent with modernity, heavily drawing from the experience of being a "free" black person in America.

This generation that began the religious movement was raised Christian but witnessed the contradictions between the words preached and a church that perpetuates injustice. African Americans after emancipation were not free; they were continually held by the chains of racism, economic dependence, and epistemic violence. They felt the intergenerational loss of their cultural roots, having remnants of their ancestors' culture passed down to them but in incomplete forms.[8] As an example, some people during the Azusa Street revival claimed that they were able to speak in African tongues they had not learned before or understand them. They said that they were able to do this through the power of the Holy Spirit.[9] This represents a desire to connect with something very tangible about intergenerational culture that was once lost, the mother tongue. Furthermore, many African American families continued African traditional religions in some form or another. Most of the time, these religious beliefs were combined with those of Christianity, to create hybrid religions. Pentecostalism, because of its focus on the individual connection with the Holy Spirit, was able to bridge this gap between African religious origins and the desire for a Christian revival. This was further reflected in African traditional music selections during the revival.[10]

When the revival movement moved to Africa, Pentecostalism was coherent with the African worldview.[11] Although African ontological views vary widely through different regions, religions, and ethnic groups, a commonality is the omniscience of religion and consequent rejection of secularity.[12] Pentecostalism is a highly emotional and interactive sect. Followers allow the Holy Spirit to flow through them and use divine gifts and the presence of the Holy Spirit to create knowledge.

Pentecostal Epistemology

> They are controlled by the fathers. Our salvation is not in some father or human instruments. It is sad to see people so blinded, worshiping the creature more than the Creator.[13]

African Pentecostals believe in biblical inerrancy. This is something that is not unique to Pentecostalism but central to many religious revival movements. Adherents to biblical inerrancy see the Bible as God's word, protected by the Holy Spirit so that the truth in the words cannot be altered by man.[14] Pentecostals believe in the worldview presented by the Bible, in terms of angels and demons, as literal rather than symbolic.[15] In particular, they believe in the ability for faith to create physical miracles. Biblical inerrancy is a complex issue, especially when considering factors of translation, ambiguous wording, and contradictory verses. It sees the Bible, not as a literary text but as an epistcmic text. That is a text which through its sacredness sets the foundation for what can and cannot be qualified as knowledge. While Pentecostals do assert biblical inerrancy, they use the tool of the Holy Spirit to interpret the text, a practice that distinguishes them from fundamentalist Christian groups.[16] In practice, they take the biblical philosophy of experientialism over fundamentalism.[17]

In terms of revival movements, Pentecostalism is often named as the first wave in a series of charismatic Christian revivals. In some cases, charismatic churches have close similarities that make them indistinguishable to Pentecostalism. A defining factor of Pentecostalism, however, is the doctrine of subsequence. This is the idea of a "spirit filling" that provides the Christians with special gifts or healing that takes place after the initial salvation.[18] Traditionally, salvation is the acceptance of Jesus as your lord and savior. Traditional Protestantism believes that radical spiritual transformation stops here. On the contrary, Pentecostalism believes that after salvation an ongoing relationship with the Holy Spirit can result in spiritual gifts. Pentecostalism acknowledges the fault of man and actively engages with the Bible in a contemporary context. This translates to the apparent demonstrations of speaking in tongues, highly emotional worship, miracles, and experience of divine gifts.[19]

Another feature of Pentecostalism and subsequent Protestant revivals is their Manichean nature. This is the religions continuous binary between good and evil, God and Satan. Pentecostal preachers talk about these forces in very individual and real terms. They urge subjects to guard themselves against the devil and work together with God and the Holy Spirit.[20] Pentecostal ways of knowing in Africa also validate the existence of witchcraft. Traditional African spirits and "occult powers" are associated with the devil and hell, put in opposition with the Father, Jesus, and the Holy Spirit.[21]

The Modern Pentecostal Megachurch

Although the Pentecostal movement started in the early 1900s, the term "megachurch" was not used until the 1980s in the United States.[22] The Azusa Street revival featured an unconventional worship space, that of a worn-down shack or even out on the streets. People traveled from across the United States to be part of the spontaneous Azusa Street services, which broke Christian tradition by not being held in an official church and not meeting only on Sunday mornings.[23] This combination of huge crowds and a breakdown of the traditional time and space restrictions of the church opened the door for what are now termed "megachurches." The term "megachurch" has multiple definitions across contexts. The Hartford Institute for Religion Research defines a megachurch as that which has more than 2,000 attendees.[24] Yet, it isn't the number of people that truly defines the megachurch but the essence of the church itself. Everything about the megachurch is big, from the ideology of a big God to the billboards and the architecture church itself.[25]

Imagine you are a Christian living in Lagos, Nigeria. You hear about a new megachurch in town that sometimes has an attendance of over 200,000. People travel across the country to visit the sermons by the famous preacher, who you have often encountered through radio, television, and signs in town. He wears Western-style clothes and has an air of success. His wife and children are beautiful and often shown with him, as he is an advocate for family values. You decide to attend one Sunday, fighting the crowds to make it into the congregation. Outside the church markets are selling religious items, asking for donations and giving out flyers. The church itself is huge but largely unmarked. It is simplistic, almost industrial. It has signs of the cross without the intricate architecture of other church you've seen before. You are greeted by several church employees before entering the service. Inside the church there are a few pews but extensive space for standing that you have never seen in a place of worship. The stage where the preacher will stand is large, with microphones and cameras. There are posters, flowers, and sayings supporting Jesus' message but minimalist decorations.

Figure 7.1. Tongues of fire descend on the apostles at Pentecost. *Source*: The Wellcome Collection. Accessed July 29, 2020, from https://wellcomecollection.org/works/xz93vma8.

As the service begins, the lights dim and the screens around the room fill with the famous preacher. The sermon is being broadcast for live TV and the audience cheers when he comes out. After a brief sermon, the music begins. The speakers are loud, but the crowd's singing is louder. Apart from knowing the lyrics by heart, people begin to scream out "thank you Jesus!" or "amen!" spontaneously. The pastor encourages everyone to raise their hands up and give themselves over to the Holy Spirit. Several people fall to their knees in worship, others yell in praise. As the music escalates, some worshipers fall over in a trance or begin to speak in tongues. People are crying and many are laying hands on each other in prayer.[26]

Toward the end of the service, the pastor encourages you to come for upcoming events. There are stations throughout the church where you can give money. The pastor encourages you to do this and promises that God gives back much more than is given. The preacher explains the various ways you can stay connected with the church through the week: social media, TV, radio, books, or pamphlets. As you leave, the market is again open with bracelets, books, home decor, and remedies all related to the church.

PART II
GODMENTALITY OF PENTECOSTALISM

The Pentecostal Processes of Subjectivation

For the remainder of this analysis, this study will take a Foucauldian perspective to the Pentecostal Megachurch. This analysis will seek to understand how "docile bodies" are transformed into subjects of the Pentecostal church. This study seeks to explain how the Pentecostal identity is maintained, internalized, and ultimately performed by subjects.

The way this study will analyze the relationship between the Pentecostal church and the subject borrows from Foucault's idea of "governmentality." In Foucault's 1978 speech "Security, Territory and Population," he identified the state as having three types of power. The first power of the government is its sovereignty, that is, the ability for the government to ordain its own laws and authority. The second is disciplinary power, which is the ability for the government to inflict punishment on those who do not follow its rules. Bodies of discipline include jail and the military but expand to systems of fines and even schools. The final power of the government is governmentality.[27] Governmentality is not how the government disciplines the citizen but how the government conditions the subject to govern themselves. This process is essential, because the government having the power it does could not execute punishment on every individual if they were to act as they wish. Governmentality is the transfer of the responsibility of discipline, as defined by the state, to the population. In this process, individuals hold themselves accountable as well as each other to conforming to the will of the government.[28]

Governmentality relates to Foucault's knowledge-power symbiotic nexus. In this model, people who have power maintain that power through systematically reinforcing an ideology that legitimizes their rule.[29] For example, in ancient Egypt the Pharaoh was able to maintain his regime through Egyptian religion. The religion asserted that the Pharaoh was the reincarnation of Osiris, therefore an infallible God whose rule could not be questioned. Especially in a time where technology did not allow for efficient communication across the kingdom, the ideology of the Pharaoh as Osiris was essential to maintaining his rule.[30] In the same way, Pentecostalism beliefs can be viewed in the knowledge-power nexus of maintaining the power of the Pentecostal church.

In applying Foucault's idea of governmentality to Pentecostalism, the current analysis makes two underlying assumptions. The first is that Pentecostalism functions like a governing body. Often, Pentecostals refer to their community as "God's Kingdom." From this terminology and also the functioning of the Pentecostal church, this study asserts that they are a governing body. In terms of Foucault's first two definitions of power, the church has sovereignty—to an extent—as well as disciplinary power. The sovereignty of the church is different than the sovereignty of the state, in so as it does not exist within the nation-state system but within the spiritual realm and the physical within the state. Although the church is still subject to the rulings of the state, it has autonomy to create its own rules, institutions, and practices. In terms of discipline, the church does not have power over life and death but practices discipline through social and spiritual practices. That is, the church has the power to ban people from the church or to condemn them for their actions. The church also holds people accountable to a set of rules that will either lead them into an afterlife or heaven or hell.

The functionality of the Pentecostal church as a kingdom is fluid. The church's authority ranges depending on the culture, state, and context. For example, just as the nation-state may be able to limit the power of a church, cultural kingdoms such as in Nigeria have authority that intersects with that of the church in unique and complex ways. Despite the context, the Pentecostal church does act as a governing body in the way that it refers to itself as a kingdom, disciplines subjects, and exalts God as the undying king.[31] This divine authority of God is central to the power of the church. The authority of God is manifested through the actions of his son, Jesus Christ, as well as through the Holy Spirit. His authority goes through the Bible and the church, ultimately reaching the pastor. In this way, the pastor is not a God himself but ordained through God himself as His servant. The pastor has the power to "see," asking for testimony and vulnerability of the audience, without themselves being "seen." This is true in so as the pastor does not share their own struggles through the religion beyond the "before" narrative in their born-again story.[32] Although Pentecostalism rejects the automatic authority of human agents of God, talking about human error, this is still the skeletal construction of leadership in the Pentecostal church.

The second assumption being made is that Pentecostal Christians are "docile bodies." Foucault's theory of "docile bodies" comes from his work "Discipline and Punish." He describes people with power as exercising discipline through ways of surveillance that individuals are no longer aware of. In short, this refers back to the idea of ideology as maintaining power.[33] The assumption of "docile bodies" furthers the idea of governmentality. Not only is the responsibility of discipline transferred to individual regulating themselves and each other, but it happens in such subtle ways that individuals are no longer aware of the process. This is the normalization of power that leads people to unknowingly accept authority. The idea of docile bodies implies that people are subject to changing their thoughts, actions, and even physical appearance from powerful influencers. In the context of Pentecostalism, Pentecostal Christians function as subjects to the kingdom of the Pentecost. This study seeks to explain how the modern Pentecostal church acts as a powerful disciplinary body, molding the thoughts, actions, and appearances of Christians as docile bodies.

In the context of African Pentecostal churches, the idea of docile bodies has a specific context. This is the effect of the colonized mind. The "colonized mind" is a term that describes the psychological effects of the Western hegemony in today's society. The increasing "globalization" of the world has really meant "Westernization." The majority of our global society exists within the "colonial matrix of power," which reinforces those with money the previous colonial powers. This is a matrix of power in which Western systems of knowledge, especially to the extent to which they reflect secular and individualistic values, take priority over subaltern ways of knowing.[34] The effect of the colonized mind is the passive acceptance of these systems, which decoloniality seeks to dismantle.[35] In the case of Pentecostalism, the church is able to take advantage of the colonized mind to gain authority. It is able to associate the church with Westernization through church organization, dress, and beliefs. In general, the effect of the colonized mind increases the docility of bodies, the vulnerability of people to authority.

Again, this relationship between Pentecostalism and colonization is complex. This is because Pentecostalism exists within the colonial matrix of power while also rebelling against it. African Pentecostalism takes the context and inspiration from the West yet melds with traditional African beliefs and values to make something distinctly African. Still, Pentecostalism took place in an era of colonization in which the effect of the colonized mind increased the docility of African bodies and the acceptance of the new wave.

Performing Pentecostalism

Now that Pentecostalism has been analyzed from the perspective of governmentality, this chapter will refer to the subjectivation of Pentecostal followers as "godmentality." Godmentality works through changing the thoughts, actions, and appearance of Pentecostal followers as docile bodies. The ways in which this process can best be conceptualized are through reading Pentecostalism as a performance.

Performance theory starts with the very idea of the "actor" and a "performance." In the theater, an actor has memorized lines and actions to create an illusion of a certain character. In Schechner's performance theory, he describes acting as "the illusion of an illusion." Although the actor is pretending to be a certain person for the audience, the idea that this is unique from reality is false. Performance theory views reality in a social context. Individuals have a "character" that they intend to communicate to the people around them. This character is typically the individual's identity in some way, or how they want their identity to be perceived. Whether this is their ethnicity, religious views, gender, political views, or age, individuals think, act, and dress in a certain way that is able to perform their identity to others.[36]

In this way, people engage with "impression management" in which they use both props and nonverbal communication to project their image. This includes the way that one talks, dresses, acts, and reacts. In performance theory, some things are "backstage."[37] As an example, consider the Western stereotype of masculinity. This encourages men to refrain from emotion and be tough or macho. For a Western man performing masculinity, he might be strong during emotional times in front of others but when alone cry because he is unsure of what to do or lonely. The underlying assumption of performance theory is what has been called the "Thomas Theorem." This is: "if people define situations as real, they are real in their consequences."[38] The Thomas theorem shows a perspective of reality as entirely socially constructed, in which performance is of the highest importance. Yet, this performance does not translate to fakeness, as the performance becomes real as the performer internalizes their actions.

The implication of the Thomas theorem to Pentecostalism is that the church is able to execute real disciplinary power on the individual. This logic holds up, as long as the individual believes that they will be punished by God for taking certain actions. In the church context, Christianity is transferred through knowledge, memory, and identity in a "twice-behaved behavior."

This is, those who do conform to the church reinforce the sovereignty of the church through their performance while those who do not conform reinforce the power through their rebellion to it.[39]

The first way in which Pentecostalism practices godmentality is through reconstructing the identity of its subjects. That is, it changes what the individual is trying to perform. In the case of African Pentecostalism there are two features to this identity. The first is an identification with the African diaspora. During the Azusa Street revival, individuals reported that they were able to speak in "lost African tongues"; this is an example of trying to reconnect to their African roots. They are identifying with the African continent and performing this connection through speaking in African languages. In the African continent, this includes a complex merger between the Western African diaspora identity, in which Africans try to look "successful" in terms of Western clothing as well as local in terms of African indigenous religious beliefs. Therefore, an African's performance of Pentecostalism may be influenced by their identity as well as their imagination of the African diaspora.[40]

The second aspect of the African Pentecostal identity is "born-again" Christian. This traditional narrative is that in the moment that you accepted Christ into your life, everything before that was influenced by the devil and everything after that is part of your divine journey. Therefore, it represents a moment of fissure in your life. This identity of the self as the "new" or "saved" you creates the pressure to communicate this new identity to the world. The "born again" process involves several aspects of performance. The new Christian begins to dress the way they think that their new identity would dress, often in nicer clothing. Their narrative forms reflect a testimony of change accompanied by prayer and religious song. Finally, they commit to bodily performance of Pentecostalism through prayer and specific acts such as fasting or speaking in tongues.[41] Through testimony, this born-again narrative is constantly renewed and internalized.[42] The new convert has to undergo constant philosophical labor in order to understand what their new norms in the religion should be.[43]

One of the most brilliant illusions embedded within Pentecostalism is the idea that God's presence enacts actions within believers that defy explanation.[44]

Key to the Pentecostal performance is performing a relationship with God. Referring to this relationship as a performance does not take away from the realness of an individual's connection with God. On the contrary, performance of a relationship with God is the process in which the individual is able to internalize this relationship, to make it real to them. The scene described earlier in the Pentecostal megachurch clearly defines performance norms. During church, the pastor often cues to individuals what to do such as put their hands on their heads, in the air, or bow their heads in prayer. Yet the worship service allows for much more, including dancing, falling to our knees in prayer, and displays of emotion. Individuals may begin to speak in tongues or have a vision, one of the "gifts" that God bestows on them. There is a canon of Pentecostal actions and phrases, which may emerge during services. These may seem to be spontaneous but can more accurately be analyzed within the context of group social interactions.[45] The actions of Pentecostal worshippers during service can be analyzed not only as a social performance but in the context of dance itself.[46] To summarize, worshippers use bodily movements in order to appear that God is moving through them.[47] Their heightened emotional experience from the environment of the church, social context, and their own actions make them feel as if they are being communicated to by God.[48]

Unlike other religious movements, Pentecostalism does not seek to perform missionary volunteer work explicitly. Not that followers are discouraged from getting involved in charity work, but followers are encouraged to transform themselves as agents of God. It is thought that through this testimony, individuals are able to transform the world. Therefore, the performance of an individual relationship with God is the primary way in which Pentecostalism spreads.[49]

PART III
PENTECOSTALISM AS APPLIED EPISTEMOLOGY

Technologies of Godmentality

Foucault said that governmentality was not the way in which the government asserted domination overtly over the subject but a process that utilizes the "technologies of the self."[50] This is the way in which the individual applies discipline to themselves, interconnected with Pentecostal knowledge. This section will define the different technologies that Pentecostalism uses to achieve godmentality.

Prosperity Theology

Earlier, the existence of African Pentecostalism within the colonial matrix of power was explained. Nothing makes this more obvious than prosperity theology. The use of the term "prosperity theology" leads the individual to decide what prosperity is. In the way that this term is used, prosperity is defined as financial success in a system of capitalism. The way that preachers practice prosperity theology is through appearing to be financially successful, through their physical appearance, objects they own, and speech.[51] This definition of prosperity often intersects with coloniality as Western dress such as suits become symbols of capitalistic financial success. Preachers show off this money, or illusion of money, in a way that encourages followers of the church that God will also make them prosperous. In this way, preachers are not only spreading the gospel but also urbanism and modernization.[52] The advent of prosperity theology has created a "Pentecostal economy" in which spirituality itself is a commodity that can be bought. In this context, preachers start off as "spiritual entrepreneurs" trying to build up a megachurch as a business.[53]

One of the first Pentecostal leaders to engage with prosperity theology was Benson Idahosa. His iconic role as a televangelist in the megachurch was reinforced by his personal success. Idahosa ironically claims, "The keys to success and prosperity are grace, faith and hard work."[54] In this, the emphasis is put on the role of the Holy Spirit in delivering people to success, and Idahosa himself is the case study to prove his own point. Prosperity theology entices individuals into Pentecostalism and encourages them to identify with business, or a faith-based financial prosperity. Pentecostal subjects perform prosperity theology through the way that they dress, giving money to the church and emphasizing their financial successes.

An important contradiction of prosperity theology is the "paradox of the occult." This refers to the depiction of Satan as tempting followers of God with individual wealth in exchange for their souls. Oftentimes in Africa, Satanic rituals are represented by traditional healing practices or old religions, which are discouraged in light of the Pentecostal idea of God. It is problematic that the same prosperity offered by the megachurch through God is also offered by Satan.[55] Africans may feel an identity crisis if "occult powers" are overgeneralized, surpassing witchcraft beliefs and discouraging the world of traditional healing. In this case, they may feel torn that their cultural roots and social context require them to accept the "occult powers" they are warned against.[56]

Branding

Another way that the church influences the identity and performance of Pentecostal subjects is through missional branding. Branding in the age of capitalism depends on a simple, clear message. Yet, branding is also complex in that it can associate the church with certain types of Christianity, certain generations, or cultural groups. Churches tend to adopt a sort of brand identity that permeates through all marketing materials that they have. This includes physical items such as shirts, posters, and signs as well as media marketing.[57] It also especially includes the advent of social media, which allows churches to put their branding out to followers around the world. This new "cyberchurch" can transcend borders without political boundaries.[58]

Church branding impacts individual's identity and performance in relation to Pentecostalism. A simple message can cause Pentecostal followers to identify the church with certain ideas or groups. For example, branding may emphasize the family versus individualism, urban versus rural areas, women in leadership versus women in supporting roles, and so on. The branding of the church does not need to cite the words of God to impact how its followers perceive holiness. And therefore, the followers will perform that which has been identified with in the church. Their performance is also extended to their ability to push the marketing of the church through knowledge about and sharing of Pentecostal media.

Music

Music has the notorious power to cause great emotion. Pentecostal Christian music is able to invoke emotions both through the instrumental line and the lyrics. In the world of megachurches, Christian music has taken on its own character with megachurch favorites such as Hillsong United becoming Pentecostal anthems. Hillsong United started off as a small church in New South Wales, Australia. They took their music to production and as their appeal widened, they went through huge rebranding and message changes. It has grown so far as its own record label, which had reportedly sold more than 12 million albums globally by 2011.[59] In the Pentecostal tradition, Hillsong's old songs used the term "spirit" very often. Consider the following lyrics from Hillsong United's popular song "Oceans":

> Spirit lead me where my trust is without borders
> Let me walk upon the waters
> Wherever You would call me

However, in recent times, they opt for simple "God" or "Jesus" more often. The reasoning is likely to appeal to non-Pentecostal church audiences.[60] Apart from the messages within the emotional music, churches often have live bands play music or huge speakers. A Pentecostal church service can often feel more like a sort of rock concert.

The influence of loud, emotional music with high audience participation is the subject is put into a physiologically heightened state. This heightened state is often interpreted as a spiritual experience.[61] Music becomes part of the Pentecostal identity, changing the way in which subjects believe they should see themselves in relation to God. The music tells of how the individual should serve Him. In performing the music, the individual is internalizing the messages of the lyrics and governing themselves as a subject of God. They are also communicating to others that they are a follower of the Pentecostal church.

Televangelist

Televangelists are based all over the world, ranging from America to Nigeria. They are able to use the powers of TV, the internet, and social media to share their messages all over the world. Archbishop Benson Idahosa is often known as the father of Pentecostalism in Nigeria and also the first Nigerian Televangelist. His use of the TV to preach African Pentecostalism was able to reach preachers all over the continent, growing the movement from his city or country to international.[62] In Nigeria today, there are dozens of televangelists who not only preach the gospel but also make large amounts of money doing it, even going so far as to own the shows and TV stations themselves. Televangelists are not only clear performers of Pentecostalism but also set the identity and standard for others' performances of the religion.

Pentecostal Melodrama

The Pentecostal melodrama is another way in which TV supports the message of the Pentecost. TV dramas in which characters face everyday situations, while dealing with spiritual conflicts, are common across Africa in the format of both radio and TV. Shows are often made weekly and actors deal with issues that reflect good and evil. These dramas are not a simple transfer of information from the performers to the audience. Instead, they involve the interaction of the performers, audience, sponsors, spiritual advisors, and the Holy Spirit. The dramas are heavily influenced by the teachings of local pastors and spirits are thought to act through the shows. Complex issues of the African Pentecostal identity are explored in these shows, including relationships to indigenous beliefs. The shows often show outright showcases of witchcraft in order for the church to condemn it. It is perceived that spirits, either good or bad, are able to be transferred to the viewer through watching the show. They involve not only Christian situations but also testimonies, songs, and ceremonies.

The shows represent "mimesis in motion" in way they are not only reflective of a perceived modernity but also interact with it, since they are often produced weekly. In this way, the shows not only represent social norms in relation to Pentecostalism but they are able to set norms. For example, Pentecostal melodramas have emphasized marrying within Christianity, demonizing polygamy, adultery, and premarital sex.

The role of Pentecostal melodramas in Africa countries has been the influence of Christianity from the private into the public sphere. These programs have been successful in reshaping the African Pentecostal identity from a grassroots perspective. This includes shaping new ways that the performer can engage with Christianity and view of the actors in the shows as performing a validated Pentecostalism.[63] Part of their success stems from a pattern of censorship from African governments. This censorship encourages shows that have religious themes, with the Democratic Republic of the Congo even owning its own religious station.[64]

Architecture of the Church

Godmentality views the church not as a neutral location in which beliefs are cultivated but as a space that contributes to cultivating those beliefs. Pentecostal churches feature a very different style of architecture that is both a tool of power and an invention of necessity. They are product of placemaking that reinforces their belief systems.[65] Like traditional Christian churches, there is typically a church leader (preacher) who stands on a stage. The followers of the church are looking up at the preacher, a physical sensation that subconsciously instills a sense of the divine within the preacher. This feature and the tendency to make churches large compared to their surroundings are the few things that Pentecostal churches have in common with more traditional Christian places of worship.

The modern megachurch differs from the traditional Christian church first from its outward design. While traditional Christian churches tend to be built with intricate details, the Pentecostal megachurch is more simplistic from the outside. As in the Azusa Street Revival, they may be an informal place of worship, even a convention center or a warehouse. They might be set up in a tent or another temporary place or a large industrial-looking permanent building. The reasoning behind this may be related to a lack of funds due to the "newness" of Pentecostalism and focused location in communities of lower socioeconomic status. However, the churches do get heavy donations that seem to be spent in other ways besides creating marble structures and gold-plated crosses. The plainness of the Pentecostal church matches the philosophy of the movement, focusing on the advent of the everyday man and rejection of human leadership within the church. The role of the church in Pentecostalism in ironically not key to the religion. Followers gain their religious value, not through the preacher's message or the church community but through an individual relationship with God. This individualistic shift translates to the informality and "plainness" of the church. For example, Catholic churches tend to have architecture, not only that is grandiose but that creates the illusion of them being larger than they are. A piece of this is the tendency to build high, pointy facades that reach toward the heavens. The Catholic Church style-architecture instills a fear of God, almost an inaccessibility of God in which the preacher will enlighten the followers on how to proceed.[66] The richness, expensive paintings, and largeness of the building itself all invoke a quiet kind of restriction of behavior in the traditional church. Pentecostal churches, on the other hand, are designed with simplicity that allows individual relationships with God to take precedent over church leadership and standardized doctrine.[67] They encourage loudness, personal engagement, and a religious experience. With megachurches, everything about the church is big—just like their God. The crowds, the church itself, the multimedia broadcasting, the billboards are all disproportionately large.[68] Yet, all of these are designed with a sense of "plainness" and closeness to the ground, a focus on the people, and the accessibility of God himself.[69]

The design of the Pentecostal megachurch may have a sense of "plainness" as well not out of design but out of church doctrine. The "Nevius plan," embraced in new Pentecostal megachurches, especially in Korea, asserts that churches should be supported by local efforts and not outreaches of global entities.[70] This changes the physical church itself because a church born of global outreach will often have a Western-style design and be heavily financed. On the other hand, a local church will be more makeshift or from preexisting buildings and operate with lower initial funding. The Nevius plan also influences the architectural structures of new Pentecostal megachurches.

Disciplinary Power of the Church

Foucault identified ability to administer discipline as one of the key ways that the state achieves governmentality. The same can be said for the church. However, while the government is able to create prisons, fines, and penalties to enforce their rules, the church administers a sociospiritual violence. The church internalizes its doctrine within individuals through creating a social environment that puts shame on those who do not follow in the way of God. The powers of testimony, confession, and prayer encourage individuals to feel guilt, a feeling that encourages self-discipline. Not only the social exclusion repercussions of not following in the path of God, but the spiritual discipline that the church preaches entices followers into submission. This spiritual discipline works in realms, heaven, and earth. For those who do not follow in the ways of God, they will not get to go to heaven and be reunited with their God and their loved ones. In their life on earth, they also will not be blessed with God's grace, decreasing their potential for health and success. The Pentecostal church systematically reinforces this discipline in relation to specific Christian acts with lenience that invites Christian to return despite their interpretation of the doctrine.[71]

Effects of the "God Complex"

The God Complex has its origin in Western psychology, coined by Ernest Jones. In his book *Essays on Applied Psycho-Analysis*, Jones explained that some people think of themselves as a God, that they are infallible narcissists in their own solitary world.[72] For the purposes of this analysis, "God Complex" in this study is used not as this individual effect but as a societal belief in God reinforced by the technologies of the church. The processes of this have been described in the previous sections. However, the societal belief in God does cause a similar effect to what Jones meant by the "God Complex." This is, that for someone to believe in God is to believe in a singularity of knowledge, to believe that you know something or have experienced something others have not. Therefore, there is still a sort of narcissism within a Pentecostal belief of God. By knowing God and experiencing God, the Pentecostal subject becomes more divine themselves.

This sense of Pentecostal narcissism is evident through the spirit of missionary work. Pentecostalism, outlined in the origin of Pentecostalism in the introduction, was born in the United States by African Americans but spread throughout Africa by both Western and African missionaries. This cannot be a Western versus non-Western binary, because several important missionaries came from one African country to another, spreading God's word. This Pentecostal God Complex, or Pentecostal narcissism, reinforces certain beliefs and degrades others. Therefore, Pentecostal narcissism has political implications.

From the local to national government, all the way to the global world order, Christianity has had significant ties to power. Pentecostal churches are able to specifically reinforce political parties in African countries because they tie together Christian followers as well as followers of African indigenous religions. In addition, their Manichean properties increase their adaptability toward political situations. Pentecostalism's emphasis of God and the Devil as well as loose doctrine allows for candidates to claim personal religious knowledge or gifts that give them a divine mandate to power. Therefore, knowledge from the Pentecostal church can be used to reinforce power inequalities.[73]

Pentecostalism also has an eschatological effect on its subjects. This is the tendency for followers to focus on a type of apocalyptic thinking that causes them to disengage from the current situation in exchange for cosmic situations.[74] For example, a citizen who witnesses a malevolent regime take power may interpret this as a divine sign of the coming apocalypse. Through this thought process, there is no need to interview with the political process or organize any type of rebellion because Jesus can return any day to intervene. It also includes the tendency to pray for bad situations to resolve themselves instead of taking action. Through this perspective, a Pentecostal God Complex instills passivity.

Although Pentecostalism is often criticized for this passivity, another perspective is that the religious movement empowers individuals to be politically engaged. This perspective does not see godmentality as the process of making people passive subjects of a universal doctrine but as encouraged by the individualistic nature of the movement to think for themselves in a way that improves their community. In this way, Pentecostalism is a sort of rebellion against the top-down model of Christianity. Pentecostal followers are actively rejecting outside interpretations of the Bible and trusting in their own experience with the Bible, God, and the Holy Spirit. Therefore, individuals are more likely, through this logic, to think for themselves in political situation as well—and take action. In this way, Pentecostal discipleship encourages political engagement.[75] This may include fighting for human rights as a manifestation of fighting against sin.[76]

Seeing Pentecostalism in particular through the lens of a black theology would encourage political action and a postcolonial agenda.[77] This includes the black power movement in the United States and abroad that formalized throughout the 1960s. The term "black power" was coined during this time period, with radical black leaders taking an Afrocentric approach to Christian theology. This theology specifically rejected concepts surrounding the whiteness of Jesus and the hegemony of the West within the narrative of Christianity. Manifestations included images of black Jesus, emphasis of Afrocentric churches, and to use Christianity as a tool of liberation for oppressed peoples of African descent. This political engagement has been most visible in the opposition of the Pentecostal church in countries such as Nigeria to the corruption of politicians.[78]

Pentecostalism and Gender

An increasingly complex topic is the relationship between Pentecostal knowledge and gender. A frequently debated topic is whether the Pentecostal church is able to empower women. Those who say it does cite the way that women are able to participate by giving testimony in the church. They talk about the way that Pentecostalism focuses on the family, increasing the importance of women. Emphasis on faithfulness to partners and discouragement from drugs, crime, and alcohol encourage positive family relationships. Especially, Pentecostal churches depend on the leadership of the preacher's wife. She is often tasked with organizing social events, charitable efforts, and organizing the workings of the church. Pentecostal churches often depend on the material and spiritual labor of women, especially in black communities, that keep the interworking of the church intact.[79] Historically, the Pentecostal church has been a place that has deconstructed gender divisions and allowed for female participation.

Pentecostal ways of knowing can support women's empowerment through their emphasis on personal experience. Personal experience is a known component of a feminist epistemology, which deviates from patriarchal meta-narratives. Yet, interpretations of the Bible and of the religion itself limit the ability for Pentecostalism to be an empowering tool for women. Several Pentecostal preachers interpret the fall of man as Adam's failure to guide Eve toward salvation, reinforcing the patriarchy.[80] Pentecostalism perpetuates the gender stereotype of women as lacking sexual desire, restrictions on women's dress and actions, mostly limited to the private sphere, and a focus on men as leaders of their households. This patriarchal pattern is reinforced by God himself being a male. For these reasons, Pentecostalism may be empowering to women but is still reproductive of societal patriarchy. The claim that Pentecostalism practices gender equality represents a catachresis, a misrepresentation of the term "gender equality" as basic female inclusion.[81]

CONCLUSION: PENTECOSTAL KNOWLEDGE AS MODERNITY

Throughout this analysis Pentecostalism's unique character in African countries has been described as well as the processes it uses to subjunctivize its believers. In describing the Azusa Street Revival, the first Pentecostals were described as "discontent with modernity" in terms of Christianity and the oppressed state of African Americans. I've described the downfall of Pentecostalism as promoting eschatology and disengagement, as well as the potential for Pentecostalism to take after black theology and work toward political and social pan-African liberation. The blending of witchcraft beliefs, traditional African culture, and music as well as fusion of Western clothes and a focus on individual religious experience represent more than a religious movement. Pentecostalism is a response to globalization.[82] In the context of the African diaspora, it represents pan-African culture as well as Westernization. Therefore, Pentecostalism does not exist within modernity but is an alternative form of modern knowledge in itself.[83]

This can be interpreted, from a secular perspective, as a type of neo-exploitative modernity in which the elite of Africa are able to exploit the poorest under a religious guise.[84] However, it can also be viewed as the much-needed window of opportunity for epistemic liberation of the Global South. Pentecostalism rejects secularity and encourages pride, liberation, and morality. While it is unclear whether Pentecostal followers will consistently respond with political and moral engagement or individualism and passivity, Pentecostalism has the power to create an alternative model for development than those offered by the West.[85] While Pentecostalism in Africa has often been generalized in this chapter for the purposes of a coherent argument, the reality of a Pentecostal modernity is uncertain in a singular philosophy or application.[86] Perhaps the most valuable offer that Pentecostalism has to an alternative African modernity is the validation of the individual religious experience within itself. This is a modern notion of knowledge that restructures its economy based off of personal and religious relationships that the colonial and neocolonial projects disrupt.[87]

Part III

KINGSHIP IDEOLOGIES AND EPISTEMOLOGIES

Chapter 8

Kingship: Ideology and Epistemology

Narratives deal with such specific labels as the Alaafin, Ooni, Alake, Olubadan, Asantehene, and many others, whereby each king is described in terms of particular histories and practices. Most certainly, the labels can be configured into two terms, namely "kingship" and "monarchy," both of which are often used interchangeably. The *Oxford English Dictionary* defines kingship as a monarchical government—a type of regime distinguished by the rule of one sovereign leader, a king or a queen, over a political unit.[1] Moreover, the *Oxford Companion to the Bible* lists kingship and monarchy under the same definition and further explains both concepts via ancient Near Eastern texts and myths that accept them as a governing organization ordained by the divine.[2]

However, the *Oxford English Dictionary* also characterizes kingship as "the fact of being king," as well as "the action of reigning as a king"—specifications that suggest that kingship cannot exclusively be understood through the lens of modern-day notions of politics.[3] This definition indicates that kingship transcends decision-making and includes the institutional function and personality of kings, the institution, as well as their symbolic importance in society.

In his book, *Medieval Kingship*, Henry A. Myers examines the nuances between kingship and monarchy. He argues that while the concepts overlap (both feature one ruler, who possesses anywhere from absolute to limited power), kingship focuses on "the art or science by which such a ruler governs well."[4] Myers asserts that kings are held accountable for the overall well-being and unity of a community, whereas monarchs are relegated to a political role that largely eschews the ritual. He, above all, points to medieval Germanic kingship as representative of his definition of kingship. For instance, medieval Germanic kingship entailed serving as a mediator between the gods and humanity to secure success in war and good fortune in peace. Germanic kings were expected to possess a quality known as *Heil*, luck/ fortune achieved through careful calculation, and to have superhuman health, courage, and perception.[5] Germanic kings, as opposed to Myers' conception of monarchical leaders, were accountable for all aspects of society; their power and duty was not confined by a separation between the spiritual and the political.

In contrast to Myers' distinction, W. M. Spellman merges the terminology divide between kingship and monarchy by tracing the widespread phenomenon of monarchical structures to the earliest reaches of human history (namely, hunter-gatherer societies). This synthesis reveals kingship's meaning within the context of a monarchical structure. Spellman characterizes kingship as the culmination of foundational monarchical ideals that authorize a person to rule, such as "charismatic leadership," "victory in battle," and the maintenance of a "monopoly over alleged meditational powers between the gods and the people."[6] Spellman argues that at the center of early monarchical structures were religious obligations and popular support for the ordering of society.[7] Spellman observes that the belief in the king as a supernatural intermediary was paramount to early monarchies around the world.[8]

Consistent with Spellman's observations, early African societies were distinguished by decentralized, self-reliant villages founded on notions of tradition and kinship. Individualism was rejected in favor of coordination among the lineage community. However, after about 900 AD, power was consolidated, and African kingdoms emerged to include a broader number of clan members with the goal of mutual defense and an increase in production. The expansion of trade led to the first monarchies, as political systems were needed to address a higher population and resulting inequalities concerning the sharing of resources.[9] In regard to political leadership, a king was often chosen by an assembly of military leaders and, once confirmed, engaged in polygyny with a majority of the lineage groups to secure a comprehensive influence. African kingships concentrated on the possession of divine power, which was achieved via rituals that upheld ancestral traditions and protected the community, but they also varied widely due to the continent's diversity in climate, topography, culture, and languages.[10]

The meanings of monarchy and kingship have changed over time, and that over the past quincentenary, the fragmentation of Christianity as well as the rise of nationalism and democracy, the expansion of technology (specifically communication and industry), and the distribution of wealth and education have decreased the power and prevalence of traditional monarchies founded on kingship. The most significant source of variety in kingships is the degree in which they vary in political and religious natures. Through the following sections, the separate spheres of the political, cultural, and religious will be challenged. However, it is generally understood that in the system of modern statehood, many modern African kingdoms have remained intact separate from the formal political power of the state. Today, monarchies in many parts of the world, and therefore kingships, are often viewed as symbolic relics of a cultural past and possess relatively little political or military capital in comparison to the increasing number of democratic institutions.[11] This section challenges that notion by citing the historical and modern powers, both formal and informal, of kingships in Africa.

One notable generalization is the absorption of females as leaders into the term "king." It is true that in several cases in African history, as elsewhere, queens have filled the role of kingships. The Lovedu in South Africa, for example, are ruled by female chiefs almost exclusively. Female leaders such as Cleopatra, Queen Aminatu, Queen Nandi, and Queen Nefertiti certainly left their marks on Africa's history. Females in kingdoms throughout history have been influential as the wives, mothers, and daughters of kings.[12] A female fulfilling the role of the kingship is an exception to a convention. For the purposes of simplification, I will uniformly use the term "king" to describe the individual occupying the kingship.

CONCEPTS OF IDEOLOGY

Whichever the religious affiliation of the kingdom, kingships are religious in nature. A secular kingship has seldom, if ever, existed. A king is seen as chosen by spiritual powers to some degree through most kingship ideologies. Thus, the second terminology that I seek to define is that of ideology. The European origin of the term "ideology" was coined by Destutt de Tracy in the 1780s, during the French Revolution led by Maximilien Robespierre and his radical militaristic cohorts. De Tracy created the terminology to explain how the French people could tolerate an oppressive leader as the king. Therefore, the etymology of ideology is tied to the idea of kingship. Conventionally, however, ideology is connotated with the oppressive nature of kingship.[13] The term references the values of the enlightenment championing democracy over religious tradition.

The use of "ideology" became more popular in the nineteenth century with the work of Karl Marx. Marx emphasized that ideology was the only way to understand how historical situations were sustained in their times.[14] He related ideology and religion but did not equate them. On religion he said that "religion is the language of the oppressed creature."[15] This also shows his bias to associate ideology with oppression. Marx's work solidified the relationship between ideology and oppression in the political discourse. The etymological origins of ideology define it as a set of values shared by a group to justify institutions of power.

In the twentieth century, Max Weber brought the idea of ideology from political discourse into the field of sociology. Indeed, he did this through his analysis of modernity. Weber argued that the source of progress in history is society becoming more rational. In order for it to be more rational, it would have to be separate from elusive ideologies. Weber defined modernity as a measure of the freedom of society from ideology.[16] Critics of Weber point out his denial of his own ideology. Weber equates a lack of ideology with modernity. Yet, this value of secularization and rationality is part of a larger Western ideology.[17] Despite his contradictions, Weber established ideology as a key agent of change in historical processes. Ideology influences society's norms, values, and thought processes. It is the foundation of large-scale political systems as well as individual moral codes. Kingships were able to use ideology to support powerful institutions and facilitate historical change.

One shift in the multidisciplinary academic work of ideology is a shift in instrumentalist to social analysis. An instrumentalist perspective of ideology looks at how ideology legitimizes the power of a kingdom. This perspective does not explain the role of ideology in everyday interactions. An instrumentalist approach is limited to abstract, formal functions of society. It is able to gain the essential workings of the political system but is unable to relate it to the daily lives of people who lived there. These daily social interactions reinforced the religious ideology. The religious ideology then supported the hierarchical social structure of a kingdom. The social perspective of anthropological ideology looks at kingship from a bottom-up approach. It analyzes the daily interactions and beliefs of individual people to see how they contributed to the role of the kingship at large.[18]

The origins of the term "ideology" lie in explaining the oppression possible by a kingship. As a result, a tendency in analyzing ideology is equating ideologies with intentional oppression. As exemplified by Destutt de Tracey's and Marx's arguments, ideology can serve to perpetuate oppression. However, there are two false pretexts in equating ideology with oppression. The first is that these peoples think in a different, nonrational way. It assumes subjects of kingdoms are gullible to fall into ideologies that do not benefit them, while modern society has evolved to avoid doing so. This is a biased analysis of ideology from modern Western perspectives. Scholars possess ideologies, hence it is not possible to neutrally analyze ideologies.[19] There is always a relationship between the scholars analyzing historical ideologies to their own. The second false assumption is that ideologies are intentionally created for oppression. Ideologies are the result of natural social and religious processes that all humans possess.[20] Individuals from the top of the kingship hierarchy are often as immersed in these ideologies as their subjects. Records from art objects in ancient Egypt found references to the divine kingship in relation to Horus even in the utmost sphere of influence. This is evidence that the creators of policy believed in its power.[21] Indeed, viewing ideology as the intentional justification for oppression only warps the view of the historian, while the result is that the concept of ideology, viewed through the lens of oppression justification, leads to analysis that is biased.[22] My analysis does not portray the ideologies of kingdoms through oppression. This assumes malevolence of leaders and gullibility of the religious. Instead, I seek to understand the natural social and religious processes that lead kings to come to power and maintain that power.

An alternative framework to the oppression perspective of ideology is collective ruling. Coercive ruling is the oppression of people based solely on violence and force. Collective ruling may include some violence and force but is based on the ruler maintaining the welfare of the community. This perspective applies to African kingships. In African epistemologies, social relationships are often privileged over individual interests. Political interactions in Africa are better seen through a collective lens. Individual interests are often seen as a threat to society.[23] Power is given to the ruler, not because the individual is not capable of deviation but because they submit to what is best for society as a whole.[24] Through this model, a king does not intentionally create an ideology to support his rule. He exaggerates the social, political, and religious ideals that support the community. Creative power is the idea that a king utilizes preexisting ideology to create meaning. This meaning is often religious. It provides explicit justification for individuals to participate in the structure of the community. Creative power gives cultural and religious meaning to otherwise ordinary events. The king uses this created meaning to maintain relationships and dynamics of society and preserve a way of life.[25] By understanding ideology through the view of natural historical and religious processes, we are able to more neutrally understand how ideology supported the power of kingships.

THE CHARACTER OF AFRICAN KINGSHIPS

While displays of kingship vary across time and place, common themes, such as the sacralization of power and an emphasis on the ritual, unite them and constitute kingship as an ideology.[26] Ideology arises from the thought patterns of an individual, group, or culture. These thoughts include convictions and assumptions about the world that help an individual understand and cope with his/her reality.[27] Traditional kingship ideology rests upon a community's belief in the powers of the sovereign ruler, which are situated within an accepted spiritual framework. Moreover, the community must view these

kingly powers as necessary for protection against human, natural, and supernatural threats.[28] While kingships are united by a common ideology, differences in the importance of centralized politics, such as control over a military
or the economy, demonstrate that kingships exist along a continuum. Myths
are, therefore, created to sustain those ideologies, insulate, and preserve them
through programmed reenactment ceremonies.

This continuum is best illustrated with examples from other African
sources. For example, Mamprusi kingship in Ghana was largely ritual, with
little evidence suggesting any centralized economic or military institutions.
According to the Mamprusi, their kingdom obtained kingship from a fugi-
tive prince who became the first Mamprusi king (Nayiiri). After the first
Nayiiri, kings were enthroned via a ceremonial cycle that included a competition among chiefs (kings' sons), a secret vote among elders to determine
the successor, the forceful relocation of the successor to the former king's
palace, and ritual practices to prepare the successor for kingship. These
practices included bathing and shaving rites, animal sacrifices, blessings by
the commoner-ancestors, and a drum performance of the names of kings and
other royals (both living and dead) to celebrate the history of kingship and to
invoke the presence of their ancestors. From this process a Mamprusi king
was formed and stripped of his previous identity.

While some view monarchs as wielders of absolute authority, Mamprusi
kings were ruled by kingship. After being enthroned, the Nayiiri faced the
possibility of regicide by the Mamprusi people to symbolize the authority of
their culture over nature. If he lived, the Nayiiri was restricted to his palace
at specific times and had to separate himself from the earth via animal skins
obtained from enthronement rituals.[29] Thus, the Mamprusi kingship dominated the Nayiiri and isolated him from his people. The solitude achieved by
rituals eliminated the king's allegiances to certain groups, which generated
equal associations between him and each person within the community. This
isolation and transformation in self also separated the king from typical cultural identities related to kinship and domesticity. The Nayiiri was no longer a
member of mainstream society, maintained little power to change the institution of kingship, and, therefore, his fate was determined by rituals supported
by the people.[30]

The kingdom of Benin, in contrast, combined the ritual with military
prowess and economic might in the evolution of kingship. Benin kingship,
like that of the Mamprusi, was defined by divine authority and characterized
by extensive rituals. The Edaiken (the heir apparent to the Benin throne)
must visit key shrines and sacred Benin locations before enthronement. One
such place is Ughoton, which was the gateway to and major port of Benin
during the empire's height of power. At Ughoton, Oba Ewuare (c. 1440)
allegedly emerged victorious in a wrestling match with the goddess Olokun

for ownership of sacred coral beads. Once confirmed as king, the Ọba participates in divine kingship rituals, such as the Ugie Erha Ọba's ceremony to honor his departed father. Before partaking in the rites, the Ọba must have his hands ritually washed by a designated official using an aquamanile (see figure 8.1).[31] This reverence for ancestors displays the importance of the past in Benin culture and portrays kingship as an institution that can hold society together through tradition. While ritualized activity extends across Benin's history, the empire's kingship also involves transitions in monarchical power. Benin kingship evolved into one of military leadership due to drastic reforms enacted during the fifteenth century; these changes were generated in response to an intense power competition among the Ọba and his chiefs. Ọba Ewuare led these reforms as one of Benin's first warrior kings and consequently expanded the monarch's authority; this era lasted for about two centuries and was characterized by imperial expansion.[32] The Ọba also engaged in international trade during the European exploration of Africa in which he exchanged African slaves for firearms and other goods. However, the Benin Kingdom's power declined during the nineteenth century due to changes in trade and the Ọba's implementation of an unpopular personal export monopoly. In 1897, the kingdom fell to the British over access to Benin's resources. The British attack ended the Ọba's reign and added to the mythical nature of Benin monarchy. Although the British ruled Nigeria until 1960, the monarchy was partially restored in 1914 with the coronation of Ọba Eweka II due to the demands of the chiefs and people.[33] Although the Ọba has lost considerable political power in a postcolonial world, the Benin kingship continues to symbolize and support a unified Bini and Edo ethnic identity based on tradition and culture.[34]

A common ideology connects kingships; however, they differ in the amount of centralized military and economic power that kings possess. Some kings, such as the Mamprusi ruler, have been confined to the ritual, while other kings, such as the Ọba Ewuare, utilized the ritual to obtain greater authority from his chiefs and people. Although the number of monarchies has decreased, many cultural loyalists, specifically in Africa, continue to celebrate kingship as an important part of their history.

Africa's history includes powerful kingdoms and substantial ethnographic edifices. The Pyramids of Giza are remnants of the ancient Egyptian Empire from prehistoric times, and the city of Aksum, in the Horn of Africa region, is from the Ethiopian Empire of the thirteenth century. The Walls of Benin are one of the world's longest wall structures and evidence of the Benin Empire's greatness in the fifteenth century. Countless ruins, myths, and oral and written accounts preserve the histories and cultures of great kingdoms that once organized vast groups of diverse individuals to work toward common goals. Each kingdom developed intricate shared cultures that included languages,

Figure 8.1.   Durbar Festival Nigeria. *Source:* Toyin Falola.

art, and religion; the sheer size of these empires indicates their political and military advancements.

Effective leadership was vital for the political and cultural development of these groups. The leader at the center of each empire's culture and politics was a king, and kingship took a variety of forms across African history with distinct functions, garments, and traditions. However, there are common patterns in the way these kings used ideology to create and maintain their empires. The ideologies were understood through religious epistemologies that allowed kings to obtain, maintain, and apply their power. The nature of modern kingdoms has changed in Africa, influenced by globalization and secularization, but the ideology of kingdoms still holds implications for African epistemologies.

THE CONTEXT OF EPISTEMOLOGY

Ideology describes specific knowledge, such as values and ideals, and epistemology describes the methodological approach to that knowledge. Epistemic values determine what type of evidence qualifies as knowledge. Ideological and epistemic values are interrelated, and both influence how kings gain power.

Consider two different approaches for predicting rainfall: those of a technological weatherman and a spiritual rain-man. The weatherman's epistemic values privilege the scientific work of experts and the reliability of technology. He uses expert advice and technology, such as sonar, to predict when rain will fall. A rain-man's epistemic values privilege the holistic nature of the universe, which combines religious and scientific aspects. He will use mythology, observational knowledge, and religion to predict when rain will fall. Both are methodical approaches to prediction, but they have different epistemic foundations—the idea of knowledge for the weatherman is not the same as the idea of knowledge for the rain-man. The weatherman values empirical evidence with secular pretexts, and the ideological value of secularity in the public domain influences his empirical methodology of research. This ideology both creates and is created by epistemological approaches.

The epistemological approach of African Indigenous Religions (AIRs) provides insight into the knowledge that legitimizes African kingship. These ideologies equated natural occurrences, such as changes in health or weather, with religious events, legitimizing experiential and spiritual knowledge to understand the natural and human worlds holistically.[35] In contrast, academia values a secular epistemological approach. Secularity is often used to separate knowledge from religion, but it is not a neutral approach—the absence of religion is a "religious" philosophy.[36] Secular approaches suggest that kings create ideology to manipulate the governance of kingdoms. An epistemologically conscious approach uses African epistemologies to analyze the ideology of kingship and its divine rhetoric.

Analyzing ideology's role in African kingship can isolate historical epistemological approaches; an understanding of these approaches allows us to compare them with modern approaches. African epistemology, which is an umbrella term for all African religions, science, and philosophies, emphasizes the holistic nature of the universe and the interconnectedness of disciplines. It is never examined independently of Western epistemology and often described in contrast to it. An African epistemological approach to medicine, for example, would include social and spiritual remedies alongside different medicinal approaches. The concept of African epistemologies deconstructs the privileged role of Western epistemologies, and it serves to celebrate the benefits of African approaches to scientific problems.[37]

African kingdoms are not secular states functioning as kingdoms; they are cultural and religious social groups that often take on political responsibility. They are supported by religious epistemic values and ideology, and understanding the ideological support for these kingdoms aids in understanding history as those who lived it. It also provides a better understanding of current African epistemological approaches, offering a critical lens for viewing all epistemological and ideological values that are related to institutions of power.

THE EVOLUTION OF KINGSHIPS

Kingships form through historical, religious, and social patterns when the community values emerging from these systems allow society to have a single ruler. The king meets the society's religious and political needs, functioning as its cultural center and reinforcing that role through religious and economic processes. Through these processes, ideology reinforces the institutionalized power of kingships.

The nature of a king's power over people is an ongoing debate in anthropology. Too much focus on the religious aspect of power marginalizes the practical aspects of the kingship, but the kingship's mandate stems from the ideology of religion—it cannot function without religious symbolism. Anthropologists resolve this duality by regarding the religious and political aspects of kingship as equal. The anthropologist Ernst Kantorowicz examined

Figure 8.2.   Waribo Uranta, an Opobo chief. *Source:* **Toyin Falola.**

how subjects view their king as a mortal and the king's role as immortal;[38] the individual is not as powerful as the institutional role.

Political scientists and sociologists believe that kingdoms form naturally along social or religious lines. Ideology is only a piece of larger historical patterns in these theories. An alternate, evolutionary political theory examines how kingdoms form through societal patterns. In this model, a collection of kinship groups becomes too large to distribute resources effectively. A centralized power, usually a king, develops to perform the role of resource distribution.

Evolutionary political theory explains that the formation of centralized government is followed by the pressure to decentralize.[39] Ideology develops to support the centralized government's role in distributing resources, and bigger societies use their ideology to absorb smaller ones, creating empires. As the ideology supports the king over time, it defends the empire against the natural pressure to decentralize and justifies the inconvenience of centralization.

This theory is supported by kings who have dissociated from their kinship groups.[40] Archaeological evidence shows that kings from nonroyal families would often omit their family name from palaces and burial sites. Many kings dissociated themselves from their original families to become neutral symbols of their societies. In this pattern, kings emerge from a society of kinship groups to exist at the cultural center of a society based on rank.[41]

There are two major criticisms of evolutionary political theory. It champions rationalism as political development's ultimate goal, ignoring other epistemological approaches, such as religious studies.[42] The second problem with the theory is that it does not completely capture the king's role. In several modern kingdoms, monarchs hold little or no political power—political evolutionary theory explains how kings gain power, but it does not explain how they maintain their influence in the presence of other political systems.

In contrast, religious evolutionary theory examines how kingship emerges from the formation of religions. James Frazer, the early-twentieth-century anthropologist, is the most famous proponent of this theory. Frazer focused on the development of divine kingship ideology in ancient Western civilizations, and his basic argument was that all kingdoms began from religious cults. These cults focused on fertility and the dying or killing of a god on Earth. He argued that kings were first thought of as incarnations of the gods and the first to be sacrificed. They gradually became the center of political and cultural power, assuming the role of gods on Earth.[43] After Frazer's work was published, anthropologists applied it to other, non-Western concepts. This theory is not a flawless model, and it has attracted many critics. But it does explain how religions carry their ideology to political structures. Evidence has shown that government structures often emerge from preexisting religious ritual structures.[44] Anthropologists have also found examples of ritual killings that involve kings, supporting Frazer's idea that kingships developed from fertility cults.[45]

Religious justifications for a king's power are also practical. To command the respect necessary to head a centralized government, a king must be venerated within society. It is difficult to develop this level of respect independently and much easier to create a king from an existing source—especially when starting with a god that is already venerated.[46]

THE DIVINITY OF THE KING

Kingdoms unite people through religious ideologies and expand through ideological integration—expanding kingdoms use myth to solidify their king's divine role. The Zulu created a vast kingdom in the nineteenth century, and the great military accomplishments of South Africa's Shaka Zulu were vital for the empire's conquests. However, the empire could not have integrated diverse people without a unified ideology to explain the nature of the universe and the king's role in mediating the cosmos. Lands conquered by the Zulu embraced their culture and mythology even when the territories did not become part of the Zulu Empire. Kingdoms were created through ideological

Figure 8.3.   Housa people in Nigeria. *Source*: Toyin Falola.

integration.[47] The Mongols integrated various kingdoms through a different method: they left ideological systems intact in their conquered territories. This strategy repurposed existing religious ideologies to serve their goals, similar to the way Europeans blended Christianity with African religions to support colonialism's authority.

Ideology's importance in African kingdoms can be seen in the relationship between government and religion. In the sixteenth century, the King of Kandy in Sri Lanka believed that baptism would give him power. Through his first contact with the Portuguese, he agreed to be baptized but insisted on secrecy—he did not want to share any of the ceremony's power with those below him, and he did not want his people to turn against him for following a different ideology. Christian baptism was incompatible with the ideology of his kingship, and religion was so integral to the kingdom's structure that his reign could not continue without it.[48] Opposing religions threaten a kingdom's ideology because of the king's mythological nature. Mythological stories, taking the form of oral histories, relate true events by word of mouth to support the king's divinity. Anthropologists have used these mythologies to reconstruct world histories.[49]

Kings are often analyzed with a dual nature, having physical and spiritual bodies.[50] The king is a physical person with an individual personality and biological health, but the king is also a spiritual being who has a power relationship with the gods. This dual nature means that the king is not seen as equivalent to a god—instead, the king is an imperfect solution to the human condition that requires contact with the divine.[51] The role is more than that of a simple ruler in either politics or religion; it manages Earth and the cosmos, facilitating those relationships.[52] The king's physical powers on earth are reinforced through metaphorical power over life and death.

The king has a monopoly on violence within his kingdom's physical and spiritual worlds, able to inflict violence without repercussions. Several empires with violent histories demonstrate the king's power for creating violence, such as the Zulu, Benin, and Buganda. A famous example is the kingdom of Ganda, whose king would randomly kill his own subjects to demonstrate his power.[53] The king was expected, but not required, to use the monopoly on violence justly.

In African kingdoms, the kingship's ultimate power comes from the religious ability to mediate life and death through the spiritual world.[54] This mediation, which protects life through religious rituals and traditions, reaffirms the king's influence over the cosmos. The king's health was thought to influence the prosperity of the kingdom, meaning that the king was not required to explicitly exercise the power to protect life; it was active through his mere existence.[55] The perceived implications of the king's health explain traditions of elaborate rituals and sacrificial killings.

Many different religions link god and king, including the Christian idea of Jesus Christ, considered the "King of Kings."[56] The Pharaoh of ancient Egypt is another historical example. The title, "Pharaoh," was applied to monarchs in Egypt's first dynasty, before the influence of the Roman Empire. Egypt's first dynasty lasted from about 3100 BC until about 2900 BC, and during this period, religious ideology was inseparable from Egyptian politics. The Pharaoh was the state's political leader, with complete control over the land and its political and economic policies. He was the central commander for tax collection and all military decisions, exercising great practical power. And he was not seen merely as the ruler of a land but as the mediator between the gods and the people. The Pharaoh maintained Maat, the order of the cosmos, facilitating all religious doctrines and rituals. The king held this position as an incarnation of Horus, worshipped as a god.

THE KING'S ROLE IN SOCIETY

A king functions within society as the symbol of a kingdom and as its cultural regulator. The king is the symbol of centralized power and the manifestation of an ideology, representing cultural and religious values along with the traditions accompanying them. The king becomes a symbol by defying cultural norms and setting the royal person apart from society.[57] A king is often physically isolated and may avoid performing everyday tasks, possibly being prevented from walking or speaking under certain conditions. A king can often define social norms by defying them—in extreme examples, the king may demonstrate royal authority by performing atrocious crimes such as incest or murder. By performing taboo acts that defy traditional ideology, the king achieves separation from traditional ideology.

The king's actions create cultural norms that affect the kingdom's ideology. When the king's health is considered to influence the entire kingdom—indicative of larger forces in the cosmos—individual people and communities begin to see their health also connected with religious matters. Individuals may see their sickness as indicative of a larger evil.

The king also exerts explicit control over social norms, defining how social structures, sexuality, and the flow of resources should be treated. Historically, the Bemba of modern-day Zambia linked the king's sex life with the overall well-being of the kingdom. Sexual dysfunction was thought to harm the kingdom, and this notion was projected into Bemba culture on a smaller scale. The sexual misconduct of individuals could negatively affect those around them, just as with the kingship.[58] The king could control the larger kingdom through his personal life by imposing ideological values.

Because the king is believed to influence the fortunes of his people, the fate of a kingdom can affect how the king is perceived. The "scapegoat" sociological theory of kingship views the king as the manifestation of a time period within a kingdom, and all of the historical events taking place during a king's reign are personified by the monarch's existence.[59] This role makes the king vulnerable to being blamed for hardship—famines that take place while a king is in power could be punishments for a king's misdeeds or deficiencies. During times of great stress, the king may be blamed as the cause of all evils in the kingdom; the people may channel their frustration into the demise of their king. As in Frazer's cult theory of fertility sacrifices, the king is sacrificed and a new king is chosen, which can happen through ritual killing or dethronement. The demise of the king becomes a symbol of renewal.[60]

Scapegoat theory explains how kingdoms endure for thousands of years as political systems: blame is placed on a specific king, without criticizing the institution of kingship. Failure within the kingdom was an individual king's failure to uphold royal responsibilities—the failure of the king was not a failure of government—and the ascension of a new king restored hope in the system. As historical forces drove different kings to rise and fall, the ideology continued and the underlying structure of the system remained stable. The king's symbolic nature was equivalent to that of a scapegoat in waiting.[61]

The scapegoat theory of kingship is comparable to India's caste system, a social hierarchy that ties into the country's unique religious and cultural traditions. Priests are at the highest tier of the system, and peasants, or "the untouchables," are at the lowest. Traditional religious interpretations of the caste system have the untouchables absorbing society's spiritual filth, embodying society's evil while the priests embody its sacredness. In kingships and in the caste system, society blames a single role for the sins of an entire generation, condemning the scapegoats to hold themselves in higher regard. In both cases, blame is a function of social psychology shaping political institutions of power.[62]

Evidence for the scapegoat theory of kingship is also present in the religious epistemology of Christianity. Jesus Christ, the son of God incarnate, provides life and fertility on earth and spreads the word of his father before he is sacrificed for the sins of humanity. This is consistent with Frazer's idea about the origin of religions and kingships; Jesus is frequently called the "king of kings" and his kingdom is described as all humanity. In the story of Christianity, Jesus not only functions as a model of fertility cult sacrifices, but he also serves as a scapegoat. The death of Jesus symbolizes the cleansing of humanity's sins—by paying the ultimate price, he saves all who follow him.

Christianity provides insight into the ideology of kingship and serves as an example of Frazer's theory in a modern religious kingdom. Just as kings were sacrificed to gods, Jesus as king was also sacrificed to his Father—God to forgive the sins of his people. Kings take on the sins of their nation, either through their symbolic death or outright assumption of blame in the same way that Jesus absorbed and absolved the sins of all humankind.

THE RITUALS OF KINGSHIP

The mythological foundation of kingship ideology establishes the king's connection with deities and proves that the king deserves the respect of kingship.[63] Ritual reinforces this mythology through ceremonies and repeated oralities that maintain its relevance, and each reinforces the other.[64] Ritual killings—made famous through Frazer's theory of the origin of religions—are one such ritual that supports the ideology of the king, but they are controversial in anthropology. Pritchard is one such critic who has argued that the ritual killing of kings is rare. He asserts that the idea is a symbolic tale used to ensure a smooth transition of power from one king to the next.

The king's dual nature provides the symbolism for ritual killings. As both a divine and a physical person, the king's failing health has a negative effect on the kingdom. In many kingships, it is ideal for the king to avoid poor physical health—subjects might suffocate the king intentionally once his health starts failing, minimizing the potential for the king's gradual decline to have ill effects on the kingdom. This shocking act, performed on a venerated figure, supports the religious ideology of the kingship. Historical records of ritual killings exist among the Shilluk,[65] who believed that their king was possessed by the Nyikang, the first monarch who held the kingship. A ritual was performed to transfer the spirit of Nyikang properly, killing the existing king and transferring the spirit into a wooden effigy that would hold the spirit until the coronation of the next Reth. There are also many kingdoms in which ritual killings rarely, if ever, occurred.

The repetition of oralities, which reinforce the role of mythology and ritual, passes down cultural values that influence the nature of ideology. To understand this influence, consider the cultural influence of Yoruba women. In the patriarchal culture of ancient Yorubaland, women were subordinate to the males who held dominant roles in society. However, the responsibility of child-rearing gave women the power to change the way that society treated them through oralities. By sharing their stories through these oralities, they made a lasting change on Yoruba society.[66] Kings can also use oralities to support the ideology of kingship. In the same way that Yoruba women changed their society, kings can change the ideology of their kingdoms, incorporating legitimizing mythology into oralities that support their rule.

The ideology of kingship can also be supported through physical objects. In preliterate societies, symbolic objects were the primary way of communicating power.[67] The materialization of culture created shared experiences and provided a physical way to control the ideology that was shared.[68] Symbolic objects frequently took the form of cultic objects, such as weapons, tools, and ornaments that symbolized power. They could also be more specific symbols, such as the giraffe seen in several AIRs, which indicates an orator who can see the future.[69]

Communities used masks in rituals to symbolize individuals possessed by spirits.[70] Kings used similar items, such as the golden stool of the Asante or the large beaded crowns of Yoruba rulers, to demonstrate their closeness to the gods and their power on earth. Both examples show how kingships changed ordinary people into kings through rituals and symbolism.[71] The rituals could involve the installation of new monarchs, the reconfirmation of monarchs for a new year, or cult activities at royal tombs.

The unification of Upper and Lower Egypt exemplified links between material symbolism, politics, and religion in ancient Egypt. It was heralded as an event that pleased the cosmos and marked the beginning of a new empire. For hundreds of years, the kings of lower Egypt had traditionally worn a red crown and kings of upper Egypt had worn a white crown. After unification, the new Pharaoh wore a red and white crown to acknowledge the unification, representing the Pharaoh's central role as the symbol of the entire empire and its justification in the cosmos.

Rituals demonstrate a bottom-up approach to ideology, especially at the community level. They show how the daily lives of individuals supported the larger ideology of the king's power.[72] Kings also supported their power through demonstrations of wealth. Mansa Musa, the king of Mali, undertook a journey from Timbuktu to the Holy Mecca that showcased his great riches, gaining much respect for his empire across the continent.

Other symbols of the king's power were included in the king's death and burial. In the Pyramids of Giza, Pharaohs were buried along with their possessions in a ritualistic way to aid them after death. In life, the king's dwelling was a strong symbol of power. These dwellings could be large palaces, such as in Giza, or they could be shrines to the gods, such as with the Buganda, Sakalava, and Lozi.

Kings can support their ideology by allocating economic goods. In sub-Saharan Africa, metal was a very important resource for household activities, farming, and war. Metallurgy was vital to the survival of kingdoms, and it became synonymous with power in places such as Rwanda and Burundi. Kings were trained in metallurgy, and the king's crest incorporated the sign of the metallurgist. These kings moderated the flow of power to various population centers through their decisions to mine, trade, and allocate metal.[73]

The Zulu Empire's allocation of milk is another example. Milk was one of the primary sources of nutrition for the Zulu, and this cultural norm spread as their empire grew. Shaka Zulu controlled his empire's population and social structure by allocating milk. Cows belonged to the king, and Shaka was the first one to receive the milk. After royal assistants had taken Shaka Zulu's share of milk, young men received their shares to reinforce their importance to society. Older men and the rest of society received their milk after that. By changing the distribution of cows, and how much milk people received, Shaka Zulu controlled population growth.[74] Milk was so integrated into the Zulu kingdom that the verb "kleza," to drink milk, was equated with being young.

MODERN KINGDOMS

The processes of globalization and secularization have affected modern kingdoms in Africa. The traditional institution of kingship held the explicit ability to declare and enforce orders, and the political powers of the king included authority over a state's political, economic, and military decisions.[75] These powers frequently provided monopolies on violence and the circulation of goods.[76] Kings also held the power to seek alliances and resources to bolster their political power.[77]

Modern kings in Africa live in the contexts of states and they have not retained their explicit political powers; the primary sources of a modern king's influence are religious and cultural authority. This authority is legitimized through conventions and tradition, and its influence can be as significant as power that has physical manifestations. While power is explicit, authority is more dependent on ideology. It can shape behavior preventatively, without the need for repercussions.[78] Although modern kings can use their authority to influence their people and protect the interests of their cultural groups, this authority is challenged by globalization and secularization.

Global pressures for secularization and statehood have disintegrated the fabric of kingdoms over time. African kings resisted changing their empires to monotheism because religious values and views of the world were integral to their roles—change was detrimental to the king's rule. The idea of a statehood is a modern invention when compared to the whole of human history. Kings of the past were cultural, religious, and political leaders; separating religious and political processes poses challenges to the way kingdoms function.

Colonialism changed kingdoms in Africa. The "Indirect Rule" system retained traditional systems of government so that Europeans spent less effort on administration. However, Europeans also worked to teach Christianity, which undermined the ideology of traditional ruling systems. And European exploitation of resources and people further undermined faith in the traditional rulership of kingdoms. The result was ideological chaos.

Some African kingdoms, such as the kingdom of Oyo, showed great resilience and continued into modern times. They preserved their culture through mythology, tradition, and religion for hundreds of years. However, postcolonial Africa became divided into secular states where traditional kingdoms created a duality between statehood and kingship. States did not hold monopolies over the faith and ideology of their people, and the kingdoms lacked the political ability to enforce their authority.

Various cultural kingdoms have needed to function together under one government. Statehood is supposed to accommodate a large variety of religions, but secularism is often incompatible with the ideology of religious kingdoms. The colonization and secularization of groups within Ghana show how the pressures of secularization have changed the nature of kingdoms in Africa over time. In 2002, attempts to increase the secularization of Ghana's government resulted in great confusion over the heir to the crown of the Dagbon.[79] The government's inability to resolve the issue was perceived as a failure of the state, causing conflict and division that did not previously exist.[80] Secularization created instability.

THE CHANGING NATURE OF KINGSHIP

A few kingships still function as states in Africa, although in many cases the king's role has been diminished. Modern kingdoms in Africa are based on religious authority and political influence, and the destruction of modern kingdoms creates conflict. Two colonial formations, Lesotho and Swaziland, are governed by kings under modern constitutional frameworks. Modern kingdoms are different from historical kingdoms and current states—historical kingdoms had religious and political power, but current states solely wield political power.

The religious power and political influence of modern kingdoms is exercised through their cultural influence.[81] Kings add voices that complicate the already complex political processes under dispute in modern states, and it is tempting to exclude the influence of modern kingdoms when considering efforts to create institutional change. However, kingdoms must be included in modern political processes because their interests represent African epistemic concerns. Many African communities still respect and defer to their religious kingdoms for cultural norms and direction.

The tension between kingdoms and governments is a conflict between new and old traditions. It also represents the conflict between urban and rural areas. Most people live in rural areas where the authority of kingship is strongest, responding to local problems directly. These cultural leaders must be included in large-scale conversations so that they can provide insights that are missing from secularization. Some scholars have declared that the modern state should serve as a place for collaboration among traditional government systems.[82] Kings preserve culture and unite communities, facilitating peace by connecting religious values with other humanitarian initiatives.

Some Western perspectives insist that the only way for individuals to receive justice is through democratic governments. By understanding the religious nature of kingships, we can understand how a king functions within a society by working for the interests of the people. The king is a protector of life who functions not as a dictator but as an advocate for cultural continuity and religious perseverance. An analysis performed by Clastres, an anthropologist who studied the lives of Central American ethnic organizations, concluded that the chief protects the lives of those within his community. Ultimately, Clastres found that chiefdoms or kingdoms can be more egalitarian than democracies.[83] This idea has been cited as a landmark non-Western perspective, used to analyze leaders in non-Western contexts.

Integrating kingdoms and secular states can have dire consequences. Botswana's ancient ideology held that the king must be prevented from gaining too much power over his people and that ritual sacrifice could protect him. Botswana attempted to force modernity into its political systems through centralization and democracy, which largely failed. Rural villages saw increased poverty, and the clash of new politics and old ideology led to a rise in crime. During the turmoil, there were shocking returns to old, ritualistic crimes.

In Botswana's traditional ideology, the chief is entrusted with the highest form of magic for protection from malevolent forces. The chief must also be monitored and prevented from using these powers to satisfy personal greed. This belief has been changed by contact with the motivations of capitalist systems, and current rituals are performed to simultaneously increase the power of politicians and protect against their greed. Such rituals can involve the mutilation and murder of children to invoke the gods and limit the power of businessmen.[84]

Botswana's shifting attitudes are an example of rituals and symbolism changing over time as they adapt to the duality of the secular state and the religious kingdom. The secular state's influence changes the circulation of ideology and so does the growing influence of education and globalization: education changes how people think about religious values, allowing them to evaluate different ideologies. Ideological tensions are exacerbated by the prominence of Western curriculums, and the role of kingships can be undermined. Globalization spreads ideas that can contradict indigenous ideologies, which undermines the authority of religious kingships.[85]

The emergence of nongovernmental organizations (NGOs) also makes it difficult for kingships to maintain authority in modern societies. NGOs supply aid ranging from food assistance to education and shelter. NGO models provide services directly to the people, discouraging them from engaging with their government—such work can create unsustainable cycles alongside job opportunities and poverty relief. These NGOs are usually more successful when working in conjunction with the chief or local government. In capitalist contexts, corporations can have similar effects, creating both positive and negative outcomes when they ignore the established channels of existing governance.[86]

APPLIED EPISTEMOLOGY: THE ALAAFIN OF OYO

To tie together my analysis of the ideology of kingship, consider the Alaafin of Oyo's leadership. This kingdom was an influential force in Western Africa from the fourteenth century until the late eighteenth century. The Alaafin held political power not only among the Yoruba but also in other parts of West Africa to influence kingdoms such as the Kingdom of Dahomey, now in the modern Republic of Benin. Oyo controlled a large portion of the Yoruba area and absorbed many territories to expand its power; its centralization of power stabilized politics in the region. This political stability, and the spread of Yoruba culture, was enabled by the Alaafin of Oyo—the region thrived due to ideology used as a unifying force.

Oyo's ideology was legitimized through religious epistemological approaches. The king's justification for ruling stemmed from his ancestry, claiming to be the descendant of an "original" prince of the "founding" Yoruba city of Ife-Ife. The religious ideology supporting the kingship conforms with Frazer's ideas about fertility cults: the king was an incarnation of Oranyan, the empire builder and son of Oduduwa, and this property was passed down through blood. The king was a physical leader and spiritual being, entrusted with leadership of the empire and the maintenance of religious affairs. The king held power over life and death, and it was understood that reckless abuse of this power would diminish faith and bring injustice to the kingdom.[87] The monarch's power was reinforced by the army, and the economy was dependent on production, long-distance trade, and the Atlantic slave trade.

The Alaafin's power changed with history. The Old Oyo Empire fell in the nineteenth century, which was an era marked by political instability and too many wars. Oyo was replaced by Ibadan, and the reduced empire survived along with the Alaafin, who escaped involvement in many wars.[88]

The Alaafin enjoys great influence among the Yoruba today, helping to maintain *itàn*, the Yoruba culture, and maintaining peace. The kingship's ideology is strengthened by ritual and symbolism that include an extensive coronation ceremony involving sacrifices that happen over the course of several days. In old Oyo, the king was secluded from society to protect his sacred role. Tradition insisted that the king's departure from the palace required the entire city to leave their homes. One physical object that reinforced the power of the Alaafin was the Koso, a drum used only for the Alaafin as he danced at festivals.

Although the Oyo Empire collapsed, its cities and cultural influences remained intact. Yorubaland came under British rule and the indirect governance of colonialism, and the Alaafin remained the ruler of metropolitan Oyo and its adjoining territories. This influenced the course of history in Yorubaland. Chiefs under the Alaafin paid tribute to him, and many followed the religious traditions of the Yoruba, paying homage to the gods in times of disaster. Prominent politicians, other ọbas, and senior chiefs—typically those with a rank lower than that of the Alaafin—used the Alaafin as a scapegoat for Yorubaland's problems during some periods of Yoruba history, bolstering their own prestige.[89] The political and religious influences of the Alaafin of Oyo confirm historical patterns in kingship.

Over time, colonialism and modern politics reduced the power of the Alaafin and the kingdom of Oyo diminished. However, the 1920s marked the emergence of a new power for the Alaafin of Oyo.[90] He was the symbol of cultural revitalization and living heir to the great rulers of the past. Oyo's influence was based on political and cultural leadership instead of religious power. The Alaafin's powers coexisted with those of the state.

The Alaafin's ancient model of kingship faces new challenges in the modern age, but its role has been tied to the political power of statehood since colonial times. It is an example of a kingdom that is independent from statehood. The king no longer wields absolute political power, but his status allows him to retain significant authority.

The Alaafin of Oyo is a powerful leader today. Understanding the ideological and epistemological mechanisms of Oyo's power, and how they have been changed by modern processes such as globalization, gives insight into the current domain of his power. It also explains why historical debates about the legitimacy of the Oyo Empire and the Alaafin are relevant to current politics.[91] The position of Alaafin—currently held by Ọba Lamidi Olayiwola Adeyemi III, a preeminent leader in Yoruba religion and culture—has significant political influence in Nigeria. Many have argued that the Alaafin of Oyo should be included in political discussions because of his significant influence over his kingdom; the Alaafin represents the cultural heritage of the Yoruba, and he serves as an advocate for development through Yoruba culture.[92]

Chapter 9

Sacred Kingship: Power, Politics, and Ritual Knowledge

This chapter is, indeed, not about the historical narratives of kings and their kingdoms over time; but, instead, it is about the ideology and epistemology of kingship, especially as it is manifested in the body of the king, the rituals of power, the "arts" around the king, the spaces over which the power is exercised, as well as the people over whom it is exercised upon, the insurgencies that kingship generate. In "totalizing" the discourse on kingship and power, I combine the past with the present because both are sacrosanct and, to a large extent, relevant.

Conceptual and theoretical ideas are, of course, driven by, and grounded in narratives but theories as well as epistemologies can exclusively and implicitly elevate analysis beyond the interpretations of specific regional events, episodes and historical timelines, and particularistic or localized attributes of kings. A conceptual analysis, such as the "second-order" level that I present here, cumulates into narratives that belong to different parts of the world and historical eras, distilling them into theoretical and philosophical categories of analysis. I want to articulate a series of divergent and mutually reinforcing conceptual ideas on kingship in general, drawing on the Alaafin and hundreds of other noble kings in a comparative framework, with their long historical moments, and within a larger geographic space in Africa and other parts of the world.

Narratives on African kingships and chieftaincies tend to focus on peculiarities in association with cities, as in the power of the Alaafin in the eighteenth century, the Alake of Abeokuta in the nineteenth century, the Olubadan of Ibadan in the twentieth century, and the powerful anti-colonial Asantehene, King of the Asante. Sometimes, the narrative can focus on the sources of power, as in the case of Islam and the Sultan of Sokoto or the traditional as in the case of the Aku-Uka of Wukari. There is nothing wrong with such micro-studies and many more of them are needed. Two critiques of the micro-studies approach with respect to Africa must be noted. The first is that the characteristics of roles and responsibilities of kings, as in the case of Yoruba Ọbas, are presented in a descriptive manner, thus adding very little to the literature other than new names and titles. Second, kingship, as it must be understood, is not peculiarly African but has a global reach. That global traditions and histories of kings are sometimes analyzed comparatively, which colonial anthropology and British officials attempted in creating hierarchies among kings in Nigeria. However, this was an unsounded comparison and false hierarchy as they compared the Emirs of the North with the Ọbas of the South.

Kingship is not confined to the Yoruba people as there were, and still are, kings (going by different names) in hundreds of other places, nations, and also in different civilizations and empires. The long history of kingship, from state formations, to its predemocracy antecedents, to its apogee in different historical periods (as in the case of Africa before the colonial conquest), to the rise of modern democracies, and the subsequent decline of kingship in modern politics, has been a subject of long historical narrations in different parts of the world.

There are countless stories on the activities of kings in different societies, which I will use as some of my examples, but there are also common denominators that allow us to construct a "second-order" epistemological analysis of kingship(s). Narrations, as those on the Alaafin of Oyo, in combination with those of other kings in other places, supply the data that drive this conceptual piece. For the most part, I will skip those narratives on the specific deeds of kings and the histories on their kingdoms.

I will relate the very idea of kingship to that of the ideology that produced it, the ideology that kingship itself manifested, and the knowledge that kingly power—in its conception and uses—produced and profited from. Power is a product of an intellectual political philosophy, deeply held and very keenly contested. As power becomes manifested in governance and conflicts, it generates a complicated set of events that feed the production of knowledge. My primary interest here is the interface of kingship, as a concentrated form of power, with knowledge, ideology, and epistemology.

SUBSIDIARITY

It is difficult to talk about the good without touching on the bad, as in the *ejigbede* binary vision of Ifa, whereby reality has two sides: birth and death, heaven and earth, men and women, evil and good, bad destiny and good destiny, and so on. Kingship also has its binary: power and resistance.

Oppositional forces must form part of the critical understanding of kingship and power. Building a kingdom or an empire required wars, conquests, and processes of subjugation and incorporation. The power in that success of building a state would generate serious oppositional elements and movements. Kingdoms and empires fall, many times along with their kings and emperors.

Kingship everywhere generated resentments, resistance, and alternative forms of nationalism. What drove resistance and subnationalism is the larger notion of subsidiarity, a concept that is never fully developed in African historical narratives. Where a king presided over a kingdom or an empire, clusters of colonies emerged, with citizens whose ethnicities could be different from those of the king. In addition, kingship meant that there was social stratification as it explains how resources were not just produced but also distributed: Who controlled the lucrative aspects of trade? Who did the farming and who collected most of the products? Who enjoyed the key status of prestige? Who was treated as poor, underprivileged, and powerless? As society became more and more stratified, ideas of oppression and domination were formed with the focus of criticisms and attacks directed at kings and members of the ruling elite. A notion of fragmented citizenship would, therefore, emerge, in which the privileges and/or the ethnicity of the king and those who governed along with him could be different from those of their subjects. Even where a king governed a city-state and the ethnicity was the same, as with many Yoruba city-states, kingship could represent a different political subgroup and subsocial identity with its own agenda and aspirations. Subsidiarity—as an idea that argued that local communities, the colonies, and large kinships should take the major decisions on what affected them—would ultimately develop into critical voices and nationalism that would threaten the king and the palace and question the decisions emanating from the centralized government. Thus, there was no such a thing as a king without opposition and enemies—within the capital where royal siblings and other chiefs competed, sometimes leading to the fall of the kingdom, the city-state, or the empire itself—and in the provinces or colonies where subsidiarity notions would ultimately emerge. Subsidiarity would catastrophize its own conditions and cleverly represent the body and body politics of the king as catastrophes.

THE POLITICS OF SACRED KINGSHIP

In the preceding section, the relationship between kingship and rituals was made in a number of places and times, but it was without its relevant elaboration. That is why this connection, the idea of power based on rituals, is to be fully spelt out as it was key to the definition of kingship in Africa and the ideology of power in general. The subjectivity of kingship—an agency that controlled power; the acceptance of that power by citizens under the control of the king; and the institutions of regulations, rights, and duties that mediated the relationship between the king and his subjects—was dominated by the realm of the rituals as well as the physical exercise of power in terms of the use of violence. Similarly, it is difficult to understand subsidiarity—in its formation, articulation, and insurgency—and the responses by kings—in acts of domination, incorporation, and conquest—without understanding how the notion of the sacred became the instrumentality of both politics and power.

While there are many other forms of symbolic government in world history, an absolute monarchy through sacred kingship is perhaps the most symbolic of them all. Particularly for African cultures, their rituals of sacred kingship[1] (many of which are maintained to the present day) are evidence of the great power, control, and influence of the belief that a divine force has over the people, land, and activity. This segment will examine the general notion of sacred kingship and various African sacred kingships, with a particular focus on the Alaafin of Oyo's station and legacy. By examining the ways in which rituals are used as a means of maintaining the Alaafin's legacy, my objective is to show and conclude that the African sacred kingship is both an epistemology and ideology that is long-standing as long as the people continue to exercise or believe in tradition.

The concept of a "sacred kingship" has existed since the beginnings of prehistoric human-created governments. Though it has some different manifestations depending on culture, it is ultimately defined as the understanding that there is a king who serves as the agent of a divine or otherworldly source. Simply put, this king is a mediator between the supernatural and natural worlds in some form, either as a human being or a god himself; he is also, in a sense, granted "divine right" as ruler. Throughout the majority of human history, when religion and politics were inseparably intertwined, no kingdom could exist unless it was considered sacred and under the rule of a sacred king.[2]

However, while this sort of cultural ideology seems archaic, it has actually been reexamined by modern historians for its implications in modern governments. As might be expected, it was explained by ancient philosophers like Aristotle in the fourth century BC,[3] but it was first studied in an academic setting by Sir James Frazer in *The Golden Bough*.[4] It is because of this work, among other modern works from other scholars, that one begins to realize that sacred kingships do actually have implications for the present day.[5]

In a sacred kingship of ancient civilizations, only one man—the sacred king—held power in the form of a divinely mandated absolute monarchy, while all others had to invariably obey him. This one person had the divine right to control his people both physically and spiritually, ordering their every move and belief (at least in theory). In more literal concepts of "sacred kingship" in some cultures, the king was not merely a mediator or agent for something divine; the king was actually a god himself and a mediator for no other god but himself.

TYPES OF SACRED KINGSHIPS

Overall, it has been agreed that there have been three main forms of sacred kings across cultures in history. The first form is a ruler with supernatural power. The second form is a divine or semi-divine god. The third form is an agent of sacred acts.

In this god-king's "god-kingdom," there were historically three forms of a polity: preliminary, primary, and secondary. In the preliminary form, the chieftain was considered divine. In its primary form, the god-kingdom was made up of such huge empires as those of the ancient Iran, East Asia, and the Middle East. Finally, the secondary form took place in European, Hellenistic, and Persian empires. Between these three forms, of course, there were multiple transition forms.

The king, as the holder of supernatural power, could not only exercise his power on his people but also on all areas of his community, affecting its fertility, food, weather, and victories. Some scholars speculate that this kind of king was the actual manifestation of the state of the kingdom, meaning that his health meant the kingdom's prosperity and his lack of health meant the kingdom's doom. In other words, the king's health actually represented the "life" of his magic. If, for example, he was a young and healthy ruler, his powers would be considered strong. If, on the other hand, the king fell ill or sprouted grey hairs, his powers would be considered weakened. This sort of king has been identified mainly in "ethnic" kingdoms, such as the rain-maker king in Africa. Granted, this king may not exactly even be a king at all; even so, he was no less sacred. He may instead be a divinely inspired shaman, chief, or medicine man.

Meanwhile, the divine or semi-divine king was found in great empires or kingdoms, such as those in Egypt or Persia. In early Egypt, it was believed that the king was the same as the sky god, Horus, and the sun god—Re, Aton, or Amon. In Hittite societies, the sun was often artistically portrayed as the symbol for the king. Furthermore, according to Hittite rock inscriptions, it was common to refer to the king as "my sun." With this understanding of the king as a god, his successors were understood to be the sons of a god. Finally, the king who was the agent of sacred acts was believed to literally carry out the intentions of the gods on Earth. This means that the "sacredness" of the king was not so much associated with the king as an individual but rather with his station. This belief was found in Mesopotamia and China. There, the actual gods were considered to be the rulers, and the king was merely the gods' instrument.[6]

Regardless of the sacred king's believed nature, the king was considered to be a beneficial influence to society. The sacred king was often described as shepherd, judge, warlord, or priest, with each title having its own significant affirmative meaning. The king as a shepherd guided his people to protection and prosperity. The king as a judge carried out justice throughout his land. The king as a warlord protected his people from all enemies and harm. The king as a priest led all religious activities, festivals, and offerings to the gods.[7] Scholars who have studied African kingship acknowledge that the system was ritualized in part because of the use of poignant metaphor previously described.

THEORIZING THE RITUALIZATION OF KINGSHIP

There are two historically predominant academic theories that explain the ritualistic nature of African "sacred kingship." The first is from James Frazer who adhered to the notion that the public believed that the physical health of the king corresponded to his power. The second is from Émile Durkheim, a French sociologist, who said that the ritualism was an expression of sociopolitical factors as opposed to personal factors. Durkheim's view was popular in the 1940s in the academic world, but by the 1960s, Frazer's view was resurrected, reconsidered, and reconstructed (as mentioned previously). Frazer hypothesized that because ancient people were constantly concerned about a prosperous agriculture for means of survival, they turned to their "divine" leader for help and hope. Their king's vitality ensured a plentiful harvest and vice versa. For these people, there was no other explanation for their triumphs and trials.[8] Consequently, according to Frazer's theory, if a king's health was deemed unfit for the throne, he would be conquered by a stronger alternative. Indeed, there were early reports of the Sudan's Shilluk people committing ritual regicide.

Frazer's view came from his studies of Africa, but they also applied to his findings among people in the Middle East and Europe. He supposed, then, that the concept of sacred kingship was more of a cultural evolution that was unavoidable, irrespective of location. However, some scholars have since concluded that his observations are more relevant to the Middle East and Europe than they are to Africa.[9] These same scholars criticize Frazer's thesis further by saying that it only really describes African kingship but not African kingdoms themselves. E. E. Evans-Pritchard in 1948 theorized that the African king did not have any control of consequence and that the morality of an

African nation could only be enforced by the king's identity with spirituality. As a result, there was an odd paradox of the Shilluk people being unified and yet capable of factions and insurrection. Evans-Pritchard did not find any irrefutable evidence for a ritualistic regicide among the people. He said that any sort of violent death of a king was due to any challenger besting the king and taking the land as his own—for simple reasons and not for any reason related to the king losing his power.[10]

Meyer Fortes, an anthropologist from South Africa, modified Evans-Pritchard's theory by saying that it was the station of the king, not the individual king himself, that mattered the most in maintaining and reinforcing African rituals. Similarly, in a symbiotic fashion, the rituals were a way of maintaining or reinforcing a king's station. This means that rituals were not merely impulsive or random. They were instead an effective way to justify the king's role and instill in the king a sense of confidence that would serve him well as a leader and divine entity. Any sort of fortune that fell upon the king was then a means of confirming the rituals of the institution and station.[11]

However, not all scholars see rituals in the same way. Max Gluckman, a British-South African anthropologist, had another sociological theory relating to the rituals of the Swazi people that said that their rituals were not to confirm or justify the king but rather to condemn him. The Ncwala ceremony of the Swazi people, occurring every year, was a sort of "ritual of rebellion" in that it was used for the people to publicly state their criticism of the king. To

Figure 9.1.   Leopard Aquamanile. *Source*: The Metropolitan Museum of Art, accessed August 3, 2020, from https://www.metmuseum.org/art/collection/search/316524.

Gluckman, this ceremony did not so much offset the political system as it did stabilize it, for it gave the people a voice and, unexpectedly, some power of their own. However, more contemporary reexaminations of the Swazi culture suggest that Gluckman misinterpreted the hymns at the Ncwala ceremony. According to T. O. Beidelman, a professor of anthropology at New York University, the ritual definitely serves to set the king apart—but not to his detriment. Beidelman cited the fact that the king is nude during the ritual and that his right hand is empty. There is also always a black ox that is sacrificed during the ceremony. These factors, said Beidelman, are aligned with Swazi symbolism and cosmology. The nude king before the black ox symbolizes how the king is the "bull of the nation" who must constantly serve as a mediator between the supernatural world and the natural world. The black ox itself represents a sort of commanding but unwieldy sexuality that the king must control.[12] These points are particularly reassuring because they show how and why kingship was maintained for so long. If not for these symbolic and inherently positive rituals, why would the king's station ever be allowed to remain?

Other scholars confirm that rituals were to demonstrate the king's true authority rather than make up for the lack of his true authority. In fact, rituals of kingship also maintained respect for the king's position, even if the nature of the king's authority changed over time. How the king was respected, of course, was subjective to culture. For the Nyakyusa people of Tanzania, for example, the king earned respect because he was seen first and foremost as a priest. Among the Ngonde people, on the other hand, the king was respected because of his influence on the ivory trade. Successors who earned the respect of the king also came about differently according to culture. The Rukuba people in Benue, Nigeria, for example, had their priests chose a successor. In Bunyoro, princes physically fought one another in order to usurp the throne. In any of these cases, Frazer's thesis, while compelling, has since become less plausible because there are so many variables that exist between cultures. While a king's health might have certainly been a positive sign for all cultures, it was not the only explanation for a king's validity across cultures. Furthermore, regicide cases are difficult to verify, even though it was common for many kings not to die a natural death.[13]

Nonscholar Africans themselves often discuss how the power of the kings is an independent force that occurs naturally. With the Lega people of the Congo, this power (known as *bwami*) is thought to be forever renewed in each king (known as *mwami*). This means that the kingship rituals for the Lega are important because they allow the power of the king to be strengthened for the public good. Even if the king does not remain a king for whatever reason (for instance, death), it is the independent power inside of him that is an infinite continuance that passes on to future kings. This power is even passed on through relics of dead kings. The jawbone of the Buganda (otherwise known as Uganda) king, or *kabaka*, was preserved after he died. Similarly, in Nigeria, a Yoruba ọba was alleged to eat the dissolved heart of his predecessor as part of succession rites. These African stories are consistent with Fortes' theory of rituals, thereby perhaps unearthing the real truth about African regicide. The station of a king or the institution of kingship was seen as immortal, in a sense. This immortality, however, existed in cycles of life and death. Therefore, the living king was significant because it symbolized the immortality of the kingship. Yet the king's death was just as significant because it showed how, though bodies die, the kingship is renewed in a new living king. Similarly, agricultural harvests go through times of plenty and of famine. However, with the promise of a new king comes the promise of new agricultural prosperity.[14]

APPLIED POLITICS AND RITUALS: ALAAFIN OF OYO

Let us now examine, more specifically, the role of the Alaafin of Oyo, first through a discussion of his history. Governmentally speaking, his position was that of an absolute monarch. Metaphorically and culturally speaking, he's *ikú bàbá yèyé, aláṣẹ èkejì òrìṣà* ("the almighty, the ruler, and companion of the gods").[15] In practice, he governed with eight senior chiefs known as the Oyo Mesi. Peter Morton-Williams added the influence on power of the Ogboni secret cult.[16] Writing in the late nineteenth century, Samuel Johnson provided a complex institution of the king, political institutions, symbols of authority, and the ritual basis of power.[17] In awe, Johnson concluded that the "King is more dreaded than even the gods."[18]

The Alaafin still resides where the Oyo Empire first stood: in the Yoruba state north of Lagos in today's southwestern Nigeria. At the Oyo Empire's height from 1650 to 1750, the territory was presented in oral traditions as ranging between the eastern Niger River and the western Volta River. At this time, the Oyo Empire was the most prominent and powerful of all early Yoruba entities. Its influence and status were described in exaggerated proportions by many writers, including British officers in the early decades of the twentieth century. Samuel Johnson, the preeminent chronicler of the Old Oyo Empire, gave a description of the size of Oyo that covered most of Yorubaland and Dahomey.[19] Robin Law's detailed description of the boundaries of Oyo incorporated three levels of subjects, which attests to the reach and influence of a great empire:

1. The area that, to use Ajayi's phrase, "owed direct allegiance to the Alafin," and was subject to a relatively centralized administration from the capital. The Oyo Yoruba formed the core of this area, but it also came to

include some of the Igbomlna and Ekiti Yoruba to the east and some of the Egbado, Awori, and Anago Yoruba in the south.

2. The kingdoms whose dynasties were traditionally supposed to be descended from Oduduwa, the legendary king of Ile Ife, and over whom the Alafin claimed authority as the legitimate successor to Oduduwa's kingship. Of these perhaps only the Egba were in any real sense subject to Oyo, but others (such as the Ijesa) were prepared to acknowledge loosely the suzerainty (or at least the senior status) of the Alafin.

3. States outside the Ife dynastic system which paid tribute to Oyo, such as Dahomey.[20]

The narratives by Yoruba influential Western-educated elite like Johnson led to the British elevation of the Alaafin to the status of the most preeminent king between 1894 and 1934, the subject of the book by J. A. Atanda.[21] The analysis of the power of the Alaafin covered different historical eras—the Old Oyo Empire analyzed by Robin Law,[22] the rebuilt Oyo Empire by Alaafin Atiba in the nineteenth century,[23] and the supremacy of the Alaafin in an Indirect Rule system by Atanda.

However, the early days of the empire were not especially prosperous.[24] In the early sixteenth century, Oyo was a minor state that was under the dominance of Nupe and Borgu to the north. These two regions actually even conquered Oyo in c. 1550. However, it was by the end of the sixteenth century that Alaafin Orompoto utilized Oyo's convenient trading location to gain the empire's wealth. This wealth was then used to establish a trained military presence. At this point, the empire was thriving financially, with the conquering of the Dahomey kingdom and trades with the Europeans. The rulers of Oyo during this period either saved the great wealth in order to amass it further or expanded Oyo's territories because they had the resources.[25]

By the end of the rule of Alaafin Abiodun from 1770 to 1789, the empire began to fail.[26] Abiodun was a brilliant leader in war, conquering his enemies in a brutal civil war. He also was a tactful economic developer, for he focused on European coastal trade. Yet, for all of these virtues, he neglected his economy, which in turn weakened the empire's and government's best asset: the army. As a result, Abiodun's successor, Awole, had to hold back violent revolts from the public. His administration, without a strong army, was barely stable. It merely got by with an overly complicated public service system and lack of powerful chiefs. His own advisors even quarreled with him. These conflicts between the chiefs and the king continued even past his reign and with future Alaafins throughout the eighteenth and early nineteenth centuries. By this point in time, to make matters worse, the empire lost control of its trading routes. By 1800, after the Fon of Dahomey invaded, the empire was attacked by Fulani Muslims from the northeast. Thus, came the end of a glorious empire.[27] But, of course, since 1800, Oyo has existed as a Yoruba city, with its own continued kingship: the "Alaafin" is still the official title of the ruler of the contemporary Oyo people.

Now that we have examined the history of the Alaafin of Oyo, let us explore how rituals specifically maintaining the Alaafin of Oyo's kingship are relevant historically and in modern times. Before this is examined, it is important to remember that such rituals are groundless unless they are established with some kind of sacred myth. As such, we must now thoroughly inspect the myths of the Oyo people. According to Yoruba creation legend, the Yoruba High God, Olodumare, had a son, Oduduwa, who was destined to claim Yorubaland and became the father of the Yorubaland (hence why any descendants of Oduduwa as kings are automatically deemed rightful and sacred).[28] At this point, the world was covered in water, so Oduduwa placed a patch of soil with a rooster on top of the water. The rooster then spread out the soil with his talons until it filled up enough room to create Oduduwa's sacred spot of Ile-Ife. It was here where Oduduwa became the first Yoruba ruler and had sixteen sons, one of whom became the first official Alaafin of Oyo.[29]

However, it is interesting that multiple non-Oyo Yoruba migration legends try to undermine the original Oyo supernatural origins by infusing the story with hints that the first Oyo king was from outside of Ile-Ife—thus suggesting that any outside political entity can, based on mythologies, overthrow the Alaafin of Oyo. Some of these migration legends say that Oduduwa came from the east, and others say that he came from Egypt, Medina, Mecca, or Nupeland. The legend that says Oduduwa came from Mecca is particularly worth noting. In this version, Oduduwa overthrew his Meccan, Islamic father and then fled to Ile-Ife to found the kingship. Yet, if this version is true, the legitimacy of the kingship is entirely faulty, not founded upon the required supernatural foundation that is resurrected in Oyo ritual.[30] For this reason, the Alaafins of Oyo have always resisted the non-Oyo legends so that they could fit their own personal, supposedly deity-blessed legend.[31] By maintaining such a legend through ritual and symbolism, the Alaafin's position has also been maintained.

The greatness of the divine West African Yoruba *oba* (meaning "ruler"), otherwise known as the *Alaafin* in Oyo, is exemplified through his crowns that embellish the extravagance of his rituals. The foremost crown that the *oba* wears as a traditional leader is a crown embedded with beads and a beaded veil.[32] While the crown is undoubtedly aesthetically interesting to look at, it also is a representation of the significance of the kingship institution, bolstered by ancestry and the exposure of the king's morality. The beads are also to represent something godlike or divine in their shimmering quality. Tradition says that the father of Yorubaland, Oduduwa, was the first to wear this sort of crown.[33] Consequently, this is another reason why

Figure 9.2. Beaded crown from Nigeria. *Source*: Wellcome Collection, Museum of Ethnic Arts, University of California, Los Angeles. Height 11", as cited in Robert Farris Thompson, "The Sign of the Divine King: An Essay on Yoruba Bead-Embroidered Crowns with Veil and Bird Decorations," *African Arts* 3, no. 3 (1970): 8.

all the kings of Yorubaland say that they are descendants of Oduduwa[34] or "seconds of the gods."[35]

Crown embroidery is still practiced in many centers, including Oyo, Ilesa, Oyo, Abeokuta, Ile-Ife, and Efon-Alaiye. The skilled bead embroiderers working at these centers must make the frame of the crown by using cardboard or wickerwork. The frame is almost always a cone when the crown is made at Efon-Alaiye, one of the most prominent centers. This cone is the dominant part of the crown, and it dwarfs all other Yoruba headpieces. Once a relief is molded onto the cone, the arduous task of embroidering begins. The beads may be placed horizontally, vertically, or diagonally. They also can be formulated in any sort of geometric design, increasing or decreasing in size.[36] There of course is room for individual creativity with the crowns, but the embroiderer must honor some traditional elements. For example, the crowns must either be framed into a cone, "elliptical helmet," or into a cone with a vertical stem on top where embroidered birds are laid.[37]

The following illustrated or named criteria must also be met: faces set in the relief, birds' images set round about the frame, and a fringed veil. The veil is particularly important because it serves in state occasions where the king exhibits divine power. During such occasions, it is believed that if someone gazes upon the bare face of the king without his veil, he or she will be in danger. The crown must also not fall over the eyeline of the king, for the crown is said to have magic on the inside that could potentially cause blindness.[38]

It is important to note that the beginnings of the crown's traditions are somewhat unclear. In the city of Ile-Ife, the sculpture of Yoruba antiquity (dated around 960–1160 AD) does not show a beaded crown of any kind. The faces in this sculpture wore head pieces, to be sure, but they are also without frontal faces and birds. It was only about 400 years later, scholars speculate, when the more "modern" crown began to become popularized.[39]

Let us now consider what the significance of the frontal faces and birds actually are. Usually the faces are somewhat generic in appearance, but they often can be associated with an ancestral group if they have the same distinctive markings. Usually, the Yoruba crowns have faces with lips closed—perhaps to show a sign of dignity—but at Tada and Ile-Ife, the crowns have been shown to have faces with clenched teeth. This expression could suggest something fierce and almost snake-like—a way of showing intimidating power.[40] It is also possible that these frontal faces represent sacrificed enemies, whether they be militant challengers or witches. If this is the case, then the heads represent a victorious king over his indignant foes.[41] However, if this is true, then it is odd that many of the faces often appear peaceful. It is possible that these faces merely embody the common people or even the divining board of Yoruba that are messengers of the gods. It is also possible that all these theories are correct in their own right: the crown could represent an amalgamation of the living and the dead. Because of this, the king serves as something like a "living ancestor"—indeed perhaps even Oduduwa himself, the possessor of both the worldly and otherworldly.[42]

The birds on the crowns bring about even more interesting theories. While it is plausible that specific bird species are depicted on the crowns, it is difficult to prove that this is irrefutably true because artists could potentially make the choice to distort the birds for some aesthetic reasons. For this reason, many scholars say that the birds are simply generalized. Even throughout Yorubaland, there are disagreements among the rulers as to what the birds represent and why they are so important to the culture. For instance, in 1962, the ruler of the Egbado, a Yoruba town of Oke-Odan, said that the birds were pigeons that are symbolic of victory. However, another chief said that the birds were most certainly fish eagles. Even more interestingly, both an Oyo Yoruba priestess and prominent member of the "cult of the earth" at Olúpònnà said that the birds were egrets. These last two sources are particularly worth investigating, for their agreement and status show that they are reliable. They both said that these birds are "earth spirits," worshipped by the cult of the earth (otherwise known as the Ogboni). These spirits are said to put egret feathers on their own crowns, as indeed some Yoruba kings still do. The egret feathers are culturally recognized as signs of neatness and order, which is the greatest virtue of the cult. According to the cult's legend, the ancient egrets were able to talk and settle arguments among other creatures.[43] The way the birds seem to always converge, however, is not entirely subjective and up to the artist's discretion. They seem to be gathered at a site of meditation, which suggests that they are worshipping at an altar before their crown wearer and the faces of the wearer's ancestors on the crown. This means that the birds are also communicating with the gods, as the king does.[44]

According to John Pemberton III and Funso S. Afọlayan, the otherworldly significance of the crown cannot be overstated. This crown, like the creation legend of Yorubaland, is symbolic of the continuance of kingship, for it has been divinely received. When a new Yoruba ọba is installed to the throne, he must wear one of the crowns, thereby inhabiting a sort of sacred power in his own physical nature, a "power like that of the gods": *aláàse èkejì òrìsà*. This means that, even when an ọba dies, he does not entirely perish; instead, he merely "sinks into the ground." He does not vanish but instead changes his status as an even more commanding *òrìsà*. For this reason, no one ever mentions that an ọba has died. People say instead that "the ọba has departed" (*Oba gbésè* or *ọba wàjà*), suggesting that he has left this world and rejoined his ancestors in another otherworldly dimension to which he always belonged. Meanwhile, the title of ọba lives on in earthly form, never ceasing, all in part because of the crown's continued usage (and endowed significance) for hundreds of years.[45] It is notable that here symbolic relic and mythology are endlessly intertwined, as is appropriate and necessary for sustained passion among the people and sustained power of the Alaafin.

The process of selecting a new king is ritualistic in nature, bolstered by myth. To take the Ila-Orangun example analyzed by Pemberton III and Afolayan, once the previous ọba dies, the kingmakers send a message to the head of the princes (Alasan to the *ọmọba*). In theory, any prince from the three royal houses can succeed the last *Orangun*. However, among the lineages in the three houses, there are rotations of bestowed kingship. In other words, the selection of the Oba moves from one house to another. It is the *Alasan* who suggests to the kingmakers who among the nominated in the royal houses should be potential candidates and which house's "turn" it is for major consideration.[46] All potential candidates, to be sure, must exhibit certain qualities. They must all be in good physical health, without any noticeable defects or disabilities. They must also be considered to be of good, kingly character, capable of listening to others and judging others with fairness and intellectual caution. They also, interestingly enough, must be neither too tall nor too short. If they are too short, they shall not be taken seriously and shall be looked down upon. If they are too tall, they will appear to be egotistical, always looking down upon others.⁴⁷ All of these required qualities appear to strengthen some scholars' theory that kingship has an "image" that must be kept—either for posterity's, luck's, or heaven's sake. If the future king does not embody a certain "image," he would never be chosen by the kingmakers.

Once the *Orangun* is formally selected by one of the lineages, the ritualistic ways in which he is treated while wearing his crown indicate that he truly is revered as something otherworldly and thus deserving of respect for all eternity. All who approach him and his crown know that they must do so with reverence and, in many ways, fear. Both men and women must prostrate before the king and not dare to look at his face. Even chiefs must remove their shoes before they speak with him. Servants are to roll about in the dirt, rubbing the dirt on their foreheads as a gesture of complete servility. The servants who make the king's bed must be naked, and they must be supervised so that they are not tempted to poison him. Even when the king leaves his palace while wearing his crown (which used to be incredibly rare hundreds of years ago), he has his palace servants inform others to step aside when they are in his path.⁴⁸

Yet even the king himself is not free to behave in any way he wants. As one with the "power like that of the gods," he must in a sense "perform" as such. Granted, not all of these "performances" are still maintained, but many of them are. Traditionally, while in his palace, the king drinks water from a stream that was fetched just before dawn by naked virgin maidens. Traditionally, a king is not to consume food or drink in the presence of others. If he wishes to do so, he must be placed behind a curtain and then cough when he is finished and ready to be exposed once again. To this day, however, the king cannot see his children be born, nor can he see his newborn children's hair because they are "hairs of the spirit realm" (*irun ọrun*). Today, the king also cannot touch a dead body, see a dead body, or look into a grave. In fact, a dead body in the palace (other than the king's) is considered to be a portent of evil, for it threatens the "life-giving power" of the king.⁴⁹

As we have seen through these many examples, the very force (man-made or otherwise) that granted the Alaafin—as well as any other sacred king—his power carries on through every ritual and symbol in the present day. For this reason, sacred kingship is not a dead mythology; it is a living mythology that creates an epistemology and ideology. Whenever one prostrates before the Alaafin or whenever the Alaafin wears his sacred crown, there is a confirmation of the need to respect and venerate him. The Alaafin is thus also confirmed as a god, as well as the face of Yorubaland and its various misfortunes or blessings. Through the ritualization of the Alaafin, the Yoruba people create the sort of paragon of virtue and morality. The Alaafin is the sort of person all royals should aspire to be, for his word comes from a divine source.

However, this living mythology and epistemology/ideology will perish as soon as the people stop encouraging it and experiencing it through ritual. It is only when the people live a traditional ritual that the traditional ritual appears valid and part of their very own identity. In other words, the ritual gives form to the epistemology/ideology and in turn the epistemology/ideology gives form to the ritual. Each entity feeds the other in a continuous cycle that relies totally on the other.

Chapter 10

Kingship and Creativity

The far-reaching legacy of the Roman Empire was its ability to create a civilizing mission, made up of the spread of education, language, literature, sports, and religion over a large landmass, and for various aspects of it to continue to this day. Sports, music, dance, and all other aspects of entertainment define a palace. Kings constituted the centers of culture. This linkage between kingship and the creation of great civilizations is yet to be studied in many parts of Africa. Oyo would not have survived for so long without the ability of its kings to establish a set of common culture over a wider region, eventually leading to a cultural pan-Yorubana in language, beliefs, dress, music, and vision. And without creating an acceptable set of rules and regulations, it would not have been possible to establish a political order. Oyo's religious cult[1] also spread widely, as in the importance of Sango—the god of lightning and thunder—also credited as one of the earliest Alaafin of Oyo.[2] It must be noted that the palace served as the center of great culture in murals, gables, and decorative sculptures in all media—metals, wood, and terracotta. So, too, were the shrines, combining religious ideas with the artistic. Richard Lander supplied an eye witness account recorded in 1826, describing one of the shrines as

the largest and most fancifully ornamented of any of a similar kind in the interior of Africa. It is a perfect square building, each side of which is at least 20 yards in length. Directly opposite the entrance is an immense figure of a giant bearing a lion on its head, carved in wood, and beautifully executed. About twenty-six or twenty-seven figures, in bass-relief are placed on each of the sides of the hut, but all in a kneeling posture, with their faces turned towards the larger figure, to which they are apparently paying their devotions. On the heads of the small figures are wooden images of tigers, hyenas, snakes, crocodiles, etc., exquisitely carved and painted, or rather stained, with a variety of colors.[3]

THE ART OF THE KINGSHIP

The institution of Yoruba kingship is maintained through not only ritual and oral tradition but also art—more specifically, art for the king. This part will examine multiple forms of Yoruba art for the king, as well as how Yoruba creativity serves an essential part in the king's legacy and the people's reverence for him. Art is a language that binds a culture together in its values and beliefs. Because of this, a Yoruba king utilizes art to serve not just an aesthetic purpose but also a practical purpose. With creativity in service to him, he can unite his people with the values and beliefs of kingship.

One of the most notable artistic spectacles of the Yoruba ọba is his palace. It is the most iconic, culturally sacred architectural marvel of the community. It is believed that no secular phenomenon could desecrate it. It is for this the Yoruba say, "The burnt palace only births its greater beauty." Today, Ààfin Oyo is the largest and most extravagant palace in Yorubaland,[4] comprised of seventeen acres. It is the home of the current Alaafin of Oyo, Ọba Lamidi Olayiwola Adeyemi III. This particular palace, because of its grandeur, has been of special interest to artists and scholars alike. Back in the summers of 1971 and 1973, the Alaafin permitted some scholars to take measurements of the palace. During this time, the scholars rediscovered an exquisitely painted mural, as well as three mud relief murals. The painted decoration is located on the wall by the main entrance gate known as Abata Aremo. Two of the mud relief murals, while still a notable discovery, had already been generally known by the Afin Oyo's residents. One of these murals is located in Káá Bàbá Elesin's east interior wall. The second mural is in the Káà Ìyá Ọlọ́ya Courtyard of the Ọya Priestess, who protects the wife of the Shango's shrine. Finally, the third mud relief, which had not been known for many years, is located under a warped roof on the Kaba Bàbá Elesin's north interior wall. No one had remembered this mural's existence because this section of the palace was in such disrepair.[5]

The painted mural consists of black, traced people and animal figures on an ample space of 3.66 meters in height and 40.23 meters in length. The scholars learned from one of the oral historians (also known as the *arọkin*) that Oyo's English section officer, Captain Ross, had encouraged artwork to be placed in the palace between 1915 and 1930. These same scholars believed that he might very well have been the reason why the painted mural is in the palace in the first place. The man who created this mural, Salami Alabebe, most likely built this mural sometime between 1915 and 1917. Interestingly, while he had been painting the mural, the entrance to the front gate was hidden, for in Yoruba culture, the creation of this type of art is deemed to be a religious act that is not for public observation. To scholars, it is clear that the mural represents a theme of kingship, for there are images of elephants (traditionally

Figure 10.1. Murals at Afin Oyo. *Source:* Toyin Falola.

representative of ọba). There are also formal parades of swordsmen, royal umbrellas, ostriches, monkeys, serpents, and peacocks depicted.[6]

To scholars, it also seems clear that Alabebe wanted to not only represent kingship in general but even homage of praise to the king's authority. Alabebe depicted not only parades of animals but also an elephant tethered to a post. This is particularly significant because there is a Yoruba proverb that says: *Àjànàkú kò ní èèkàn, Ọba ti í mú erin so kò sí* (the elephant has no post to which it can be tethered; no king is capable of tethering the mammoth beast). The elephant, amid a kingly spectacle in the mural, clearly contradicts this. Thus, Alabebe expressed how his mighty Alaafin is the one—the exception—who can tether the elephant.[7]

The mud relief murals, on the other hand, were not created by Salami but rather by women in what used to be their quarters. All three of these murals were completed during Alaafin Siyanbola Ladigbolu's reign. No one knows for sure who created the smaller two murals, but Faderera Fatoba created the third mural (the largest) in the Káà Bàbá Elesin's rear exterior wall. This mural is about nineteen meters in length and three meters in height. In the mural, there is depicted a scene quite like the painted murals. There are figures of men and animals set in relief. The men are carrying royal umbrellas for the ọba. There are a variety of animals: ostriches, birds, snakes, lizards, and monkeys. There are also multiple swords and canes set in relief. There are also words on the mural: "Faderera Fatoba" and "CMG—Alaafin Oyo" (which likely means Commander of the Order of St. Michael and St. George). This mural was probably created to honor Ọba Ladigbolu I for being accepted into the order of St. Michael and St. George and for his civic service between 1911 and 1944. There are also some remnants of black, indigo, and white paint on the mural; however, almost all the color in the mural is now gone.[8]

Undoubtedly, all the art discussed so far has been to the Yoruba kings' benefit. This is, of course, to be expected. In Yoruba culture, the ọba is considered to be the embodiment and preservation of culture. There is a Yoruba proverb that says *Ilé Ọba t'ó jó, ẹwà ni ó bù kun un* (the razing of the king's house by fire adds beauty to it), meaning that even when a great fire destroys a ruler's house, there is no need to be saddened because now there is an opportunity to offer more beauty and more improvements to the ruler's home. Throughout history, the Oba is often associated with exquisite art. Still, of course, the amount of art and extravagance of the art in any royal space depends in significant part on the taste of the current ọba. More extravagant ọbas are not uncommon in Yoruba history, however.[9] For example, an early Alaafin named Aganju (fifteenth century) purportedly placed brazen posts in his Old Oyo palace.[10] Admittedly, there is no definitive evidence of such posts. However, the current New Oyo palace's most significant courtyard with carved posts is named after this Alaafin, suggesting that legend was a good enough reason to call the courtyard so. Yet even with such rumored rich taste, Aganju is not Yoruba legend's most profligate Alaafin. This unofficial "title" of sorts still belongs to Siyanbola Ladigbolu. According to Salami Alabebe, Ladigbolu had sent out officials to ensure that no other ọba's palace was as beautiful as his.[11]

ART, ORATURE, AND POWER

It was also during Ladigbolu's time as Alaafin that corrugated metal sheets were installed onto the palace's physical structure. Not only this, but Oba Ladigbolu also had every post in sight carved. The people of Oyo were so impressed by this that they composed a celebratory song:[12]

A dé 'lé Ọba	We got to the King's house
Ọpó f'ẹ̀hìn pọn 'mọ	Post carry babies on their back
Àrà t'á ò rí rí	The wonder or novelty that we never saw before
L'Adejumo ń dá	Is being created by Adejumo (the Ọba)
A dé 'lé Ọba	We got to the king's house
Ọpó f'ẹ̀hìn pọn 'mọ	Post carry babies on their backs

What is particularly noteworthy about the preceding song is that there may be a hint of pride and sarcasm to it. In reality, while there is no definitive evidence of Old Oyo architecture containing carved posts, there is some evidence that what scholars believe is sufficient to make this deduction valid. For this reason, in this song, the people were hinting that the greatness of New Oyo harkened back to the glory of Old Oyo—a move by the Alaafin that was deserving of respect. This is an indication, then, that the people see art in general as a form of reverence for kingship and their ruler. Furthermore, there is even more reverence when art pays homage to the past.[13]

Even the word "àrà" from the people's song supports this theory. There are two meanings of the word that can be found in two Yoruba dictionaries. Oxford University Press' dictionary translates the word into many English words, including "fashion," "form," "custom," and "repetition of a journey." However, only "fashion" and "form" are indisputably correct. More Yoruba people prefer *àṣà* for "custom" and *àdrà* or *òòyì* for "repetition of a journey."[14] Abraham's *Dictionary of Modern Yoruba* offers similar meanings. In this dictionary, *àrà* refers to something novel or newly fashioned[15] as well as the equivalent of the English word "wonder."[16]

Hugh Clapperton attested to the architecture of Old Oyo before its collapse by saying that the people of Katunga liked to decorate their doors and posts with carvings. The carvings usually involved animals (for instance, a hog with an antelope in its mouth or a boa snake). Clapperton also said that the king's houses (along with his various women's homes) all had posts that supported verandahs and that they were also carved.[17] Scholars have also discovered carved wooden posts from the site of Old Oyo, some of which have purportedly been utilized for building new houses in Ilorin in the early 2000s.[18]

Oral tradition also describes the importance of the carved posts of Old Oyo, thereby giving even more evidence to the hint of sarcasm in their song of Ladigbolu's palace.[19] All Oyo Yoruba families are referred to with this saga:[20]

Òpó mú 'lérò, Majà Àlekàn	The post that supports the house, *Majà Àlekàn*
Ọmọ esú iré	The children of good locust
Ọmọ òpó kọrọbítí kọrọbítí	The children of fat posts
Ọmọ òpó kọrọbìtì kọrọbìtì	The children of fat posts
Ọmọ òpó ró 'ṣọ òpó gbà'já	The children of the post that ties wraparound and belts it
Òpó kàn dudu níwájú Ọba	The post that appears gorgeous before the king

Thus, with the archeological evidence as well as community belief, Old Oyo's assumed architecture revived again and again in art is of great importance because it represents reverence for not just the current king but kingship as an institution.

PERFORMANCE AND POWER

The ọba are not just associated with visual art, of course. They are also related to performative art through chant, theater, and poetry. For instance, Yoruba Masque Theatre (more commonly known as the Alárìjó) began with the Egúngún masquerade troupe in the early seventeenth century. At this time, Ologbin Ologbojo was the Arokin (the primary cymbalist, rhapsodist, and singer of ballads), and Ologbo was the staff bearer. They both were under the orders of King Ogbolu, the Alaafin of Oyo Igboho, and together they established the troupe of entertainers for the happiness of the king. To this day, the legacy of the entertainers lives on, still at the service of the Alaafin and the people. This type of theater specializes in poetry, in the Yoruba style of chanting. The Yoruba Masque troupe takes on the role of other guild masqueraders by using the poetry form known as *ẹsà*: a Yoruba poetical focus on descriptions of settlements, specific people, and moments in myth. Esa Ogbin, who supposedly lived in the eighteenth century during the reign of the Alaafin Abiodun, was the very first dramatist of the Yoruba Masque Theatre. He performed the poetry as designed by Ologbojo, which was intended not to have a rigid form. Even so, however, to this day, the poems are usually consistent with a specific pattern established by Ologbojo. Each poem is to be divided into four sections: Prologos, Ludus, Interludus, and Epilogos.[21]

The Prologos, as might be expected, is the first song—a prologue of sorts. Two types of Prologos songs occur in a certain order: first the *oríkì orílè* and then the *ìjúbà*. The *oríkì orílè* is the "salute to the settlement." This song is believed to awaken the settlement's spirit and praise its distinctive features. It is usually performed at the entrance to a village or town, followed by the troupe dancing in rhythm to signal their procession into this village or town. It is necessary for every member of the troupe, upon entering the gate of the community, to gesture with a certain salute. Next comes the *ìjúbà*, which is a pledge that pays tribute to the beginnings of the Yoruba Masque Theatre, as well as its first dramatist.[22] The second sequence of the *ẹsà* is Ludus, consisting of improvised masque plays. It is somewhat like a variety show in style in that it lends itself to various dances, chants, and songs accompanied by the *bàtá* orchestra. Yet while there is variety in the Ludus, depending on the troupe performing, there must always be chanting, for chanting is the driver of the plot.

The Interludus then follows, composed of poetic chants, usually satirical, which are typically used simply to pass the time. The chants illustrate Esa Ogbin's way of assuming the role of Ologbojo, for Ogbin truly believed that he was a reimagining of Ologbojo when he performed the poetry style Ologbojo himself founded.[23] Finally comes the Epilogos, or the epilogue. It is a recessional chant that follows the last Interludus masque. The *bata* orchestra begins the closing:[24]

> It's enough for us to go home
> It's time we went home
> No masque-actor ever carried on his show
> And forgot home

The troupe subsequently dances its way out of the community, past the gate again, carrying with them their costume and prop boxes.[25] Some things are evident regarding the Yoruba Masque Theatre. Poetry, through song and chant, is the heart of it all. The improvisational performances give the individuality and soul to the story. And the performative pattern is the spine that holds the body of the plot together. With these three elements—poetry, improvisation, and pattern—the Masque takes its shape. All of this, of course, traces back to King Ogbolu. Over 200 years later, the Masque continues to delight the king and the people. Consequently, Yoruba kingship, as an institution, also continues to serve as an instigator of public art.

THE ROYAL BARD

Yoruba royal poetry, while it has changed over the years, still plays a vital role in maintaining the ọbas' social and cultural influence. While, of course, a Masque troupe may sing the king's praises, it is usually the royal bards who traditionally have done so informally, royal settings. There are two types of royal bards who serve their ọba: those who chant with "gourd rattles" (bulbous instruments with thin skin and a hollow center, usually filled with seeds) and those who chant with metal clavicles. Regardless of the instrument used, however, the bards always focus on proclaiming the goodness and awesomeness of their ọba.[26] For example, one particular chanted poem in honor of the ruler of Iseyin says that he is an "offspring of warriors" and "benevolent king," as well as "one-who-is-not-deceitful."[27] All of these names of praise are referred to as *oriki* and have been used on behalf of the king since the precolonial Yoruba era. These *oriki* used to be chanted every day when the sun rose; for this reason, the royal bards used to live in the palaces of their ọbas.[28] According to Karin Barber, the *oriki* for the king are of the highest significance to him because such words are believed to awaken inner powers within the subject. They allow the best aura of the subject—in this case, the king—to be realized and, in some cases, even become visibly noticeable on the subject's body.[29] Of course, because of the status of the king and the symbol of good fortune for the people, having his aura released would likely not just benefit himself but also his society. Thus, the belief that the king is second to a god and a bringer of good news encourages the *oríkì*, and the *oríkì* nurtures the belief that the king is second to a god and a bringer of good news.

Yoruba royal poetry has several distinct characteristics that make it different from other types of Yoruba performative art. Traditionally, other than *oríkì* (referring to the king or the king's lineage), this form of poetry involves the proclamation of names, kingship terms, history, and epithets. The proclamation of names is, in many ways, the greater context that envelopes the *oríkì*, so it is useful to examine this characteristic first. In Yoruba culture, a person's name is of the utmost importance. When children are named, parents are careful to choose the "right" name, for the name will embody the child's upbringing and fortunes, as well as the family's history and identity.[30] The peoples' names that encompass all these qualities are known as *orúkọ àbísọ* (personal names) or *oríkì àbísọ* (personal praise names). However, it is not just parents or other relatives who bestow names upon children or other individuals. It is also other supporters and well-meaning passersby who give these people names as a way of showing praise and their happiness. For instance, in Yoruba culture, it is not uncommon for one child to have five names from throughout his or her community. This sort of "phenomenon" is also shown in royal bards' poetry for their king. They may use suffixes or prefixes such as *Ọlá* (honor), *Adé* (crown), and *Oyè* (chieftaincy or royalty) to describe their king and his family to show the king's majesty and goodness that should be respected.[31]

By using kingship terms in their poetry, royal bards can connect their kings with their relations and kin, all to demonstrate how their kings are righteous and family-oriented. Royal bards will use terms like *ọmọ* (child of), *ọkọ* (husband of), and *bàbá* (father of) because, in Yoruba society, the greater a man's family, the higher his virtues.[32] However, it is essential to note that *ọmọ* may not always mean "child of." Depending on the context, it could be just an expedient term that connects the king to his forefathers and lineage. Overall, with these kingship terms, the royal bards show the validity of the king's past and succession, as well as the efficacy of the institution of kingship.[33]

Of course, the royal bards also depict historical events in their poetry to tell a story and capture the interest of their audience. More than this, scholars have found that the bards' songs are a way to document and rebuild Yoruba history.[34] With these references, the royal bards often (consciously or subconsciously) depict the Yoruba people's "psychological attitude" toward them. For this reason, the listener or scholar must listen for biases that distort the facts.[35] According to Jan Vansina, "The kind of historical information transmitted by [the] poetry is usually of a rather vague, generalized nature and it is often impossible to attribute it to any definite period of the past."[36] Yet even while some of the histories may be skewed, this method serves an essential purpose because it is to show how the king "should be" perceived—almost always for the better. Consequently, the institution of kingship continues with good graces and agreement from the people.

Finally, the royal bards use epithets for their kings, mostly about their emotional and physical qualities, as well as their general greatness. When the bards present the *oríkì* for their king, they almost always use his epithets as well, for both are intertwined and interrelated. For instance, Prince Àtìbà garnered much fame and epithets from the Yoruba nineteenth-century wars after the disintegration the Old Oyo Empire (reigning from 1797 to 1893).[37] These epithets were then used in his royal bards' poems after he became the Alaafin:[38]

Àtìbà, kínkín ò gbọdọ̀ gbin.	Àtìbà, in whose presence total silence is maintained.
Adébísí A-romọ-jogbo . . .	*Adébísí,* one who scolds the child mercilessly. . .
Àtìbà, Janganjangan . . .	Àtìbà, *Janganjangan* . . .
Ó gbóná girigiri . . .	One who is extremely tough,
Ó tutù nininini,	One who is extremely quiet.
Àtìbà lẹ rí	Because of Àtìbà
Lẹ kápó lápó;	You took quivers upon quivers;
Mọ́bòòṣàjẹ́ lẹ rí	Because of the one-who-will-not-bring-the-gods-into-disrepute
Lẹ kọ́fa lọ́fa;	You took arrows upon arrows;
Tẹ́ẹ kóbọn lùbọn	You took guns upon guns
Tẹ́ẹ kápata lápata . . .	You took shields upon shields . . .
Gbógun-nídè . . .	One-who-wins-a-war-tactfully . . .
Ọmọọ Atẹ́ní-ìjà bẹbẹ	Offspring of the one who is never tired of fighting

The bolded, italicized words show the epithets used for this Alaafin. "Adébisi" is one of the personal names of the Alaafin, translating to the "crown has increased." This name is supposed to show how a child's parents wish that the birth of their child is a validation of their right to the institution of kingship. The name "Janganjangan" is an onomatopoeic title for the king, and it is supposed to resemble the sound of the charms that rustled and jangled on his garb before he became the Alaafin.[39]

The preceding five elements that are present in the royal bard poetry can overlap in many ways. Still, they each serve a unique purpose to help one common goal: celebrating the king and allowing him to be presented in the most praiseworthy light as possible. By doing this, the people see the institution of kingship as worthy and good, and they comply with its rules. They also can make kings themselves appear mightier and feel mightier. For instance, during the Yoruba wars, the royal bards held the great responsibility of chanting for the warlords and encouraging them to fight on to victory. Because of this great responsibility, the bards were considered to be quite prestigious and honorable.[40] However, after the wars ended and democracy overthrew the African peoples' traditional form of government, the circumstances and nature of the bards changed. The economic sector of the kings and their warlords collapsed, meaning that the kings could no longer serve as hosts and patrons for their bards. Many kings and warlords fired their bards out of financial necessity; only a select few kept their bards to maintain a certain favorable political image. As a result, most bards even today live independently and may chant as a second job. When they do the chant, they primarily perform in front of the general public in big crowds, rather than at royal events, because this leads to a more lucrative performance.[41]

Even with these new circumstances, the bards have managed to survive and thrive in their ways with some changes to their poetry. The vast majority of the bards' chanting now focuses on their subjects' (including their kings') lineage *oríkì*, in part because of a practical reason: the lineage is a more stable topic that is much easier to memorize.[42] Besides, the lineage has a concrete set of memorable, generally unchanging images that form the foundation of Yoruba pride and the essential components of varied performances.[43] This form of *oríkì* is also useful for contemporary royal bards because they "draw on personal *oríkì*, prayers, blessings, proverbs, and topical comments."[44] Even though the bards now usually omit citation of names and history of the kings, their focus on the lineage *oríkì* allows royal poetry to remain relevant and popular to the Yoruba people, so much so that collections of the poetry are published[45] and featured in obituaries.[46] Thus, even though arguably the royal poetry has lost some of its creative "flairs," it still serves an essential purpose in Yoruba society that propagates positive attitudes surrounding the values and beliefs of kingship.

The physical artists, Masque performers, and royal bards have shown that, even with changes in Yoruba culture and the rise of globalism, some traditions—with some recycling—are not only possible but also practical in maintaining the Yoruba identity and the institution of kingship. All forms of Yoruba art in service to the king are purposefully and thoughtfully crafted. They allow people to rally about the king and sense the power of his symbolic presence. They also allow for the king to remain a valid, useful entity in the lives of the Yoruba people. Ultimately, the art confirms the king's eminence and worth. Without such art, there would be no visible representation of just what the Yoruba king's belief system and self are made of.

CREATIVITY AND THE ALAAFIN

I have elaborated upon creativity and power not only to show how various aspects defined the majesty of the king but also how many practices became the markers of identity, which they became the source of unity among the people, and how citizens were also able to accept the power of the king. Much more so, pan-Yorubana—the agency of Yoruba cultural impact over a wider region—could not have been possible without Oyo's influence and its ability to contribute to the flowering of a great Yoruba civilization in West Africa and across the Atlantic. Indeed, the Alaafin had significant festivals, like the Ifa, Orun, and Bere,[47] which united him with his people to share and enjoy performance, gifts, and loyalty. S. A. Akintoye reflected upon these creative and cultural practices to reach significant conclusions:

> The Oyo homeland in the era of the Oyo Empire, then, was a land of great and dynamic culture. Its huge cultural outflow played a very important part in promoting the image and influence of the Alaafin in the rest of Yorubaland and much of West Africa. The royal festival named Bebe served as the occasion to put on show the beauty of Oyo-Ile and the glory of the Alaafin and Oyo-Ile chiefs. Celebrated by the Alaafins who reigned long or whose reigns were adjudged by them and their chiefs to be successful and prosperous, Bebe was the biggest and loudest royal festival ever designed by any Yoruba kingdom. At its best, it was an ambitious royal jubilee supposed to last a full 10 years, during which rulers and chiefs of the Oyo homeland, vassal rulers and chiefs from all the tributary states of the empire, very senior messengers of kings of other Yoruba kingdoms, ordinary citizens, rich and poor, from all over Yorubaland and the Oyo Empire, were invited to converge on Oyo-Ile, to honor the Alaafin and give gifts to him, to bask in the greatness and beauty of Oyo-Ile and gaze with awe at the palace and its great king, to join in mammoth dancing celebrations and parades, and to partake of the surprisingly rich hospitality of the Alaafin's government and royal city. The Alaafin and his kingdom, sitting atop a sprawling and prosperous empire, took the beauty of Yoruba civilization to very great heights.[48]

Those Yoruba in the Yoruba colonies in far-flung places—Kanuri, Nupe, Hausa cities to the North, in Benin to the southeast, in Aja-speaking areas to the west, in the valley of Senegal—must have participated in several aspects of Yoruba culture. These Yoruba in the diaspora spread Yoruba language and cultural institutions to the Edo and Aja. By the nineteenth century, as part of the impact of the Atlantic slave trade, Yoruba culture had reached Sierra Leone. About 1.12 million Yoruba were taken as slaves across the Atlantic, with sizable numbers in the province of Bahia in Brazil, Saint Domingo, and Cuba. In these places, Yoruba cultural impact was very clearly established, enduring to this day.[49]

Alaafin Adeyemi III, the current occupant of the throne, has continued to relive elements of the culture of the past in the maintenance of the palace, in his food and the way he eats them, in the award of meaningful chieftaincy titles, in belief in herbal medicine and *gbẹ̀rẹ́ sínsín* (medicinal incisions), in praise songs that depict him as a spiritual and political figure as well as the body of the king, in his attire, both in private and public appearances, and in drums, those in the palace and those that accompany him to public events. In private, each morning, the drum announced to the world that the Alaafin is well and healthy:

> Dìde, dìde Layiwola.
> Dìde kí o bọ ṣòkòtò
> Layiwola dìde kí o bọ ṣòkòtò
> Atanda, kí o bọ ṣòkòtò

> Get up, get up, Layiwola
> Get up and put on (your) trousers
> Layiwola, rise up and put on (your) trousers
> Atanda, get up and put on your trousers

When the drummers stop, the Akunyungba (women singers) take over, singing praise songs. Whether recited men or women, the royal poetry is elaborate in words, and limitless in compositions, as the major book by Akintunde Akinyemi points out.[50] Many of the songs and poems reference the Alaafin's key motto: *Ikú Bàbá Yèyé*, the core cognomen used only for the Alaafin. In these three-letter words is the merger of creativity with cultic power, the merger of "heaven" and earth. As the Alaafin himself explains in his own words:

When an Alaafin is to be crowned, he is made to go through rituals, cleansing and sacrifice. He is inducted to the Sango mystery, the Ifa corpus and other mysteries of the gods. The Ọba becomes a beneficiary of death, sorrow, predicaments at home and outside. They term him "Iku ('death') personified." Since you've come to the world, you know (that) you are going to die; why don't you do your duties that are assigned to you by tradition? You come to the world as a mortal; you will be afflicted by ailments; why can't you forget the ailments and become a beneficiary of the ailments? Now, when you are crowned the Alaafin, and you are to do your duties . . ., the travails inside and the travails outside must come always, and the Alaafin must be controversial. So, why are you running away from your responsibilities? You've become *omo iku, omo arun, omo ofo, omo adaba ile, omo adaba ita, omo ti iku npa tii gbe ru baba e, omo ti iku n pa tii gbe ru iya re.* (lit. "the child of death," "the child of disease," "the child of loss/waste," "the child who, while dying gradually, helps to lift a load to his mother's head)." You are the beneficiary of all these as the Alaafin, and as a human being, you have no more sorrow, no more death, you don't fear predicaments, you go and do your duties. That is why the Alaafin is described as death personified . . . he is a beneficiary of the person who is dead; . . . and you ascend the throne. If he is not dead, you cannot ascend the throne; so you can now die . . . so that other people can ascend the throne.[51]

CONCLUSION

Chapter 11

Rethinking the Discipline: Africanity and Belief Systems

From the foregoing, we have explored the boundaries and ambiguities of knowledge systems. We've done this by demonstrating how each system of knowledge holds embedded values and beliefs. Societies have often tried to absolve themselves from possible critical onslaught from their dissidents that believe differently. Each of their knowledge systems, namely religious and scientific arguments (specifically those coming from Western backgrounds), inundate the intellectual community with strong evidentiary bases that may appear objective and convincing. These lines of argument require reflexivity, beyond simply the limits of in-group bias, to define the inelastic and limited capabilities they have to provide the answers they seek. What makes all these knowledge-generating sources more compelling for keen engagement is their history rooted in rationalism. The mere fact that science comes with results after carefully invested observation and justified logic, ditto religious sources, makes each of them a provider of light for the advancement of human society.

It is regrettable, however, that both of these structures believed to generate knowledge for mankind are contentiously leaving African knowledge production sources behind over an erroneous assumption that these African epistemologies are inherently illogical. This attitude is deep-rooted in the culture of universalism; the universalist epistemic perspective reflects Western hegemony by supplementing subaltern epistemologies with Western philosophy without ever augmenting the Western philosophies themselves. In the same way that Euro-Arabic relationships are rooted in attitudinal rebellion, the same pattern can be applied to established Afrocentric worldviews, ideologies, and ultimately epistemologies. Africa, like the West and Arabic world, has attached her knowledge generation to belief systems. This unity is grounded in the great importance of religion and social activities in African worldviews. Through these knowledge systems, Africans often base their understandings and advancements of human geography, medicines, astronomy, sociology, and moral ideas. These examples are few among the many other subjects that Africans instrumentalize to the advancement and development of their individual cultures and societies.

Apart from the relatively recent ascension of scientific inquiry—in the modern usage of the phrase—into general knowledge production of the contemporary world, every race of people has always maintained a level of scientific and logical scenarios or processes of getting truth. This is valid as long as we align with the definition that science does allow for observation, replication, and experimentation. Similar to *other* domains of knowledge production, science often finds shield under the cover of inaccessibility to equipment. This elitism and inaccessibility of scientific knowledge may be the reason for making, at times, unveracious projections. While the superiority of modern sciences is often claimed, scientists also admit that science is not infallible. When mistakes are made, their propensity to misfire is excused by the ability to update their positions when superior arguments backed with solid evidence surface. Could this be taken as an alibi created to give scientists a soft landing? If anything, it is evidence that the hegemonic truth of science is a smokescreen; despite its self-admitted fallibility, science suffocates the intellectual community through asserting itself as the incontestably strongest knowledge system with impenetrable standards.

Perhaps, the most educative way to understand the unstable nature of scientific inquiry is through historical analysis of discoveries past. Many scientific studies, previously accepted as truth, have found difficulty remaining in public relevance after being debunked by superior scientific arguments. For example, the Blank Slate theory (or Tabula rasa), which was widely popularized by John Locke in 1689, argued that individuals are born without any intrinsic knowledge. That is, our brains are empty at the point of birth, and that all human knowledge is built from experience and perception. However, contemporary scientific research challenges this theory through the discovery that genes and other genetic information congenitally inherited have important roles to play in human memory.[1] Another insightful example of a debunked scientific assertion is the assumption (or conclusion) that humans evolved from apes. Scientific proposition such as this floods the intellectual space of the twentieth century by scientists who arrogate to themselves an unparalleled sense of pride for having a different path to conventional understanding. However, this is rendered invalid by the current discovery that humans and apes do not actually share a father/mother relationship; instead, they share common ancestors.[2]

Curiously, one may be compelled to ask if our journey to identify the shortfalls of science could be motivated by malicious intent to discredit it. Our current interrogation of science is not motivated by such intent. However, what is primary to this intellectual exercise is to critically place in perspectives the alternative source of knowledge generation provided by science and then objectively evaluate the method to see if it is foolproof. From all indications, science, like the "other" knowledge production sources, is prone to making errors. This reinforces the assumption that religiously and culturally motivated truth can be sometimes factual and in other times laden with sentiments that are pushed to be arbitrarily accepted over time. What this is tending toward is that humans can accept science and other emerging sources of knowledge generation—especially those that do not conform with science or religious ones. Mention must be made, however, that the attitude of arrogance arrogated to science today has been tasted unchallenged in the past by religious institutions when they equally were the sole determinant of knowledge economy for the human populace. It is therefore incumbent on religious teachings and institutional structures to understand, instead of condemn, the scientific approach to generating truth as a worthy alternative.

Now that the content of knowledge production that comes from the African continent today has achieved a comparative success, its enduring confrontation with the Eurocentric ideology and Abrahamic religious knowledge economy is to be understood within the context of essentialism where it seeks to establish itself as, like others, noteworthy knowledge sources. Science is not explicitly particularly credited to any group of people in particular, as long as you can engage in any research that satisfies the basic tenets of scientific enquiry. African systems of knowledge have been used to develop environmental and human resources from time immemorial. However, there is certain underlying assumption that Africans are incapable of engaging scientific research because of the likelihood of some interference of their culture into data gathering. Therefore, it the duty of African scholars—who are witnesses to the African style and method of knowledge generation—to educate the world about the outstanding characteristics of African knowledge production. These scholars must advocate for rethinking the academic disciplines to expand the applications of African knowledge systems for the usefulness of mankind as this book has elaborated.

CAN SCIENCE TEACH MORALITY?

As has been established in this work, cultural or religious knowledge that corroborates scientific knowledge is often, and arrogantly, overlooked as coincidence. Modern science is regrettably limited, offering a narrow pathway to truth that often only recognizes a set of procedures known as the scientific method as the *only* acceptable one. This leads us to a soul-searching question about those human engagements that cannot be actually affected by science. Given the understanding that science only validates existential and natural knowledge through observation, evaluation, and rationalism, can science therefore teach morality, or enhance it? Or does the pursuit of objective knowledge through scientific research transcend the human pursuit of morality? If we conclude that humanity needs morality and that it is not logically within the domain of science to provide, then science needs the intervention of a human moral architecture.

Logically, we have concluded without any fear of contradiction that science really observes nature. Additionally, it gives adequate attention to events before coming to conclusions through the use of instruments that have the capacity to enhance reliable results. It is, however, undeniable that the preexisting methods were also credited for following similar steps before arriving at their truth in Africa, and fortunately the religious truths as offered by Abrahamic religions are not exempted. However, the point of their divergence can be seen in that African knowledge production, despite a round of critical onslaught generated that its own form of truth is devoid empirical backings, provides the compass for the moral architecture, spiritual behavior, social security and mental sanity, emotional intelligence, and ideological contents of the people. This represents humanistic dimensions to knowledge that contemporary scientific information cannot ascertain, using the method that is corroborated by Christian and Islamic religious ideologies. The fact that many things are written, ranging from history, culture, and attitudes of the African people, by Europeans without having adequate social and cultural exposure to these people expatiates the attitudes of arrogance of the European world in jumping to conclusions about Africans and their epistemologies.

This lack of insight and adequate knowledge about African practices inspires them, Eurocentric viewers of African events, to make sweeping generalizations about Africans, not minding those available cultural and social exigencies that give power to the establishment of certain institutions, for example, witchcraft. The attitude of universalizing human experiences continues to deprive Western and culturally weaned African scholars (who obviously were immersed in Eurocentric culture) of the opportunity to understand Africans who tenaciously hold in their hearts the essentialism of these institutions that are held under skepticism by outsiders. Without straying from the question about the capability of science to provide moral structures, we consider it invaluable to add that knowledge production is best appreciated when the sources are diverse and inherently convincing. And then we swerve swiftly again to the actual discussion that morality is as important to humanity as science and its unveiling discoveries. Also, the existence of science does not hibernate the age-long human capacity to launch corrosive content to vulnerable civilizations. In fact, it intensifies the probability. Scientific and technological inventions have historically been employed to silence vulnerable civilizations.

An encouraging aspect of modern science is how it has evolved to dislodge heretofore erroneously held beliefs, allaying people's fear over mythical composition. By taking hard knocks on falsely generated truth, people renew a confidence to develop a thinking mindset to culturally believed ideologies. For example, foreign religions, chief of which are Islam and Christianity, have sects that have strongly prevailed that the earth is flat. Without remorse, they have held this position for centuries and are not apparently interested in dissenting opinions whether they are logically proved or emotionally motivated. To accentuate their position, they have silenced very many thinkers who held the belief that the position of the earth is actually different from the position agreed upon by religious institutions. During this period, the religious institutions enjoyed unequal freedom, giving it the privilege to decide what it believed to be the truth on astronomical matters as in this example. By bringing the existence of people who suggested otherwise, banking on their findings, into an untimely erasure, many potentially versatile minds with brewing scientific skills and knowledge were give compulsory censorship. Eventually, the myth is debunked after the surge of scientific and intellectual inquiry made into the phenomenon of space knowledge. This, we must admit, is one out of the many other scientific inputs to modern knowledge that faced severe onslaught before finding foot eventually.

The appropriate question to ask therefore is, "Is this type of *scientific* truth about the earth new to Africa?" To get into a logical end, let us examine a few of African epistemologies on space matter. Coming from the knowledge of Ifa, the compendium of the Yoruba people's history, physics, arts, and aesthetics, ecological understanding, and also where their understanding about human life and universe is sourced, what is then their perception of the shape of the earth? According to a documentary where Professor Sophie Oluwole, professor of African philosophy, discusses the concept of Olodumare (the Yoruba God) in a TV program, Opomulero TV, she gives an insightful information about the position of Yoruba people regarding their understanding of the planet. She prevails that the concept of God in Yoruba epistemology gives educative signals about the knowledge of the people on astronomy issues. To her, the word Olodumare is a coinage of different lexicons, with the breakdown of the word into Ol-odu-mare where ODU is the base word. This base word, ODU, means a pot, and one needs to be familiar with the Yoruba culture to have a clue about how and what their pot looks like in precolonial time. Descriptively, it is spherical in shape. MARE, the last lexicon in the neologism, has a clausal value if it is condensed into the English language and it literally means "that cannot be exhausted."[3]

Following this sequential arrangement, the OL attached as a prefix simply means "the possessor" of something. Therefore, Olodumare, the Yoruba God, means the owner of a pot that cannot be exhausted. It must be borne in mind that the *pot* that already comes as representative of the spherical earth is synonymous with the scientific position on earth, which says that it is truly spherical and not flat, as propounded by different religious knowledge productions. Given this level of scientific exactitude, one is compelled to consider acknowledging such knowledge generation method that has been in existence for more than 10,000 years. To understand the enormity of the Yoruba epistemology, one cannot but see how the submission of science about the galaxy, or universe, continues to take different turns in accordance to the available scientific tools, changing, evolving, and updating their position at quick succession. Despite this, however, the position of the Yoruba people about the shape of the earth is not invalidated. Even though scientists are predictably clinging to their default escape root where they would ascribe such claim made by the Yoruba as being a produce of coincidence, their ignorance of how things are organized from another end should not be excused to accommodate arrogance, or masked under it.

All these elucidations are geared toward the understanding of science as an alternative source of generating truth. By attuning itself to the already popular understanding of it, science confirms that humans can generate knowledge through attentive observations of universal laws, adequate experimentation to verify or falsify developed hypothesis, and the tenacity of result to withstand critical evaluation. In a simple arithmetic, such methods are not lacking in the African knowledge production method used before their contact with external bodies. Having shed some light on the issue at hand, it is instructive that we address the question of morality, which is the primary concern of this angle of education about science. For anyone to arrive at a scientific result, there usually is the need to generate hypothesis that will serve as the foundation of inquiry. For example, the early humans after noticing that the universe is structured in ways that go beyond their own comprehension would make unconfirmed assertions about different phenomena that they believed would be sorted out after considerable observation, examination, and rationalization. In this spirit, they would expunge held beliefs when overcome by superior scientific arguments that question or challenge the validity of their conclusions.

Their discovery, for example, that the earth is spherical does not, however, contribute to human moral life, and neither does it debase it. Instead, it gives the human race a reliable information about the universe, which essentially shapes their conception about some natural events. Human morals come from their lived experiences, shaped through continuous practice of behavior that are acceptable among that particular group. It is this definition of morality that makes it a relative possession because what is morally acceptable to an African man may be unacceptable to an American. The fact that the moral architectures of a people are different across cultures attests to this subtle summary. However, scientific conclusions about some phenomenon can sometimes occupy universal or global definitions, as seen in the example of the planet earth. And in some instances, it could be streamlined to specific demographic. If it is a scientific truth that the sun burns some human skins especially those from American race, such truth may not necessarily apply to Africans and all their racial family because of their melanin nature. So, science is good and does not seem to be in contention with African knowledge-generating sources. In the opposite, it can actually be integrated into them for a powerful synergy. Against the campaign of mainstream scientists, we do not need to discard indigenous information and knowledge in order to become informed. In other words, they are not mutually exclusive.

SCIENCE, RELIGIONS, AND EPISTEMOLOGIES

Now that we have attempted to situate the place of science in knowledge production in modern thinking, we are duty-bound to address how the alternative knowledge economy, as introduced through African knowledge system, can be incorporated and recognized to occupy its deserved position. It is inconsequential to collapse African epistemologies into the mainstream, making it to operate from the background when other sources of knowledge generation are enthusiastically accepted in intellectual engagements. Apart from this condition being an extension of Western hegemonic agenda that silences other sources other than universalist ideas, an attitude espoused by mainstream academic despite the degrading effects it has on the "other," it also aims to force Africans to adopt the lens of the European society to view the world around them. What is very pertinent in this process is that Africans primarily need to understand that variation in geography, culture, religion, and social reality, among others, condition people to expressly think in the way that they have particularly chosen to. Even when humans are liable to accept change when confronted with superior encounters, some things would rather be modified than abandoned. Despite that obvious level of modernity prevalent in the Americas, a large number of the population are still operating within their religiously dictated moral philosophy.

In spite of the numbers of African religions in their preliterate time, none was able to challenge the imported religions when they came because of the methods used by the machineries that exposed the indigenous ones to be swept away after a long campaign of calumny against them. By promising an instant relief to the overwhelming problems facing the people, they succeeded in uprooting these indigenous religions and shortchanged them with Western ones. Except for those people who clung stubbornly to their belief systems, there was a gradual erosion of the knowledge that the people used to derive from their African religion sources. Thus, having been clothed under various deprecating garment, the indigenous knowledge productions lack the strength to sustain themselves in the turbulent environment that is hostile to their survival. Their knowledge economy was derided as lacking empirical information, devoid of logic and starved of due diligence. Temporarily, this would be immediately replaced by the imported religion knowledge sources, which comes to tell Africans "about the things they do not know." Such knowledge about natural phenomenon begins to flood the African space where they do not particularly share similar convictions. For example, the religious knowledge about the existence of God and the position of the planet, among others, came from Islam and Christianity.

All this time, science has been a tool of political power in control of the knowledge economy, especially in the West. As a consequence, in the global political economy, indigenous African sources of knowledge were marginalized. For a very long period, many Africans considered their acquired indigenous knowledge as an incontestable truth. This determined the ways through which their social activities, moral architecture, and ideological policies were then structured. Looking at this history of suppression that African knowledge economy has been a constant victim of, it would amount to outright epistemic violence to discredit the source when there has not been any thorough examination of it from the people who intend to keep it perpetually silent. The mere fact that African scholars who are well read usually do consistently affirm the knowledge production coming from Africa as tenable, observable, and replicable enables an understanding that their indigenous knowledge systems are worthy of recognition. African knowledge epistemology therefore may not conform with the mainstream—scientific—definition or knowledge acquisition; however, it does relate to the people and address their contemporary trends. What therefore could be done to rethink the discipline would be explored momentarily.

SCIENTIFIC ESSENTIALISM

The first step to rethinking African knowledge production is by acknowledging other sources of knowledge generation, including scientific and religious. By understanding that these two sources are not in competition for the survival or effacement of any of them, the African mind versed in indigenous African knowledge will navigate their ways properly without losing their face. As explained in this book, the line of difference between magic and miracle is determined by the position of the analyst. These two phenomena function within the same circumference; Africans can therefore leverage on what is available to them to contribute to the body of knowledge existing in the global society to advance the course of humanity. When these knowledge sources are acknowledged, it would propel the people to understand why contemporary society deserves diverse approach to information gathering. We have identified instances where science upgrades its position when superior instruments become available and at the disposal of the scientists. This identification is not meant to fault the reliability of scientific processes; rather, it is a way to affirm the nature of truth, which sometimes could be unstable just like the universe itself.

Science has educated us generally that it is not constrained to function within a specific discipline and we have notably seen the rise of scientific behavior in various disciplines such as in politics, geography, and sociology, among many others, where people are recognized by using scientific approaches to arrive at their conclusions. This means that while conventional science is leading the ways of discovery in important things such as getting additional information about constellations, making further expeditions into pharmaceutical research and understanding the world generally, there could exist a complementary knowledge production. This complementary system may be offered by African epistemologies and religious sources. There are established items of information that have been considered as true for millennium, regarding constellations in the African worldviews; however, there is an absence of empiricism in the method. This makes the patterns of observation, evaluation, and rationalism, as espoused by modern scientists, difficult to achieve. The absence of this therefore does not invalidate the truth discovered using indigenous methods, as long as they are not rendered invalid by modern scientific researches. For example, the concept of the planet, as understood by the Yoruba people.

All these notwithstanding, the usefulness of science as propagated by the Western interests will never be underestimated. Within the relatively short period of time that it has enjoyed in human knowledge generation, it has challenged *existential truth* and age-long held beliefs by providing a more logical and empirical evidence to substantiate all the claims it makes. As such, it becomes difficult, if not impossible, to relegate the essentialism of scientific approach to truth finding to the background. In essence, the collaboration of science with the other available sources where knowledge is generated is necessary. Creating such synergy will foster human development both in moral and philosophical existence. The symbiotic essence of the collaboration holds different benefits for mankind for the advancement of knowledge and its application cannot bring about devastating consequences. Science itself is an appeal to the intellectual community that usually determines the direction of the society through the knowledge they produce. Even though science is susceptible to fallibility owing to the available instruments at its disposal, it has still historically been relatively reliable.

RELIGION IN A MODERN WORLD

Apparently, religious establishments, especially Christianity and Islam, have dominated the world for ages now making assiduous attempts to convince humans about their individual truth. While their submissions about existential truth can be contradictory sometimes, they have demonstrated similar capacity to sway the global audience about having the exclusive pathway to generating universal truth. Of course, in the previous submission, we have indicated how each of the religions claims itself as the *only* way to reaching truth. Owing to the vast acceptance of these religious beliefs, it is therefore relatable why we stipulate that people who are convinced of the religious ideologies would hold tenaciously the truth as espoused by the religious doctrines. This explains why, even till today, the majority of the adherents of Christian and Islamic faiths are strong believers of a flat earth. Despite the increasing scientific evidence used to support the claim of a spherical earth, people convinced of the infallible status of their religion still believe that science has given a contrary position not because of any falsity found in the claim of the religion but because they are committed to bring the influence of the religion to naught.

Taken as the words of God by believers of these religions, their social, political, and moral systems of the people in Africa have been shaped. Many countries seek for both moral and objective truth from religious books, making their continued reliance on these religious structures guaranteed the more. Therefore, this stresses the importance of religious epistemology and insight, as the source of knowledge and the decider of their social relationships, even though the promulgation of other different religions challenges the value of truth as showcased by a particular religious group. Accepting these religious statements as truth is rooted in the conviction that the Supreme Being inspired their writings. Even when there are emerging historical and scientific arguments that contradict these conclusions of the religious truth, they continue to gain relevance because the followers have developed unbeatable reverence for the religion. Therefore, when worshipers are obviously manipulated, they easily conclude that it has a divine coloration. To discard the known influences of religion because of the rise of scientific inquiry would remain contextually difficult for obvious reasons. In spite of the number of conclusions reached by science that contrasts claims made by the religion, people are still convinced to follow their religious part if it brings no harm.

Although many of the African religions do not enjoy such popularity as the Abrahamic ones, the fact that Africans are rooted in religious issues attests to the inherent religiosity of the cultures even before the incursion of the external influencers. Rethinking religion to suit the demands of the current world system requires that religion shows readiness to accept scientific truths that are gathered through empiricism, to avoid leading people astray or keeping them uninformed about important things that concern their existence in a quest to remain in forever dominance. Religion has retained modern relevance partially because of the work of religious scholars, who are educated in epistemological arguments and the logic of modern science. These religious scholars combine the knowledge they gather through their religion and scientific knowledge to navigate their individual or collective realities. Thus, the integration of scientific findings to suit religious truth becomes relatively easy as people are convinced further that religious positions, which in some instances contradict any scientific finding, result from the unsophisticated materials available at the time of writing the conclusions and not as a result of the unintelligibility of the writers. With this mindset therefore, obscuring religious truth entirely could be difficult. The integration of scientific findings with religious truth and information would achieve beautiful results.

REINVENTING AFRICAN EPISTEMOLOGIES

When closely observed, it would be clear that native knowledge production systems stem from the culture of observation and examination, for it is strenuously difficult to project knowledge into existence. The quest for truth demands a pattern of behavior that involves this method because it is the nature of knowledge generation to make hypothesis, view the things of nature very keenly before depending on eventual conclusions. In other words, indigenous knowledge too must have had a systemic pattern followed before arriving at their current status of becoming unchallenged truth. It is undeniable that Africans lost a chunk of their historical artifacts the moment they had a contact with colonial imperialists. The people only rely on verbal sources to retrieve many of the lost information about themselves—a gesture that was not only derided by Western audience but also desecrated as fatuous. Although Africans in preliterate era depended heavily on oral rendition of history because of an absence of the writing science, even when there are indigenous methods of inscription not totally regarded as writing. As diverse as the African cultures, so also are the diversity status of their epistemological understanding. Their native knowledge provides for them the level of civilizations they could lay claim to—technology, arts, mathematics, physics, and many others.

Using the Yoruba culture, for example, there is a division of knowledge production and acquisition into very clear terms, which make people to identify their strengths and pursue knowledge in that regard. Among them, this division helps to build and develop competent minds with vibrant energy who would handle developmental issues ranging from academics, technology, philosophy, art, and aesthetics within their society making it easy to have knowledge production from quality minds to move the society to the next level. This is basically how their nonformal education system transcends generation and helped them to build civilizations worthy of recognition. For example, among them, there is the group they call Alágbède (the irons smith) who are exclusively in charge of their technology; there is another called Gbénàgbénà equivalent to civil engineers in English language; there also exists another group called Babalawo/Iyanifa who are in charge of pharmaceutical research engagements handling health-related events. In fact, this system developed so that families are identified by their trades and such systems build competent hands who in turn make overwhelming contributions to the advancement of the Yoruba society. The maintenance of this style further cements the people's confidence in their native knowledge.

Comparatively, the method was very productive because of its result-oriented nature. Countless issues are handled by hands with technical know-how that enabled the experts to learn further through practice and experience. They in turn become pioneers offering expertise knowledge and sound judgment over what they have acquired in the process. Going by the potency of their information, it is inconsequential that this is not recognized in modern knowledge production method where the survival of cultural identity is dependent on how they can organize knowledge themselves and turn their lives around. The people in charge of say pharmaceutical study devised means by which their discipline would experience notable differences and changes; the ones in technology understand the task ahead of them and embrace the attitude of record making and keeping in the line. There are encouraging improvements made in accordance to the speed of development kept by those people generally. When this generation decides to take further interest in the African knowledge economy, such expedition will uncover important things that will be relevant to the contemporary world generally.

It is possible that one day the world will understand that the level of scientific inquiry concentrated on finding about constellations and stars, about geography and ecology, by the modern Western scientists, is not far from what the indigenous people of Africa did when they conduct researches on trees to see how they can be used for human benefits. When this day comes, we would therefore accept the reality that knowledge generation should not have to follow identical ways before it could be given that scientific status. Any attempt to infantilize one in favor of the other would result into a hegemonic attitude that pervades the intellectual space generally and this would disallow a level ground that can foster genuine development. In other words, Africans are saddled with the responsibility to ensure that their native knowledge production must be reinvented to suit the emerging realities and demands, if they would ever lay claim to international respect. There are numerous aspects of African knowledge that can be explored, patented, and would add value to the global society entirely. The world keeps showing us that we just must be ready to challenge our collective style and methods of knowledge production and acquisition. As an example, the world can learn some new things about African pharmaceutical knowledge.

THINKING OUTSIDE THE BOX

The contemporary world is filtered with compelling Eurocentric biases arranged deliberately to enable further hegemonic culture of imperialism. When we look keenly into all fora of knowledge and information generation, there are unfurling Eurocentric permutations, which would expose the underlying attitude of superiority in everything. The foundation for this is set, beginning from the era of colonization that saw to the establishment of educational structures that conditioned the minds of the people to function in an insidiously preconceived way. The most potent thing and instrument employed to execute this assignment is language, a diversionary approach used to harvest the minds of the already colonized people. By speaking the language of their erstwhile colonial invaders and using them in their educational engagement, the African mind is wired to think in a particular direction. The potency of language would be properly understood within the context of thought generation and eventually their reality formulation. The moment the African people are conditioned to use the language of these occupiers of their geographical space, they become victims of epistemic conquest who straddle between two opposing identities.

The problem is extensively complex because of some existential factors, which of course were not put into perspective by the generations that inherited the colonial tongues. One of these facts is the reality that the newly Western schoolgoers began with the thought of being *like* the European or the Arabic man, depending on the side that colonized them, carelessly tossing their African identity to suffer utter abandonment. Aided by the potency of language, other artifacts of European cultures (apart from their languages), such as dress, food, living style, marriage system, legal methods, and invariably the chunk of their cultures entirely, became transported into the bloodstream of African nations, without caution. When all these have crisscrossed their ways into African indigenous systems, it automatically sets the whole stage for mental colonization, where all the phenomena usually handled by indigenous system are forced to take up the toga of the European color, with amazing turn-in. As a result, the African methods and styles appeared obsolete to these new set of Africans with Western culture and education, and unfortunately, they were the potential leaders of their respective countries with the political power to determine things.

As a result of this, there was an immediate change in the ways that things were hitherto done in general. African governing styles became instant victims to be obscured, even when they clearly have difficulty understanding properly the new ones bequeathed and how they can fit into these countries. Largely, African values are now defined by Western perception adopted by the schoolgoers immediately after independence, and by the ones who succeeded the generations that survived colonialism. However, the African man is unaware that all the thought generation that gives way to the formation of their ideologies and realities is a product of continuous examination and evaluation of their environment. In other words, the creation of dress, food, government systems, marriage, and other customs results from their ecological and social consideration of events. Therefore, the inheritance and the adoption of these things without considering their contextual importance or compatibility status makes things more difficult for the African man. Even till today, we would notice that European style of education takes Africans far away from their indigenous knowledge systems because of a misconception that African knowledge production is evil or incapable of meeting up with the contemporary dictates.

Let us consider as an example the adoption of democracy by African countries; succumbing to the pressures coming from the Western world, it affirms that Africans who have gone through the Western education system think that whatever is of European making would automatically fit into their African system to achieve African agenda. Even though countries like America who now campaign for the global adoption of democracy accepted it in relatively recent history, also facing emerging challenges until the system was probably domesticated to suit native American agenda, the contemporary African is in haste to appropriate these imported ideologies. This is just a mere example, amidst all other aspects of Western culture that creep into the African space. All these are boxes—the established standards—with which Africans measure their development or conceive what development should be. The sad reality, however, is that Africans and other parts of the world have dissimilar realities that demand unequal method to the application of solutions to existential challenges. Even in intellectual environment, Africans hardly use their yardstick to measure their growth; instead, they rush immediately to invoke Western standards to determine a number of things. As such, the people are discouraged from looking into their own indigenous knowledge system.

This continues to serve as a nagging impediment to African progress because of the reality that the contemporary Africa is a shadow of their precolonial ancestors and leeches to Eurocentric ideologies. Here, several people contend that Africans have truly advanced considerably by applying the Western method to the administration of African concerns. For the people who share this mindset, it is not impossible that they defend their position by citing the progress they think Africa has made in education, medical science, legal system, government system, and social architecture, among others, all of which are open to objective contentions. However, they would likely be oblivious to the staggering reality that we have education but less morality and this becomes the foundation for the perennial challenges Africans have in contemporary time especially at leadership front. Hardly would there be any succession of government in Africa since postindependence that is not extensively immoral in their dealings. However, this conclusion could generate a reaction leading to the question, "Is the precolonial time free from immoral engagement?" Fine question if we have it. Quite simply, the time was actually not rid of immoral actions in the corridor of power; however, there were indigenous solutions to problems arising from that angle. Unlike today, we have a justice system that does not give swift response to emerging issues; more so, they are susceptible to corruption.

Logically, all these trends are clear indicators that African knowledge economy should be given the needed attention, not only for the continent to be recognized but also to assist in thorough decolonization process. A cursory journey into the education curriculum of the American and their European counterparts reveals that they are deliberately taking away the histories of their exploit in other people's countries to configure a generation of Americans and Europeans who would be absolved of any emotional guilt of their ancestors. Curiously, the Africans in their own sense of liberalism having acquired Western education think in similar way. In essence, Africans of the contemporary world do not think independently for their thoughts are always hovering around what has already been conditioned by the Western interests. Thinking outside the box requires that Africans would identify their recurrent challenges, conduct findings on how similar issues have been handled by their ancestors, develop new ways from the systems they left behind, and then apply African solutions to African problems. The fact that many Africans care a little less about their language today shows that they still do not prioritize their worldviews. Sadly, this mindset continues to keep them inside the box.

ANCESTORHOOD/ELDERHOOD KNOWLEDGE SOURCE

Another source of knowledge generation in Africa is through the elders or the aged ones in the society. The opportunity to serve as stakeholders of knowledge impartation is bestowed to them by their lived experiences and involvements that cannot be purchased by money. Elderhood that has been used interchangeably with ancestorhood in this writing can be understood from two important philosophical perspectives. First, it has a conceptual structure that talks about numerical value of people's age. Here, aged people in the society are revered not actually because of their acquired competence or knowledge on a particular field of study. Instead, they are regarded because important activities have occurred in the society and they are witnesses to them. These accumulated experiences therefore qualify them to provide valuable information and judgment when similar situations surface in future dealings. In other words, they are identified as the public memory, keeping interrelated events as data, upon which they interrogate, analyze, and then evaluate to sift out something important for the collective society generally, meant to be used to their general benefits.

Second, elderhood is understood within the context of artistry got from a profession through the dedicated time of service in the said profession. Under this, wisdom is not automatically conferred by a person's age; rather, it is dictated by the acquired knowledge and skills that they have had over a particular period of time. This means that the numerical value of a person does not clearly bestow on them the ability of be well informed on every aspect of knowledge generation source. For example, age does not automatically confer on one the ability to be vibrant or competent in an aspect that one does not engage one's times and services. Therefore, people who have spent or dedicated their time and intellectual services into a profession are bound to be more vibrant and competent than the people who have not. If a person of twenty-five years has spent seven years learning iron smiting, it would be very difficult for an older person of thirty-five years who have only spent six weeks in the same profession to have a comparatively better or more reliable skills that the former, particularly when these two individuals are biologically and mentally sound in similar capacity. Therefore, the wisdom of age is best understood from social angle when the knowledge bothers on social issues, while it has to do with numbers spent on profession when it has to do with a particular field.

On social knowledge economy, even the less brilliant members of the society are still certain to possess important information about the society because their age has made it easy for them to internalize events that happen while they are growing up. An underage, no matter how brilliant, cannot lay claim to this form of knowledge because it is not bequeathed through mental strength or intellectual brilliance. The sole requirement is the accumulation of age. It is, therefore, on this basis that the aged ones are highly revered in the African worldview as reliable repository of the people's knowledge and their source of information gathering. Their closeness to exit route from the physical world places them directly to the ancestral ways and are conceived as getting their motivation and inspiration from ancestors believed to roam the African space in spiritual forms. Therefore, the African people consider elders as respectable because of the unending messages they pass to the younger generations, which are always philosophically embedded with useful content. Through experience, the African elders can predict the future of an event with doubtless exactitude by merely glancing through the data.

Every family in Africa usually has a head who is saddled with the responsibility to guide the ones coming up from making wrong life decisions that can threaten their existence. In fact, it is very common among African elders to see them interested in sacrificing their lives for anything that can threaten the lives of the younger ones. This is because it is socially considered inconsequential for the younger ones to pass away when elders are living healthy. Such elders lose their common regard and are debased for being unlucky, or not spiritually observant of their own downgrading. So, when elders give their contributions on natural, social, or philosophical issues, their inputs are always seen as devoid of emotional biases, unlike the younger generations who are predisposed to arriving at a conclusion based on their emotional involvement. African elders occupy important position in African world because they have, through their age, acquired numerous knowledge that can guide the younger ones from making wrong choices and decisions that can stand in the way of collective progress. They mediate between or among warring individuals or societies to strengthen the bond existing among them to ensure solid growth.

The emergence of modernity, however, challenges the concept of adulthood and ancestorhood in the African worldview. There are continuous demands to differentiate between the experience, competence, and intellectual brilliance in managing the contemporary concept of society, which obviously takes a different form from the ancient ones. Today, there are metropolis, city-states, and urban settlements grounded in technological wiring that obviously requires more than what the African elders' experience can be totally relied on for requisite knowledge or input. This then demands that there is a paradigm shift in the conception of elders' knowledge generation owing to the political philosophies that have taken over in contemporary world. This is because there are some African elders who have the primitive understanding of their roles and always want to exert this sociological influence in all aspects of African world, especially in the political circles. Whereas what is needed to maintain maximum functionality in the current world is not actually an experience bequeathed by age; rather, it is a competence that is validated by intellectual and mental strength acquired through learning. A cursory look at the world political leaders making important strides will confirm this assertion.

Does this therefore relegate the usefulness of the African elders to nothing? It is actually far from it. Instead, their elder's positions could be transformed to be useful to the society in very different manifestations. For example, they can offer priceless information and ideas that are key to the formulation of international relations and internal coordination, all in an effort to promote these social values to the global world. They would, therefore, function to the maximum by constituting the advisory bodies to government agencies on diplomatic issues and relations. Although mode politics might have considerably changed from its primitive prototype, its structures are an exclusive preserve of the traditional methods, where important things that are instrumental to the advancement of the society are cautiously managed by the elders. What is different remains the global persuasion of economic and political expediencies, which of course require different or innovative ideas to engage them. The project of globalization demands that the involvement of elders in political matters takes different dimensions so as not to lose touch with important global events. For example, climate change is the core concern of the global security challenges but many African elders at the political front are unaware of its gravity.

How then do we incorporate elder's knowledge into the contemporary sources of knowledge and information generation? To answer this, there is a need to understand that information gathered from elders on any topic usually serves profound purposes because they provide crystal-clear ideas that could help in conceiving the modern world when placed side by side with history. The fact that all the contemporary happenings are mere modifications of what has happened in the historical past accentuates the importance of elders in modern indulgence. War? The aged ones have witnessed surplus of them. Political affairs? They have encountered numerous examples that they can offer expert knowledge about potential ways of handling them. This, rather than reduce their functionality in the contemporary world, improves it. They are the primary contacts that individuals who eventually go out to have social input meet for knowledge and ideas. Thus, the deference to the elders should be reinforced because they have the tendency to communication their experience to the younger ones without allowing personal sentiments to come in their way of judgment. Again, elders are not disposed to making hasty political decisions, unlike the younger ones, because they have witnessed horrible consequences of hasty conclusions.

INDIGENOUS THOUGHT PROCESS AS A PRECURSOR TO GROWTH PATTERNS

The exploration of rote thinking that has been institutionally activated in Africans seeks to achieve some clearly structured goals. First, it aims to identify how Africans have mindlessly accelerated their thought processing in wrong directions. The occurrence of colonialism does not necessarily forestall a people's progress if they are aware of their problems and how to deal with them using their self-guided methods; after all, the Chinese, Japanese, and Indians were all colonized and are making significant progress today. Second, it has helped to identify how languages are potent instruments used to condition a people's thoughts, revealing why generations of Africans have been a silhouette of their colonial invaders instead of being Africans in the actual definition of it. Now, after the recurrent challenge facing the continent, it becomes the primary responsibility of the intellectual spectrum of the African world to search for likely solutions to the myriad of problem facing them collectively. In this spirit, we offer useful alternative to engaging the concerns through reverting back to the available indigenous knowledge systems of Africa to reclaim the lost identity, integrate them with modern trends, and then claim their deserved position in the scheme of things. What therefore does it mean to think like an African man? Answering this question is not a straightforward as it could be thought of and, given the very many ways that the precolonial Africans conduct their activities, Africans are also diverse in their thinking.

The preliterate African societies are not, in the long run, devoid of having some advantages. The projection of the downsides of lacking written documentation eclipses the other sides of African reliance on oral legacy. When the Europeans make sweeping conclusions that African archives cannot be recognized as reliable source of information gathering, they were only directing their aversion to African preservation methods because they are unaware of how things actually work in Africa. Elders in Africa have always been their repository of knowledge, history, mathematics, and physics amidst other items of their cultures who then in turn download all these into the subconscious of those younger ones through proverbs, folktales, riddles, and moonlight plays, among other methods, usually recognized by the people. Thus, knowledge generation process is an interplay of mutual respect from the givers and the receivers. This stresses the importance of every demographic in society ranging from the geriatrics, the middle-aged, and the younger ones, owing to the understanding that everyone has their roles to play in moving the society to the next level. Through this, a good sense of communalism is birthed for the enhancement of desirable future.

A striking example of knowledge production source is the Ifa, the compendium of the Yoruba's mathematics, epistemology, metaphysics, history, ecological compass, and aesthetics, among other things. This has been preserved by the custodians of the system from generations to generations through the oral methods in that chain of events. Naturally, it would be nothing short of amazing to nonpractitioners of the Yoruba culture to understand that something as enormous as the Ifa divination system was an exclusive preserve of people who did not attend Western education outlets. Oral legacies extracted from the communal archives are usually derided because they continue to defy Western logic. And interestingly, they are just the routine styles of the Yoruba people, for example. Ifa is consulted when the society is confronted with overwhelming and acute challenges; it is their source of moral philosophy; it helps in strengthening the bonds that appear slicking for known or unknown reasons; it is their source of inspiration to advance their general courses of action, among many other things it does for them collectively. Everyone has a clear definition of responsibility and what is expected of them as their quota to the society.

For millenniums, Ifa remains the source of knowledge for the people concerning their lifestyle and it is always regulated by internal arrangements to avoid occasions of subjective permutations where an individual cunningly arrogate power to themselves. For the outsiders, the wonderment of the system makes them conclude that it is either built on mere hallucinations or orchestrated to deceive the multitude. But when we come to the realization that Ifa divination system has been in existence for thousands of years, guiding and guarding the people, our innocent curiosity will be aroused. This is in addition to the fact that the territorial integrity of the Yoruba people has always been maintained and sustained by the people who obviously practice the indigenous and native knowledge. Virtually all the aspects of human life are touched and explained using their native divination system. In fact, Yoruba coding system was manufactured by the custodians of this indigenous system, which further accentuates the importance of native knowledge and how it provides extensive avenue to make great impact, give the people a direction, and prepare them to be of value addition to their society.

In this society, therefore, the spread of indigenous knowledge is credited to the socialization of people among themselves where the individuals acquire information from members of their society. Knowledge is coordinated by people who have inherited adequate information from the ancestors for the development of their society, and this is usually refined to meet up with the standards of the contemporary world. The reinforcement of native knowledge production could actually dislodge the institutionally entrenched systems of Eurocentrism that always seeks to discredit it because of its indigenous coloration African. The fact that this knowledge generation method is communally prioritized with the tenacity to accommodate various contributions from the people stresses why it prevails in the traditional African society. Unlike the modern method that infantilizes those considered as incapable of producing outstanding knowledge, the African society in the preliterate era was not stratified along these class lines. Coupled with the alienation of the people from their indigenous sources, the modern knowledge sources decapacitates the people who are unprivileged to acquire Western education, from contributing to the knowledge production of the society.

Just like many other sources of knowledge production such as those found in the Christian and Islamic religion, the philosophy of Ifa is designed to preserve extant Yoruba cultures and mores to reflect their collective values. They have recorded a history of consultancy of Ifa as their major source of innovation with the assurance of offering reliable solutions to address their pressing concerns. As such, the thought process of the Yoruba people springs from the close relationship they maintain with their indigenous knowledge provider, which usually propels them to develop the necessary pathway to solution finding. Ifa corpus houses a number of activities that attune the people with the changing society so that up-to-date ideas can be formed to address different emergencies. Getting a Western education, however, draws many Africans farther away from their own native knowledge because of the internalized colonization that is activated when one solely relies on Western education methods. The end product of this is that people become distant by applying Western philosophies that are always proving inapplicable to the challenges of the African people. Every aspect of Yoruba knowledge is sourced from their understanding of Ifa and this has proven potent for a long period.

From this, the South, North, East, West, and Central Africa should consider appropriating indigenous knowledge systems into their engagements and develop a generation of Africans who can address the African challenges using the African methods. Virtually all aspects of human discipline today will always identify with different corners of native knowledge production where additional information can be extracted for the common good of the people. To really embark on a genuine decolonization process, native ideas must be encouraged. These alternative worldviews are key to challenging the box—standards of thinking and measurements of progress created by orientalists—that has carefully been institutionalized by the Western politics. The majority of Africans who get Western education run to adopting Western standards to judge the African progress in terms of technological development and scientific innovations, doing damage to the African minds whose reality does demand for something more urgent and practical. Today, Africans barely can lay claim to contributing to the growing global advancement and the reason is obvious. By developing the African minds to reflect European values, Africa incarcerates itself the more.

AFRICAN WITCHCRAFT: AN AFRICAN UNDERSTANDING

The continued inability of Africans to define the epistemic standards of their world gives undue advantage to the hegemonic power to impose their definition on some concepts that they believe share similarities with their own existential truth. Witchcraft is one of the many angles of outright, apparent misappropriation of image that Africans have had to contend with in modern time. There appears to be growing fear among some Africans who have made insufficient efforts to decode majority of the phenomenon around them, including outsiders with passive understanding of the same events. The West, in their unrepentant ethical desecration of anything contrary to their *truth*, imposed Western definition of witchcraft and appropriated their foreign characteristics on these African witches. In this expedition, the African witchcraft is a target of acidic dehumanization and their names are sullied irretrievably in the process. Findings reveal that a large number of Africans accept witchcraft as a reality that has continued to shape their world, in many ways. Their existence is defined by an understanding that there are some groups of individuals with the spiritual wherewithal that can influence their world for provincial reasons.

In the contemporary times, the treatment of the witches especially in areas where they gather much recognition, albeit negative ones, conveys that modern Africans conceive of them as predatory beings deserving of hostile decapitation or condemnatory abuse. In plain language, the current Africans, rather than hold unproductive government accountable for their swelling woes in consistent with the Marxist ideology, usually redact to attacking the witches over a misconception that their lack of employment, success, and entrepreneurial advancement has some connections with the activities of the demographic. This conceptual understanding stems from the Western-induced definition of witches circulated by missionaries who have a dangling responsibility to extend the colonial degeneration of African values. After prolonged battering of this foreign understanding into the bloodstream of the African people, they would eventually be alienated from their sociocultural reality. Instantly, a people who have successfully lived with witches for millennium now begin to see the phenomenon through the viewing lenses of their European allies, depending on which country colonized who. Not minding the inherent lack of empathy for the group, the process of identifying and attacking the witches especially in the modern society is fraught with inconsequential shortcomings.

For anyone who is versed in the African epistemology, the witches apart from answering the call of nature to undertake certain responsibilities within their different societies, they constitute a spiritual social group that challenges the misuse of power by the people invested with authority in the society, contrary to the hegemonic assumption that they are inherently wicked. In Africa, it remains difficult to separate the people's spiritual life from their social realities as these are an interrelationship of variegated experiences where people navigate their existence by giving relative attention to them all. The spiritual life is useful and can be the sole decider of their social life. Their economic status is equally understood from the angle of politics. Therefore, the formation of such social groups as witchcraft is hinged upon the conviction that they could mobilize their influence and charge the leadership to be observant of their sociological duties that would especially enhance virile development and smooth running of collective activities. The enduring difficulty to establish empirical evidence to substantiate the conclusion that African witches chiefly perpetuate evil is a proof that they have been helplessly misconstrued.

In this way, the activities of the African witches can be understood within the context of power and a history of challenging authorities leveraging on the spiritual, social, and cultural values they are societally recognized with. This tells a story of the system of development adopted by these Africans in preliterate era, as the decentralization of power in politics and spiritual matters helps to reduce the excessive pressure that could have naturally erupted from the center, that is, the monarchs and their power proxies. From this understanding, the witches constitute a check-and-balance groups in the African societies, and in some instances, they extend their responsibilities to capture individual immoral engagements, giving deserving reprimand where needed. Witchcraft in Africa becomes a victim of desecration by the Western interests who are obviously oblivious of its cultural symbolism, and these contemporary Africans are unhelpful in their conscientious ignorance. Looked at from the sociopolitical angle, they are the spiritual police that timely remind the power holders of their political mandate, forcing them to cultivate good attitudes to cater for the needs of the powerless community members. Africans who immediately jump on the bandwagon to prosecute the witches are always guilty of malicious manhunt for the continuous failure to substantiate their claims when they conclude that African witchcraft is irreparably evil.

As has been argued in this segment, understanding African witches from the viewpoint of the African people is necessary if genuine decolonization of Eurocentric permutations would ever encounter any sustainable chance. To redeem the lost information about these people, there must be some intellectual engagement that seeks to search from the untainted truth, contrary to the popular ones always masterminded by European anthropologists. By realizing that the first set of Europeans usually relied on in the past for giving information about the African people are unmistakably pursuing a malicious agenda that enabled them to make many horrible conclusions about Africa and Africa as being savage, barbaric, and backward, we cannot therefore comfortably accept their definitions and conclusions about many African realities. The work of Joseph Conrad, those writings of Herbert Spencer, and the narratives of Francis Galton all culminated to the image incarceration Africans have to contend with for a very long period. In essence, as many of their conclusions about the people are fraught with apparent inconsistencies, relying on their literatures about African witchcraft would be ideologically difficult. The witches in Africa, given their survivalist tactic and how they evolve with the fast-changing societies, cannot be adjudged as evil in generalizing term for they have contributed to the African issues beyond what can be underestimated or measured.

KINGSHIP STUDIES

One advantage of my approach, in focusing on ideologies and epistemologies of kingship, is that it can lead to the creation of African Kingship Studies, which would cumulate the narratives around all the kingdoms and their kings into rigorous intellectual studies and teaching of kingships, the examination of older and alternative political systems, the meanings of networks of power, and the relevance of past institutions in contemporary societies. Kingship Studies is not about whether the older forms of kingship should be kept, revived, or abandoned but about studying an institution that governed Africa and many other parts of the world for centuries, much longer than the contemporary colonial and postcolonial ones. Kingship Studies can be located in various departments: Anthropology, Sociology, History, Cultural Studies, Religious Studies, Philosophy, and others. It provides the junction to engage in comparative analysis, international relations (among and between empires), intergroup relations, cultural analysis, and many more.

Kingship Studies will definitely provide a unique opportunity to discover the strange in the familiar within accepted notions of modernization and, thus, to conceptualize Africa's reality within the context of history. While the expansion of modern secular democracy is often viewed as correct or fated, it deviates from the larger historical trends of monarchies that blended the religious with the political. Indeed, a majority of political structures around the world from the Neolithic era to the Industrial Revolution were characterized by kingship; consequently, early political prudence must be understood by its emphasis on the sacred. This historical frame of reference demonstrates that secular thinking is not innate to the human experience and those perceptions of what designates as commonsense change over time. Therefore, the push for modernity through democratization is only one of many possible outcomes that could have arisen from the decline of kingship.[4] With this in mind, a valuable opening emerges to reconsider Western value judgments that presume secularized democracy is the only viable structure for civil society. Kingship Studies, combined with my other ideas on "ritual archives," will lead us in the direction of what I had previously developed and termed as pluriversalism, thus taking ideas that originate from Africa, that are then refined by African scholars, that are decolonial, and seeing the extent to which epistemologies deriving from them can drive scholarship.

Kingship Studies will, as well, examine the creation, evolution, and current manifestations of kingship in Africa through the lens of power politics and culture. Through the investigation of Kingship Studies, students will achieve a greater understanding of African cultures within the context of their sociopolitical histories. Students will also have the opportunity to evaluate notions of modernization that rely on the spread of secular democracy and to discover the role of sacred rituals in politics and society. Potential course contents include, among others, the global nature of kingship, how kingships operate (examples drawn from places where the students come from, the Qba of Benin, the Nayiiri of Mamprusi, the Alaafin of Oyo, and many more), the historic role of the ritual in politics, the divine right of kings and its functions, the transformation of kingships over time, and the role and perceptions of kingships in an increasingly democratic political atmosphere.

Kings gain their influence from the power of ideology, uniting groups of people sharing common values through the flow of economic and cultural materials. This relationship exemplifies the potential for knowledge to create power, and the epistemology of kingship provides critical analysis of general epistemological approaches. It gives special perspectives into African epistemologies and their holistic nature. Kingships are maintained through holistic understandings of religion, science, and social relationships. They are supported by mythology and tradition, ritual, and kinship. These are common ideas for understanding the fundamentals of African epistemologies. Thomas Hobbes famously said that the state is "a moral god,"[5] and this role of divine government was the essence of kingship in Africa. Kings remain, although the ideology has shifted, and a new epistemological foundation must be built.

Naturally, in Africa and across existing sacred kingships, the extent of the cycle of power varies depending on location. But the cycle has yet to be broken completely. It makes up a significant part of the history and even the modern culture of the African people. The youth of Africa should understand sacred kingship and its influence, especially within the context of a globalizing world where democracy is the globalized ideal.

If a syllabus were to be created for kingship courses in universities and colleges, the following is a starting point:

I. Instructors must discuss the use of mythology in creating and bolstering an ideology and epistemology of a people. Without mythology, there would be no foundation for any kind of symbolic sacred kingship. Instructors must review the various mythologies either supporting or contradicting the use of the sacred king, noting that any mythology must necessarily serve a certain agenda.

II.   Concepts of indigenous governance in various societies (afọbajẹ, ijòyè, adé, ìtẹ́, and others among the Yoruba, for example) must be taught and understood as first step to understanding the notion of ọbaship.

III.   After reviewing the various mythologies of ancient sacred kingship, students must be given a thorough history of how sacred kingship has been perceived and how it has evolved over time.

IV.   Similar to point II, instructors must ensure that all theories on the significance of and purposes for sacred kingship are covered. There is a continuous cycle of renewal between ritualization and epistemology/ ideology, but the history of the proposed methods of kingship is an important part of this understanding.

V.   There must be an emphasis on the meaning of symbolism in culture. Objects are merely physical entities on the surface, but they carry memories, emotions, and identities. Before students understand the use of symbolism in sacred kingship, they must understand and appreciate the use of symbolism across history, recognizing why symbolism resonates with cultures. Symbols can communicate an unspoken language that is not understood verbally, but emotionally, between peoples who have similar struggles and experiences.

VI.   Once the students understand the general significance of symbolism, they must examine how and why specific symbols, like those found on Yoruba ọbas' crowns, are culturally significant to specific people. The instructors must inform the students that symbols, while powerful, only convey an important message if the message is relevant for the intended audience.

VII.   After they learn about the history of symbolism and sacred kingship, students must study the various rituals found in sacred kingships across the African continent. Seeing the rituals with a new lens will allow them to grasp just how profoundly integral these rituals are to perpetuating ideology, epistemology, and identity.

VIII.   Students must leave the course understanding the cycle of ritual and epistemology/ideology. Without a true grasp of this cycle, the student will fail to understand how living mythologies have continued for hundreds of years.

IX.   Students can study transitions of power in different historical formations, learning how the present takes elements from the past. Colonialism terminated the sovereignty of kingdoms, but not their kingships. Not all modern kings are grounded in rituals, and many have even become Muslims and Pentecostalists. After their subordination to colonial and post-colonial authorities, previously land-based kingdoms became part of expansive, sea-based imperial powers. Kingships can teach comparative histories of kings, kingdoms, and empires. Although

Oyo and other African empires and kingdoms became part of new colonial territories, many old, land-based empires survived for much longer, such as the Ottoman Empire in Russia. The greatest land-based empire, the Soviet, collapsed in the 1990s—it endured longer than the sea-based empires, which all collapsed rapidly between the Second World War and the 1970s.

This course would show students how the concept of a sacred kingship is not primitive or unrelated to their own worldviews; it is entirely compatible with them. Sacred kingship forms the backbone of their civilization and a cultural identity they should be proud of. Sacred kingship's ability to unify people and continue significant communal traditions involve activities that make us human—capable of deep understanding, creativity, and emotional communication. As long as the next generation respects the benefits of this concept, the benefits shall continue.

Kingship Studies represents an opportunity to teach history over a long historical period. As many as 4,000 years ago, Hammurabi and Sargon the Akkadian emerged as kings in Asia who conquered vast areas and created centralized authorities. The Assyrians developed an imperial ideology based on conquest and kingly prestige. Trading posts established by the Greeks between 750 and 550 BC resembled twentieth-century colonial systems in many ways. Egypt became one of the longest multiethnic empires, with powerful kings ensuring stability, collecting tributes, and levying taxes. Contemporary politics and systems can be compared with older polities; many problems faced by modern states had equivalences in the older regimes of kings.

Kingships are systems of government interwoven with religion, philosophy, history, and culture. From ancient Egypt, the Aztec Empire, and the Kingdom of Oyo, kingships have been a driving force in history. They are unique institutions that require multidisciplinary perspectives. They use ideology to support institutions of power in unique ways, and their ideologies rely on religious epistemological approaches. Kingship Studies gives an integrated perspective on diverse disciplines in the humanities working together. Its interdisciplinary approach will allow students to understand historical perspectives and non-Western epistemologies.

Kingship Studies would introduce students to a variety of topics through discussions of kingship, including examples of kingships and their historical patterns. An introduction to philosophy would discuss epistemological justifications of power. It would explore theories of religion, including anthropological theories about the religious origin of civilization. Kingship Studies would also explore the sociology of kingdoms, the formation of social hierarchies, and theories of civilization. Kingship Studies involves theories that can be applied to literature, archaeological evidence, and modern issues in international relations. It could be developed into a master's program with a well-developed curriculum. A number of kings in Nigeria could give endowments and create fellowships for this.

Kingship Studies could educate students about epistemological and political diversity. At the end of the course, students would use perspective-taking skills to interpret primary historical documents. The fieldwork component would include oral interviews with kings, chiefs, citizens, and people connected to the specifics of governance. And students could apply their knowledge of kingships to contemporary issues in international relations, becoming more critical of their own epistemological approaches to justifying power and more tolerant to those of others.

With respect to the humanities, Kingship Studies will achieve the same general ends as the study of great works in literature, or any topic in history or religion that supports knowledge and the need to develop critical thinking skills and impressive writing abilities. Kingship Studies is an approach and method for building and practicing analytical thinking, improving on the skills of written and verbal communications and understanding one's culture and the cultures of others. These studies enable students to be inspired by the great minds of the past while learning to criticize foolish acts and behaviors, understanding excesses and abuses of power.

In relation to their times, they can evaluate the meaningless in the past and the meaningful in the present. As students engage with those meanings, they will be drawn into the intellectual, spiritual, and moral aspects of the complicated world where we live. Their wisdom of the past and present will deepen, widening the sources of wisdom and learning not just about current ways but also about how those in the past dealt with obstacles, success and failures, adversities, and triumphs. In the process, they will imbibe the spirit of empathy taught by humanities, and they will have clarity of values by comparing their own to those of others.

To understand great kings of the past is to understand the complexities of politics. To understand King Mansa Musa is to understand the global order at his time and the global reach of finances. To understand the Pharaohs and the pyramids is to understand ways of life and culture centuries ago. To be at Ibadan and understand Shaka Zulu is to appreciate the cultures of the Zulu and how they think. To compare the Alaafin with the Buganda is to understand the interconnectedness of knowledge, and how ideas that are treated separately can actually fit together. To understand the Sèkèrè Alaafin is to understand how creativity develops, how it is appreciated, how it is repackaged for the contemporary moment, and, above all, how it is important for you and I to promote arts and museums. To understand King Solomon and his biblical psalms is to develop the habits of being human. To understand Caliph Bello is to ask questions about Islam and the world. To understand kings and their wars is to engage in difficult intellectual arguments about cause and effect, dealing logically with human motivations. And to debate both sides of wars and their execution is to recognize how knowledge is driven by complex stories and information, biased mythologies, and imperfect data. Understanding dynastic rivalries and competition for the throne is to develop the ability to weigh evidence, to understand that there is no one side of a question or one side of an answer. And for those who lack this understanding, the transparent values in Kingship Studies will teach them that any subject, any field that is well developed and well taught will lead to informed citizens who are also critical of knowledge and society. Without critical, informed citizens who can apply knowledge from the past and a variety of sources, Nigeria itself—which has replaced kings with politicians—may not even flourish.

ALAAFINOLOGY

By deploying the conceptual framing of kingship power as Alaafinology, I am offering a conversation that is less about the narrative of this specific kingship but a lot more about it as a "system" of politics, institution of governance, and political philosophy. I am doing so not within just the Oyo data, as useful as this may be, but within a larger African setting as well as the world beyond Africa that speaks to kingship. In this larger setting, the ingenuity of a system receives substantial theoretical analysis in terms of its representation, justification, ideology, and relevance. In my approach, the African concept and ideologies of power may begin to receive an attention that they have not yet received. One advantage of such an approach is that this discourse can be built upon to move the contributions of Africa to a higher level of analysis, approximating it to what is called the "universal." Indeed, narratives on Oyo as well as other African kingdoms and empires treat them as localities and peculiarities; my study treats them beyond that, with the further suggestion that theoretical ideas can be formulated around the Alaafin and other kings to talk about the constitution of political ideologies, ontologies of power, and the epistemologies around domination and subjectivity.

Alaafinology may also be renamed as "Obalogy"; however, my reasons will still be the same. Historical narratives, as rich as they can be, are not enough to create intellectual permanence, to organize memory, to build museums, to build ideologies, and to universalize knowledge. Many essays on different aspects of kingship have become ephemeral. Labels and definitions are the tools of power, knowledge dissemination, and the means to spread ideas over a wider region. Taking the great stories of the Alaafin outside of the Yoruba region may not necessarily connect with such people as the Igbo (Nigeria), Asante (Ghana), Vai/Kru/Grebo (Liberia), or Zulu (South Africa).

However, labels and definitions connect; therefore, they enable others to study their own histories and events in relations to those labels. Where the label fits, it enables the "universalizing" of narratives; whereby it does not fit, it allows narrative departure points.

A label is a shortcut to a library. It allows the creation of a subject, a field, a specialization, as in PhD in Alaafinology, which may be on a group of people in faraway Gambia. Disciplines have their roots in labels, as in History, Literature, and the subspecializations within them. Elsewhere, I have argued that if we had created Ifalogy in the 1950s and 1960s, many universities would have been awarding degrees on it. Such a degree would have attained virtually everything that the humanities stand for as in critical thinking and pedagogy. Labels have been created to understand institutions, processes, places, and so on. For instance, we now use the Sultanate as a label to describe many kings in Muslim countries. We now use Egyptology to describe the study of ancient Egypt and its antiquities, and we label those who engage in it as Egyptologists. A highly specialized branch on language within Egyptology is known as Demotic Studies, and they refer to themselves as Demotologists. Studies on Ifa could be labeled as Ifalogy while those who engage in it can be called Ifalogists to designate a highly dense and specific field.

We must create labels and define them, their meanings, methodology, and tools. Thus, I can say that Alaafinology means the following: kingship and the exercise of power, kingship and the civilizing mission of culture, kingship and the collapse of kingdoms, the body of the king, and so on.

We can then apply the meaning to specific cases over time. For instance, the label can be a way to understand history, as in the study of the Pharaohnic state—the king and his ability to expand the polity. After the decline of Egypt, monarchies developed in Napata and Meroe (Sudan) and a greater success story in Ethiopia, which survived the modern era. Alaafinology can speak to the forms of monarchies, their strengths, and decline. To speak of Alaafinology, in whatever form kingship is defined, is to speak to ideas about the centralization of power, the forms of government, and the theory of power (distributive, absolutist, divine, monarchical, predatory, premodern, modernist, etc.). Alaafinology can speak to the theory of checks and balances, but with moments of ruptures to the system and the move toward absolutism.

Alaafinology can be used as a label to understand land-based kingdoms. The Alaafin and Oyo illustrate the characteristics of land-based empires, in some ways different from the far more expansive sea-based empires with larger conception of global imperialism and modernism.[6] Land-based empires emerged in China, in the Americas (Maya, Tiahuanaco, and Huari), Aztec in Mexico and Inca in Peru, both later destroyed by the Spaniards. How did they emerge? Who destroyed the kings? How did the fall of kings connect with the role of outsiders with better weaponry? Why did some like China survive for a longer time and able to work its long successful past into its impressive present, based on a solid long-standing bureaucracy? How did land-based empires generate resources to fund emperors and fight their wars?

Alaafinology is about the ability to manage conflicts and wars. Conflicts were very endemic to the kingship system. It was hard to manage an extensive empire. Similarly, it was certainly hard to manage the competing forces within the palace and capital. It was hard to manage sibling rivalries. Take, for instance, the succession to a vacant throne, which was (and now) always very complicated. Rivalries were intense by the aspirants, in spite of being related by blood. *Oye didu*—competing for the throne—reveals the ability of a candidate to master the skills of negotiations and survival, the understanding of the forces that exercise control, and the ability to project one's character. The competition was tough in the past, and tough in the present.[7] Having ascended to the throne, its maintenance was equally difficult—one needs political acumen to handle men and women with competing interests and a lot of money to sustain a lifestyle.

Alaafinology is about the understanding of African power systems before the imposition of colonial rule. Power revolved around the king, his palace, the household, officials and retainers, and powerful chiefs and kin groups. The strategies of kings to maintain dominance were never the same. Many African kingdoms were fragile, while some were strong. Migrations away from power centers undermined the power of many kings. Loss of the control of trade routes, long-distance trade, and labor weakened many kings. The impact of the king on everyday life of citizens was never the same everywhere. Not all kingdoms were able to be successful as Egypt in establishing legal systems and bureaucracies. Not all were also greater than the Roman emperors to use religious institutions to establish a cultural dominance.

Alaafinology is a label to understand the processes of state formation in different parts of the world. Sometimes, state formation involved an access to an ideology of power, as in the case of Islam in the Sokoto Caliphate. The success in building a strong military, which must be ensured by access to weapons, means of mobility, and horses (as in the case of Oyo). Warrior kings emerged in some places, as in the case of Shaka, the founder king of the Zulu. Between the sixteenth and nineteenth centuries, Oyo and many other West African kingdoms, especially those along the coast, had to deal with the opportunities and destructions of the Atlantic slave trade. The supplies of slaves to the Atlantic—which produced access to guns and gunpowder, while allowing them to consolidate power—also destroyed them in the long run.

One final example is about death and transition in the context of royal life. The body of the king, in death, creates mysteries, and in some sense miseries as well where, in the past, it warranted human sacrifices. In secular terms, the death of the king was a calamity around the continuity of the system and the ruptures that were created. Whether it be Oyo or Mali, the death of the king generated serious uncertainties. There were reasons for this. Performance and effectiveness were very much tied to the person of the king. Indeed, the health and fortune of the state was the same as those of the king. Death could immediately undermine the state itself. Speaking about death, the study around death, including suffering and agonies, has come under the label of thanatology, which has given rise to scholars on this topic who call themselves thanatologists.

I expect a vigorous challenge to my intellectual creation of Alaafinology as a label. If objections are raised to the suggestion on its wider application to cover long historical eras in different parts of the world, it can, at least, be applied to the study of Oyo in the *longue durée*. The label will certainly work for Oyo where, as in a study by Abdullahi Smith on the fall of the Old Oyo Empire, the label of "Alafinate" had previously been coined.[8] Pending the affirmation or rejection of my idea, I am using Alaafinology in its broader sense that I defined previously. In this application, I am not just dealing with Oyo but kingship in general within a broad ideological and epistemological canvas. To fully understand what I am driving at, it has to be seen as an epistemic enterprise in the decolonization of African knowledge. The proposal has a very strong scholarly potential to open the traditional archive to unfold a richer understanding of institutions.

CREATING LABELS TO SUSTAIN AFRICAN EPISTEMOLOGIES

African history obviously did not start from their contact with the West. There are innumerable items of history that can be studied and the timeless knowledge that can be excavated from the African archives when appropriate energy is dedicated to the purpose. Just like the Egypt Empire was an awe that attracted the intellectual attention of the curious ones after its occupation by the Roman imperialists even till modern day, there are other African cultures and communities whose gigantic posture of history would unfurl a constellation of values, ranging from their great political organization, social philosophies, and technological inventions, all that could sufficiently prove beneficial to the contemporary world. Like we have suggested, creating such labels as Ifalogy, for example, would bring about getting expertise knowledge about the nature and components of Ifa in relation to how it became very influential in designing the Yoruba world. In another case, the previous chapter argued that the creation of Alaafinology as a label will enunciate the political theory adopted to control vassals for centuries with competent economic designs that assisted in upholding the empire for long. Creating them into modern discipline is not premature for it would automatically inspire a revelation of the ingenuity of precolonial Africans, who unfortunately have been labeled on the wrong side of history, by revisionist historians.

The other available alternative is, however, not helpful. The failure to create such labels would lead to the complete obliteration of African epistemologies, obscuring what should naturally have been a compass to their modern reality. In a clearer term, what will Africans gain from the template of education provided by non-Africans who, in the truest representation, are not especially interested in their psychological, political, and economic freedom? By refusing to revisit past history to explore the exploits of the past Africans who have demonstrated versatile mental capacity, to what extent can Africans advance themselves using their inherited European templates to navigate their realities? Going by the understanding that Africans have been appropriating the Eurocentric models of social development for almost a century now, are there comparative advantages that would inspire instantaneous nostalgia if dropped? Development is a complex interplay of analysis of recorded progress made in every facet of individual life. If the adoption of an economic system or philosophy, for example, advances a country's financial status but destroys its moral architecture, has negative consequences on its social lifestyles, crumbles its political views, and crashes other areas of its worldviews, what has been developed?

To arrive at this utopian African future, fundamental questions should be asked and convincingly responded to. How does such label as Alaafinology unveil the intricate powerplay among potential power contenders who are qualified by blood to occupy the seat of power? One powerful thing that we would uncover from this is that the council of chiefs are usually statutorily empowered to determine who succeeds the throne, and here, the phenomenon of election comes into play that allows the vested authority to choose who represents them in the political department. Contrary to popular narratives peddled by the orientalists, such process showcases democratic engagement where leaders are chosen based on their qualification to the throne and their satisfaction of lay down rules. Such label, therefore, would enable Africans and outsiders to understand that the application of native and traditional knowledge has been very useful in advancing the course of the people, especially the Yoruba people in this sense. Today, the American model of government and democracy is learnt in different institutions, whereas such systems have been in practice in many of the African city-states before their contact with the European world. Therefore, it also deserves learning.

The benefits of creating labels could be interminable. As people learn about the intellectual and mental brilliance that enabled the then people to have such admirable level of organization, they would equally learn about the reason for its decline; why it fazes out during the invasion of some external civilizations? The Empire of Benin, for example, resisted aggressive attacks of invasive civilizations for centuries because of its military policy and competence. Therefore, civilizations such as the Oyo and Benin did not collapse because of their inferior weapons used to engage the colonial imperialists; instead, their defeat was a complex network of internal politics, power tussle, and social infractions. The Europeans cashed in on this weakness to penetrate to almost all the African civilization and this gave them the opportunity to infiltrate them and inflict maxim pains. If appropriate attention is deployed to the learning of these historical artifacts, sufficient education would be gained on how to create, manage, and sustain empires, bearing in mind the negative consequences of bitter internal politics of mudslinging and the effects of fragmented unity, as these are potential sellouts for the people generally.

It is undeniable, therefore, that the creation of labels will definitely help to understand many things as regard the progress of the African people. Apart from it allowing retrospective reflections on past events in relation to how they can have unnegotiable influence on the future, it would also enable retroactive considerations of activities, to consolidate their balance. Politics, technology, war, and philosophies all can be learned from the historical archives of the African people when the academic discipline is created to answer to these unfolding questions. Labels like Ifalogy would continue to help illuminate how a body of knowledge and information can be structured into the social codes that would be studied and decoded by the succeeding generation. It reveals things about the people that European knowledge generation methods cannot ensure. Although there are stories that Ifa is a component of knowledge that emanated from the unusual ingenuity of Orunmila having been touched by Celestial bodies and inspired by them. Beyond this, however, we should marvel at the documentary prowess of the people that survived many centuries in the absence of a writing culture. Therefore, creating a label of discipline to the study of such a phenomenon would most predictably show the elastic capacity of people to store information, without using Western methods.

REVIVING AFRICAN CREATIVITY

Information sharing and its generation occupy an important position in human life and it has been known as an integral part of African civilizations, just like every other. Although there persist the allegations by Western world that the African's failure to have a writing culture affirms their conclusion of them being savagery in nature—a conclusion reached to justify imminent predation. Despite the absence of a writing culture, however, different African city-states communicated using conventions accepted by them and this transcends generations. One of such examples is the Aroko method of information exchange by the Yoruba people. This method exclusively uses semiotic arrangements to share messages, which cannot be decoded by non-members. Before expanding the nitty-gritty of Aroko, the chapter explained the sensitivity of information sharing, even in contemporary world. People trade information and its lack of control can essentially implicate person-alities and destroy civilizations. Today, the security architecture of Western nations is guided strictly by the code of silence. The continuation of secrecy in communication exchange determines the safety of a people in today's world. Therefore, the inherent rule that guided the creation and use of Aroko still lingers in today's world—secrecy.

The communicative and semiotic value of Aroko hints further about the sense of creativity of Africans because of their understanding that their safety index is largely proportional to the secrecy that can be maintained and sustained by their communicative systems. Driven by native awareness, the objects of communication in Aroko medium are a department of knowl-edge acquisition that can be resuscitated for modern use. Civilizations in the modern world do not reveal their inner potentials to others because of the tendency to become predatory over them. Once one's security architecture is exposed to external knowledge, its occupation is therefore imminent. Coding has become an important part of the current global system and this can duly be leveraged as reason to embark on historical soul-searching. Each object included in Aroko coding system has their meaning that cannot be understood in isolation. Without phones, without technology, communication was unim-peded in the primordial Yoruba society. By theorizing that the journey to the exploration of this knowledge production will most likely lead to the discov-ery of important things about the African communicative system, my position would therefore generate mixed reactions, and we are ready to defend this.

Using objects as indexes of information sharing and gathering, the people with such knowledge economy are automatically carried along, making it easy for them to grab messages passed within their community. Choosing these objects, like picking up codes in the modern computer system, involves amazing creativity that enables people to relate objects to real-life situations. Therefore, the revival of this system would presumably place the foot of the African people toward sturdy security architecture formulation. By learning more about the sociopolitical conditions that did necessitate the people to come up with such communicative system, by understanding cultural para-digms that gave rise to it, more ingenuity will be unlocked to create alterna-tive perspective to the security management of the people. A long-standing culture of consumerism clearly has reconfigured the African minds to feel unchallenged when others make unprecedented progress in different walks of life and this is ominous.

We should recall that the Yoruba woodcarving is an art of aestheticism that shares characteristic with Aroko coding system. Africans communicate in various ways and their arts generally qualified as a medium to understanding this. From visual arts to performative arts, the African people are unmistakably great in their communication dexterity. Using some types of drum at certain event, the Yoruba people can communicate different occurrence to the public without saying a word. It is resident in African cultures that their lack of writing science does not impede them from the proper sharing of information. Today, African arts are transported beyond the shores of continent, attracting swelling interests by global audience. Therefore, nothing is there to lose if the creative ingenuity of the African people is reawakened. How can Aroko, for example, be integrated into computer system when Africans—Yoruba especially—begin to manufacture their own forms of information storage and retrieval system? How will African knowledge production reinforce the existing global knowledge economy for African advantage? All these questions would be duly explored at the time when Africans reinvent their knowledge production through the modern disciplines.

FINAL WORDS

This writing has demonstrated the importance of native knowledge production and provided the basis for recoiling into an expedition of self-assertion. By squinting our intellectual vision to observe the most minimal details of how scientific knowledge works, we have thus offered systematic symmetry between the knowledge economy of science, native knowledge production, and religious knowledge generation, all of which share a commonality of approach—observation, examination, data gathering before arriving at their truth. Truth to its outstanding characteristics, science, despite its relatively short popularity in human history, has spearheaded unprecedented progress in knowledge production, even though, like other sources, it is open to making errors. It is an unassailable fact, however, that the nature of knowledge, in other words truth, does preclude perfection because things of nature, as we know it, continue to change beyond the control of anyone. Save for the hegemonic attitude of the modern scientists, the scientific approach is actually reliable and could be confided in to guarantee sound knowledge—and truth—about phenomenon in the context of learning.

However, we must be careful not to eradicate other sources of knowledge generation because we suddenly want to invest all our trust into science, even if science is infallible, which it is really not. For one thing, science can be likened to a brilliant child who understands the nitty-gritty of what he is taught in school but cannot bring himself to educate others about what he knows. As such, the child is trapped in the feeling of self-denial because his brilliance is not converted into something measurable for others but him. As such, his knowledge is only valid as to the level of self-reliance. Science can always untie itself from its self-generated knot, in the first instance. Looked from the moral perspective, nevertheless, science is not imbued with the structural competence to guide humans on the part of moral uprightness. In fact, the happenings around the world today reveals that the interconnection between science and technology has ignited advancement and development, almost at the same rate that it has enabled acute discordance among the humans. We have seen allegations of the development of virus from various labs to infect certain population target in an effort to make financial profits. There have been various instances of chaos orchestrated by the people because of their control of scientific power and information.

Apparently, humanity and their sense of morality is not dependent on their scientific advancement; in the contrary, it is in spite of it. While science does not cater for this aspect of knowledge and information generation, other sources of knowledge production such as the religious and African ones are stakeholders of moral development system. Coming from the knowledge base that controls all the aspects of human life, spiritual, political, social, cultural, and epistemic behavior, these two sources have shown generational usefulness to advance the course of humans across the globe. Are they fallible? Yes. Do they evolve to meet up with the latest trends? Definitely, yes. Therefore, it is inconsequential to think that African knowledge sources should not be promoted to occupy its deserved position in the scheme of things. In a carefully worded explanation, these have been explained in the angle where the romanticization of these indigenous knowledge sources can be used to advance the African course when they are arranged under appropriate labels capable of inspiring scholarly engagements for discovery, and education.

Since the elders are understood as having requisite knowledge and experience, it is not unlikely that they have the knowledge of the environment that could rival scientific reasoning in their reservoir. After all, all the knowledge of the African world is preserved through an oral legacy and the elders are usually the ones with trusted source of information gathering. Growth in the African context should encapsulate all the aspects of human existence and not to be limited to the knowledge of science, especially as relentlessly made obvious by the Western science community. Therefore, the knowledge of the elders is greatly needed to boost the African values and ideas. It is not coincidental that the primitive Africans are always seen at their home and settings dishing out knowledge to the younger ones virtually every day. They function in the development of the society till they give up the ghost. Elders in the African sense are seen as walking libraries of the people because of their numerous knowledge that they have acquired with their age. Even though the missionaries have forced a meaning down the throat of the African man to see the aged ones as evil, it still does not eclipse the face that they are very important to the formulation of the African societies we have today.

As against the popular opinion that Africans, either in the preliterate, colonial, or postcolonial era, are incapable of making scientific contributions to the global body of knowledge, unfurling findings dislodge this assertion by showing us the symmetrical base of African native knowledge attuning itself with scientific methods. It is not impossible, however, that if African knowledge production systems have not been challenged by the colonial imperialism, it would predictably have assumed a greater position because it certainly advances with time. As such, there is an urgent need for true decolonization that will see to the incorporation of African knowledge production and their epistemologies into modern discipline to see how they would combine to inspire new ways of thinking, and how they can influence all-round development of the African mind to begin to see things from the viewpoint of Africans. In other words, using the European standards as the measurement of progress in Africa limits the functionality of the African mind and brains, since this would only portray them as a silhouette of their counterparts in the world around. Developing the African child for African advantage is a project that would lead to true emancipation where their full potentials could be unlocked.

Notes

CHAPTER 1

1. Josiah Hesse, "Flat Earthers Keep the Faith at Denver Conference," *The Guardian*, November 18, 2018, https://www.theguardian.com/us-news/2018/nov/18/flat-earthers-keep-the-faith-at-denver-conference.

2. Fakhr al-Dīn Rāzī, "19/131," *Al-Tafsīr Al-kabīr*, translated by Sohaib Saeed (Cambridge: Royal Aal al-Bayt Institute for Islamic Thought, 2018).

3. Neil deGrasse Tyson, Twitter post, June 14, 2013, 7:41 AM, https://twitter.com/neiltyson/status/345551599382446081.

4. *The Holy Bible*, John 14:6, New International Version and English Standard Version, accessed December 26, 2019, from https://www.biblegateway.com/.

5. *The Holy Quran*, 10:100, Sahih International, accessed December 26, 2019, from https://quran.com.

6. David Coady and Miranda Fricker, "Introduction to Special Issue on Applied Epistemology," *Journal of Applied Philosophy* 34, no. 2 (2017): 153–56.

7. Larry Laudan, *Truth, Error, and Criminal Law: An Essay in Legal Epistemology* (Cambridge: Cambridge University Press, 2006).

8. Thomas G. West, *Plato's "Apology Of Socrates": An Interpretation, with a New Translation* (Ithaca, NY: Cornell University Press, 1979).

9. Aristotle, *Posterior Analytics*, translated by Jonathan Barnes (Oxford: Clarendon Press, 1994).

10. René Descartes and Laurence J. Lafleur, *Meditations on First Philosophy* (Indianapolis, IN: Bobbs-Merrill, 1960).

11. Francis Bacon, *Novum Organum Scientiarum* (Cambridge: Cambridge University Press, 2000).

12. Michele Marsonet, "Philosophy and Logical Positivism," *Academicus* MMXIX, no. 19 (2019): 32–36.

13. B. Blanshard, *The Nature of Thought* (London: George Allen and Unwin, 1939).

14. Bas C. van Fraassen, *The Empirical Stance* (New Haven, CT: Yale University Press, 2002).

15. Edmund L. Gettier, "Is Justified True Belief Knowledge?" *Analysis* 23, no. 6 (1963): 121–23.

16. Ted Honderich, "Ideology," in *The Oxford Companion to Philosophy*, edited by Ted Honderich, 2nd ed. (Oxford: Oxford University Press, 2005).

17. Karl Marx and Joseph J. O'Malley, *Critique of Hegel's "Philosophy of Right"* (Cambridge: Cambridge University Press, 1970).

18. Michel Foucault, *Power/Knowledge: Selected Interviews and Other Writings, 1972–1977*, edited by Colin Gordon, translated by Colin Gordon (Harlow: Longman, 1980).

19. Max Weber, *Max Weber Readings and Commentary on Modernity*, Modernity and Society, vol. 3, edited by Stephen Kalberg (Malden, MA: Blackwell, 2005).

20. Herbert Spencer, *The Principles of Sociology*, vol. 6. (New York: Appleton, 1895).

21. T. T. Cele, "Qualities of King Shaka as Portrayed in Zulu Oral Testimony and in Izibongo," *South African Journal of African Languages* 21, no. 2 (2001): 118–32.

22. Conrad Hackett and David McClendon, "Christians Remain World's Largest Religious Group, but They Are Declining in Europe," Pew Research Center, April 5, 2017, http://www.pewresearch.org/fact-tank/2017/04/05/christians-remain-worlds-largest-religious-group-but-they-are-declining-in-europe/.

23. Dave Meadors, "The Bible and Its Influence," *Journal of Church and State* 48, no. 3 (2006): 711.

24. J. K. H. Tse, "Grounded Theologies: 'Religion' and the 'Secular' in Human Geography," *Progress in Human Geography* 38, no. 2 (2014): 201–20.

25. Walter D. Mignolo, "Introduction: Coloniality of Power and De-Colonial Thinking," *Cultural studies* 21, no. 2–3 (2007): 155–67.

26. Ramón Grosfoguel, "The Epistemic Decolonial Turn: Beyond Political-Economy Paradigms," *Cultural Studies* 21, no. 2–3 (2007): 211–23.

27. Gayatri Chakravorty Spivak and Rosalind C. Morris, *Can the Subaltern Speak?: Reflections on the History of an Idea* (New York: Columbia University Press, 2010).

28. Rolando Vazquez, "Translation as Erasure: Thoughts on Modernity's Epistemic Violence," *Journal of Historical Sociology* 24, no. 1 (2011): 27–44.

29. B. de Sousa Santos, *Epistemologies of the South: Justice against Epistemicide* (New York: Routledge, 2014).

30. Mignolo, "Introduction."

31. Scott Plous, *The Psychology of Judgment and Decision Making*, McGraw-Hill Series in Social Psychology (New York: McGraw-Hill, 1993), 233.

32. Scott Plous, "The Availability Heuristic," in *The Psychology of Judgment and Decision Making,* McGraw-Hill Series in Social Psychology (New York: McGraw-Hill, 1993).

33. Daniel Kahneman, *Thinking, Fast and Slow* (London: Allen Lane, 2011).

34. Donald M. Taylor and Janet R. Doria, "Self-Serving and Group-Serving Bias in Attribution," *Journal of Social Psychology* 113, no. 2 (1981): 201–11.

35. Aaron M. McCright and Riley E Dunlap, "Bringing Ideology In: The Conservative White Male Effect on Worry about Environmental Problems in the USA," *Journal of Risk Research* 16, no. 2 (2013): 211–26.

CHAPTER 2

1. Nations Online, "Official and Spoken Languages of African Countries," accessed August 5, 2019, https://www.nationsonline.org/oneworld/african_languages.htm.

2. Benjamin Radford, "Belief in Witchcraft Widespread in Africa," *LiveScience*, August 30, 2010, https://www.livescience.com/8515-belief-witchcraft-widespread-africa.html.

3. BBC News, "Tanzania 'Witchcraft' Murders: 'Our Son Was Robbed of His Future'," February 9, 2019, https://www.bbc.com/news/av/world-africa-47174329/tanzania-witchcraft-murders-our-son-was-robbed-of-his-future.

4. Jean La Fontaine, "Witchcraft Belief Is a Curse on Africa," *The Guardian*, March 1, 2012, https://www.theguardian.com/commentisfree/belief/2012/mar/01/witchcraft-curse-africa-kristy-bamu.

5. Brian Rath, "Believe It or Not: Witchcraft in Kenya," *Voices of Africa*, May 2, 2013, https://voicesofafrica.co.za/believe-it-or-not-witchcraft-in-kenya/.

6. Jane Parish, "West African Witchcraft, Wealth and Moral Decay in New York City," *Ethnography* 12, no. 2 (2011): 247–65.

7. BBC News, "Is Witchcraft Alive in Africa?" July 27, 2005, http://news.bbc.co.uk/2/hi/africa/4705201.stm.

8. Aleksandra Cimpric, "Children Accused of Witchcraft," UNICEF, April 2010, https://www.unicef.org/wcaro/wcaro_children-accused-of-witchcraft-in-Africa.pdf.

9. K. Wiredu, "Toward Decolonizing African Philosophy and Religion," *African Studies Quarterly* 1 (1998): 17–46.

10. Bruce Kapferer, "Outside all Reason: Magic, Sorcery and Epistemology in Anthropology," *Social Analysis (Adelaide)* 46, no. 3 (2002): 1–30.

11. Dale Wallace, "Rethinking Religion, Magic and Witchcraft in South Africa: From Colonial Coherence to Postcolonial Conundrum," *Journal for the Study of Religion* 28, no. 1 (2015): 23–51.

12. Frederick Kakwata, "Witchcraft and Poverty in Africa: A Pastoral Perspective," *Black Theology* 16, no. 1 (2018): 22–37.

13. Robin Horton, "African Traditional Thought and Western Science," *Africa* 37, no. 2 (1967): 155–87.

14. Pew Research Center's Religion & Public Life Project, "Projected Religious Population Changes in Sub-Saharan Africa," May 10, 2016, https://www.pewforum.org/2015/04/02/sub-saharan-africa/.

15. Molefi K. Asante, "African Ways of Knowing and Cognitive Faculties," in *Encyclopedia of Black Studies*, edited by Molefi Asante and Ama Mazama, 40 (Thousand Oaks, CA: Sage, 2005).

16. Stephen Ellis and Gerrie ter Haar, "Religion and Politics: Taking African Epistemologies Seriously," *Journal of Modern African Studies* 45, no. 3 (2007): 385–401.

17. Wallace, "Rethinking Religion."

18. James George Frazer, *The Golden Bough* (London: Palgrave Macmillan, 1990).

19. Claude Lévi-Strauss, "The Sorcerer and His Magic," in *Understanding and Applying Medical Anthropology*, edited by Peter J. Brown and Svea Closser, 129–37 (London: Routledge, 1963).

20. Alfred Schutz and Thomas Luckmann, *The Structures of the Life-World*, vol. 1 (Evanston, IL: Northwestern University Press, 1973).

21. Henrietta L. Moore and Todd Sanders, eds., *Magical Interpretations, Material Realities: Modernity, Witchcraft and the Occult in Postcolonial Africa* (London: Routledge, 2003).

22. Wallace, "Rethinking Religion."

23. Edward E. Evans-Pritchard, *Witchcraft, Oracles and Magic among the Azande* (London: Oxford, 1937).

24. Parish, "West African Witchcraft."

25. Wallace, "Rethinking Religion."

26. J. Z. Smith, *Relating Religion: Essays in the Study of Religion* (Chicago, IL: University of Chicago Press, 2004).

27. Mary Douglas, *Natural Symbols* (London: Routledge, 2002).

28. Kapferer, "Outside all Reason."

29. Walter D. Mignolo, *The Darker Side of the Renaissance: Literacy, Territoriality, and Colonization* (Ann Arbor: University of Michigan Press, 1995).

30. J. K. H. Tse, "Grounded Theologies: 'Religion' and the 'Secular' in Human Geography," *Progress in Human Geography* 38, no. 2 (2014): 201–20.

31. Arthur M. Schlesinger, Jr., *The Disuniting of America: Reflections on a Multicultural Society* (New York: W. W. Norton, 1992).

32. Horton, "African Traditional Thought and Western Science."

33. Silva, "Mind, Body and Spirit in Basket Divination."

34. Evans-Prichard, *Witchcraft, Oracles and Magic among the Azande*

35. Howard Sankey, "Witchcraft, Relativism and the Problem of the Criterion," *Erkenntnis (197)* 72, no. 1 (2010): 1–16.

36. Adam Ashforth, "Muthi, Medicine and Witchcraft: Regulating 'African Science' in Post-Apartheid South Africa?" *Social Dynamics* 31, no. 2 (2005): 211–42.

37. Malcolm Ruel, "Witchcraft, Morality, and Doubt," *HAU: Journal of Ethnographic Theory* 7, no. 1 (2017): 579–95.

38. Silva, "Mind, Body and Spirit in Basket Divination," 1175–87.

39. John Mack, "Fetish: Magic Figures in Central Africa," *Journal of Art Historiography* 5 (2011): 53.

40. Evans-Prichard, *Witchcraft, Oracles and Magic among the Azande*.

41. Ibid.

42. Schutz and Luckmann, *Structures of the Life-World*.

43. Lévi-Strauss, "The Sorcerer and His Magic."

44. Ryan Schram, "Witches' Wealth: Witchcraft, Confession, and Christianity in Auhelawa, Papua New Guinea," *Journal of the Royal Anthropological Institute* 16, no. 4 (2010): 726–42.

45. Huib van de Grijspaarde, Maarten Voors, Erwin Bulte, and Paul Richards, "Who Believes in Witches? Institutional Flux in Sierra Leone," *African Affairs* 112, no. 446 (2013): 22–47.

46. Jason Hickel, "'Xenophobia' in South Africa: Order, Chaos, and the Moral Economy of Witchcraft," *Cultural Anthropology* 29, no. 1 (2014): 103–27.

47. Jean Comaroff and John L. Comaroff, eds., *Modernity and Its Malcontents: Ritual and Power in Postcolonial Africa* (Chicago, IL: University of Chicago Press, 1993).

48. Schram, "Witches' Wealth."

49. Julien Bonhomme, "The Dangers of Anonymity: Witchcraft, Rumor, and Modernity in Africa," *HAU: Journal of Ethnographic Theory* 2, no. 2 (2012): 205–33.

50. Felicity Wood, "Kinship, Collegiality and Witchcraft: South African Perceptions of Sorcery and the Occult Aspects of Contemporary Academia," *Tydskrif Vir Letterkunde* 51, no. 1 (2014): 150–62.

51. Moore and Sanders, *Magical Interpretations, Material Realities.*

52. David T. Ngong, "Stifling the Imagination: A Critique of Anthropological and Religious Normalization of Witchcraft in Africa," *African and Asian Studies* 11, no. 1–2 (2012): 144–81.

53. Jerome Brooks, "Chinua Achebe, the Art of Fiction No. 139," *The Paris Review*, December 11, 2018, https://www.theparisreview.org/interviews/1720/chinua-achebe-the-art-of-fiction-no-139-chinua-achebe.

54. Knut Rio Michelle MacCarthy and Ruy Blanes, *Pentecostalism and Witchcraft: Spiritual Warfare in Africa and Melanesia* (Cham: Palgrave Macmillan, 2017).

55. J. Kwabena Asamoah-Gyadu, "Witchcraft Accusations and Christianity in Africa," *International Bulletin of Missionary Research* 39, no. 1 (2015): 23–27.

56. Julie Parle, and Fiona Scorgie, "Bewitching Zulu Women: Umhayizo, Gender, and Witchcraft in KwaZulu-Natal," *South African Historical Journal* 64, no. 4 (2012): 852–75.

57. Tanja Kleibl and Ronaldo Munck, "Civil Society in Mozambique: NGOs, Religion, Politics and Witchcraft," *Third World Quarterly* 38, no. 1 (2017): 203–18.

58. Michela Wrong, "World View: Writing about Africa without Mentioning the Role of Tribalism and Witchcraft Is Like Writing about British Fox-Hunting without Mentioning Class," *New Statesman* 134, no. 4722 (2005): 24.

59. Adam Ashforth, "Human Security and Spiritual Insecurity: Why the Fear of Evil Forces Needs to be Taken Seriously," *Georgetown Journal of International Affairs* 11 (2010): 99.

60. Claude Ake, *Social Science as Imperialism: The Theory of Political Development* (Ibadan: Ibadan University Press, 1982).

61. Wallace, "Rethinking Religion."

62. Schram, "Witches' Wealth."

63. Malcolm Ruel, "Witchcraft, Morality, and Doubt," *HAU: Journal of Ethnographic Theory* 7, no. 1 (2017): 579–95.

64. Rose Kisia Omondi and Chris Ryan, "Sex Tourism: Romantic Safaris, Prayers and Witchcraft at the Kenyan Coast," *Tourism Management* 58 (2017): 217–27.

65. Dirk Kohnert, "Magic and Witchcraft: Implications for Democratization and Poverty-Alleviating Aid in Africa," *World Development* 24, no. 8 (1996): 1347–55.

66. Eirik Saethre and Jonathan Stadler, "Malicious Whites, Greedy Women, and Virtuous Volunteers," *Medical Anthropology Quarterly* 27, no. 1 (2013): 103–20.

67. Elliott P. Currie, "Crimes without Criminals-Witchcraft and Its Control in Renaissance Europe," *Law & Society Review* 3 (1968): 7.

68. Annette B. Weiner and Jane Schneider, eds., *Cloth and Human Experience* (London: Smithsonian Institution, 2013).

69. Arthur Evans, *Witchcraft and the Gay Counterculture: A Radical View of Western Civilization and Some of the People It Has Tried to Destroy* (Boston, MA: Fag Rag Books, 1978).

70. Anne Llewellyn Barstow, "On Studying Witchcraft as Women's History: A Historiography of the European Witch Persecutions," *Journal of Feminist Studies in Religion* 4, no. 2 (1988): 7–19.

71. Jeffrey Burton Russell, *Witchcraft in the Middle Ages* (Ithaca, NY: Cornell University Press, 1972).

72. Nicholas P. Spanos, "Witchcraft in Histories of Psychiatry: A Critical Analysis and an Alternative Conceptualization," *Psychological Bulletin* 85, no. 2 (1978): 417.

73. Barbara Ehrenreich and Deirdre English, *Witches, Midwives, & Nurses: A History of Women Healers* (New York: Feminist Press at CUNY, 2010).

74. Rosalind I. J. Hackett, "Women, Rights Talk, and African Pentecostalism," *Religious Studies and Theology* 36, no. 2 (2017): 245–59.

75. Paul Thomas, "Religious Education and the Feminisation of Witchcraft: A Study of Three Secondary Schools in Kumasi, Ghana," *British Journal of Religious Education* 34, no. 1 (2012): 67–86.

76. UN Women, "Facts & Figures," accessed September 5, 2019, https://www.unwomen.org/en/news/in-focus/commission-on-the-status-of-women-2012/facts-and-figures.

77. UNESCO Institute for Statistics, "Adult and Youth Literacy: Trends in Gender Parity," September 2010, http://uis.unesco.org/sites/default/files/documents/fs3-adult-and-youth-literacy-global-trends-in-gender-parity-2010-en.pdf.

78. UNICEF, "Child Marriage: Latest Trends and Future Prospects," Resources, United Nations, July 2018, https://data.unicef.org/resources/child-marriage-latest-trends-and-future-prospects/.

79. Emmanuel N. N. Dzama and Jonathan F. Osborne, "Poor Performance in Science among African Students: An Alternative Explanation to the African Worldview Thesis," *Journal of Research in Science Teaching* 36, no. 3 (1999): 387–405.

80. Boris Gershman, "Witchcraft Beliefs and the Erosion of Social Capital: Evidence from Sub-Saharan Africa and Beyond," *Journal of Development Economics* 120 (2016): 182–208.

81. Thomas Aneurin Smith, "Witchcraft, Spiritual Worldviews and Environmental Management: Rationality and Assemblage," *Environment and Planning A* 49, no. 3 (2017): 592–611.

82. Edward Fottrell, Stephen Tollman, Peter Byass, Frederick Golooba-Mutebi, Kathleen Kahn, Medicinska fakulteten, Institutionen för folkhälsa och klinisk medicin, Epidemiologi och global hälsa, and Umeå universitet, "The Epidemiology of 'Bewitchment' as a Lay-Reported Cause of Death in Rural South Africa," *Journal of Epidemiology and Community Health* 66, no. 8 (2012): 704–9.

83. Ediomo-Ubong E. Nelson and Ifureuwem J. Uko, "Ethnomedical Beliefs and Utilization of Alcohol Herbal Remedy for Malaria in South-Coastal Nigeria," *International Quarterly of Community Health Education* 39, no. 2 (2019): 119–26.

84. Lamin Sidibeh, "Diviners and Diagnosticians in the Gambia: Psychological Functions and Traditional Healers," *Fourth World Journal* 14, no. 1 (2015): 5–12.

85. Elizabeth J. and Harrison M. K. Maithya, "Bewitching Sex Workers, Blaming Wives: HIV/AIDS, Stigma, and the Gender Politics of Panic in Western Kenya," *Global Public Health* 13, no. 2 (2018): 234–48.

86. Vikram Patel, "Traditional Healers for Mental Health Care in Africa," *Global Health Action* 4, no. 1 (2011): 7956–62.

87. Heike Behrend, "The Rise of Occult Powers, AIDS and the Roman Catholic Church in Western Uganda," *Journal of Religion in Africa* 37, no. 1 (2007): 41–58.

88. Eduard Grebe and Nicoli Nattrass, "AIDS Conspiracy Beliefs and Unsafe Sex in Cape Town," *AIDS and Behavior* 16, no. 3 (2012): 761–73.

CHAPTER 3

1. A. Sagner and P. Kowal, "Defining 'Old Age' Markers of Old Age in Sub-Saharan Africa and the Implications for Cross-Cultural Research," Discussion Paper, The Minimum Data Set (MDS) Project on Ageing and Older Adults in sub-Saharan Africa, no. 1, 2002.

2. W. H. Sangree, "Pronatalism and the Elderly in Tiriki, Kenya," in *African Families and the Crisis of Social Change*, edited by T. S. Weisner, C. Bradley, and P. L. Kilbride, 184–207 (London: Bergin & Garvey, 1997).

3. P. M. Baker and G. G. Eaton, "Seniority versus Age as Causes of Dominance in Social Groups," *Small Group Research* 23, no. 3 (1992): 322–43.

4. Ibid., 323.

5. Ibid.

6. O. Adeboye, "The Changing Conception of Elderhood in Ibadan, 1830–2000," *Nordic Journal of African Studies* 16, no. 2 (2017): 261–78.

7. Baker and Eaton, "Seniority versus Age."

8. I. Ogo, "Enhancing Youth-Elder Collaboration in Governance in Africa," Discussion Paper, Minds Annual African Youth Dialogue, 2015.

9. F. A. Eboiyehi, "Perception of Old Age: Its Implications for Care and Support for the Aged among the Esan of South-South Nigeria," *Journal of International Social Research* 8, no. 36 (2015): 340–56.

10. Adeboye, "Changing Conception of Elderhood in Ibadan, 1830–2000."

11. J. Kenyata, *Facing Mount Kenya* (New York: Vintage Books, 1965).

12. Adeboye, "Changing Conception of Elderhood in Ibadan, 1830–2000."

13. Ibid.

14. U. Okoye, "Traditional Values and Mechanisms for the Care of the Elderly among the Igbos of South Eastern Nigeria: Implication for Social Policy," Paper Presented at the Conference on "Healthy Aging," University of Ibadan, June 24, 1999.

15. N. A. Apt, "Rapid Urbanization and Living Arrangements of Older Persons in Africa," in *Living Arrangements of Older Persons: Critical Issues and Policy Responses*, 288–310, United Nations, population division, *Population Bulletin of the United Nations*, 2001.

16. Igor Kopytoff, "Ancestors as Elders in Africa," *Journal of the International African Institute* 41, no. 2 (1971): 129–42.

17. Ibid., 129.

18. Okoye, "Traditional Values and Mechanisms."

19. B. A. Yanker, T. Lu, and P. Loerch, "The Aging Brain," *Annual Review of Pathology Mechanisms of Disease* 3, no. 1 (2008): 241–66.

20. J. Mbele, "The Elder in African Society," *Journal of Intergenerational Relationships* 2, no. 3–4 (2004): 53–61, 54.

21. Eboiyehi, "Perception of Old Age."

22. Okoye, "Traditional Values and Mechanisms."

23. Eboiyehi, "Perception of Old Age."

24. Okoye, "Traditional Values and Mechanisms."

25. S. L. Amosun and P. Reddy, "Healthy Ageing in Africa," *World Health* 50, no. 4 (1997): 18–19.

26. C. K. Brown, "Research Findings in Ghana: A Survey on Elderly in Accra Region," *Gerontologie Africaine* 4 (1985): 11–33.

27. M. Udvardy and M. Cattell, "Gender, Aging and Power in Sub-Saharan Africa: Challenges and puzzles," *Journal of Cross-Cultural Gerontology* 7, no. 4 (1992): 275–88.

28. Eboiyehi, "Perception of Old Age."

29. C. Bambra, D. Fox, and A. Scott-Samuel, "Towards a New Politics of Health," *Health Promotion International* 20, no. 2 (2005): 187–93.

30. F. Fukuyama, "What Is governance?" *Governance* 26, no. 3 (2013): 347–68.

31. Ogo, "Enhancing Youth-Elder Collaboration in Governance in Africa."

32. R. M. Berton and S. Panel, "Elderhood and Compliance: How Aging Dictators Affect Civil Wars," Working Paper, Sciences Po Grenoble, 2014, accessed February 10, 2020, from https://hal-mines-paristech.archives –ouvertes.fr.

33. J. Mbele, "The Elder in African Society," *Journal of Intergenerational Relationships* 2, no. 3–4 (2004): 53–61, 54.

34. Ibid.

35. J. O. Adebayo, "Gerontocracy in African Politics: Youth and the Quest for Political Participation," *Journal of African Elections* 17, no. 1 (2018): 140–61.

36. V. Khasandi-Telewa, M. Wakoko, J. Mugo, E. Mahero, and F. Ndegwa, "What an Old Man Sees While Sitting a Young Man Cannot See while Standing: Utilizing Senior Citizens to Achieve Peace," *International Journal of Research and Social Sciences* 2, no. 2 (2013): 44–49.

37. Adebayo, "Gerontocracy in African Politics," 149.

38. Ogo, "Enhancing Youth-Elder Collaboration in Governance in Africa."

39. Ibid.

40. Adebayo, "Gerontocracy in African Politics," 141.

41. Ibid., 4.

42. T. A. Olaiya, "Youth and Ethnic Movements and Their Impacts on Party Politics in the ECOWAS Member States," *Sage Open* 4, no. 1 (2014): 1–12.

43. Ogo, "Enhancing Youth-Elder Collaboration in Governance in Africa," 7

44. Adebayo, "Gerontocracy in African Politics," 150.

45. Ogo, "Enhancing Youth-Elder Collaboration in Governance in Africa."

46. Ibid., 8.

47. K. T. Sung, "Elder Respect among Adult: A Cross-Cultural Study of Americans and Koreans," *Journal of Aging Studies* 18 (2004): 215–30.

48. B. Bytheway and J. Johnson, "On Defining Ageism," *Critical Social Policy* 10, no. 29 (1990): 27–39.

49. Pierre L. Van den Berghe, *Power and Privilege at an African University* (Piscataway, NJ: Transaction Publishers, 1973).

50. Ibid.

51. Ibid.

52. Eboiyehi, "Perception of Old Age."

53. Van Den Berghe, *Power and Privilege at an African University*.

54. Ibid.

55. Eboiyehi, "Perception of Old Age," 340.

56. Van Den Berghe, *Power and Privilege at an African University*.

57. Ibid.

58. Ibid.

59. Pierre Lienard, "Age Grouping and Social Complexity," *Current Anthropology* 57 (2016): 105–17.

60. Ogo, "Enhancing Youth-Elder Collaboration in Governance in Africa."

61. Ibid.

62. Baker and Eaton, "Seniority versus Age."

63. A. Shankar, M. A. Ansari, and S. Saxena, "Organizational Context and Ingratiatory Behavior in Organizations," *Journal of Social Psychology* 135, no. 5 (1994): 641–47.

64. Ibid.

65. Adeboye, "Gerontocracy in African Politics."

66. Peter C. W. Gutkind, "The Socio-Political and Economic Foundations of Social Problems in African Urban Areas: An Exploratory Conceptual overview," *Civilizations* 22, no. 1 (1972): 18–34.

67. J. O. J. Nwachukwu-Agbada, "The Igbo Folktale: Performance Conditions and Internal Characteristics," Bloomington: Department of Folklore and Ethnomusicology, Indiana University, 1991. Accessed on October 16, 2019, from https:www.scholarworks. iu.edu

68. G. M. Chen and J. Chung, "Seniority and Superiority: A Case Analysis of Decision Making in a Taiwanese Religious Group," *Intercultural Communication Studies* XI-1 (2002): 41–56.

69. Ibid.

70. Ibid.

71. Ibid.

72. K. Martinez-Carter, "How the Elderly Are Treated around the World," July 23, 2013, retrieved from https://www.theweek.com/articles-amp/462230/how-elderly-are-treated-around-the-world. accessed 5th February 2020.

73. Eboiyehi, "Perception of Old Age," 341.

74. Sung, "Elder Respect among Adult," 221.

75. A. Kusserow, "Western Education, Psychologized Individualism and Home/School Tensions: An American Example," Proceedings of the Fourth International Conference on Gross National Happiness, 468–69 (2008), accessed June 24, 2020, from http://citeseerx.ist.psu.edu/viewdoc/download?doi=10.1.1.729.6731&rep=rep1&type=pdf.

76. Ibid.

77. Ibid.

78. Y. Gorodnichenko and G. Roland, "Understanding the Individualism-Collectivism Cleavage and Its Effects: Lessons from Cultural Psychology," *Institutions and Comparative Economic Development* (2012): 213–326.

79. Ibid.

80. D. Todd, "How Do East and West Really Treat Seniors," 2010, accessed February 8, 2020, from https://vancouversun.com>news.

81. Adeboye, "Gerontocracy in African Politics."

82. Ibid.

83. S. J. Fenton and H. Draper, "Older People Make Contributions to Society. Some Communities and Faith Groups Draw on This Contribution in Responding to the Needs of All Their Members," *Birmingham Policy Commission* (2014): 1–7.

CHAPTER 4

1. Edmund L. Gettier, "Is Justified True Belief Knowledge?" *Analysis* 23, no. 6 (1963): 121–23.

2. O. F. Olusegun, A. T. Akinwale, R. O. Vincent, and B. Olabenjo, "A Mobile-Based Knowledge Management System for 'Ifa': An African Traditional Oracle," *African Journal of Mathematics and Computer Science Research* 3, no. 7 (2010): 114–31.

3. Olusegun, 2015, 1.

4. Ibid.

5. Ibid., 3.

6. M. Karenga, *Ethical Insights from Odu Ifa: Choosing to Be Chosen* (Los Angeles, CA: Sentinel, 2008).

7. S. Olu-Osayomi, "Dramatic Aspects of Ese Ifa in Yorubaland," *International Journal on Studies in English Language and Literature* 5, no. 10 (2017): 12–18. Accessed March 30, 2020, from http://dx.doi.org/10.20431/2347-3134.0510003.

8. H. J. Drewal, J. Pemberton, R. Abiodun, and ed. A. Wardwell, *Yoruba: Nine Centuries of African Art and Thought* (New York: Center for African Art and Harry N. Abrams Inc., 1989).

9. Ibid.

10. W. Abimbola, *Ifa Divination Poetry* (New York: Nok Publishers Ltd., 1977), 1.

11. Ibid.

12. Ibid.

13. O. Ogunnaike, *Sufism and Ifa: Ways of Knowing in Two West African Intellectual Traditions* (Cambridge, MA: Harvard University, 2015), 322.

14. O. Adegbindin, ed., T. Falola, and A. Akinyemi, *Encyclopedia of the Yoruba* (Bloomington: Indiana University Press, 2016), 100.

15. Ibid.

16. Abimbola, *Ifa Divination* Poetry, 14.

17. Ibid.

18. Ruth Finnegan, "Religious Poetry," in *Oral Literature in Africa*, 165–200 (Cambridge: Open Book Publishers, 2012), accessed March 30, 2020, from www.jstor.org/stable/j.ctt5vjsmr.17, 190.

19. Ibid., 191.

20. Ibid.

21. Ibid.

22. Ibid., 192.

23. Ibid.

24. K. A. Ilori, "Ifa: The Yoruba God of Wisdom," *The African Guardian* (1986), accessed on March 30, 2020, from https://www.academia.edu/28340608/IFA_-_THE_YORUBA_GOD_OF_WISDOM, 5.

25. Ibid.

26. Abimbola, *Ifa Divination* Poetry, 11.

27. Ibid.

28. Ogunnaike, *Sufism and Ifa*, 393.

29. Finnegan, "Religious Poetry," 188.

30. B. Oluwade and O. Longe, "On the Code Characteristics of Ifa Divination," *Journal of Computer Science & Its Applications* 9, no. I (2003): 23–28, accessed March 30, 2020, from https://www.researchgate.net/publication/327161021, 25.

31. Ilori, "Ifa."

32. Finnegan, "Religious Poetry," 188.

33. Ibid., 188–89.

34. Ilori, "Ifa," 17.

35. Finnegan, "Religious Poetry," 188.

36. Ibid.

37. Abimbola, *Ifa Divination* Poetry, 15.

38. O. I. Pogoson and A. O. Akande, "Ifa Divination Trays from Isale-Oyo," *Cadernos de Estudos Africanos* 21 (2011): 15–41.

39. Ibid.

40. Karenga, *Ethical Insights from Odu Ifa*, 1.

41. Ibid.

42. Ilori, "Ifa," 3.

43. Ibid.

44. Ibid.

45. J. D. Y. Peel, "Divergent Modes of Religiosity in West Africa," in *Christianity, Islam, and Orisa-Religion: Three Traditions in Comparison and Interaction*, 71–87 (Oakland: University of California Press, 2016), accessed March 30, 2020, from www.jstor.org/stable/10.1525/j.ctt1ffjng5.9, 77.

46. O. Adegboyega, "The Metaphysical and Epistemological Relevance of Ifa Corpus," *International Journal of History and Philosophical Research* 5, no. 1 (2017): 28–40, 363.

47. Ibid.

48. Peel, "Divergent Modes of Religiosity in West Africa," 77–78.

49. Ibid.

50. Abimbola, *Ifa Divination* Poetry, 10.

51. Ibid., 8.

52. Ibid.

53. Ibid.

54. Ibid., 5.

55. Ibid., 6.

56. Ibid.

57. Ibid., 8.

58. Ibid., 7.

59. Ibid.

60. W. Abimbola, *Awon Oju Odu Mereerindinlogun.* (Ibadan: University Press PLC, 2014), 13.

61. Ibid., 38.

62. Ibid., 41.

63. Abimbola, *Ifa Divination* Poetry, 122.

64. Ibid., 126.

65. Ibid., 102–4.

CHAPTER 5

1. *The Holy Quran* 13:1, Sahih International, accessed December 6, 2018, from https://quran.com.

2. Michael Lipka and Conrad Hackett, "Why Muslims Are the World's Fastest Growing Religious Group," Pew Research Center, April 6, 2017, http://www.pewresearch.org/fact-tank/2017/04/06/why-muslims-are-the-worlds-fastest-growing-religious-group/.

3. Drew Desilver and David Masci, "World Muslim Population More Widespread Than You Might Think," Pew Research Center, January 31, 2017, http://www.pewresearch.org/fact-tank/2017/01/31/worlds-muslim-population-more-widespread-than-you-might-think/.

4. Pew Research Center, "Europe's Growing Muslim Population," November 29, 2017, http://www.pewforum.org/2017/11/29/europes-growing-muslim-population/.

5. Shadi Hamid, "Is Islam 'Exceptional'?" *The Atlantic,* June 6, 2016, https://www.theatlantic.com/international/archive/2016/06/islam-politics-exceptional/485801/.

6. Ibid.

7. Andrew Buncombe, "Islamophobia Even Worse under Trump Than after 9/11 Attacks Says Top Muslim Activist," *Independent*, December 27, 2017, https://www.independent.co.uk/news/world/americas/us-politics/trump-islam-muslim-islamophobia-worse-911-says-leader-a8113686.html.

8. Thomas G. West, *Plato's "Apology of Socrates": An Interpretation, with a New Translation* (Ithaca, NY: Cornell University Press, 1979).

9. Aristotle, *Posterior Analytics*, translated by Jonathan Barnes (Oxford: Clarendon Press, 1994).

10. René Descartes and Laurence J. Lafleur, *Meditations on First Philosophy* (Indianapolis, IN: Bobbs-Merrill, 1960).

11. Edmund L. Gettier, "Is Justified True Belief Knowledge?" *Analysis* 23, no. 6 (1963): 121–23.

12. Francis Bacon, *Novum Organum Scientiarum* (Cambridge: Cambridge University Press, 2000).

13. Karl Popper, *Conjectures and Refutations: The Growth of Scientific Knowledge* (New York: Basic Books, 1962).

14. Ibrahima Diallo, "Introduction: The Interface between Islamic and Western Pedagogies and Epistemologies: Features and Divergences," *International Journal of Pedagogies and Learning* 7, no. 3 (2012): 175–79.

15. Ali Paya, "What and How Can We Learn from the Qur'Ān? A Critical Rationalist Perspective," *Islamic Studies* 53, no. 3/4 (2014): 175–200.

16. *The Holy Quran* 42:51.

17. Isaiah Goldfeld, "The Illiterate Prophet (Nabi Ummi)," *Der Islam: Zeitschrift für Geschichte und Kultur des Islamischen Orients* 57 (1980): 58.

18. Adday Hernández López, "Qur'Anic Studies in Al-Andalus: An Overview of the State of Research on qirā'āt and Tafsīr," *Journal of Qur'Anic Studies* 19, no. 3 (2017): 74–102.

19. Paul E. Walker, "The Pillars of Islam: Daaim al-Islam of al-Qadi al-Numan, Vol. 1," *Journal of the American Oriental Society* 123, no. 2 (2003): 467.

20. Khaled Abou El Fadl, "The Epistemology of the Truth in Modern Islam," *Philosophy & Social Criticism* 41, no. 4–5 (2015): 473–86.

21. Diallo, "Introduction."

22. Abou El Fadl, "Epistemology of the Truth in Modern Islam."

23. Ibid.

24. Paya, "What and How Can We Learn from the Qur'Ān?"

25. Ibid.

26. Yedullah Kazmi, "The Qur'Ān as Event and as Phenomenon," *Islamic Studies* 41, no. 2 (2002): 193–214.

27. Ibid.

28. Nasr Abu-Zayd, "The Dilemma of the Literary Approach to the Qur'an," *Alif: Journal of Comparative Poetics* no. 23 (2003): 8.

29. Firas Alkhateeb, "How the Quran Is Protected from Any Change, Corruption," *Arab News*, June 4, 2015, http://www.arabnews.com/islam-perspective/news/756976.

30. *The Holy Quran* 4:48.

31. *The Holy Quran* 4:153.

32. Barbara Stowasser, "The Qur'an and Its Meaning," *Arab Studies Journal* 3, no. 1 (1995): 4–8.

33. Paya, "What and How Can We Learn from the Qur'Ān?"

34. *The Holy Quran*, 17:36.

35. Aref Ali Nayed, "The Radical Qur'anic Hermeneutics of Sayyid Qutb," *Islamic Studies* 31, no. 3 (1992): 355–63.

36. *The Holy Quran*, 2:29.

37. Jules Janssens, "Al-Kindī: The Founder of Philosophical Exegesis of the Qur'an," *Journal of Qur'anic Studies* 9, no. 2 (2007): 1–21.

38. Kazmi, "Qur'Ān as Event and as Phenomenon."

39. Saleh Omar, "Ibn Al-Haytham's Theory of Knowledge and Its Significance for Later Science," *Arab Studies Quarterly* 1, no. 1 (1979): 67–82.

40. Michael Sweeney, "Greek Essence and Islamic Tolerance: Al-farabi, Al-ghazali, Ibn Rush'd," *Review of Metaphysics* 65, no. 1 (2011): 41–61.

41. Nicolai Sinai, "Al-Suhrawardī's Philosophy of Illumination and Al-ghazāl," *Archiv Für Geschichte Der Philosophie* 98, no. 3 (2016): 272–301.

42. Ibid.

43. Mohammad Iqbal, *The Reconstruction of Religious Thought in Islam* (Stanford, CA: Stanford University Press, 2013).

44. Nidhal Guessoum, "Science, Religion, and the Quest for Knowledge and Truth: An Islamic Perspective," *Cultural Studies of Science Education* 5, no. 1 (2010): 55–69.

45. Masudul Alam Choudhury, "Conclusion: The Ultimate Nature of Qur'anic Socioscientific Abstraction," in *Absolute Reality in the Qur'an*, 209–25 (New York: Palgrave Macmillan, 2016).

46. Mahdī Hā'irī Yazdī, *The Principles of Epistemology in Islamic Philosophy: Knowledge by Presence* (New York: State University of New York Press, 1992).

47. M. A. Muqtedar Khan, "Introduction: Islam and Epistemology," *American Journal of Islamic Social Sciences* 16, no. 3 (1999): 81.

48. Ibid.

49. Abu-Zayd, "Dilemma of the Literary Approach to the Qur'an."

50. Joseph Schacht, *The Origins of Muhammadan Jurisprudence*, 3rd ed. (London: Oxford University Press, 1959).

51. "Qur'Ān as Event and as Phenomenon."

52. Michael G. Carter, "'Blessed Are the Cheese Makers': Reflections on the Transmission of Knowledge in Islam," *Journal of American Oriental Society* 133, no. 4 (2013): 597–605.

53. Ibn Warraq, *Why I Am Not a Muslim* (Amherst, NY: Prometheus Books, 1995).

54. Ghulam Ahmad Parwez, *Islam: A Challenge to Religion* (Lahore: Tayyeb Iqbal Printers, 2012).

55. Stowasser, Qur'an and Its Meaning."

56. Wilfred Cantwell Smith, "The True Meaning of Scripture: An Empirical Historian's Nonreductionist Interpretation of the Qur'an," *International Journal of Middle East Studies* 11, no. 4 (1980): 487–505.

57. Nidhal Guessoum, *Islam's Quantum Question: Reconciling Muslim Tradition and Modern Science* (New York: IB Tauris, 2010).

58. Christer Hedin, "Islam and Science: Tensions in Contemporary Epistemology," *Temenos* 31 (1995): 55–76.

59. *The Holy Quran* 6:57.

60. John Harney, "How Do Sunni and Shia Islam Differ?" *The New York Times,* January 3, 2016, https://www.nytimes.com/2016/01/04/world/middleeast/q-and-a-how-do-sunni-and-shia-islam-differ.html.

61. Abu Bakr Siraj Al-Din, "The Origins of Sufism," *Islamic Sciences* 13, no. 2 (2015): 59.

62. Anshumali Shukla, "Wahhabism and Global Terrorism," *International Journal of Innovation and Applied Studies* 9, no. 4 (2014): 1521.

63. Rüdiger Seesemann, "Embodied Knowledge and the Walking Qur'an: Lessons for the Study of Islam and Africa," *Journal of Africana Religions* 3, no. 2 (2015): 201–9.

64. Fatima Mernissi, *The Fundamentalist Obsession with Women: A Current Articulation of Class Conflict in Modern Muslim Societies* (Lahore: Women's Resource and Publication Centre, 1987).

65. Solomon A. Nigosian, *Islam: Its History, Teaching, and Practices* (Bloomington: Indiana University Press, 2004).

66. Michael Bonner, "Ja 'ä'il and Holy War in Early Islam," *Der Islam* 68, no. 1 (1991): 45–64.

67. Shin Chiba and Thomas J. Schoenbaum, eds., *Peace Movements and Pacifism after September 11* (Northampton, MA: Edward Elgar, 2008).

68. *The Holy Quran* 2:190.

69. James L. Rowell, "Abdul Ghaffar Khan: An Islamic Gandhi," *Political Theology* 10, no. 4 (2009): 591–606.

CHAPTER 6

1. John 14:6 (New International Version).

2. This was conducted by four research assistants, two in Lagos and two in Atlanta, both covering flights by Delta over a two-week period in July 2017.

3. Conrad Hackett and David McClendon, "Christians Remain World's Largest Religious Group, but They Are Declining in Europe," Pew Research Center, April 5, 2017, http://www.pewresearch.org/fact-tank/2017/04/05/christians-remain-worlds-largest-religious-group-but-they-are-declining-in-europe/.

4. Joseph Liu, "Global Christianity: A Report on the Size and Distribution of the World's Christian Population," Pew Research Center's Religion & Public Life Project, December 19, 2011, http://www.pewforum.org/2011/12/19/global-christianity-exec/.

5. "Bible Translated into 2,454 Languages, 4,500 to Go - Europe - International - News," *Catholic Online*, October 15, 2008, https://www.catholic.org/news/international/europe/story.php?id=30064.

6. Hebrews 4:12.

7. Liu, "Global Christianity." Some argue that Islam is increasing exponentially in numbers due mainly to high birth rates in its major regions in Asia. Only a relatively small portion of its expansion, according to some arguments, is due to conversions based on a better vision of "truth." See, for example, http://graphics.wsj.com/catholics-world/.

8. The Bible and Christianity are linked but can also be treated as separate analytical categories. Christianity's power derives not only from the Bible but also from other additional sources—politics, leadership, class relations, a history of imperialism and colonialism, and so on. The Bible has intrinsic power but also derives additional power from Christianity as a social phenomenon. The Bible and Christianity can be conflated and treated as separate.

9. The issue of the linkage between faith and truth is very complicated. The link has been questioned by many Christian groups. For instance, many Catholics have long abandoned this rule. Some modern Catholics even have Bibles different from the original Catholic Douay version, which are substantially different from the Bible that the rest of Christians use—written especially to change this faith versus reason rule! There are other Christian denominations, too, that no longer rely completely on the faith as truth principle. Another section of Christianity operates with an assumption of the Bible as requiring a mixture of faith and reason, not necessarily a faith-versus-reason template. Some Pentecostal churches, such as Mensa Otabil's large congregation based in Ghana, are in this category. I would also count here many of the mainline churches—Anglicans, Baptist, Methodists, perhaps in this group. They didn't start as such; they evolved into this mode of reasoning. To be included are also the Jehovah's witnesses who use the Bible but many question their Christian credentials. Then there are Christian believers (as in the case of charismatic offshoots of mainline churches) who preach faith without caveat, and shun science and discounts reason.

10. David Coady and Miranda Fricker, "Introduction to Special Issue on Applied Epistemology," *Journal of Applied Philosophy* 34, no. 2 (2017): 153–56.

11. Mario Augusto Bunge, *Philosophical Dictionary* (Amherst: Prometheus Books, 1998).

12. Tina Beattie, *The New Atheists: The Twilight of Reason and the War on Religion* (London: Darton, Longman and Todd, 2007).

13. Richard Dawkins, *River out of Eden: A Darwinian View of Life* (New York: Basic Books, 1995).

14. Proverbs 3:5–6 (New International Version (NIV)).

15. Luke 21:33 (New International Version (NIV)).

16. 2 Timothy 3:16–17 (New International Version (NIV)).

17. "Why Bible Translation | International Missions | Christian Mission Organizations," Wycliffe Bible Translators, accessed July 11, 2018, https://www.wycliffe.org/about/why.

18. Dave Meadors, "The Bible and Its Influence," *Journal of Church and State* 48, no. 3 (2006): 711.

19. Proverbs 30:5 (New International Version (NIV)).

20. Andrew F. Smith, "Secularity and Biblical Literalism: Confronting the Case for Epistemological Diversity," *International Journal for Philosophy of Religion* 71, no. 3 (2012): 205–19.

21. "What Is a Christian Testimony?" GotQuestions.org, February 21, 2018, accessed July 11, 2018, from https://www.gotquestions.org/Christian-testimony.html.

22. "Philosophy of Religion," Philosophy of Religion: The Argument from Fine Tuning Comments, accessed July 11, 2018, from http://www.philosophyofreligion.info/.

23. Lawrence Pasternack, "Kant's 'Appraisal' of Christianity: Biblical Interpretation and the Pure Rational System of Religion," *Journal of the History of Philosophy* 53, no. 3 (2015): 485–506.

24. Alan Sell, "The Bible and Epistemology," *Journal of Reformed Theology* 3, no. 2 (2009): 219–26.

25. Smith, "Secularity and Biblical Literalism," 2012.

26. 1 Peter 2:18 (New International Version (NIV)).

27. 1 Timothy 2:12 (New International Version (NIV)).

28. 1 Samuel 15:3 (English Standard Version (ESV)).

29. Leviticus 24:14 (New International Version (NIV)).

30. 1 John 4:8 (New International Version (NIV)).

31. Bertram Eugene Schwarzbach, "Reason and the Bible in the So-Called Age of Reason," *Huntington Library Quarterly* 74, no. 3 (2011): 437–70.

32. Ibid.

33. Ibid.

34. Kenneth L. Pearce, "Berkeley's Lockean Religious Epistemology," *Journal of the History of Ideas* 75, no. 3 (2014): 417–38.

35. Andrew F. Smith, "Secularity and Biblical Literalism: Confronting the Case for Epistemological Diversity," *International Journal for Philosophy of Religion* 71, no. 3 (2012): 205–19.

36. Jeffrey L. Morrow, "The Acid of History: La Peyrère, Hobbes, Spinoza, and the Separation of Faith and Reason in Modern Biblical Studies," *The Heythrop Journal* 58, no. 2 (2017): 169–80.

37. John Blake, "Half of the New Testament Forged, Biblical Scholar Says," CNN Belief Blog, May 13, 2011, http://religion.blogs.cnn.com/2011/05/13/half-of-new-testament-forged-Bible-scholar-says/.

38. Harry Freedman, *The Murderous History of Bible Translations: Power, Conflict and the Quest for Meaning* (New York: Bloomsbury, 2016).

39. George A. Wells, "How Destructive of Traditional Christian Beliefs Is Historical Criticism of the Bible Today Conceded to Be?" *Think* 10, no. 29 (2011): 91–109.

40. B. Wood, "Museum of the Bible: Questionable Science," *Science* 358, no. 6367 (2017): 1142–1142.

41. Robert D. Branson, "Science, the Bible, and Human Anatomy," *Perspectives on Science and Christian Faith* 68, no. 4 (2016): 229.

42. Brooke Alan Trisel, "God's Silence as an Epistemological Concern," *The Philosophical Forum* 43, no. 4 (2012): 383–93.

43. Antony Flew, R. M. Hare, and Basil Mitchell, "Theology and Falsification: The University discussion," in *New Essays in Philosophical Theology* (New York: Macmillan, 1964).

44. Russell, *Witchcraft in the Middle Ages*, 1997.

45. Descartes and Lafleur, *Meditations on First Philosophy*.

46. William E. Carroll, "Creation, Evolution, and Thomas Aquinas," *Revue des Questions Scientifiques* 171, no. 4 (2000): 319–47.

47. Matt Slick, "How to Interpret the Bible," accessed July 16, 2018, from https://carm.org/how-interpret-Bible.

48. Bryan Enderle, "Science vs God," filmed at TEDxUCDavid 2013, Davis, CA, video, 2:24, published June 22, 2013, https://www.youtube.com/watch?v=sn7YQOzNuSc.

49. Amir Aczel, "Why Science Does Not Disprove God," *New York Times*, April 27, 2014, http://time.com/77676/why-science-does-not-disprove-God/.

50. Richard Krejcir, "Genres in the Bible," *Into Thy Word*, accessed July 22, 2018, http://www.intothyword.org/apps/articles/default.asp?articleid=31435.

51. Lydia Willsky, "The (Un)Plain Bible: New Religious Movements and Alternative Scriptures in Nineteenth-Century America," *Nova Religio: The Journal of Alternative and Emergent Religions* 17, no. 4 (2014): 13–36.

52. Ibid.

53. Nicholas Humphrey, *Soul Dust: The Magic of Consciousness* (Princeton, NJ: Princeton University Press, 2011).

54. Gerhard Andersson, "Atheism and How It Is Perceived: Manipulation of, Bias against and Ways to Reduce the Bias," *Nordic Psychology* 68, no. 3 (July 2016): 194–203.

55. S. Schimmel, *The Tenacity of Unreasonable Beliefs* (Oxford: Oxford University Press, 2008).

56. Darren E. Sherkat, "Religion and Scientific Literacy in the United States," *Social Science Quarterly* 92, no. 5 (2011): 1134–50.

57. Avner Segall and Kevin Burke, "Reading the Bible as a Pedagogical Text: Testing, Testament, and Some Postmodern Considerations about Religion/the Bible in contemporary education," *Curriculum Inquiry* 43, no. 3 (2013): 305–31.

58. Stephen Ellis and Gerrie ter Haar, "Religion and Politics: Taking African Epistemologies Seriously," *Journal of Modern African Studies* 45, no. 3 (2007): 385–401.

59. 1 Samuel 17; *Leviticus 19:11 NIV Bible Gateway*, Bible Gateway Blog, www.biblegateway.com/passage/?search=1%2BSamuel%2B17.

60. 2 Samuel 11; *Luke 6 NIV*, www.bibles.org/eng-GNTD/2Sam/11.

61. Reza Aslan, *Zealot: The Life and Times of Jesus of Nazareth* (New York: Random House, 2013).

62. "Jews in Roman Times," *PBS*, 2006, www.pbs.org/empires/romans/empire/jews.html.

63. "The Roman Republic," *Ushistory.org*, Independence Hall Association, www.ushistory.org/civ/6a.asp.

64. Jon Wiener, "Contributing Edition," *The Nation*, July 25, 2013.

65. Ibid.

66. Aslan, *Zealot*.

67. Richard A. Horsley, *Jesus and the Politics of Roman Palestine* (Columbia: University of South Carolina Press, 2014).

68. History.com Staff, "Martin Luther and the 95 Theses," *History.com*, A&E Television Networks, 2009, www.history.com/topics/martin-luther-and-the-95-theses.

69. David Vandrunen, "The Two Kingdoms Doctrine and the Relationship of Church and State in the Early Reformed Tradition," *Journal of Church and State*, 49, no. 4 (Autumn 2007), 743–63.

70. Leviticus 19:11 NIV.

71. Ibid.

72. See various works on Christian missionary activities by J. F. Ade Ajayi, *Christian Missions in Nigeria: 1841–1891* (London: Longmans, 1965); and E. A. Ayandele, *The Missionary Impact on Modern Nigeria, 1842–1914: A Political and Social Analysis* (London: Longman, 1942). For an accessible synthesis, see Julius Adekunle, "Christianity," in *Africa, Vol 5: Contemporary Africa*, edited by by Toyin Falola, pp. 583–603.

73. E. A. Ayandele, *The Missionary Impact on Modern Nigeria, 1842–1914: A Political and Social Analysis* (London: Longman, 1942).

74. Ibid.

75. Walter Rodney, *How Europe Underdeveloped Africa* (London: Bogle-L'Ouverture, 1973).

76. See, for instance, Lamin Sanneh, *Translating the Message: The Missionary Impact on Culture* (Maryknoll, NY: Orbis Books, 2009).

77. William E. Phipps, "Christianity and Nationalism in Tropical Africa," *Civilisations* 22, no. 1 (1972): 92.

78. James S. Coleman, *Nigeria: Background to Nationalism* (Berkeley: University of California Press, 1961), 91; James S. Coleman, *The Politics of the Developing Areas* (Princeton, NJ: Princeton University Press, 1961), 78; David A. Kimble, *A Political History of Ghana* (Oxford, Clarendon Press, 1963), 166; George Kimble, *Tropical Africa*, Vol. II, *Society and Polity* (New York: Twentieth Century Fund, 1960), 274; and René Lemarchand, *Political Awakening in the Belgian Congo* (Berkley: University of California Press, 1964), 122.

79. Phipps, "Christianity and Nationalism," 94.

80. Lemarchand, *Political Awakening in the Belgian Congo*, 127.

81. Coleman, *Politics of the Developing Areas*, 348.

82. *New American Bible*, revised ed. (Totowa: Catholic Book Publishing Corporation, 2011).

83. G. W. Carpenter, "The Role of Christianity and Islam in Contemporary Africa," in *Africa Today*, edited by Charles Grove Haines, 111; Coleman, *Nigeria*, 103; Ndabaningi Sithole, *African Nationalism* (Capetown: Oxford University Press, 1959), 58; and Frederick B. Welbourn, *East African Rebels* (London: SCM Press Limited, 1961), 6, 133–34.

84. Charles Pelham Groves, *1914–1954*, Vol. IV, *The Planting of Christianity in Africa* (London: Lutterworth Press, 1958), 204.

85. *New American Bible*, revised ed.

86. Ibid.

87. Thomas Masaji Okuma, *Angola in Ferment: The Background and Prospects of Angolan Nationalism* (Boston, MA: Beacon Press, 1961), 43.

88. *New American Bible*, revised ed.

89. Ibid.

90. Sithole, *African Nationalism*, 53, cited in Phipps, "Christianity and Nationalism," 96.

91. J. F. Ade Ajayi, *Christian Missions in Nigeria, 1841–1891: The Making of a New Elite* (Evanston, IL: Longman, 1965), 174; and Catherine Hoskyns, *The Congo since Independence* (London: Oxford University Press, 1965), 34.

92. Coleman, *Nigeria*, 103; and Lemarchand, *Political Awakening*, 132.

93. Kimble, *A Political History*, 203.

94. Ibid.

95. Phipps, "Christianity and Nationalism," 99.

96. Thomas Lionel Hodgkin, *Nationalism in Colonial Africa* (London: Muller, 1956), 97.

97. Azikiwe, quoted in Herbert J. Spiro, *Politics in Africa: Prospects South of the Sahara* (Englewood Cliffs, NJ: Englewood Cliffs, 1962), 146.

98. Spiro, *Politics*, 146.

99. *New American Bible*, revised ed.

100. Spiro, *Politics*, 8.

101. Emma George Ross, "African Christianity in Kongo," *Metropolitan Museum of Art*, October 2002, https://www.metmuseum.org/toah/hd/acko/hd_acko.htm.

102. Alexander Ives Bortolot, "Women Leaders in African History: Dona Beatriz, Kongo Prophet," *Metropolitan Museum of Art*, October 2003, https://www.metmuseum.org/toah/hd/pwmn_4/hd_pwmn_4.htm.

103. Ibid.

104. Religion Library: African Independent Churches, "Overview," *Patheos*, n.d., http://www.patheos.com/library/african-independent-churches.

105. Ibid.

106. E. Bolaji Idowu, "The Predicament of the Church in Africa," in *Christianity in Tropical Africa*, edited by Christian G. Baëta (London: Oxford University Press, 1986), 427.

107. State Journal, "Teach the Bible as Secular Text? Impossible," *The State Journal*, May 11, 2014, accessed July 20, 2018, from https://www.state-journal.com/2014/05/10/teach-the-bible-as-secular-text-impossible-2/.

108. Brian Edgar, "Eight Core Christian Values," *Evangelical Alliance Faith & Politics*, http://www.ethos.org.au/site/Ethos/filesystem/documents/In-depth/Politics/Eight-Core-Christian-Values-Brian-Edgar.pdf.

109. GracefulAtheist, "Secular Grace," *Graceful Atheist*, October 21, 2016, https://gracefulatheist.wordpress.com/2016/10/21/secular-grace/.

110. Edgar, "Eight Core Christian Values."

111. Jack Wellman, "What Is the Biblical or Christian Definition of Hope?" *Faith on the Couch*, November 23, 2016, http://www.patheos.com/blogs/christiancrier/2014/05/26/what-is-the-Biblical-or-christian-definition-of-hope/.

112. "What Do Atheists Hope For?" *Big Think*, October 17, 2017, https://bigthink.com/hope-optimism/what-do-atheists-hope-for.

113. Henry M. Morris III, "The Power of Love," The Institute for Creation Research, January 31, 2014, http://www.icr.org/article/power-love/.

114. "Biblical Justice," *The Bible Project*, 2018, https://thebibleproject.com/explore/justice/.

115. David Mathis, "Joy Is Not Optional," *Desiring God*, February 3, 2016, accessed July 29, 2018, https://www.desiringgod.org/articles/joy-is-not-optional.

116. Edgar, "Eight Core Christian Values."

117. John MacArthur, "The Gift of Peace," *Grace to You*, August 18, 2016, https://www.gty.org/library/articles/P21/the-gift-of-peace.

118. Adrian Wilson, "What Is A Text?" *Studies in History and Philosophy of Science Part A* 43, no. 2 (June 2012): 341–58.

119. William M. Schniedewind, *How the Bible Became a Book: The Textualization of Ancient Israel*, 1st ed (Cambridge: Cambridge University Press), 2005.

120. Ibid.

121. Ibid.

122. Ibid.

123. Ibid.

124. Ibid.

125. David W. Kling, *The Bible in History: How the Texts Have Shaped the Times* (Oxford: Oxford University Press, 2004).

126. Leland Ryken, *How to Read the Bible as Literature* (Grand Rapids, MI: Zondervan, 2016).

127. Robert Alter, *Art of Biblical Narrative*, 1st ed. (New York: Perseus Books Group, 2011).

128. Ibid.

129. J. H. Gardiner, *The Bible as English Literature*, 1st ed. (Whitefish, MT: Kessinger Pub., 2010).

130. Ryken, *How to Read the Bible as Literature*, 2016.

131. Gardiner, *Bible as English Literature*, 2016.

132. Ryken, *How to Read the Bible as Literature*, 2016.

CHAPTER 7

1. Pew Research Center, "Christian Movements and Denominations," Pew Research Center's Religion & Public Life Project, July 10, 2019, https://www.pewforum.org/2011/12/19/global-christianity-movements-and-denominations/.

2. Africa Churches, "Top 10 Biggest Churches in Africa 2018," *Africa Churches.com News Portal*, October 11, 2018, https://africachurches.com/top-10-biggest-churches-in-africa-2018/.

3. André Corten and Ruth Marshall-Fratani, *Between Babel and Pentecost: Transnational Pentecostalism in Africa and Latin America* (London: Hurst, 2001).

4. Ibid.

5. Marne L. Campbell, "They Were All Filled with the Holy Ghost!: The Early Years of the Azusa Street Revival," in *Making Black Los Angeles: Class, Gender, and Community, 1850–1917* (Chapel Hill: University of North Carolina Press, 2016).

6. Allan Anderson, "The Azusa Street Revival and the Emergence of Pentecostal Missions in the Early Twentieth Century," *Transformation: An International Journal of Holistic Mission Studies* 23, no. 2 (2006): 107–18.

7. Joël Noret, "On the Inscrutability of the Ways of God: The Transnationalization of Pentecostalism on the West African Coast," in *Religion Crossing Boundaries: Transnational Religious and Social Dynamics in Africa and the New African Diaspora*, Religion and the Social Order, vol. 18 (Boston, MA: Brill, 2010).

8. Campbell, "They Were All Filled with the Holy Ghost!"

9. Ibid.

10. Anna Wickham, "That Old Time Religion: The Influence of West and Central African Religious Culture on the Music of the Azusa Street Revival," Master's dissertation (University of Arizona, 2014).

11. Ogbu Kalu, *African Pentecostalism: An Introduction* (Oxford: Oxford University Press, 2008).

12. Stephen Ellis and Gerrie ter Haar, "Religion and Politics: Taking African Epistemologies Seriously," *Journal of Modern African Studies* 45, no. 3 (2007): 385–401.

13. William Seymour, "River of Living Water," Sermon Index Audio Sermons, accessed November 19, 2019, http://www.sermonindex.net/modules/articles/index.php?view=article&aid=39711.

14. Solomon Schimmel, "Christian Biblical Fundamentalism," in *The Tenacity of Unreasonable Beliefs* (Oxford: Oxford University Press, 2008).

15. Willis Newman, "Evangelical and Pentecostal: What Is the Difference?" Bible-teaching-about.com (blog), accessed November 19, 2019, http://www.bible-teaching-about.com/evangelicalandpentecostal.html.

16. Schimmel, "Christian Biblical Fundamentalism."

17. Corten and Marshall-Fratani, *Between Babel and Pentecost*.

18. Robert Lionel Elkington, "The Doctrine of Subsequence in the Pentecostal and Neo-Pentecostal Movements," Master's dissertation (University of South Africa, 1998).

19. Kalu, *African Pentecostalism*.

20. Katrien Pype, *The Making of the Pentecostal Melodrama: Religion, Media and Gender in Kinshasa*, vol. 6 (Oxford: Berghahn Books, 2012).

21. Corten and Marshall-Fratani, *Between Babel and Pentecost*.

22. Warren Bird, "World's First Megachurch?" Leadership Network (blog), May 4, 2012, https://leadnet.org/worlds_first_megachurch/.

23. Campbell, "They Were All Filled with the Holy Ghost!"

24. Barney Warf and Morton Winsberg, "Geographies of Megachurches in the United States," *Journal of Cultural Geography* 27, no. 1 (2010): 33–51.

25. J. Kwabena Asamoah-Gyadu, "God Is Big in Africa: Pentecostal Megachurches and a Changing Religious Landscape," *Material Religion* 15, no. 3 (2019): 390–92.

26. Samuel Krinsky, "The Pan-African Church: Nation, Self, and Spirit in Winners' Chapel, Nigeria," in *Religion Crossing Boundaries* (Leiden: Brill, 2010), 227–51.

27. Michel Foucault, *Security, Territory, Population: Lectures at the Collège de France, 1977–78*, edited by Michel Senellart (New York: Springer, 2009).

28. Michel Foucault, *The Foucault Effect: Studies in Governmentality*, edited by Graham Bruchell, Colin Gordon, and Peter Miller (Chicago, IL: University of Chicago Press, 1991).

29. Michel Foucault, "Truth and Power: An Interview with Alessandro Fontano and Pasquale Pasquino," in *Michel Foucault Power/Truth/Strategy*, edited by M. Morris and P. Patton (Sydney: Feral, 1979), 29–48.

30. Luděk Vacín, *Experiencing Power, Generating Authority: Cosmos, Politics, and the Ideology of Kingship in Ancient Egypt and Mesopotamia*, edited by Jane A. Hill, Philip Jones, and Antonio J. Morales (Penn Museum International Research Conferences: University of Pennsylvania Museum of Archaeology and Anthropology, 2013).

31. Karen J. Brison, "Kingdom Culture?" *Social Sciences and Missions* 30, no. 1–2 (2017): 143–62.

32. Sarah Jeanette Dove, "The Choreography and Performance of Religion: Power and Ritual within American Pentecostal Worship Practice in the U.S," Master's dissertation (University of North Carolina at Greensboro, 2015).

33. Michel Foucault, *Religion and Culture*, selected and edited by Jeremy R. Carrette (New York: Routledge, 1999).

34. Walter D. Mignolo, *Local Histories/Global Designs: Coloniality, Subaltern Knowledges, and Border Thinking* (New York: Princeton University Press, 2000).

35. Frantz Fanon, "Black Skin, White Masks [1952]," *Contemporary Sociological Theory* (2012): 417.

36. Richard Schechner, *Performance Theory* (London: Routledge, 2003).

37. Erving Goffman, *Interaction Ritual: Essays in Face-to-Face Behavior* (New York: Routledge, 2017).

38. William I. Thomas, "Situational Analysis: The Behavior Pattern and the Situation," *Publ Am Sociol Soc* 22 (1927): 1–13.

39. Schechner, *Performance Theory*.

40. Nimi Wariboko, "Pentecostal Theology as a Discursive Site for the Weight of Blackness in Nigeria," *Pneuma* 36, no. 3 (2014): 417–31.

41. Ruth Marshall-Fratani, "Mediating the Global and Local in Nigerian Pentecostalism," *Journal of Religion in Africa* 28, no. 3 (1998): 278–315.

42. Corten and Marshall-Fratani, *Between Babel and Pentecost*.

43. Girish Daswani, *Looking Back, Moving Forward: Transformation and Ethical Practice in the Ghanaian Church of Pentecost* (Toronto: University of Toronto Press, 2015).

44. Dove, "Choreography and Performance of Religion,"

45. Ibid.

46. Susan Leigh Foster, ed. *Choreographing History* (Bloomington: Indiana University Press, 1995).

47. Kimerer LaMothe, "Enlivening Spirits: Shaker Dance Ritual as Theopraxis," *Théologiques* 25, no. 1 (2017): 103–24.

48. Joel Inbody, "Sensing God: Bodily Manifestations and Their Interpretation in Pentecostal Rituals and Everyday Life," *Sociology of Religion* 76, no. 3 (2015): 337–55.

49. Jerry M. Ireland, "A Classical Pentecostal Approach to Discipleship in Missions," *Journal of Pentecostal Theology* 28, no. 2 (2019): 243–66.

50. Michel Foucault, *Technologies of the Self: A Seminar with Michel Foucault*, edited by Luther H. Martin, Huck Gutman, and Patrick H. Hutton (Boston: University of Massachusetts Press, 1988).

51. Katsaura, "Theo-Urbanism: Pastoral Power and Pentecostals in Johannesburg," *Culture and Religion* 18, no. 3 (2017): 232–62.

52. Daswani, *Looking Back, Moving Forward*.

53. Katsaura, "Theo-Urbanism."

54. Benson Idahosa, *I Choose to Change: The Scriptural Way to Success and Prosperity* (Godalming: Highland Books, 1987).

55. Corten and Marshall-Fratani, *Between Babel and Pentecost*.

56. Daswani, *Looking Back, Moving Forward*.

57. Peter White, "Missional Branding: A Case Study of the Church of Pentecost," *HTS Teologiese Studies/Theological Studies* 75, no. 4 (2019): E1–e7.

58. Peter White, Fortune Tella, and Mishael Donkor Ampofo, "A Missional Study of the Use of Social Media (Facebook) by Some Ghanaian Pentecostal Pastors," *koers* 81, no. 2 (2016): 1–8.

59. Leesha McKenny, "Money Christmas: Hillsong Ensures Show in Tune with Spirit of Season," *Sydney Morning Herald*, retrieved 26 December 2011, from https://www.smh.com.au/entertainment/money-christmas-hillsong-ensures-show-in-tune-with-spirit-of-season-20111218–1p0vd.html.

60. Tanya Riches and Tom Wagner, "The Evolution of Hillsong Music: From Australian Pentecostal Congregation into Global Brand," *Australian Journal of Communication* 39, no. 1 (2012): 17.

61. Inbody, "Sensing God."

62. Kalu, *African Pentecostalism*.

63. Pype, *Making of the Pentecostal Melodrama*.

64. Ibid.

65. Katsaura, "Theo-Urbanism."

66. Albert Babajide Adeboye, "Characteristics of Modern Ecclesiastical Architecture in Nigeria: A Case Study of Some Selected Church Buildings," *International Journal of Research in Engineering & Technology* 3, no. 1 (2015): 1–10.

67. Ed Stetzer, "Trends in Church Architecture, Part 1," The Exchange (blog), July 18, 2016, https://www.christianitytoday.com/edstetzer/2016/july/trends-in-church-architecture-part-1.html.

68. J. Kwabena Asamoah-Gyadu, "God Is Big in Africa: Pentecostal Mega Churches and a Changing Religious Landscape," *Material Religion* 15, no. 3 (2019): 390–92.

69. Baba Oladeji, "House on the Rock?: Finding an Architectural Language for the Pentecostal Church by Baba Oladeji," *livin spaces*, March 5, 2018, https://www.livinspaces.net/interviews-and-articles/house-rock-finding-architectural-language-pentecostal-church-baba-oladeji/.

70. Jonathan D. James, *A Moving Faith: Mega Churches Go South* (New Delhi: Sage, 2015).

71. Bruno Reinhardt, "Discipline (and Lenience) beyond the Self: Discipleship in a Pentecostal-Charismatic Organization," *Social Analysis* 62, no. 3 (2018): 42–66.

72. Ernest Jones, *Essays in Applied Psycho-Analysis*, International Psycho-Analytical Library, no. 40, 41 (London: Hogarth Press, 1951).

73. Darío Rodríguez, "The God of Life and the Spirit of Life: The Social and Political Dimension of Life in the Spirit," *Studies in World Christianity* 17, no. 1 (2011): 1–11.

74. D. Jacobsen, "Political Spiritualities: The Pentecostal Revolution in Nigeria," *Choice* 47, no. 5 (2010): 973.

75. Selina Stone, "Pentecostal Power: Discipleship as Political Engagement," *Journal of the European Pentecostal Theological Association* 38, no. 1 (2018): 24–38.

76. Rodríguez, "God of Life and the Spirit of Life."

77. Frederick L. Ware, "On the Compatibility/Incompatibility of Pentecostal Premillennialism with Black Liberation Theology," in *Afro-Pentecostalism: Black Pentecostal and Charismatic Christianity in History and Culture*, edited by Yong Amos and Alexander Y. Estrelda (New York: NYU Press, 2011).

78. Jacobsen, "Political Spiritualities."

79. Judith Casselberry, *The Labor of Faith: Gender and Power in Black Apostolic Pentecostalism* (Durham, NC: Duke University Press, 2017).

80. Jane Soothill, "Gender and Pentecostalism in Africa," in *Pentecostalism in Africa: Presence and Impact of Pneumatic Christianity in Postcolonial Societies*, edited by Martin Lindhardt (Boston, MA: Brill, 2014).

81. Adriaan S. van Klinken, "God's World Is Not an Animal Farm—or Is It? The Catachrestic Translation of Gender Equality in African Pentecostalism," *Religion and Gender* 3, no. 2 (2013): 240–58.

82. Kalu, *African Pentecostalism*.

83. Corten and Marshall-Fratani, *Between Babel and Pentecost*.

84. Ibid.

85. Robert Herner and Peter L. Berger, *Global Pentecostalism in the 21st Century* (Bloomington: Indiana University Press, 2013).

86. Daswani, *Looking Back, Moving Forward*.

87. Michael D. Palmer, "Abundant Life or Abundant Poverty?" in *Wiley-Blackwell Companions to Religion* (Chichester: John Wiley & Sons, 2012).

CHAPTER 8

1. "Monarchy," *Oxford English Dictionary*, http://www.oed.com.ezproxy.lib.utexas.edu/view/Entry/121100?redirectedFrom=monarchy#eid.

2. Baruch Halpern, "Kingship and Monarchy," in *The Oxford Companion to the Bible*, edited by Michael D. Coogan and Bruce M. Metzger (New York: Oxford University Press, 1993), 413–16.

3. "Kingship," *Oxford English Dictionary*, http://www.oed.com.ezproxy.lib.utexas.edu/view/Entry/103550?redirectedFrom=kingship#eid.

4. Henry A. Myers, *Medieval Kingship* (Chicago, IL: Nelson-Hall, 1982), 1.

5. Ibid., 2–4.

6. W. M. Spellman, *Monarchies 1000–2000* (London: Reaktion Books, 2001), 12.

7. A. M. Hocart, *Kings and Councillors: An Essay in the Comparative Anatomy of Human Society* (Chicago, IL: University of Chicago Press, 1970).

8. Spellman, *Monarchies 1000–2000*, 12–13.

9. Philip Curtin, Steven Feierman, Leonard Thompson, and Jan Vansina, *African History* (Boston, MA: Little Brown, 1978), 35–35.

10. Spellman, *Monarchies 1000–2000*, 71–83.

11. Ibid., 21–23.

12. O. B. Jegede, "Women, Power and Subversion in Orature: A Palace Performance in Yorubaland, Nigeria," *Journal of Gender Studies* 15, no. 3 (2006): 253–66.

13. Lorna Finlayson, "On Mountains and Molehills: Problems, Non-Problems, and the Ideology of Ideology," *Constellations* 22, no. 1 (2015): 135–46.

14. Karl Marx, "The German Ideology: Part 1," translated by Robert C. Tucker from *The Marx Engels Reader*, 2nd ed. (New York: Norton, 1978).

15. Karl Marx, "Religion, the Opium of the People," *World Treasury of Modern Religious Thought* (1990): 79–91.

16. Max Weber, *The Protestant Ethic and the Spirit of Capitalism* (New York: Routledge, 2001).

17. Finlayson, "On Mountains and Molehills."

18. Jeffrey Fleisher and Stephanie Wynne-Jones, "Authorisation and the Process of Power: The View from African Archaeology," *Journal of World Prehistory* 23, no. 4 (2010): 177–93.

19. Petar Ramadanovic, "No Place Like Ideology (on Slavoj Žižek): Is there a Difference between the Theory of Ideology and the Theory of Interpretation?" *Cultural Critique* 86, no. 86 (2014): 119–38.

20. Louis Althusser, "Ideology and Ideological State Apparatuses (Notes towards an Investigation)," *Anthropology of the State: A Reader* 9, no. 1 (2006): 86–98.

21. Jane A. Hill, Philip Jones, and Antonio J. Morales, eds., *Experiencing Power, Generating Authority: Cosmos, Politics, and the Ideology of Kingship in Ancient Egypt and Mesopotamia* (Philadelphia: University of Pennsylvania Press, 2013).

22. Finlayson, "On Mountains and Molehills."

23. Susan Keech McIntosh, ed., *Beyond Chiefdoms: Pathways to Complexity in Africa* (New York: Cambridge University Press, 2005).

24. Fleisher, "Authorisation and the Process of Power."

25. Ibid.

26. Declan Quigley, "Introduction: The Character of Kingship," in *The Character of Kingship*, edited by Declan Quigley (New York: Berg, 2005), 1–11.

27. Michael H. Hunt, "Ideology," *Journal of American History* 77, no. 1 (June 1990): 108.

28. Spellman, *Monarchies 1000–2000*, 12–13.

29. Susan Drucker-Brown, "Horse, Dog, and Monkey: The Making of a Mamprusi King," *Man* (NS) 27, no. 1 (March 1992): 71–79.

30. Quigley, "Introduction," 3–5.

31. William Fagg, *Divine Kingship in Africa* (London: Trustees of the British Museum, 1970), 22.

32. Osarhieme Benson Osadolor, "The Military System of Benin Kingdom, c. 1440–1897" (PhD diss., University of Hamburg, 2001).

33. Osarhieme Benson Osadolor, "The Benin Royalist Movement and Its Political Opponents: Controversy over Restoration of the Monarchy, 1897–1914," *International Journal of African Historical Studies* 44, no. 1 (2011): 45–59.

34. Joseph Nevadomsky, "Kingship Succession Rituals in Benin. 3: The Coronation of the Oba," *African Arts* 17, no. 3 (May 1984): 57.

35. Stephen Ellis and Gerrie ter Haar, "Religion and Politics: Taking African Epistemologies Seriously," *Journal of Modern African Studies* 45, no. 3 (2007): 385–401.

36. J. K. H. Tse, "Grounded Theologies: 'Religion' and the 'Secular' in Human Geography," *Progress in Human Geography* 38, no. 2 (2014): 201–20.

37. Kiatezua Lubanzadio Luyaluka, "An Essay on Naturalized Epistemology of African Indigenous Knowledge," *Journal of Black Studies* 47, no. 6 (2016): 497–523.

38. Ernst Kantorowicz, *The King's Two Bodies: A Study in Medieval Political Theology*, vol. 22 (Princeton, NJ: Princeton University Press, 1957; reprint 2016).

39. Herbert Spencer, *The Principles of Sociology*, vol. 6. (New York: Appleton, 1895).

40. Pierre de Maret, "From Kinship to Kingship: An African Journey into Complexity," *Azania: Archaeological Research in Africa* 47, no. 3 (2012): 314–26.

41. Edward Evan Evans-Pritchard, *The Divine Kingship of the Shilluk of the Nilotic Sudan* (Cambridge: Cambridge University Press, 1948; reprint 2014).

42. Dennis C. Rasmussen, "Burning Laws and Strangling Kings? Voltaire and Diderot on the Perils of Rationalism in Politics," *Review of Politics* 73, no. 1 (2011): 77–104.

43. James George Frazer, *The Golden Bough* (London: Palgrave Macmillan, 1990).

44. Arthur Maurice Hocart, *Kingship* (Oxford: Oxford University Press, 1927).

45. David Graeber, "The Divine Kingship of the Shilluk: On Violence, Utopia, and the Human Condition, or, Elements for an Archaeology of Sovereignty," *Hau: Journal of Ethnographic Theory* 1, no. 1 (2011): 1.

46. Marshall Sahlins, "The Stranger-King or, Elementary Forms of the Politics of Life," *Indonesia and the Malay World* 36, no. 105 (2008): 177–99.

47. Temesgen G. Baye, "The Evolution and Development of Kingship and Traditional Governance in Ethiopia: A Case of the Kefa Kingdom," *Journal of Asian and African Studies* 47, no. 2 (2012): 190–203.

48. Alan Strathern, "Drawing the Veil of Sovereignty: Early Modern Islamic Empires and Understanding Sacred Kingship," *History and Theory* 53, no. 1 (2014): 79–93.

49. Jan Vansina, "A Comparison of African Kingdoms," *Africa* 32, no. 4 (1962): 324–35.

50. Kantorowicz, *King's Two Bodies*.

51. Graeber, "The Divine Kingship."

52. Hill et al., *Experiencing Power*.

53. Thomas Blom Hansen and Finn Stepputat, "Sovereignty Revisited," *Annual Review of Anthropology* 35 (2006): 295–315.

54. Megan Vaughan, "'Divine Kings': Sex, Death and Anthropology in Inter-War East/Central Africa," *Journal of African History* 49, no. 3 (2008): 383–401.

55. Abdou Maliq Simone, *For the City Yet to Come: Changing African Life in Four Cities* (London: Duke University Press, 2004).

56. Graeber, "The Divine Kingship."

57. Luc De Heusch, *Drunken King, or, the Origin of the State (African Systems of Thought)* (Bloomington: Indiana University Press, 1982).

58. Vaughan, "Divine Kings."

59. Declan Quigley, "Scapegoats: The Killing of Kings and Ordinary People," *Journal of the Royal Anthropological Institute* 6, no. 2 (2000): 237–54.

60. Frazer, *The Golden Bough.*

61. Jean-Claude Muller, "12 'Divine Kingship' in Chiefdoms and States. A Single Ideological Model," *Study of the State* 35 (1981): 239.

62. Quigley, "Scapegoats."

63. De Heusch, *Drunken King.*

64. Ibid.

65. Graeber, "The Divine Kingship."

66. Jegede, "Women, Power and Subversion in Orature."

67. Hill et al., *Experiencing Power.*

68. J. Calabrese, "Metals, Ideology and Power: The Manufacture and Control of Materialised Ideology in the Area of the Limpopo-Shashe Confluence," *South African Archaeological Society Goodwin Series* 8 (2000): 100–11.

69. Hill et al., *Experiencing Power.*

70. Manuela Palmeirim, "Masks, Myths, Novels, and Symbolic Ambiguity: Dialogues between Verbal and Visual Arts," *African Arts* 41, no. 3 (2008): 74–77.

71. Gillian Feeley-Harnik, "Issues in Divine Kingship," *Annual Review of Anthropology* 14, no. 1 (1985): 273–313.

72. Fleisher, "Authorisation and the Process of Power."

73. Calabrese, "Metals, Ideology and Power."

74. Paul K. Bjerk, "They Poured Themselves into the Milk: Zulu Political Philosophy under Shaka," *Journal of African History* 47, no. 1 (2006): 1–19.

75. Georges Dumézil, *The Destiny of a King* (Chicago, IL: University of Chicago Press, 1988).

76. Hill et al., *Experiencing Power.*

77. McIntosh, *Beyond Chiefdoms.*

78. Michel Foucault, Meaghan Morris, and Paul Patton, *Michel Foucault Power, Truth, Strategy* (Sydney: Feral, 1979).

79. Wyatt MacGaffey, "Death of a King, Death of a Kingdom? Social Pluralism and Succession to High Office in Dagbon, Northern Ghana," *Journal of Modern African Studies* 44, no. 1 (2006): 79–99.

80. Timo Kallinen, "Christianity, Fetishism, and the Development of Secular Politics in Ghana: A Dumontian Approach," *Anthropological Theory* 14, no. 2 (2014): 153–68.

81. Peter Skalnik, "Chiefdoms and Kingdoms in Africa: Why They Are neither States nor Empires," 2012, accessed July 31, 2018, http://www.ascleiden.nl/Pdf/chiefdomsandkingdoms.pdf.

82. Jean-François Bayart, "Democracy and the Challenge of Tradition in Sub-Saharan Africa," *Pouvoirs* 2 (2009): 27–44.

83. P. Clastres, *Society against the State* (New York: Zone, 1974; reprint 1989).

84. Ørnulf Gulbrandsen, "The Discourse of 'Ritual Murder': Popular Reaction to Political Leaders in Botswana," *Social Analysis: The International Journal of Social and Cultural Practice* 46, no. 3 (2002): 215–33.

85. Hansen and Stepputat, "Sovereignty Revisited."

86. Ibid.

87. Jegede, "Women, Power and Subversion in Orature."

88. J. F. A. Ajayi and R. S. Smith, *Yoruba Warfare in the 19th Century* (Cambridge: Cambridge University Press, 1964); and I. A. Akinjogbin, "Prelude to the Yoruba Civil Wars of the Nineteenth Century," *Odu: University of Ife Journal of African Studies* 1, no. 2 (1965): 24–46.

89. Samuel Johnson, *The History of the Yorubas: From the Earliest Times to the Beginning of the British Protectorate* (Lagos: C.M.S., 1921; reprinted 1960), 40–78.

90. For details, see Atanda, *New Oyo Empire.*

91. Insa Nolte, "Chieftaincy and the State in Abacha's Nigeria: Kingship, Political Rivalry and Competing Histories in Abeokuta during the 1990s," *Africa* 72, no. 3 (2002): 368–90.

92. Daniel Anazia, "Yoruba Indigenous Knowledge Should Be Basis of Development, Says Alaafin," *The Guardian*, October 12, 2017, https://guardian.ng/news/yoruba-indigenous-knowledge-should-be-basis-of-development-says-alaafin/.

CHAPTER 9

1. See, for instance, P. C. Lloyd, "Sacred Kingship and Government among the Yoruba," *Africa* XXX, no. III (1960): 221–37.

2. Claus Westermann, "Sacred Kingship: Religious and Political Concept," *Encyclopaedia Britannica*, n.d., https://www.britannica.com/topic/sacred-kingship.

3. To learn more on this aspect, see, for example, P. A. Vander Waerdt, "Kingship and Philosophy in Aristotle's Best Regime," *Phronesis* 30, no. 3 (1985): 249–74.

4. Read the following: Encyclopaedia Britannica, "The Golden Bough: Work by Frazer," *Encyclopaedia Britannica*, n.d., https://www.britannica.com/topic/The-Golden-Bough. This work was a study of comparative religion that was originally published in 1890 in two volumes. It was later expanded and republished into twelve volumes. This work examines the progression of kingdoms under the beliefs of magic, religion, and science.

5. Westermann, "Sacred Kingship: Religious and Political Concept."

6. Ibid.

7. Ibid.

8. Thomas Gale, "Kingship: Kingship in Sub-Saharan Africa," *Encyclopedia.com*, 2005, https://www.encyclopedia.com/environment/encyclopedias-almanacs-transcripts-and-maps/kingship-kingship-sub-saharan-africa.

9. Ibid.

10. Ibid.

11. Ibid.

12. Ibid.

13. Ibid.

14. Ibid.

15. See, for instance, J. A. Atanda, *The New Oyo Empire: Indirect Rule and Change in Western Nigeria, 1894–1934* (London: Longman, 1973), 15.

16. Peter Morton-Williams, "The Ogboni Cult in Oyo," *Africa*, XXX, no. 4 (Oct. 1960): 362–74.

17. Samuel Johnson, *The History of the Yorubas from the Earliest Times to the Beginning of the British Protectorate* (Lagos: C.M.S., 1921; reprinted 1960), 40–78.

18. Ibid., 40.

19. Ibid., 179.

20. Robin Law, *The Oyo Empire, c. 1600–c. 1836: A West African Imperialism in the Era of the Atlantic Slave Trade* (Oxford: Clarendon Press, 1977), 84–85.

21. Atanda, *New Oyo Empire*.

22. Law, *Oyo Empire, c. 1600–c. 1836*.

23. S. O. Babayemi, *The Fall and Rise of Oyo, c. 1706–1905: A Study in the Traditional Culture of an African Polity* (Ibadan: Lichfield, 1990).

24. B. A. Agiri, "Early Oyo History Reconsidered," *History in Africa* 2 (1975): 1–16.

25. Encyclopedia Britannica, "Oyo Empire: Historical Kingdom in Western Africa," *Encyclopedia Britannica*, n.d., https://www.britannica.com/place/Oyo-empire.

26. I. A. Akinjogbin, "The Oyo Empire in the Eighteenth Century: A Reassessment," *Journal of the Historical Society of Nigeria* 3, no. 3 (1966): 449–60.

27. Ibid.

28. For creation mythologies, see Johnson, *History of the Yorubas*, Chapter 2.

29. Andrew Apter, "The Historiography of Yoruba Myth and Ritual," *History in Africa* 14 (1987): 3.

30. Ibid.

31. Ibid.

32. Headdress. Wellcome Collection, Museum of Ethnic Arts, University of California, Los Angeles. Height 11", as cited in Robert Farris Thompson, "The Sign of the Divine King: An Essay on Yoruba Bead-Embroidered Crowns with Veil and Bird Decorations," *African Arts* 3, no. 3 (1970): 8.

33. Thompson, "Sign of the Divine King," 8.

34. For more information on this subject, see Peter Lloyd, "Sacred Kingship and Government among the Yoruba," *Africa* 30, no. 3 (1960): 221–37.

35. Thompson, "Sign of the Divine King," 8.

36. Ibid.

37. Ibid., 10.

38. Ibid.

39. Ibid.

40. Ibid.

41. Father L. K. Carroll, "Yoruba Craftwork at Oye-Ekiti, Ondo Providence," *Nigeria* 35 (1950): 353.

42. Thompson, "Sign of the Divine King," 16.

43. Ibid.

44. Ibid.

45. John Pemberton III and Funso S. Afọlayan, *Yoruba Sacred Kingship: "A Power Like That of the Gods"* (Washington, DC: Smithsonian Institution Press, 1996), 73.

46. Ibid., 77.

47. Ibid., 78.

48. Ibid., 92–93.

49. Ibid., 93–94.

CHAPTER 10

1. P. Morton-Williams, "An Outline of the Cosmology and Cult Organization of the Oyo Yoruba," *Africa* 34 (1964): 243–61.

2. J. Westcott and P. Morton-Williams, "The Symbolism and Ritual Context of the Yoruba Laba Shango," *Journal of the Royal Anthropological Institute* 92 (1962): 23–37.

3. Richard Lander, *Records of Captain Clapperton's Last Expedition to Africa*, vols. 1 and 2 (London: Henry Colburn and Richard Bentley, 1830), 197–200.

4. For a useful and competent study of Yoruba palaces, see G. J. A. Ojo, *Yoruba Palaces: A Study of Afins of Yorubaland* (London: University of London Press, 1966).

5. Anne Bisci Bowen, "Murals at Afin Oyo," *African Arts* 10, no. 3 (1977): 42.

6. Picture from ibid., 43.

7. C. O. Adepegba, *"Ara*: The Factor of Creativity in Yoruba Art," *Critical Interventions* 2, no. 3–4 (2008): 224.

8. Bowen, "Murals at Afin Oyo," 44.

9. Adepegba, *"Ara,"* 223.

10. A. Johnson, *The History of the Yorubas*, reprint (Westport, CT: Negro Universities Press, 1970), 155.

11. Adepegba, *"Ara,"* 223.

12. Ibid., 224.

13. Ibid., 224–27.

14. Oxford University Press, *A Dictionary of the Yoruba Language*, 1913 reprint (London: Oxford University Press, 1976), 39, as cited in Adepegba, *"Ara,"* 227

15. R. C. Abraham, *A Dictionary of Modern Yoruba* (London: University of London Press, 1958), 61, as cited in Adepegba, *"Ara,"* 227.

16. Adepegba, *"Ara,"* 227.

17. H. Clapperton, *Journal of a Second Expedition into the Interior of Africa from the Bight of Benin to Soccatoo* (Philadelphia, PA: Grey, Lean and Carey, 1829), 48, as cited in Adepegba, *"Ara,"* 224–25.

18. R. Soper, "Carver Posts at Old Oyo," *The Nigerian Field* 43, no. 1 (1978): 17. See also J. D. Clarke, "Carved Posts at Old Oyo," *Nigeria Magazine* 18 (1999): 248–49.

19. Adepegba, *"Ara,"* 225.

20. Ibid., 226.

21. Joel Adedeji, "The Poetry of Yoruba Masque Theatre," *African Arts* 11, no. 3 (1978): 62.

22. Ibid.

23. Ibid., 63.
24. Ibid., 64.
25. Ibid.
26. Akintunde Akinyemi, *Yoruba Royal Poetry: A Socio-Historical Exposition and Annotated Translation*, vol. 71 (Bayreuth: Bayreuth University, 2004), 9.
27. Ibid., 9–12.
28. Ibid., 13.
29. Karin Barber, "Yoruba *Oríkì* and Deconstructive Criticism," *Research in African Literature* 15, no. 4 (1984): 503–5.
30. Akinyemi, *Yoruba Royal Poetry*, 14.
31. Ibid., 14–15.
32. Ibid., 20.
33. Ibid., 22–23.
34. Ibid., 25.
35. Ibid., 29.
36. Jan Vansina, *Oral Tradition: A Study in Historical Methodology*, translated by H. M. Wright (London: Routledge and Kegan Paul, 1965), 150, as cited in Akinyemi, *Yoruba Royal Poetry*, 29.
37. Samuel Johnson, 1901, 188–95.
38. Akinyemi, *Yoruba Royal Poetry*, 23–24.
39. Ibid., 23.
40. Ibid., 34–35.
41. Ibid., 39.
42. O. Olatunji, *Features of Yoruba Oral Poetry* (Ibadan: University Press Limited, 1984), Chapter 4, as cited in Akinyemi, *Yoruba Royal Poetry*, 40.
43. S. A. Babalola, *The Content and Form of Yoruba Ijálá* (Oxford: Clarendon Press, 1966), 50; O. Olajubu, "The Yoruba Artists and Their Work," in *Seminar Series*, Department of African Languages and Literatures, University of Ife, II, 1977, 384–418; Olatunji, *Features of Yoruba Oral Poetry*, 57, as cited in Akinyemi, *Yoruba Royal Poetry*, 40.
44. Olatunji, *Features of Yoruba Oral Poetry*, 73fff, as cited in Akinyemi, *Yoruba Royal Poetry*, 40.
45. S. A. Babalola, *Àwọn Oríkì Orílè* (Glasgow: Collins, 1967), as cited in Akinyemi, *Yoruba Royal Poetry*, 41.
46. Karin Barber, *I Could Speak until Tomorrow* (Edinburgh: Edinburgh University Press, 1991), 167, as cited in Akinyemi, *Yoruba Royal Poetry*, 41.
47. Johnson, *History of the Yorubas*, 48–50.
48. S. Adebanji Akintoye, *A History of the Yoruba People* (Dakar: Amalion, 2010), 259.
49. Toyin Falola and Matt Childs, eds., *The Yoruba Diaspora in the Atlantic World* (Bloomington: Indiana University Press, 2004).
50. Akinyemi, *Yoruba Royal Poetry*, 2004.
51. Kola Owolabi and Sayo Alagbe, *The Alaafin of Oyo, Oba Lamidi Adeyemi III: His Life History and His Philosophy* (Ibadan: Universal Akada Books, 2008), 103–4.

CHAPTER 11

1. NA. Famous Scientists: *The Art of Genius*. https://www.famousscientists. org/10-most-famous-scientific-theories-that-were-later-debunked/.

2. For additional information about this, see David Ferrer, *25 Popular Science Myths Debunked*, Edited by Forrest M. Mims. https://thebestschools.org/magazine/ 25-popular-science-myths-debunked/.

3. Professor Oluwole Sophie was a lecturer on African philosophy in the University of Lagos in Nigeria. See the interview session with Professor Sophie Oluwole on Opomulero TV.

4. Francis Oakley, *Kingship: The Politics of Enchantment* (Oxford: Blackwell, 2006), 1–9.

5. Thomas Hobbes, *Leviathan* (Longman Library of Primary Sources in Philosophy) (New York: Routledge, 2016).

6. I am adopting here the controversial classifications of kingdoms/empires into land-based and sea-based. For their meaning and adoption, see Stephen Howe, *Empire: A Very Short Introduction* (Oxford: Oxford University Press, 2002).

7. For how the current Alaafin, Oba Lamidi Adeyemi III, ascended the throne, see Kola Owolabi and Sayo Alagbe, *The Alaafin of Oyo, Oba Lamidi Adeyemi III: His Life History and His Philosophy* (Ibadan: Universal Akada Books, 2008), 60–81.

8. Abdullahi Smith, "A Little New Light on the Collapse of the Alafinate of Yoruba," in *Studies in Yoruba History and Culture: Essays in Honour of Professor S. O. Biobaku*, edited by Gabriel Olusanya, 42–71 (Ibadan: University Press Limited, 1983).

Bibliography

A Dictionary of the Yoruba Language. 1913. Reprint, London: Oxford University Press, 1976.

Abimbola, W. *Awon Oju Odu Mereerindinlogun.* Ibadan: University Press PLC, 2014.

Abimbola, W. *Ifa Divination Poetry.* New York: Nook, 1977.

Abou El Fadl, Khaled. "The Epistemology of the Truth in Modern Islam." *Philosophy & Social Criticism* 41, no. 4–5 (2015): 473–86.

Abraham, R. C. *A Dictionary of Modern Yoruba.* London: University of London Press, 1958.

Abu-Zayd, Nasr. "The Dilemma of the Literary Approach to the Qur'an." *Alif: Journal of Comparative Poetics* no. 23 (2003): 8.

Aczel, Amir. "Why Science Does Not Disprove God." *New York Times*, April 27, 2014. http://time.com/77676/why-science-does-not-disprove-God/.

Adebayo, J. O. "Gerontocracy in African politics: Youth and the Quest for Political Participation." *Journal of African Elections* 17, no. 1 (2018): 140–61.

Adeboye, Albert Babajide. "Characteristics of Modern Ecclesiastical Architecture in Nigeria: A Case Study of Some Selected Church Buildings." *International Journal of Research in Engineering & Technology* 3, no. 1 (2015): 1–10.

Adeboye, O. "The Changing Conception of Elderhood in Ibadan, 1830–2000." *Nordic Journal of African Studies* 16, no. 2 (2017): 261–78.

Adedeji, Joel. "The Poetry of Yoruba Masque Theatre." *African Arts* 11, no. 3 (1978): 62.

Adegbindin, O. *Encyclopedia of the Yoruba*, edited by T. Falola and A. Akinyemi. Bloomington: Indiana University Press, 2016.

Adegboyega, O. O. "The Metaphysical and Epistemological Relevance of Ifa Corpus." *International Journal of History and Philosophical Research* 5, no. 1 (2017): 28–40.

Adepegba, C. O. "Ara: The Factor of Creativity in Yoruba Art." *Critical Interventions* 2, no. 3–4 (2008): 224.

Africa Churches. "Top 10 Biggest Churches in Africa 2018." *Africa Churches.com News Portal*, October 11, 2018. https://africachurches.com/top-10-biggest-churches-in-africa-2018/.

Ajayi, J. F. A., and R. S. Smith. *Yoruba Warfare in the 19th Century*. Cambridge: Cambridge University Press, 1964.

Ake, Claude. *Social Science as Imperialism: The Theory of Political Development*. Ibadan: Ibadan University Press, 1982.

Akinjogbin, I. A. "Prelude to the Yoruba Civil Wars of the Nineteenth Century." *University of Ife Journal of African Studies* 1, no. 2 (1965): 24–46.

Akintoye, S. Adebanji. *A History of the Yoruba People*. Dakar: Amalion, 2010.

Akinyemi, Akintunde. *Yoruba Royal Poetry: A Socio-Historical Exposition and Annotated Translation*, vol. 71. Bayreuth: Bayreuth University, 2004.

Ali Nayed, Aref. "The Radical Qur'anic Hermeneutics of Sayyid Qutb." *Islamic Studies* 31, no. 3 (1992): 355–63.

Alkhateeb, Firas. "How the Quran Is Protected from Any Change, Corruption." *Arab News*, June 4, 2015. http://www.arabnews.com/islam-perspective/news/756976.

Althusser, Louis. "Ideology and Ideological State Apparatuses (Notes towards an Investigation)." *Anthropology of the State: A Reader* 9, no. 1 (2006): 86–98.

Amosun, S. L., and P. Reddy. "Healthy Ageing in Africa." *World Health* 50, no. 4 (1997): 18–19.

Anazia, Daniel. "Yoruba Indigenous Knowledge Should be Basis of Development, Says Alaafin." *The Guardian*, October 12, 2017. https://guardian.ng/news/yoruba-indigenous-knowledge-should-be-basis-of-development-says-alaafin/.

Anderson, Allan. "The Azusa Street Revival and the Emergence of Pentecostal Missions in the Early Twentieth Century." *Transformation: An International Journal of Holistic Mission Studies* 23, no. 2 (2006): 107–18.

Andersson, Gerhard. "Atheism and How It Is Perceived: Manipulation of, Bias against and Ways to Reduce the Bias." *Nordic Psychology* 68, no. 3 (July 2016): 194–203.

Apt, N. A. "Rapid Urbanization and Living Arrangements of Older Persons in Africa." In *Living Arrangements of Older Persons: Critical Issues and Policy Responses*, 288–310. United Nations, Population Division. *Population Bulletin of the United Nations*, 2001.

Aristotle. *Posterior Analytics*. Translated by Jonathan Barnes. Oxford: Clarendon Press, 1994.

Asamoah-Gyadu, J. Kwabena. "Witchcraft Accusations and Christianity in Africa." *International Bulletin of Missionary Research* 39, no. 1 (2015): 23–27.

Asamoah-Gyadu, J. Kwabena. "God Is Big in Africa: Pentecostal Megachurches and a Changing Religious Landscape." *Material Religion* 15, no. 3 (2019): 390–92.

Asante, Molefi K. "African Ways of Knowing and Cognitive Faculties." In *Encyclopedia of Black Studies*, edited by Molefi Asante and Ama Mazama, 40. Thousand Oaks, CA: Sage, 2005.

Ashforth, Adam. "Human Security and Spiritual Insecurity: Why the Fear of Evil Forces Needs to Be Taken Seriously." *Georgetown Journal of International Affairs* 11 (2010): 99.

Ashforth, Adam. "Muthi, Medicine and Witchcraft: Regulating 'African Science' in Post-Apartheid South Africa?" *Social Dynamics* 31, no. 2 (2005): 211–42.

Atanda, Joseph Adebowale. *The New Ọyọ Empire: Indirect Rule and Change in Western Nigeria, 1894–1934*. Harlow: Longman, 1973.

Babalola, S. A. *The Content and Form of Yoruba Ìjálá.* Oxford: Clarendon Press, 1966.

Babalola, S. A. *Àwọn Oríkì Orílẹ̀.* Glasgow: Collins, 1967.

Bacon, Francis. *Novum Organum Scientiarum.* Cambridge: Cambridge University Press, 2000.

Baker, P. M, and G. G. Eaton. "Seniority versus Age as Causes of Dominance in Social Groups." *Small Group Research* 23, no. 3 (1992): 322–43.

Bambra, C., D. Fox, and A. Scott-Samuel. "Towards a New Politics of Health." *Health Promotion International* 20, no. 2 (2005): 187–93.

Barber, Karin. "Yoruba Oríkì and Deconstructive Criticism." *Research in African Literature* 15, no. 4 (1984): 503–5.

Barber, Karin. *I Could Speak until Tomorrow.* Edinburgh: Edinburgh University Press, 1991.

Barstow, Anne Llewellyn. "On Studying Witchcraft as Women's History: A Historiography of the European Witch Persecutions." *Journal of Feminist Studies in Religion* 4, no. 2 (1988): 7–19.

Baruch Halpern. "Kingship and Monarchy." In *The Oxford Companion to the Bible,* edited by Michael D. Coogan and Bruce M. Metzger, 413–16. New York: Oxford University Press, 1993.

Bayart, Jean-François. "Democracy and the Challenge of Tradition in Sub-Saharan Africa." *Pouvoirs* 2 (2009): 27–44.

BBC News. "Is Witchcraft Alive in Africa?" *Africa,* July 27, 2005. http://news.bbc.co.uk/2/hi/africa/4705201.stm.

BBC News. "Tanzania 'Witchcraft' Murders: 'Our Son Was Robbed of His Future'." *Africa,* February 9, 2019. https://www.bbc.com/news/av/world-africa-47174329/tanzania-witchcraft-murders-our-son-was-robbed-of-his-future.

Beattie, Tina. *The New Atheists: The Twilight of Reason and the War on Religion.* London: Darton, Longman and Todd, 2007.

Behrend, Heike. "The Rise of Occult Powers, AIDS and the Roman Catholic Church in Western Uganda." *Journal of Religion in Africa* 37, no. 1 (2007): 41–58.

Berton, R. M., and S. Panel. "Elderhood and Compliance: How Aging Dictators Affect Civil Wars." Working Paper, Sciences Po Grenoble, 2014. Accessed February 10, 2020, from https://hal-mines-paristech.archives –ouvertes.fr.

Bird, Warren. "World's First Megachurch?" Leadership Network (blog). May 4, 2012. https://leadnet.org/worlds_first_megachurch/.

Bjerk, Paul K. "They Poured Themselves into the Milk: Zulu Political Philosophy under Shaka." *Journal of African History* 47, no. 1 (2006): 1–19.

Blake, John. "Half of the New Testament Forged, Biblical Scholar Says." Belief (blog), CNN. May 13, 2011. http://religion.blogs.cnn.com/2011/05/13/half-of-new-testament-forged-Bible-scholar-says/.

Blanshard, B. *The Nature of Thought.* London: George Allen and Unwin, 1939.

Bonhomme, Julien. "The Dangers of Anonymity: Witchcraft, Rumor, and Modernity in Africa." *HAU: Journal of Ethnographic Theory* 2, no. 2 (2012): 205–33.

Bonner, Michael. "Ja 'ä'il and Holy War in Early Islam." *Der Islam* 68, no. 1 (1991): 45–64.

Bortolot, Alexander Ives. "Women Leaders in African History: Dona Beatriz, Kongo Prophet." *Metropolitan Museum of Art*, October 2003. https://www.metmuseum.org/toah/hd/pwmn_4/hd_pwmn_4.htm.

Bowen, Anne Bisci. "Murals at Afin Oyo." *African Arts* 10, no. 3 (1977): 42.

Branson, Robert D. "Science, the Bible, and Human Anatomy." *Perspectives on Science and Christian Faith* 68, no. 4 (2016): 229.

Brison, Karen J. "Kingdom Culture?" *Social Sciences and Missions* 30, no. 1–2 (2017): 143–62.

Brooks, Jerome. "Chinua Achebe, the Art of Fiction No. 139." *The Paris Review*, December 11, 2018. https://www.theparisreview.org/interviews/1720/chinua-achebe-the-art-of-fiction-no-139-chinua-achebe.

Brown, C. K. "Research Findings in Ghana: A Survey on Elderly in Accra Region." *Gerontologie Africaine* 4 (1985): 11–33.

Buncombe, Andrew. "Islamophobia Even Worse under Trump Than after 9/11 Attacks Says Top Muslim Activist." *Independent*, December 27, 2017. https://www.independent.co.uk/news/world/americas/us-politics/trump-islam-muslim-islamophobia-worse-911-says-leader-a8113686.html.

Bunge, Mario Augusto. *Philosophical Dictionary*. Amherst: Prometheus Books, 1998.

Bytheway, B., and J. Johnson. "On Defining Ageism." *Critical Social Policy* 10, no. 29 (1990): 27–39

Calabrese, J. "Metals, Ideology and Power: The Manufacture and Control of Materialised Ideology in the Area of the Limpopo-Shashe Confluence." *South African Archaeological Society Goodwin Series* 8 (2000): 100–11.

Campbell, Marne L. "They Were All Filled with the Holy Ghost!: The Early Years of the Azusa Street Revival." In *Making Black Los Angeles: Class, Gender, and Community, 1850–1917*. Chapel Hill: University of North Carolina Press, 2016.

Carroll, William E. "Creation, Evolution, and Thomas Aquinas." *Revue des Questions Scientifiques* 171, no. 4 (2000): 319–47.

Carter, Michael G. "'Blessed Are the Cheese Makers': Reflections on the Transmission of Knowledge in Islam." *Journal of American Oriental Society* 133, no. 4 (2013): 597–605.

Casselberry, Judith. *The Labor of Faith: Gender and Power in Black Apostolic Pentecostalism*. Durham, NC: Duke University Press, 2017.

Catholic Online. "Bible Translated into 2,454 Languages, 4,500 to Go." Europe. International News. October 15, 2008. Accessed June 22, 2020, from https://www.catholic.org/news/international/europe/story.php?id=30064.

Cele, T. T. "Qualities of King Shaka as Portrayed in Zulu Oral Testimony and in Izibongo." *South African Journal of African Languages* 21, no. 2 (2001): 118–32.

Chen, G. M., and J. Chung. "Seniority and Superiority: A Case Analysis of Decision Making in a Taiwanese Religious Group." *Intercultural Communication Studies* XI-1 (2002): 41–56.

Chiba, Shin, and Thomas J. Schoenbaum, eds. *Peace Movements and Pacifism after September 11*. Northampton, MA: Edward Elgar, 2008.

Choudhury, Masudul Alam. "Conclusion: The Ultimate Nature of Qur'anic Socio-scientific Abstraction." In *Absolute Reality in the Qur'an*, 209–25. New York: Palgrave Macmillan, 2016.

Cimpric, Aleksandra. "Children Accused of Witchcraft." Report, UNICEF, April 2010. https://www.unicef.org/wcaro/wcaro_children-accused-of-witchcraft-in-Africa.pdf.

Clapperton, H. *Journal of a Second Expedition into the Interior of Africa from the Bight of Benin to Soccatoo*. Philadelphia, PA: Grey, Lean and Carey, 1829.

Clarke, J. D. "Carved Posts at Old Oyo." *Nigeria Magazine* 18 (1999): 248–49.

Clastres, P. *Society against the State*. 1989. Reprint. New York: Zone, 1974.

Coady, David, and Miranda Fricker. "Introduction to Special Issue on Applied Epistemology." *Journal of Applied Philosophy* 34, no. 2 (2017): 153–56.

Comaroff, Jean, and John L. Comaroff, eds. *Modernity and Its Malcontents: Ritual and Power in Postcolonial Africa*. Chicago, IL: University of Chicago Press, 1993.

Corten, André, and Ruth Marshall-Fratani. *Between Babel and Pentecost: Transnational Pentecostalism in Africa and Latin America*. London: Hurst, 2001.

Currie, Elliott P. "Crimes without Criminals-Witchcraft and Its Control in Renaissance Europe." *Law & Society Review* 3 (1968): 7.

Curtin, Philip, Steven Feierman, Leonard Thompson, and Jan Vansina. *African History*. Boston, MA: Little Brown, 1978.

Daswani, Girish. *Looking Back, Moving Forward: Transformation and Ethical Practice in the Ghanaian Church of Pentecost*. Toronto: University of Toronto Press, 2015.

Dawkins, Richard. *River out of Eden: A Darwinian View of Life*. New York: Basic Books, 1995.

de Grijspaarde, Huib van, Maarten Voors, Erwin Bulte, and Paul Richards. "Who Believes in Witches? Institutional Flux in Sierra Leone." *African Affairs* 112, no. 446 (2013): 22–47.

de Maret, Pierre. "From Kinship to Kingship: An African Journey into Complexity." *Azania: Archaeological Research in Africa* 47, no. 3 (2012): 314–26.

de Sousa Santos, B. *Epistemologies of the South: Justice against Epistemicide*. New York: Routledge, 2014.

deGrasse Tyson, Neil. Twitter post. June 14, 2013, 7:41 AM. https://twitter.com/neiltyson/status/345551599382446081.

Descartes, René, and Laurence J. Lafleur. *Meditations on First Philosophy*. Indianapolis, IN: Bobbs-Merrill, 1960.

Desilver, Drew, and David Masci. "World Muslim Population More Widespread Than You Might Think." Pew Research Center, January 31, 2017. http://www.pewresearch.org/fact-tank/2017/01/31/worlds-muslim-population-more-widespread-than-you-might-think/.

Diallo, Ibrahima. "Introduction: The Interface between Islamic and Western Pedagogies and Epistemologies: Features and Divergences." *International Journal of Pedagogies and Learning* 7, no. 3 (2012): 175–79.

Douglas, Mary. *Natural Symbols*. London: Routledge, 2002.

Dove, Sarah Jeanette. "The Choreography and Performance of Religion: Power and Ritual within American Pentecostal Worship Practice in the U.S." Master's dissertation, the University of North Carolina at Greensboro, 2015.

Drewal, H. J., J. Pemberton, and R. Abiodun, ed. A. Wardwell. *Yoruba: Nine Centuries of African Art and Thought*. New York: Center for African Art and Harry N. Abrams Inc., 1989.

Drucker-Brown, Susan. "Horse, Dog, and Monkey: The Making of a Mamprusi King." *Man (NS)* 27, no. 1 (March 1992): 71–79.

Dumézil, Georges. *The Destiny of a King.* Chicago, IL: University of Chicago Press, 1988.

Dzama, Emmanuel N. N., and Jonathan F. Osborne. "Poor Performance in Science among African Students: An Alternative Explanation to the African Worldview Thesis." *Journal of Research in Science Teaching* 36, no. 3 (1999): 387–405.

Eboiyehi, F. A. "Perception of Old Age: Its Implications for Care and Support for the Aged among the Esan of South-South Nigeria." *Journal of International Social Research* 8 no. 36 (2015): 340–56.

Ehrenreich, Barbara, and Deirdre English. *Witches, Midwives, & Nurses: A History of Women Healers.* New York: Feminist Press at CUNY, 2010.

Elkington, Robert Lionel. "The Doctrine of Subsequence in the Pentecostal and Neo-Pentecostal Movements." Master's dissertation, University of South Africa, 1998.

Ellis, Stephen, and Gerrie ter Haar, "Religion and Politics: Taking African Epistemologies Seriously." *Journal of Modern African Studies* 45, no. 3 (2007): 385–401.

Enderle, Bryan. "Science vs God." Filmed at TEDxUCDavid 2013. Davis, CA. Video, 2:24. Published June 22, 2013. https://www.youtube.com/watch?v=sn7YQOzNuSc.

Esiebo, Andrew. "The Mega Churches of Lagos: Huge Hangars Hold Hundreds of Thousands—in Pictures." *The Guardian,* February 24, 2016. https://www.theguardian.com/cities/gallery/2016/feb/24/mega-churches-lagos-nigeria-in-pictures.

Evans, Arthur. *Witchcraft and the Gay Counterculture: A Radical View of Western Civilization and Some of the People It Has Tried to Destroy.* Boston, MA: Fag Rag Books, 1978.

Evans-Pritchard, Edward E. *Witchcraft, Oracles and Magic among the Azande.* London: Oxford University Press, 1937.

Evans-Pritchard, Edward Evan. *The Divine Kingship of the Shilluk of the Nilotic Sudan.* 1948. Reprint. Cambridge: Cambridge University Press, 2014.

Fagg, William. *Divine Kingship in Africa.* London: Trustees of the British Museum, 1970.

Falola, Toyin, and Matt Childs, eds. *The Yoruba Diaspora in the Atlantic World.* Bloomington: Indiana University Press, 2004.

Fanon, Frantz. "Black Skin, White Masks [1952]." *Contemporary Sociological Theory* (2012): 417.

Feeley-Harnik, Gillian. "Issues in Divine Kingship." *Annual Review of Anthropology* 14, no. 1 (1985): 273–313.

Fenton, S. J., and H. Draper. "Older People Make Contributions to Society. Some Communities and Faith Groups Draw on This Contribution in Responding to the Needs of All Their Members." *Birmingham Policy Commission* (2014): 1–7

Finlayson, Lorna. "On Mountains and Molehills: Problems, Non-Problems, and the Ideology of Ideology." *Constellations* 22, no. 1 (2015): 135–46.

Finnegan, Ruth. "Religious Poetry." In *Oral Literature in Africa,* 165–200. Cambridge: Open Book Publishers, 2012. Accessed March 30, 2020, from www.jstor.org/stable/j.ctt5vjsmr.17.

Fleisher, Jeffrey, and Stephanie Wynne-Jones. "Authorisation and the Process of Power: The View from African Archaeology." *Journal of World Prehistory* 23, no. 4 (2010): 177–93.

Flew, Antony, R. M. Hare, and Basil Mitchell. "Theology and Falsification: The University Discussion." In *New Essays in Philosophical Theology*. New York: Macmillan, 1964.

Fontaine, Jean La. "Witchcraft Belief Is a Curse on Africa." *The Guardian*, March 1, 2012. https://www.theguardian.com/commentisfree/belief/2012/mar/01/witchcraft-curse-africa-kristy-bamu.

Foster, Susan Leigh, ed. *Choreographing History*. Bloomington: Indiana University Press, 1995.

Fottrell, Edward, Stephen Tollman, Peter Byass, Frederick Golooba-Mutebi, and Kathleen Kahn. "The Epidemiology of 'Bewitchment' as a Lay-Reported Cause of Death in Rural South Africa." *Journal of Epidemiology and Community Health* 66, no. 8 (2012): 704–9.

Foucault, Michel, Meaghan Morris, and Paul Patton. *Power, Truth, Strategy*. Sydney: Feral, 1979.

Foucault, Michel. "Truth and Power: An Interview with Alessandro Fontano and Pasquale Pasquino." In *Michel Foucault Power/Truth/Strategy*, edited by M. Morris and P. Patton, 29–48. Sydney: Feral, 1979.

Foucault, Michel. *Power/Knowledge: Selected Interviews and Other Writings, 1972–1977*, edited by Colin Gordon. Translated by Colin Gordon. Harlow: Longman, 1980.

Foucault, Michel. *Technologies of the self: A seminar with Michel Foucault*, edited by Luther H. Martin, Huck Gutman, and Patrick H. Hutton. Boston: University of Massachusetts Press, 1988.

Foucault, Michel. *The Foucault Effect: Studies in Governmentality*, edited by Graham Bruchell, Colin Gordon, and Peter Miller. Chicago, IL: University of Chicago Press, 1991.

Foucault, Michel. *Religion and Culture*, selected and edited by Jeremy R. Carrette. New York: Routledge, 1999.

Foucault, Michel. *Security, Territory, Population: Lectures at the Collège de France, 1977–78*, edited by Michel Senellart. New York: Springer, 2009.

Frazer, James George. *The Golden Bough*. London: Palgrave Macmillan, 1990.

Freedman, Harry. *The Murderous History of Bible Translations: Power, Conflict and the Quest for Meaning*. New York: Bloomsbury, 2016.

Fukuyama, F. "What Is Governance?" *Governance* 26, no. 3 (2013): 347–68.

Gettier, Edmund L. "Is Justified True Belief Knowledge?" *Analysis* 23, no. 6 (1963): 121–23.

Goffman, Erving. *Interaction Ritual: Essays in Face-to-Face Behavior*. New York: Routledge, 2017.

Goldfeld, Isaiah. "The Illiterate Prophet (Nabi Ummi)." *Der Islam; Zeitschrift für Geschichte und Kultur des Islamischen Orients* 57 (1980): 58.

Gorodnichenko, Y., and G. Roland. "Understanding the Individualism-Collectivism Cleavage and Its Effects: Lessons from Cultural Psychology." *Institutions and Comparative Economic Development* (2012): 213–326.

GotQuestions.org. "What Is a Christian Testimony?" February 21, 2018. Accessed July 11, 2018, from https://www.gotquestions.org/Christian-testimony.html.

Graeber, David. "The Divine Kingship of the Shilluk: On Violence, Utopia, and the Human Condition, or, Elements for an Archaeology of Sovereignty." *Hau: Journal of Ethnographic Theory* 1, no. 1 (2011): 1.

Grebe, Eduard, and Nicoli Nattrass. "AIDS Conspiracy Beliefs and Unsafe Sex in Cape Town." *AIDS and Behavior* 16, no. 3 (2012): 761–73.

Grosfoguel, Ramón. "The Epistemic Decolonial Turn: Beyond Political-Economy Paradigms." *Cultural Studies* 21, no. 2–3 (2007): 211–23.

Guessoum, Nidhal. "Science, Religion, and the Quest for Knowledge and Truth: An Islamic Perspective." *Cultural Studies of Science Education* 5, no. 1 (2010): 55–69.

Guessoum, Nidhal. *Islam's Quantum Question: Reconciling Muslim Tradition and Modern Science*. New York: IB Tauris, 2010.

Gulbrandsen, Ørnulf. "The Discourse of 'Ritual Murder': Popular Reaction to Political Leaders in Botswana." *Social Analysis: The International Journal of Social and Cultural Practice* 46, no. 3 (2002): 215–33.

Gutkind, P. C. W. "The Socio-Political and Economic Foundations of Social Problems in African Urban Areas: An Exploratory Conceptual Overview." *Civilizations* 22, no. 1 (1972): 18–34.

Hackett, Conrad, and David McClendon. "Christians Remain World's Largest Religious Group, but They Are Declining in Europe." Pew Research Center, April 5, 2017. http://www.pewresearch.org/fact-tank/2017/04/05/christians-remain-worlds-largest-religious-group-but-they-are-declining-in-europe/.

Hackett, Rosalind I. J. "Women, Rights Talk, and African Pentecostalism." *Religious Studies and Theology* 36, no. 2 (2017): 245–59.

Hamid, Shadi. "Is Islam 'Exceptional'?" *The Atlantic*, June 6, 2016. https://www.theatlantic.com/international/archive/2016/06/islam-politics-exceptional/485801/.

Hansen, Thomas Blom, and Finn Stepputat. "Sovereignty Revisited." *Annual Review of Anthropology* 35 (2006): 295–315.

Harney, John. "How Do Sunni and Shia Islam Differ?" *New York Times*, January 3, 2016. https://www.nytimes.com/2016/01/04/world/middleeast/q-and-a-how-do-sunni-and-shia-islam-differ.html.

Hedin, Christer. "Islam and Science: Tensions in Contemporary Epistemology." *Temenos* 31 (1995): 55–76.

Herner, Robert, and Peter L. Berger. *Global Pentecostalism in the 21st Century*. Bloomington: Indiana University Press, 2013.

Hesse, Josiah. "Flat Earthers Keep the Faith at Denver Conference." *The Guardian*, November 18, 2018. https://www.theguardian.com/us-news/2018/nov/18/flat-earthers-keep-the-faith-at-denver-conference.

Heusch, Luc De. *Drunken King, or, the Origin of the State (African Systems of Thought)*. Bloomington: Indiana University Press, 1982.

Hickel, Jason. "'Xenophobia' in South Africa: Order, Chaos, and the Moral Economy of Witchcraft." *Cultural Anthropology* 29, no. 1 (2014): 103–27.

Hill, Jane A., Philip Jones, and Antonio J. Morales, eds. *Experiencing Power, Generating Authority: Cosmos, Politics, and the Ideology of Kingship in Ancient Egypt and Mesopotamia*. Philadelphia: University of Pennsylvania Press, 2013.

Hobbes, Thomas. *Leviathan*. 1961. In Longman Library of Primary Sources in Philosophy. Reprint. New York: Routledge, 2016.

Hocart, A. M. *Kings and Councillors: An Essay in the Comparative Anatomy of Human Society*. Chicago, IL: University of Chicago Press, 1970.

Hocart, Arthur Maurice. *Kingship*. Oxford: Oxford University Press, 1927.

Honderich, Ted. "Ideology." In *The Oxford Companion to Philosophy*, 2nd ed., edited by Ted Honderich. Oxford: Oxford University Press, 2005.

Horton, Robin. "African Traditional Thought and Western Science." *Africa* 37, no. 2 (1967): 155–87.

Howe, Stephen. *Empire: A Very Short Introduction*. Oxford: Oxford University Press, 2002.

Humphrey, Nicholas. *Soul Dust: The Magic of Consciousness*. Princeton, NJ: Princeton University Press, 2011.

Hunt, Michael H. "Ideology." *Journal of American History* 77, no. 1 (June 1990): 108.

Idahosa, Benson. *I Choose to Change: The Scriptural Way to Success and Prosperity*. Godalming: Highland Books, 1987.

Ilori, K. A. "Ifa: The Yoruba God of Wisdom." *The African Guardian*, 1986. Accessed March 30, 2020, from https://www.academia.edu/28340608/IFA_-_THE_YORUBA_GOD_OF_WISDOM.

Inbody, Joel. "Sensing God: Bodily Manifestations and Their Interpretation in Pentecostal Rituals and Everyday Life." *Sociology of Religion* 76, no. 3 (2015): 337–55.

Iqbal, Mohammad. *The Reconstruction of Religious Thought in Islam*. Stanford, CA: Stanford University Press, 2013.

Ireland, Jerry M. "A Classical Pentecostal Approach to Discipleship in Missions." *Journal of Pentecostal Theology* 28, no. 2 (2019): 243–66.

Jacobsen, D. "Political Spiritualities: The Pentecostal Revolution in Nigeria." *Choice* 47, no. 5 (2010): 973.

James, Jonathan D. *A Moving Faith: Mega Churches Go South*. New Delhi: Sage, 2015.

Janssens, Jules. "Al-Kindī: The Founder of Philosophical Exegesis of the Qur'an." *Journal of Qur'anic Studies* 9, no. 2 (2007): 1–21.

Jegede, O. B. "Women, Power and Subversion in Orature: A Palace Performance in Yorubaland, Nigeria." *Journal of Gender Studies* 15, no. 3 (2006): 253–66.

Johnson, A. *The History of the Yorubas*. Reprint. Westport, CT: Negro Universities Press, 1970.

Johnson, Samuel. *The History of the Yorubas: From the Earliest times to the Beginning of the British Protectorate*, 1st ed., edited by Dr. O. Johnson. 1901. Reprint. New York: Routledge and K. Paul, 1966.

Jones, Ernest. *Essays in Applied Psycho-Analysis*. International Psycho-analytical Library, no. 41. London: Hogarth Press, 1951.

Kahneman, Daniel. *Thinking, Fast and Slow/Daniel Kahneman*. London: Allen Lane, 2011.

Kakwata, Frederick. "Witchcraft and Poverty in Africa: A Pastoral Perspective." *Black Theology* 16, no. 1 (2018): 22–37.

Kallinen, Timo. "Christianity, Fetishism, and the Development of Secular Politics in Ghana: A Dumontian Approach." *Anthropological Theory* 14, no. 2 (2014): 153–68.

Kalu, Ogbu. *African Pentecostalism: An Introduction*. Oxford: Oxford University Press, 2008.

Kantorowicz, Ernst. *The King's Two Bodies: A Study in Medieval Political Theology*, vol. 22. 1957. Reprint. Princeton, NJ: Princeton University Press, 2016.

Kapferer, Bruce. "Outside All Reason: Magic, Sorcery and Epistemology in Anthropology." *Social Analysis (Adelaide)* 46, no. 3 (2002): 1–30.

Karenga, M. *Ethical Insights from Odu Ifa: Choosing to Be Chosen*. Los Angeles, CA: Sentinel, 2008.

Katsaura. "Theo-Urbanism: Pastoral Power and Pentecostals in Johannesburg." *Culture and Religion* 18, no. 3 (2017): 232–62.

Kazmi, Yedullah. "The Qur'Ān as Event and as Phenomenon." *Islamic Studies* 41, no. 2 (2002): 193–214.

Kenyata, J. 1965. *Facing Mount Kenya*. New York: Vintage Books, 1965.

Khan, M. A. Muqtedar. "Introduction: Islam and Epistemology." *American Journal of Islamic Social Sciences* 16, no. 3 (1999): 81.

Khasandi-Telewa, V., M. Wakoko, J. Mugo, E. Mahero, and F. Ndegwa. "What an Old Man Sees while Sitting a Young Man Cannot See while Standing: Utilizing Senior Citizens to Achieve Peace." *International Journal of Research and Social Sciences* 2, no. 2 (2013): 44–49

Kleibl, Tanja, and Ronaldo Munck. "Civil Society in Mozambique: NGOs, Religion, Politics and Witchcraft." *Third World Quarterly* 38, no. 1 (2017): 203–18.

Klinken, Van, Adriaan S. "God's World Is Not an Animal Farm—Or Is It? The Catachrestic Translation of Gender Equality in African Pentecostalism." *Religion and Gender* 3, no. 2 (2013): 240–58.

Kohnert, Dirk. "Magic and Witchcraft: Implications for Democratization and Poverty-Alleviating Aid in Africa." *World Development* 24, no. 8 (1996): 1347–55.

Kopytoff, I. "Ancestors as Elders in Africa." *Journal of the International African Institute* 41, no. 2 (1971): 129–42.

Krejcir, Richard. "Genres in the Bible." Into Thy Word. Accessed July 22, 2018, from http://www.intothyword.org/apps/articles/default.asp?articleid=31435.

Krinsky, Samuel. "The Pan-African Church: Nation, Self, and Spirit in Winners' Chapel, Nigeria." In *Religion Crossing Boundaries*, 227–51. Leiden, Netherlands: Brill, 2010.

Kusserow, A. "Western Education, Psychologized individualism and Home/School Tensions: An American Example." Proceedings of the Fourth International Conference on Gross National Happiness, 468–69. (2008). Accessed June 24, 2020, from http://citeseerx.ist.psu.edu/viewdoc/download?doi=10.1.1.729.6731&rep=rep1&type=pdf.

LaMothe, Kimerer. "Enlivening Spirits: Shaker Dance Ritual as Theopraxis." *Théologiques* 25, no. 1 (2017): 103–24.

Lander, Richard. *Records of Captain Clapperton's Last Expedition to Africa*, vols. 1 and 2. London: Henry Colburn and Richard Bentley, 1830.

Laudan, Larry. *Truth, Error, and Criminal Law: An essay in Legal Epistemology*. Cambridge: Cambridge University Press, 2006.

Law, Robin. *The Oyo Empire, c. 1600–c. 1836: A West African Imperialism in the Era of the Atlantic Slave Trade*. Oxford: Clarendon Press, 1977.

Lévi-Strauss, Claude. "The Sorcerer and His Magic." In *Understanding and Applying Medical Anthropology*, edited by Peter J. Brown and Svea Closser, 129–37. London: Routledge, 1963.

Lienard, Pierre. "Age Grouping and Social Complexity." *Current Anthropology* 57 (2016): 105–17.

Lipka, Michael, and Conrad Hackett. "Why Muslims Are the World's Fastest Growing Religious Group." Pew Research Center, April 6, 2017. http://www.pewresearch.org/fact-tank/2017/04/06/why-muslims-are-the-worlds-fastest-growing-religious-group/.

Liu, Joseph. "Global Christianity—a Report on the Size and Distribution of the World's Christian Population." Pew Research Center's Religion & Public Life Project. December 19, 2011. http://www.pewforum.org/2011/12/19/global-christianity-exec/.

López, Adday Hernández. "Qur'Anic Studies in Al-Andalus: An Overview of the State of Research on qirā'āt and Tafsīr." *Journal of Qur'Anic Studies* 19, no. 3 (2017): 74–102.

Luyaluka, Kiatezua Lubanzadio. "An Essay on Naturalized Epistemology of African Indigenous Knowledge." *Journal of Black Studies* 47, no. 6 (2016): 497–523.

MacGaffey, Wyatt. "Death of a King, Death of a Kingdom? Social Pluralism and Succession to High Office in Dagbon, Northern Ghana." *Journal of Modern African Studies* 44, no. 1 (2006): 79–99.

Mack, John. "Fetish: Magic Figures in Central Africa." *Journal of Art Historiography* 5 (2011): 53.

Marshall-Fratani, Ruth. "Mediating the Global and Local in Nigerian Pentecostalism." *Journal of Religion in Africa* 28, no. 3 (1998): 278–315.

Marsonet, Michele. "Philosophy and Logical Positivism." *Academicus* MMXIX, no. 19 (2019): 32–36.

Martin, David. *Pentecostalism: The World Their Parish*. Oxford: Blackwell, 2002.

Martinez-Carter, K. "How the Elderly Are Treated around the World." July 23, 2013. Accessed February 5, 2020, from https://www.theweek.com/articles-amp/462230/how-elderly-are-treated-around-the-world.

Marx, Karl, and Joseph J. O'Malley. *Critique of Hegel's "Philosophy of Right"*. Cambridge: Cambridge University Press, 1970.

Marx, Karl. *The German Ideology: Part 1*, 2nd ed. Translated by Robert C. Tucker. New York: Norton, 1978.

Marx, Karl. "Religion, the Opium of the People." *World Treasury of Modern Religious Thought* (1990): 79–91.

Mbele, J. "The Elder in African Society." *Journal of Intergenerational Relationships* 2, no. 3–4 (2004): 53–61, 54.

McCright, Aaron M., and Riley E. Dunlap. "Bringing Ideology In: The Conservative White Male Effect on Worry about Environmental Problems in the USA." *Journal of Risk Research* 16, no. 2 (2013): 211–26.

McIntosh, Susan Keech, ed. *Beyond Chiefdoms: Pathways to Complexity in Africa*. New York: Cambridge University Press, 2005.

McKenny, Leesha. "Money Christmas: Hillsong Ensures Show in Tune with Spirit of Season." *Sydney Morning Herald,* December 19, 2011. Accessed June 24, 2020, from https://www.smh.com.au/entertainment/money-christmas-hillsong-ensures-show-in-tune-with-spirit-of-season-20111218–1p0vd.html.

Meadors, Dave. "The Bible and Its Influence." *Journal of Church and State* 48, no. 3 (2006): 711.

Mernissi, Fatima. *The Fundamentalist Obsession with Women: A Current Articulation of Class Conflict in Modern Muslim Societies.* Lahore: Women's Resource and Publication Centre, 1987.

Mignolo, Walter D. *The Darker Side of the Renaissance: Literacy, Territoriality, and Colonization.* Ann Arbor: University of Michigan Press, 1995.

Mignolo, Walter D. *Local Histories/Global Designs: Coloniality, Subaltern Knowledges, and Border Thinking.* New York: Princeton University Press, 2000.

Mignolo, Walter D. "Introduction: Coloniality of Power and De-Colonial Thinking." *Cultural studies* 21, no. 2–3 (2007): 155–67.

Moore, Henrietta L., and Todd Sanders, eds. *Magical Interpretations, Material Realities: Modernity, Witchcraft and the Occult in Postcolonial Africa.* London: Routledge, 2003.

Morrow, Jeffrey L. "The Acid of History: La Peyrère, Hobbes, Spinoza, and the Separation of Faith and Reason in Modern Biblical Studies." *Heythrop Journal* 58, no. 2 (2017): 169–80.

Morton-Williams, P. "An Outline of the Cosmology and Cult Organization of the Oyo Yoruba." *Africa* 34 (1964): 243–61.

Muller, Jean-Claude. "12 'Divine Kingship' in Chiefdoms and States: A Single Ideological Model." *Study of the State* 35 (1981): 239.

Myers, Henry A. *Medieval Kingship.* Chicago, IL: Nelson-Hall, 1982.

Nations Online. "Official and Spoken Languages of African Countries." Accessed August 5, 2019, from https://www.nationsonline.org/oneworld/african_languages.htm.

Nelson, Ediomo-Ubong E., and Ifureuwem J. Uko. "Ethnomedical Beliefs and Utilization of Alcohol Herbal Remedy for Malaria in South-Coastal Nigeria." *International Quarterly of Community Health Education* 39, no. 2 (2019): 119–26.

Nevadomsky, Joseph. "Kingship Succession Rituals in Benin. 3: The Coronation of the Oba." *African Arts* 17, no. 3 (May 1984): 57.

Newman, Willis. "Evangelical and Pentecostal: What Is the Difference?" Bible-teaching-about.com (blog). Accessed November 19, 2019, from http://www.bible-teaching-about.com/evangelicalandpentecostal.html.

Ngong, David T. "Stifling the Imagination: A Critique of Anthropological and Religious Normalization of Witchcraft in Africa." *African and Asian Studies* 11, no. 1–2 (2012): 144–81.

Nigosian, Solomon A. *Islam: Its History, Teaching, and Practices.* Bloomington: Indiana University Press, 2004.

Nolte, Insa. "Chieftaincy and the State in Abacha's Nigeria: Kingship, Political Rivalry and Competing Histories in Abeokuta during the 1990s." *Africa* 72, no. 3 (2002): 368–90.

Noret, Joël. "On the Inscrutability of the Ways of God: The Transnationalization of Pentecostalism on the West African Coast." In *Religion Crossing Boundaries:*

Transnational Religious and Social Dynamics in Africa and the New African Diaspora, Religion and the Social Order, vol. 18. Boston, MA: Brill, 2010.

Nwachukwu-Agbada, J. O. J. "The Igbo Folktale: Performance Conditions and Internal Characteristics." Bloomington: Department of Folklore and Ethnomusicology, Indiana University, 1991. Accessed October 16, 2019, from https:www.scholarworks.iu.edu.

Oakley, Francis. *Kingship: The Politics of Enchantment*. Oxford: Blackwell, 2006.

Ogo, I. "Enhancing Youth-Elder Collaboration in Governance in Africa." Discussion Paper, Minds Annual African Youth Dialogue, 2015.

Ogunnaike, O. *Sufism and Ifa: Ways of Knowing in Two West African Intellectual Traditions*. Cambridge, MA: Harvard University, 2015.

Ojo, G. J. A. *Yoruba Palaces: A Study of Afins of Yorubaland*. London: University of London Press, 1966.

Okoye, U. "Traditional Values and Mechanisms for the Care of the Elderly among the Igbos of South Eastern Nigeria: Implication for Social Policy." Paper Presented at the Conference on "Healthy Aging," University of Ibadan, June 24, 1999.

Oladeji, Baba. "House on the Rock?: Finding an Architectural Language for the Pentecostal Church by Baba Oladeji." *Livin spaces*, March 5, 2018. Accessed June 24, 2020, from https://www.livinspaces.net/interviews-and-articles/house-rock-finding-architectural-language-pentecostal-church-baba-oladeji/.

Olaiya, T. A. "Youth and Ethnic Movements and Their Impacts on Party Politics in the ECOWAS Member States." *Sage Open* 4, no. 1 (2014): 1–12.

Olajubu, "The Yoruba Artists and Their Work." In Seminar Series II, Department of African Languages and Literatures, University of Ife (1977): 384–418.

Olatunji, O. *Features of Yoruba Oral Poetry*. Ibadan: University Press Limited, 1984.

Olu-Osayomi, S. "Dramatic Aspects of Ese Ifa in Yorubaland." *International Journal on Studies in English Language and Literature (IJSELL)* 5, no. 10 (2017): 12–18. Accessed March 30, 2020, from http://dx.doi.org/10.20431/2347-3134.0510003.

Olusegun, O. F., A. T. Akinwale, R. O. Vincent, and B. Olabenjo. "A Mobile-Based Knowledge Management System for 'Ifa': An African Traditional oracle." *African Journal of Mathematics and Computer Science Research* 3, no. 7 (2010): 114–31.

Oluwade, B., and O. Longe. "On the Code Characteristics of Ifa Divination." *Journal of Computer Science & Its Applications* 9, no. 1 (2003): 23–28. Accessed March 30, 2020, from https://www.researchgate.net/publication/327161021.

Omar, Saleh. "Ibn Al-Haytham's Theory of Knowledge and Its Significance for Later Science." *Arab Studies Quarterly* 1, no. 1 (1979): 67–82.

Omondi, Rose Kisia, and Chris Ryan. "Sex Tourism: Romantic Safaris, Prayers and Witchcraft at the Kenyan Coast." *Tourism Management* 58 (2017): 217–27.

Osadolor, Osarhieme Benson. "The Benin Royalist Movement and Its Political Opponents: Controversy over Restoration of the Monarchy, 1897–1914." *International Journal of African Historical Studies* 44, no. 1 (2011): 45–59.

Osadolor, Osarhieme Benson. "The Military System of Benin Kingdom, c. 1440–1897." PhD diss., University of Hamburg, 2001.

Owolabi, Kola, and Sayo Alagbe. *The Alaafin of Oyo, Oba Lamidi Adeyemi III: His Life History and His Philosophy*. Ibadan: Universal Akada Books, 2008.

Palmeirim, Manuela. "Masks, Myths, Novels, and Symbolic Ambiguity: Dialogues between Verbal and Visual Arts." *African Arts* 41, no. 3 (2008): 74–77.

Palmer, Michael D. "Abundant Life or Abundant Poverty?" In *Wiley-Blackwell Companions to Religion*. Chichester: John Wiley & Sons, 2012.

Parish, Jane. "West African Witchcraft, Wealth and Moral Decay in New York City." *Ethnography* 12, no. 2 (2011): 247–65.

Parle, Julie, and Fiona Scorgie. "Bewitching Zulu Women: Umhayizo, Gender, and Witchcraft in KwaZulu-Natal." *South African Historical Journal* 64, no. 4 (2012): 852–75.

Parwez, Ghulam Ahmad. *Islam: A Challenge to Religion*. Lahore: Tayyeb Iqbal Printers, 2012.

Pasternack, Lawrence. "Kant's 'Appraisal' of Christianity: Biblical Interpretation and the Pure Rational System of Religion." *Journal of the History of Philosophy* 53, no. 3 (2015): 485–506.

Patel, Vikram. "Traditional Healers for Mental Health Care in Africa." *Global Health Action* 4, no. 1 (2011): 7956–62.

Paya, Ali. "What and How Can We Learn from the Qur'Ān? A Critical Rationalist Perspective." *Islamic Studies* 53, no. 3/4 (2014): 175–200.

Pearce, Kenneth L. "Berkeley's Lockean Religious Epistemology." *Journal of the History of Ideas* 75, no. 3 (2014): 417–38.

Peel, J. D. Y. "Divergent Modes of Religiosity in West Africa." In *Christianity, Islam, and Orisa-Religion: Three Traditions in Comparison and Interaction*, 71–87. Oakland: University of California Press, 2016. Accessed March 30, 2020, from www.jstor.org/stable/10.1525/j.ctt1ffjng5.9.

Pew Research Center. "Europe's Growing Muslim Population." November 29, 2017. http://www.pewforum.org/2017/11/29/europes-growing-muslim-population/.

Pew Research Center. "Christian Movements and Denominations." *Pew Research Center's Religion & Public Life Project*, July 10, 2019. https://www.pewforum.org/2011/12/19/global-christianity-movements-and-denominations/.

Pew Research Center's Religion & Public Life Project. "Projected Religious Population Changes in Sub-Saharan Africa." May 10, 2016. https://www.pewforum.org/2015/04/02/sub-saharan-africa/.

Pfeiffer, Elizabeth J., and Harrison M. K. Maithya. "Bewitching Sex Workers, Blaming Wives: HIV/AIDS, Stigma, and the Gender Politics of Panic in Western Kenya." *Global Public Health* 13, no. 2 (2018): 234–48.

Philosophy of Religion. "Philosophy of Religion: The Argument from Fine Tuning Comments." Accessed July 11, 2018, from http://www.philosophyofreligion.info/.

Phipps, William E. "Christianity and Nationalism in Tropical Africa." *Civilisations* 22, no. 1 (1972): 92–100.

Plous, Scott. *The Psychology of Judgment and Decision Making/Scott Plous*. McGraw-Hill Series in Social Psychology. New York: McGraw-Hill, 1993.

Pogoson, O. I., and A. O. Akande. "Ifa Divination Trays from Isale-Oyo." *Cadernos de Estudos Africanos* 21 (2011): 15–41.

Popper, Karl. *Conjectures and Refutations: The Growth of Scientific Knowledge*. New York: Basic Books, 1962.

Pype, Katrien. *The Making of the Pentecostal Melodrama: Religion, Media and Gender in Kinshasa*, vol. 6. Oxford: Berghahn Books, 2012.

Quigley, Declan. "Scapegoats: The Killing of Kings and Ordinary People." *Journal of the Royal Anthropological Institute* 6, no. 2 (2000): 237–54.

Quigley, Declan, ed. "Introduction: The Character of Kingship." In *The Character of Kingship*, 1–11. New York: Berg, 2005.

Radford, Benjamin. "Belief in Witchcraft Widespread in Africa." *LiveScience*, August 30, 2010. https://www.livescience.com/8515-belief-witchcraft-widespread-africa.html.

Ramadanovic, Petar. "No Place Like Ideology (on Slavoj Žižek): Is There a Difference between the Theory of Ideology and the Theory of Interpretation?" *Cultural Critique* 86, no. 86 (2014): 119–38.

Rasmussen, Dennis C. "Burning Laws and Strangling Kings? Voltaire and Diderot on the Perils of Rationalism in Politics." *Review of Politics* 73, no. 1 (2011): 77–104.

Rath, Brian. "Believe It or Not: Witchcraft in Kenya." *Voices of Africa*, May 2, 2013. https://voicesofafrica.co.za/believe-it-or-not-witchcraft-in-kenya/.

Rāzī, Fakhr al-Dīn. "19/131." In *Al-Tafsīr Al-kabīr*. Translated by Sohaib Saeed. Cambridge: Royal Aal al-Bayt Institute for Islamic Thought, 2018.

Reinhardt, Bruno. "Discipline (and Lenience) beyond the Self: Discipleship in a Pentecostal-Charismatic Organization." *Social Analysis* 62, no. 3 (2018): 42–66.

Riches, Tanya, and Tom Wagner. "The Evolution of Hillsong Music: From Australian Pentecostal Congregation into Global Brand." *Australian Journal of Communication* 39, no. 1 (2012): 17.

Rio, Knut, Michelle MacCarthy, and Ruy Blanes. *Pentecostalism and Witchcraft: Spiritual Warfare in Africa and Melanesia*. Cham: Palgrave Macmillan, 2017.

Rodríguez, Darío. "The God of Life and the Spirit of Life: The Social and Political Dimension of Life in the Spirit." *Studies in World Christianity* 17, no. 1 (2011): 1–11.

Ross, Emma George. "African Christianity in Kongo." *Metropolitan Museum of Art*, October 2002. https://www.metmuseum.org/toah/hd/acko/hd_acko.htm.

Rowell, James L. "Abdul Ghaffar Khan: An Islamic Gandhi." *Political Theology* 10, no. 4 (2009): 591–606.

Ruel, Malcolm. "Witchcraft, Morality, and Doubt." *HAU: Journal of Ethnographic Theory* 7, no. 1 (2017): 579–95.

Russell, Bertrand. *The Problems of Philosophy*. Oxford: Oxford University Press, 1997.

Russell, Jeffrey Burton. *Witchcraft in the Middle Ages*. Ithaca, NY: Cornell University Press, 1972.

Saethre, Eirik, and Jonathan Stadler. "Malicious Whites, Greedy Women, and Virtuous Volunteers." *Medical Anthropology Quarterly* 27, no. 1 (2013): 103–20.

Sagner A., and P. Kowal. "Defining 'Old Age' Markers of Old Age in Sub-Saharan Africa and the Implications for Cross-Cultural Research." Discussion Paper, the Minimum Data Set (MDS) Project on Ageing and Older Adults in sub-Saharan Africa, no. 1, 2002.

Sahlins, Marshall. "The Stranger-King or, Elementary Forms of the Politics of Life." *Indonesia and the Malay World* 36, no. 105 (2008): 177–99.

Sangree, W. H. "Pronatalism and the Elderly in Tiriki, Kenya." In *African Families and the Crisis of Social Change*, edited by T. S. Weisner, C. Bradley, and P. L. Kilbride, 184–207. London: Bergin & Garvey, 1997.

Sankey, Howard. "Witchcraft, Relativism and the Problem of the Criterion." *Erkenntnis (1975–)* 72, no. 1 (2010): 1–16.

Schacht, Joseph. *The Origins of Muhammadan Jurisprudence*, 3rd ed. London: Oxford University Press, 1959.

Schechner, Richard. *Performance Theory*. London: Routledge, 2003.

Schimmel, S. *The Tenacity of Unreasonable Beliefs*. Oxford: Oxford University Press, 2008.

Schimmel, Solomon. "Christian Biblical Fundamentalism." In *The Tenacity of Unreasonable Beliefs*. Oxford: Oxford University Press, 2008.

Schlesinger Jr., Arthur M. *The Disuniting of America: Reflections on a Multicultural Society*. New York: W. W. Norton, 1992.

Schram, Ryan. "Witches' Wealth: Witchcraft, Confession, and Christianity in Auhelawa, Papua New Guinea." *Journal of the Royal Anthropological Institute* 16, no. 4 (2010): 726–42.

Schutz, Alfred, and Thomas Luckmann. *The Structures of the Life-World*, vol. 1. Evanston, IL: Northwestern University Press, 1973.

Schwarzbach, Bertram Eugene. "Reason and the Bible in the So-Called Age of Reason." *Huntington Library Quarterly* 74, no. 3 (2011): 437–70.

Seesemann, Rüdiger. "Embodied Knowledge and the Walking Qur'an: Lessons for the Study of Islam and Africa." *Journal of Africana Religions* 3, no. 2 (2015): 201–9.

Segall, Avner, and Kevin Burke. "Reading the Bible as a Pedagogical Text: Testing, Testament, and Some Postmodern Considerations about Religion/the Bible in Contemporary Education." *Curriculum Inquiry* 43, no. 3 (2013): 305–31.

Sell, Alan. "The Bible and Epistemology." *Journal of Reformed Theology* 3, no. 2 (2009): 219–26.

Seymour, William. "River of Living Water." Sermon Index Audio Sermons. Accessed November 19, 2019, from http://www.sermonindex.net/modules/articles/index.php?view=article&aid=39711.

Shankar, A., M. A. Ansari, and S. Saxena. "Organizational Context and Ingratiatory Behavior in Organizations." *Journal of social psychology* 135, no. 5 (1994): 641–47.

Sherkat, Darren E. "Religion and Scientific Literacy in the United States." *Social Science Quarterly* 92, no. 5 (2011): 1134–50.

Shukla, Anshumali. "Wahhabism and Global Terrorism." *International Journal of Innovation and Applied Studies* 9, no. 4 (2014): 1521.

Sidibeh, Lamin. "Diviners and Diagnosticians in the Gambia: Psychological Functions and Traditional Healers." *Fourth World Journal* 14, no. 1 (2015): 5–12.

Silva, Sónia. "Mind, Body and Spirit in Basket Divination: An Integrative Way of Knowing." *Religions* 5, no. 4 (2014): 1175–87.

Simone, Abdou Maliq. *For the City Yet to Come: Changing African Life in Four Cities*. London: Duke University Press, 2004.

Sinai, Nicolai. "Al-Suhrawardī's Philosophy of Illumination and Al-ghazāl." *Archiv Für Geschichte Der Philosophie* 98, no. 3 (2016): 272–301.

Siraj Al-Din, Abu Bakr. "The Origins of Sufism." *Islamic Sciences* 13, no. 2 (2015): 59.

Skalnik, Peter. "Chiefdoms and Kingdoms in Africa: Why They Are Neither States Nor Empires." 2012. Accessed July 31, 2018, http://www.ascleiden.nl/Pdf/chiefdomsandkingdoms.pdf.

Slick, Matt. "How to Interpret the Bible." Accessed July 16, 2018, from https://carm.org/how-interpret-Bible.

Smith, Abdullahi. "A Little New Light on the Collapse of the Alafinate of Yoruba." In *Studies in Yoruba History and Culture: Essays in Honour of Professor S. O. Biobaku*, edited by Gabriel Olusanya, 42–71. Ibadan: University Press Limited, 1983.

Smith, Andrew F. "Secularity and Biblical Literalism: Confronting the Case for Epistemological Diversity." *International Journal for Philosophy of Religion* 71, no. 3 (2012): 205–19.

Smith, J. Z. *Relating Religion: Essays in the Study of Religion.* Chicago, IL: University of Chicago Press, 2004.

Smith, Wilfred Cantwell. "The True Meaning of Scripture: An Empirical Historian's Nonreductionist Interpretation of the Qur'an." *International Journal of Middle East Studies* 11, no. 4 (1980): 487–505.

Soothill, Jane. "Gender and Pentecostalism in Africa." In *Pentecostalism in Africa: Presence and Impact of Pneumatic Christianity in Postcolonial Societies*, edited by Martin Lindhardt. Boston, MA: Brill, 2014.

Soper, R. "Carver Posts at Old Oyo." *The Nigerian Field* 43, no. 1 (1978): 17.

Spanos, Nicholas P. "Witchcraft in Histories of Psychiatry: A Critical Analysis and an Alternative Conceptualization." *Psychological Bulletin* 85, no. 2 (1978): 417.

Spellman, W. M. *Monarchies 1000–2000.* London: Reaktion Books, 2001, 12.

Spencer, Herbert. *The Principles of Sociology*, vol. 6. New York: Appleton and Company, 1895.

Spivak, Gayatri Chakravorty, and Rosalind C. Morris. *Can the Subaltern Speak?: Reflections on the History of an Idea.* New York: Columbia University Press, 2010.

Stetzer, Ed. "Trends in Church Architecture, Part 1." The Exchange (blog). July 18, 2016. https://www.christianitytoday.com/edstetzer/2016/july/trends-in-church-architecture-part-1.html.

Stone, Selina. "Pentecostal Power: Discipleship as Political Engagement." *Journal of the European Pentecostal Theological Association* 38, no. 1 (2018): 24–38.

Stowasser, Barbara. "The Qur'an and Its Meaning." *Arab Studies Journal* 3, no. 1 (1995): 4–8.

Strathern, Alan. "Drawing the Veil of Sovereignty: Early Modern Islamic Empires and Understanding Sacred Kingship." *History and Theory* 53, no. 1 (2014): 79–93.

Sung, K. T. "Elder Respect among Adult: A Cross-Cultural Study of Americans and Koreans." *Journal of Aging Studies* 18 (2004): 215–30.

Sweeney, Michael. "Greek Essence and Islamic Tolerance: Al-farabi, Al-ghazali, Ibn Rush'd." *Review of Metaphysics* 65, no. 1 (2011): 41–61.

Taylor, Donald M., and Janet R. Doria. "Self-Serving and Group-Serving Bias in Attribution." *Journal of Social Psychology* 113, no. 2 (1981): 201–11.

Temesgen, G. Baye. "The Evolution and Development of Kingship and Traditional Governance in Ethiopia: A Case of the Kefa Kingdom." *Journal of Asian and African Studies* 47, no. 2 (2012): 190–203.

The Holy Bible. New International Version and English Standard Version. Accessed July 22, 2018, from https://www.biblegateway.com/.

The Holy Quran. Sahih International. Accessed December 6, 2018, from https://quran.com.

The Metropolitan Museum of Art. "Leopard Aquamanil." Accessed June 22, 2020, from https://www.metmuseum.org/art/collection/search/316524.

Thomas, Paul. "Religious Education and the Feminisation of Witchcraft: A Study of Three Secondary Schools in Kumasi, Ghana." *British Journal of Religious Education* 34, no. 1 (2012): 67–86.

Thomas, William I. "Situational Analysis: The Behavior Pattern and the Situation." *Publ Am Sociol Soc* 22 (1927): 1–13.

Thompson, Robert Farris. "The Sign of the Divine King: An Essay on Yoruba Bead-Embroidered Crowns with Veil and Bird Decorations." *African Arts* 3, no. 3 (1970): 8.

Todd, D. "How Do East and West Really Treat Seniors." 2010. Accessed February 8, 2020, from https://vancouversun.com>news.

Trisel, Brooke Alan. "God's Silence as an Epistemological Concern." *Philosophical Forum* 43, no. 4 (2012): 383–93.

Tse, J. K. H. "Grounded Theologies: 'Religion' and the 'Secular' in Human Geography." *Progress in Human Geography* 38, no. 2 (2014): 201–20.

Udvardy, M., and M. Cattell. "Gender, Aging and Power in Sub-Saharan Africa: Challenges and Puzzles." *Journal of Cross-Cultural Gerontology* 7, no. 4 (1992): 275–88.

UN Women. "Facts & Figures." Accessed September 5, 2019, from https://www.unwomen.org/en/news/in-focus/commission-on-the-status-of-women-2012/facts-and-figures.

UNESCO Institute for Statistics. "Adult and Youth Literacy: Trends in Gender Parity." September 2010. http://uis.unesco.org/sites/default/files/documents/fs3-adult-and-youth-literacy-global-trends-in-gender-parity-2010-en.pdf.

UNICEF. "UNICEF Executive Director, in Third Committee, Says 18,000 Children Still Dying Every Day, despite Dramatic Fall in Death Rate." Meetings Coverage and Press Releases. United Nations. October 16, 2013. https://www.un.org/press/en/2013/gashc4071.doc.htm.

UNICEF. "Child Marriage: Latest Trends and Future Prospects." Resources. United Nations. July 2018. https://data.unicef.org/resources/child-marriage-latest-trends-and-future-prospects/.

Vacín, Luděk. *Experiencing Power, Generating Authority: Cosmos, Politics, and the Ideology of Kingship in Ancient Egypt and Mesopotamia*, edited by Jane A. Hill, Philip Jones, and Antonio J. Morales. Penn Museum International Research Conferences: University of Pennsylvania Museum of Archaeology and Anthropology, 2013.

Van den Berghe, Pierre L. *Power and Privilege at an African University*. Piscataway, NJ: Transaction, 1973.

Van Fraassen, Bas C. *The Empirical Stance*. New Haven, CT: Yale University Press, 2002.

Vansina, Jan. "A Comparison of African Kingdoms." *Africa* 32, no. 4 (1962): 324–35.

Vansina, Jan. *Oral Tradition: A Study in Historical Methodology*. Translated by H. M. Wright. London: Routledge and Kegan Paul, 1965.

Vaughan, Megan. "'Divine Kings': Sex, Death and Anthropology in Inter-War East/ Central Africa." *Journal of African History* 49, no. 3 (2008): 383–401.

Vazquez, Rolando. "Translation as Erasure: Thoughts on Modernity's Epistemic Violence." *Journal of Historical Sociology* 24, no. 1 (2011): 27–44.

Walker, Paul E. "The Pillars of Islam: Daaim al-Islam of al-Qadi al-Numan, Vol. 1." *Journal of the American Oriental Society* 123, no. 2 (2003): 467.

Wallace, Dale. "Rethinking Religion, Magic and Witchcraft in South Africa: From Colonial Coherence to Postcolonial Conundrum." *Journal for the Study of Religion* 28, no. 1 (2015): 23–51.

Ware, Frederick L. "On the Compatibility/Incompatibility of Pentecostal Premillennialism with Black Liberation Theology." In *Afro-Pentecostalism: Black Pentecostal and Charismatic Christianity in History and Culture*, edited by Yong Amos and Alexander Estrelda Y. New York: NYU Press, 2011.

Warf, Barney, and Morton Winsberg. "Geographies of Megachurches in the United States." *Journal of Cultural Geography* 27, no. 1 (2010): 33–51.

Wariboko, Nimi. "Pentecostal Theology as a Discursive Site for the Weight of Blackness in Nigeria." *Pneuma* 36, no. 3 (2014): 417–31.

Warraq, Ibn. *Why I Am Not a Muslim*. Amherst, NY: Prometheus Books, 1995.

Weber, Max. *Max Weber Readings and Commentary on Modernity*. Modernity and Society, vol. 3, edited by Stephen Kalberg. Malden, MA: Blackwell, 2005.

Weber, Max. *The Protestant Ethic and the Spirit of Capitalism*. New York: Routledge, 2001.

Weiner, Annette B., and Jane Schneider, eds. *Cloth and Human Experience*. London: Smithsonian Institution, 2013.

Wells, George A. "How Destructive of Traditional Christian Beliefs is Historical Criticism of the Bible Today Conceded to Be?" *Think* 10, no. 29 (2011): 91–109.

West, Thomas G. *Plato's "Apology Of Socrates": An Interpretation, with a New Translation*. Ithaca, NY: Cornell University Press, 1979.

Westcott, J., and P. Morton-Williams. "The Symbolism and Ritual Context of the Yoruba Laba Shango." *Journal of the Royal Anthropological Institute* 92 (1962): 23–37.

White, Peter. "Missional Branding: A Case Study of the Church of Pentecost." *HTS Teologiese Studies/Theological Studies* 75, no. 4 (2019): E1–e7.

White, Peter, Fortune Tella, and Mishael Donkor Ampofo. "A Missional Study of the Use of Social Media (Facebook) by Some Ghanaian Pentecostal Pastors." *koers* 81, no. 2 (2016): 1–8.

Wickham, Anna. "That Old Time Religion: The Influence of West and Central African Religious Culture on the Music of the Azusa Street Revival." Master's dissertation, the University of Arizona, 2014.

Willsky, Lydia. "The (Un)Plain Bible: New Religious Movements and Alternative Scriptures in Nineteenth-Century America." *Nova Religio: The Journal of Alternative and Emergent Religions* 17, no. 4 (2014): 13–36.

Wiredu, K. "Toward Decolonizing African Philosophy and Religion." *African Studies Quarterly* 1 (1998): 17–46.

Wood, B. "Museum of the Bible: Questionable Science." *Science* 358, no. 6367 (2017): 1142.

Word of Life Bible Church. "Home." Accessed November 19, 2019, from http://www.ayo-oritsejafor.org/.

Wrong, Michela. "World View: Writing about Africa without Mentioning the Role of Tribalism and Witchcraft Is Like Writing about British Fox-Hunting without Mentioning Class." *New Statesman* 134, no. 4722 (2005): 24.

Wycliffe Bible Translators. "Why Bible Translation | International Missions | Christian Mission Organizations." Accessed July 11, 2018, from https://www.wycliffe.org/about/why.

Yanker, B. A, T. Lu, and P. Loerch. "The Aging Brain." *Annual Review of Pathology Mechanisms of Disease* 3, no. 1 (2008): 241–66.

Yazdī, Mahdī Ḥā'irī. *The Principles of Epistemology in Islamic Philosophy: Knowledge by Presence.* New York: State University of New York Press, 1992.

Index

Note: Page references for figures are italicized.

Yorubaland, 196, 202, 211, 213–15, 220, 229
Yoruba Masque Theatre, 224–25
Yoruba performative art, 226
Yoruba religion, 64, 68–69, 100
Yoruba royal poetry, 225–26
Yoruba women, 196
Yoruba woodcarving, 270

youth leadership, 47
youth-valuing society, 55, 59

Zakat, 110
Zambia, 25, 194
Zande witchcraft beliefs, 24
Zealot: The Life and Times of Jesus of Nazareth, 141

www.ingramcontent.com/pod-product-compliance
Lightning Source LLC
Chambersburg PA
CBHW050626280326
41932CB00015B/2544